Editor
DIANA SCHUTZ

Designer
CARY GRAZZINI

Publisher
MIKE RICHARDSON

USAGI YOJIMBO™ (BOOK 19): FATHERS AND SONS

This volume collects issues 69-75
of the Dark Horse comic book series *Usagi Yojimbo Volume Three*.

Visit the Usagi Dojo web site
www.usagiyojimbo.com

Published by
Dark Horse Books
A division of Dark Horse Comics, Inc.
10956 SE Main Street
Milwaukie, Oregon 97222

First edition: July 2005
ISBN 1-59307-319-4

Limited hardcover edition: August 2005
ISBN 1-59307-320-8

1 3 5 7 9 10 8 6 4 2
Printed in Canada

USAGI YOJIMBO™

— FATHERS AND SONS —

Created, Written, and Illustrated by

STAN SAKAI

Introduction by

MATT WAGNER

DARK HORSE BOOKS™

Usagi Yojimbo

Introduction

Fathers and sons.

I have one and I am one.

Actually, that statement works no matter which side of the equation I place myself.

Like a lot of fourteen-year-old boys, my son shares the usual litany of common teenaged interests with many of his friends: hot new music, the ever-ubiquitous video games, any and all things Japanese, and — of course, thank god — comic books. Now, since my son is who he is and since his dad is who *he* is, Brennan and his pals have access to a veritable treasure trove of the latter on a regular and rotating basis. They tear through whatever I give them with a rabid hunger, consuming pages and pages of material that — when I was kid — had to be unearthed with the most painstaking persistence and patience. Still, I'm overjoyed to be able to share my love of our unique medium with them, and I get a real kick out of seeing how their tastes develop and evolve.

And so it was that, about a year or so ago, they all discovered the rich and sprawling world of *Usagi Yojimbo*.

With a locust-like appetite, they consumed every available volume that I fed them — even digging up some, on their own, that I didn't have. It was fun to see how deeply involved they soon became in this distinctive, epic tale that pairs the disarming style so commonly known as "funny animals" with a narrative depth that belies that description at almost every turn. I could often hear the boys discussing not only the individual character traits of Usagi's wandering *ronin* and Jei's soul-gathering demon, but also the artist's clever use of symbolic word balloons, evocative dialogue, and smoothly paced action sequences.

One day, after I had finished work in my own home-studio, I came upstairs and heard the familiar chatter of Bren's usual posse of pals all gathered in his bedroom. On my way to a much-needed shower, I stuck my head in the room and offered my usual hellos. This time, though, as I turned to go, one of my son's oldest friends, Morgan, summoned me back. "Hey, *Matt*, wait, wait..."

I paused. "Yeah?"

"Um..." He seemed a bit embarrassed, as if he were about to ask an enormous favor of me.

"Do you..." (Here, his eyes went wide, actually twinkling with the most unfettered display of starstruck awe I think I've ever seen.) Do you... *know* Stan Sakai?"

I chuckled to myself. These guys had all been in and out of my studio for years. They'd seen me work on project after project that involved not only my own creations but also a wide variety of popular, established characters, and while surely impressed, they had never expressed this sort of enraptured delight.

"Yeah, sure," I answered. "In fact, we had breakfast together just a few weeks ago at a convention in Seattle."

To be so close, even by proxy, to his newfound hero struck my questioner utterly silent. Nearby, his comrade Peter nodded knowingly and offered the only response imaginable. "That is *so* cool!"

What else could I possibly add to that?

MATT WAGNER

CONTENTS

FOR AKIO SAKAI,
NO SON COULD HAVE HAD A BETTER ROLE MODEL.
AND FOR MATTHEW SAKAI,
NO FATHER COULD BE MORE PROUD OF A SON.

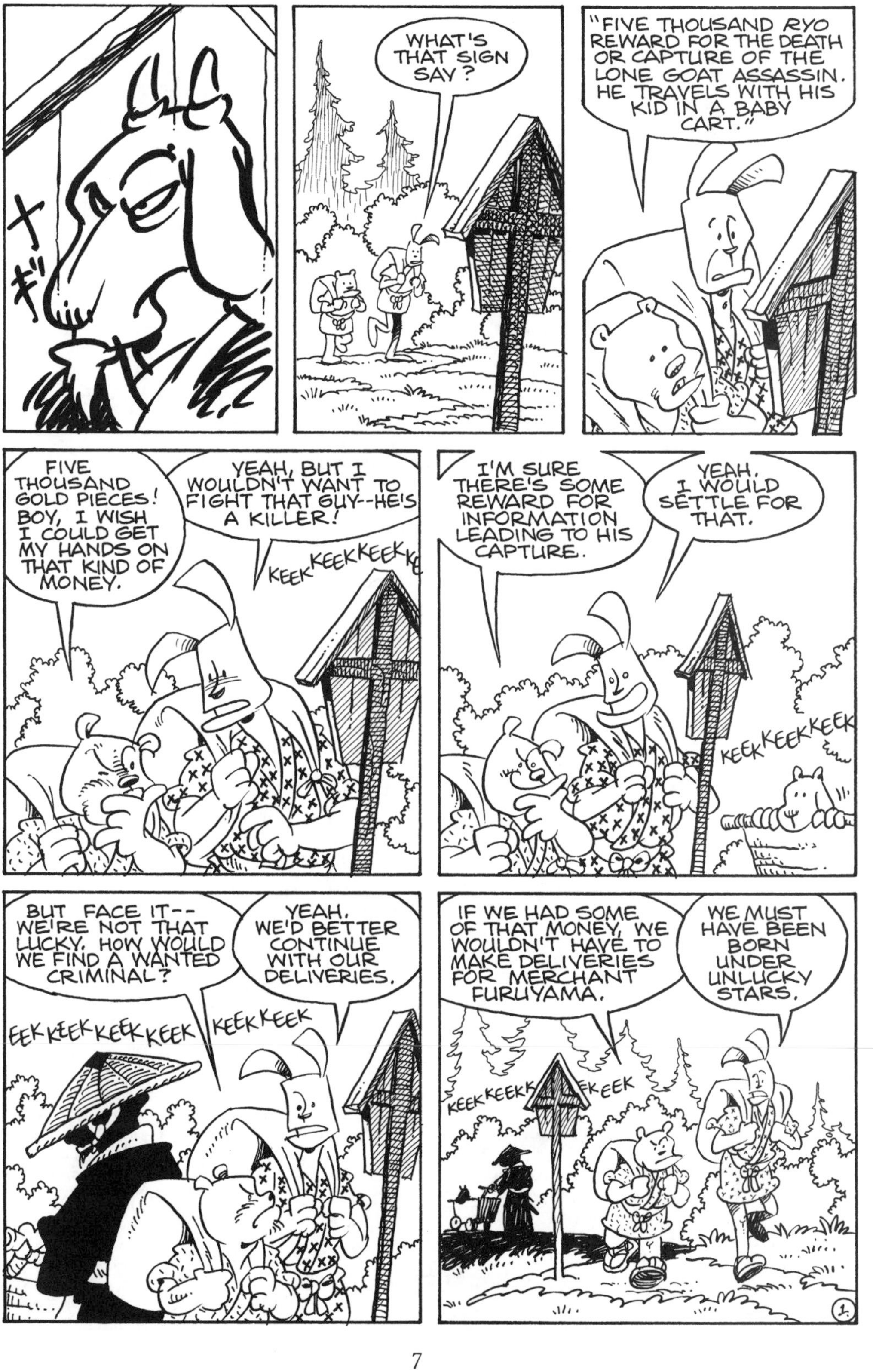
WHAT'S THAT SIGN SAY?
"FIVE THOUSAND RYO REWARD FOR THE DEATH OR CAPTURE OF THE LONE GOAT ASSASSIN. HE TRAVELS WITH HIS KID IN A BABY CART."
FIVE THOUSAND GOLD PIECES! BOY, I WISH I COULD GET MY HANDS ON THAT KIND OF MONEY.
YEAH, BUT I WOULDN'T WANT TO FIGHT THAT GUY--HE'S A KILLER!
KEEKKEEKKEEKKE
I'M SURE THERE'S SOME REWARD FOR INFORMATION LEADING TO HIS CAPTURE.
YEAH. I WOULD SETTLE FOR THAT.
KEEKKEEKKEEK
BUT FACE IT--WE'RE NOT THAT LUCKY. HOW WOULD WE FIND A WANTED CRIMINAL?
YEAH. WE'D BETTER CONTINUE WITH OUR DELIVERIES.
EEKKEEKKEEKKEEK
KEEKKEEK
IF WE HAD SOME OF THAT MONEY, WE WOULDN'T HAVE TO MAKE DELIVERIES FOR MERCHANT FURUYAMA.
WE MUST HAVE BEEN BORN UNDER UNLUCKY STARS.
KEEKKEEKK
EKEEK

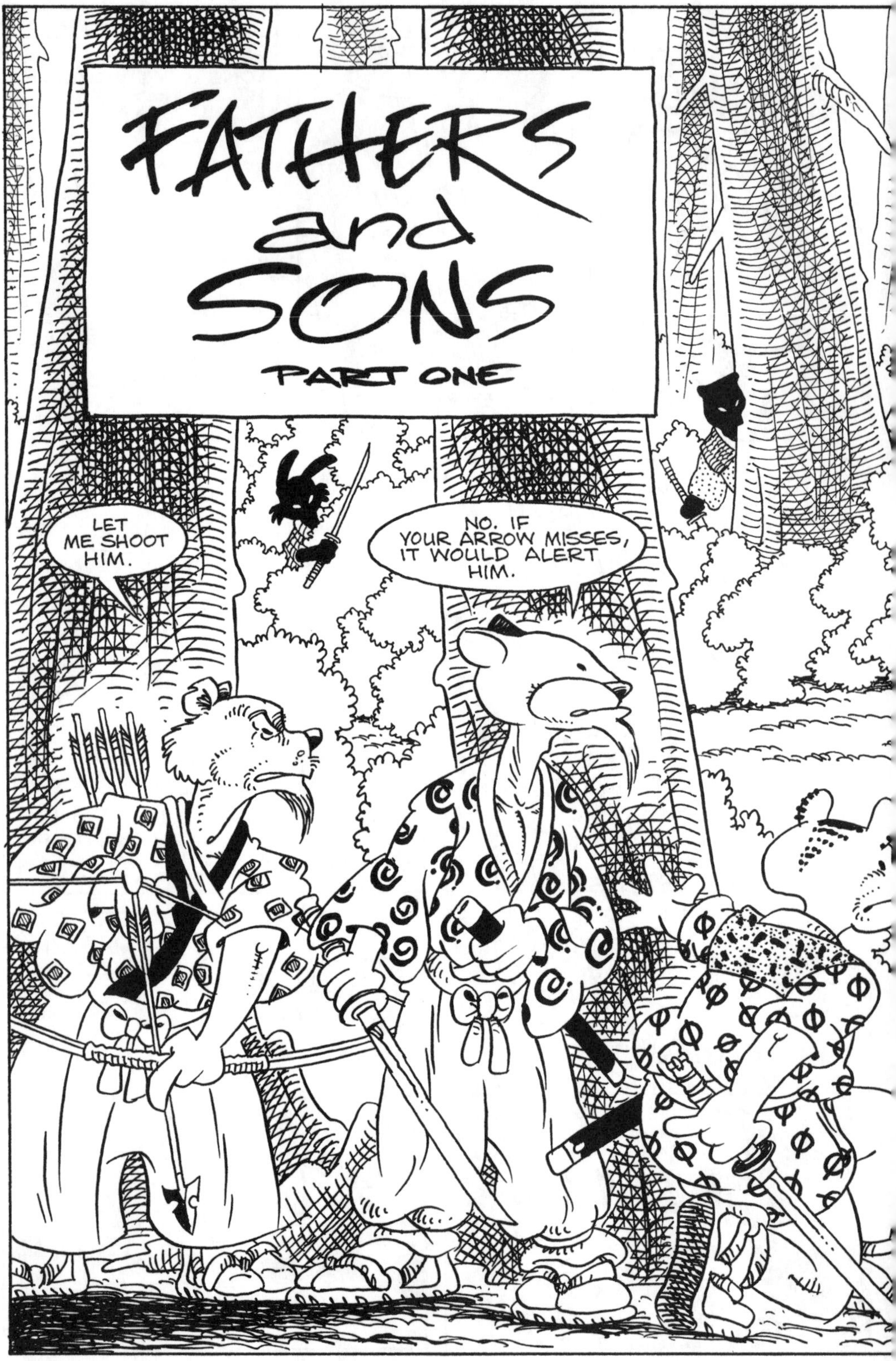
FATHERS and SONS
PART ONE
LET ME SHOOT HIM.
NO. IF YOUR ARROW MISSES, IT WOULD ALERT HIM.

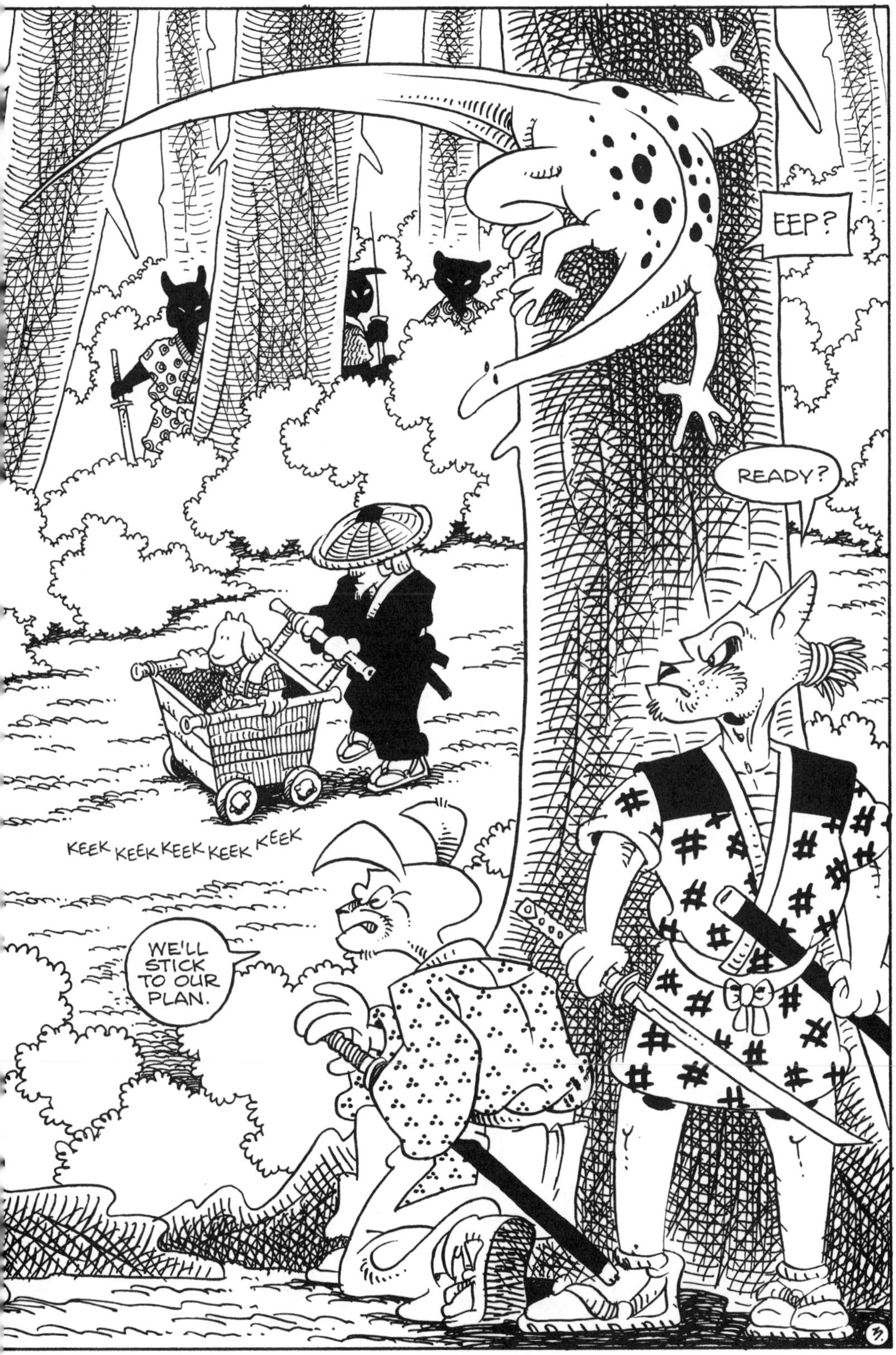
EEP?
READY?
KEEK KEEK KEEK KEEK KEEK
WE'LL STICK TO OUR PLAN.
3.

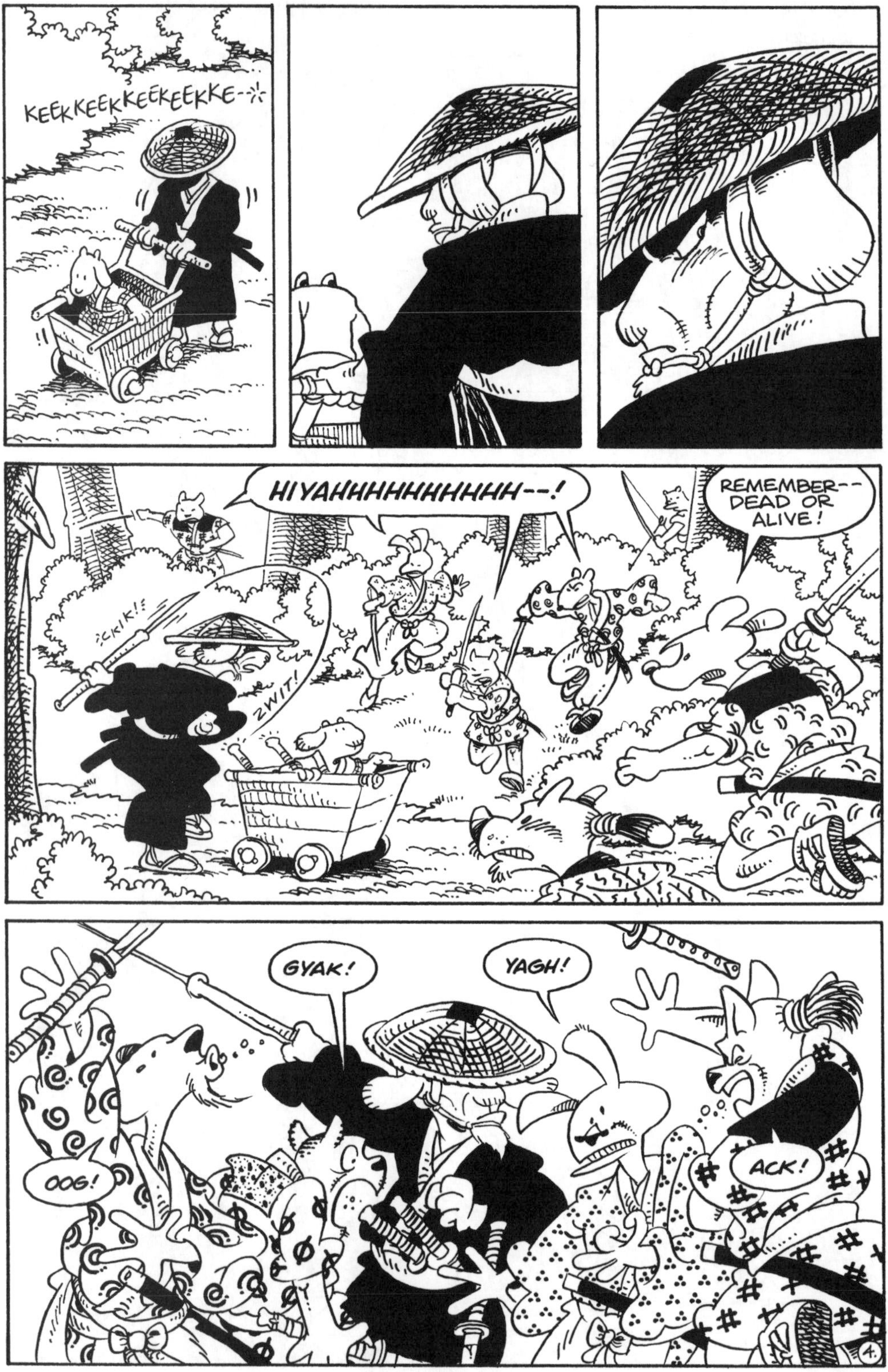
KEEKKEEKKEEKEEKKE--
HIYAHHHHHHHHHH--!
REMEMBER-- DEAD OR ALIVE!
CKIK!
ZWIT!
GYAK!
YAGH!
OOG!
ACK!

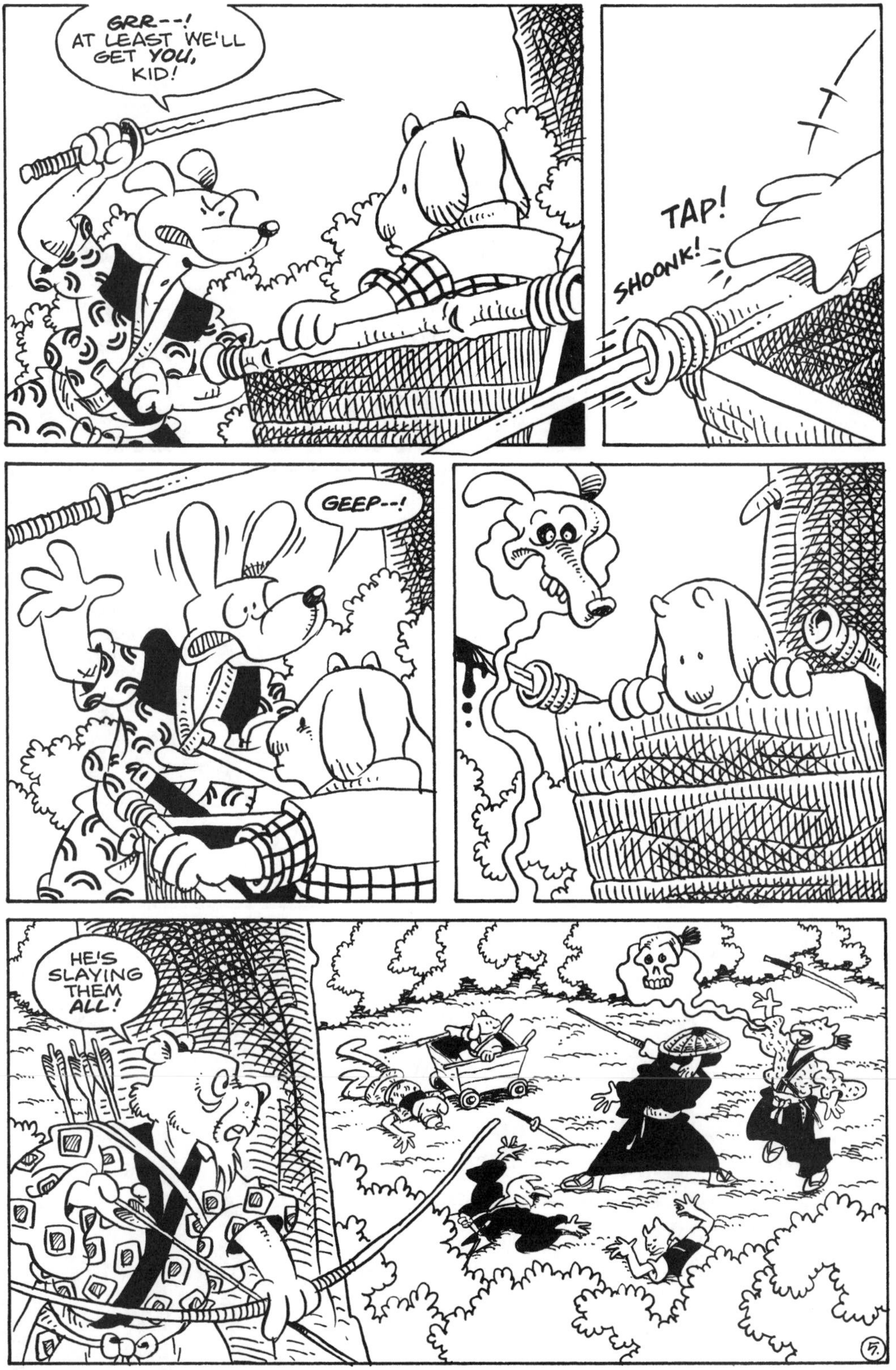
GRR--! AT LEAST WE'LL GET YOU, KID!
TAP!
SHOONK!
GEEP--!
HE'S SLAYING THEM ALL!
5.

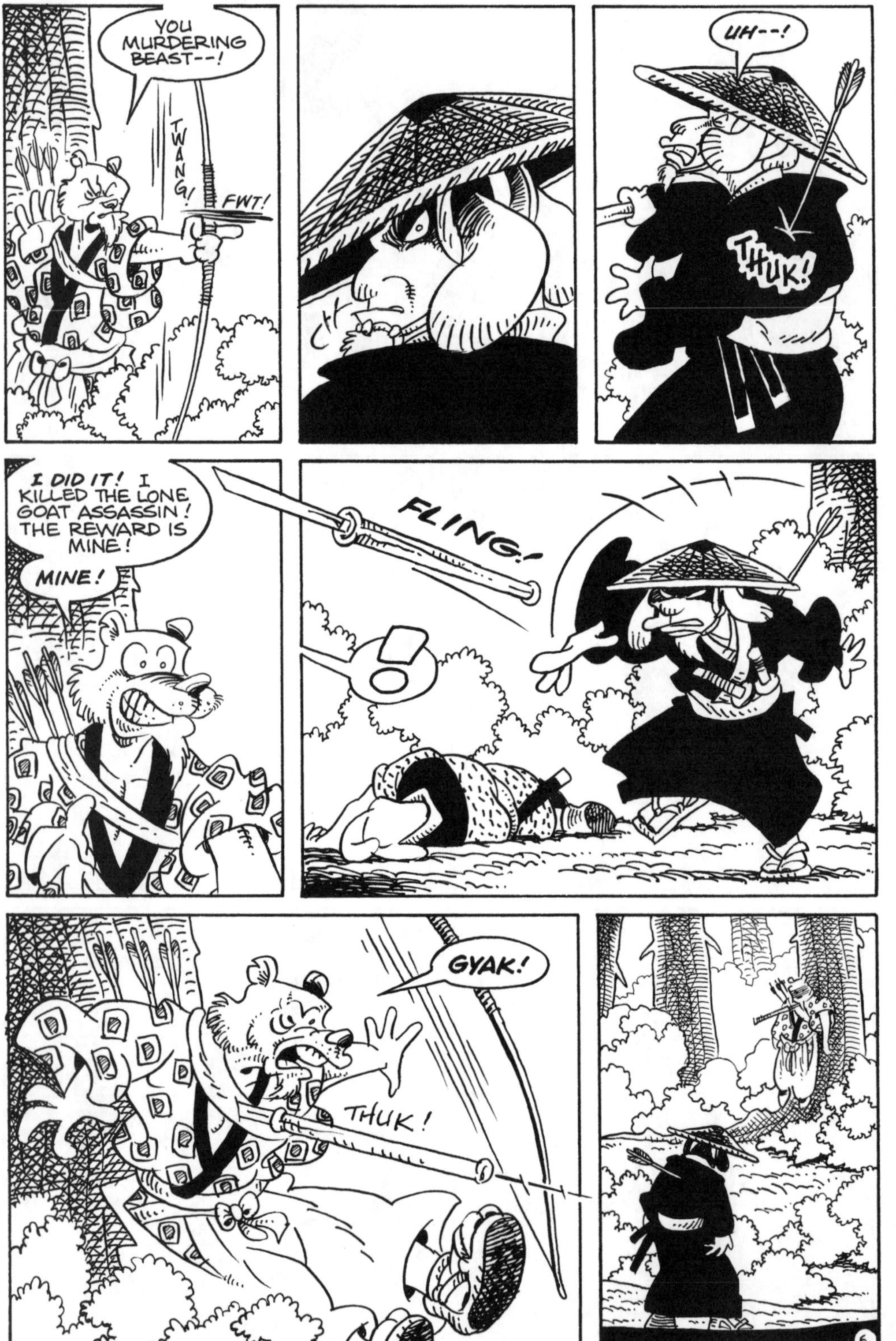
YOU MURDERING BEAST--!
TWANG!
FWT!
CH
UH--!
THUK!
I DID IT! I KILLED THE LONE GOAT ASSASSIN! THE REWARD IS MINE!
MINE!
FLING!
!
GYAK!
THUK!
6.

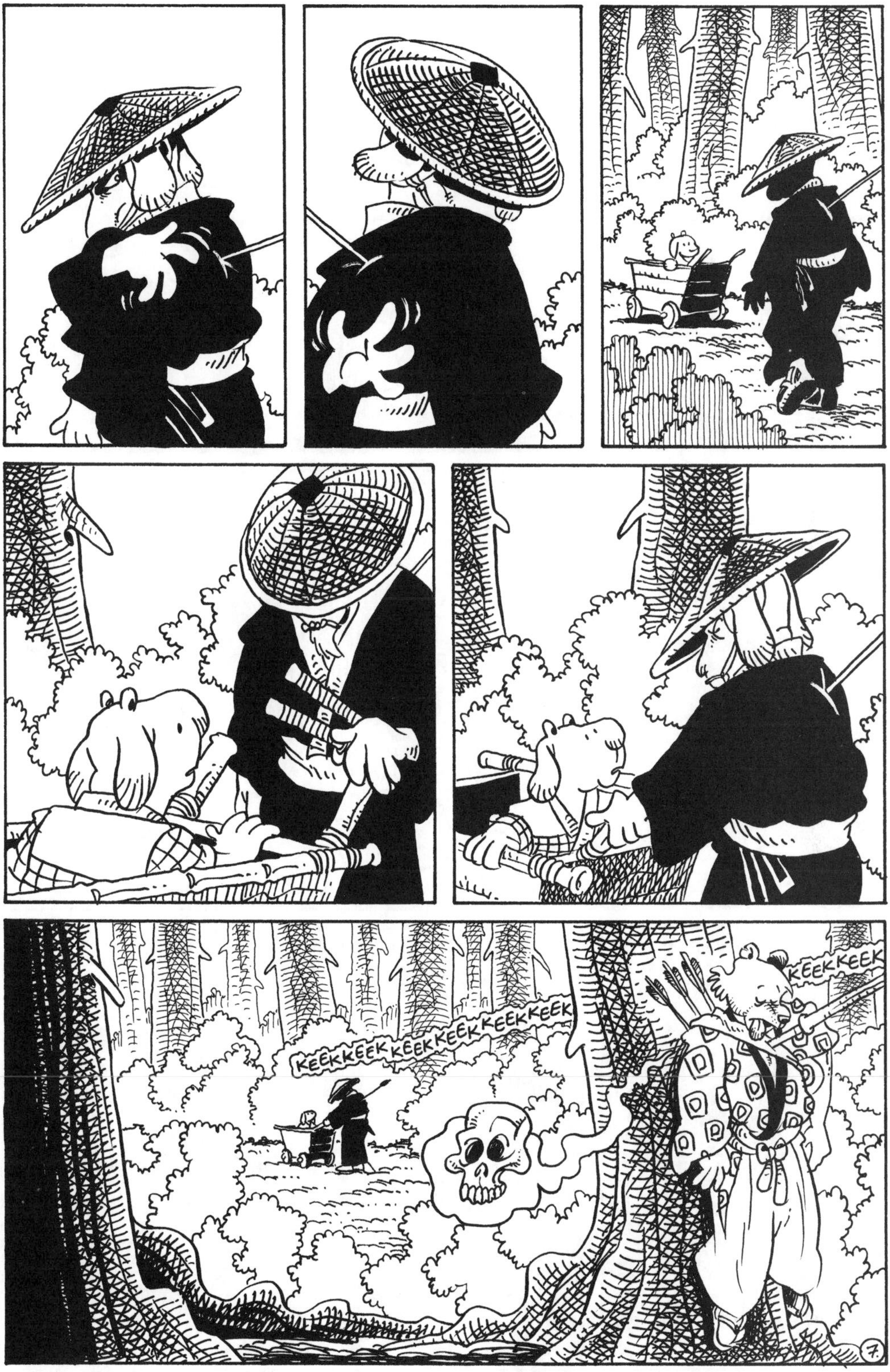
KEEKKEEK
KEEKKEEKKEEKKEEKKEEKKEEK
7.

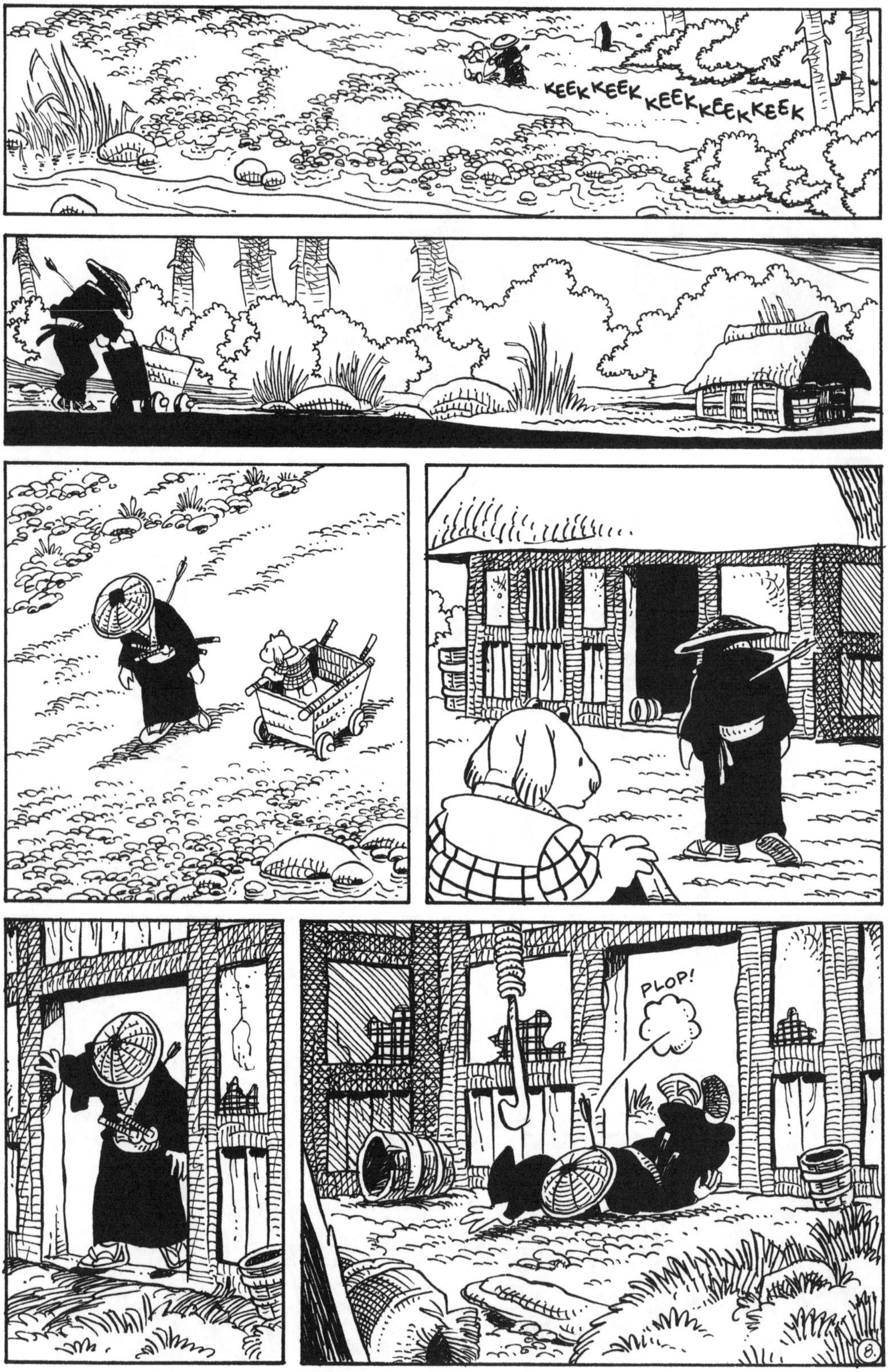
KEEK KEEK KEEK KEEK KEEK
PLOP!
8.

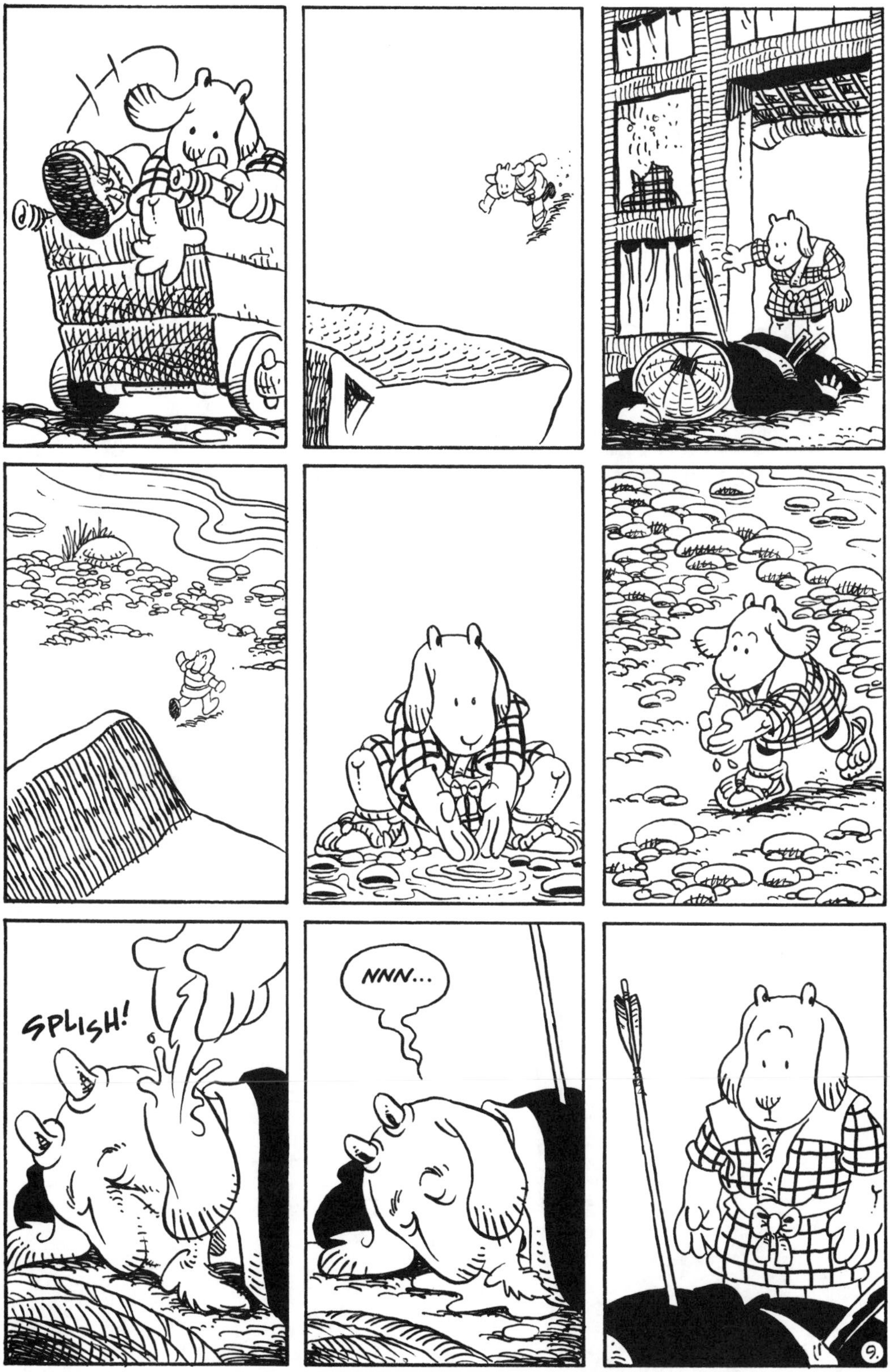
SPLISH!
NNN...
9.

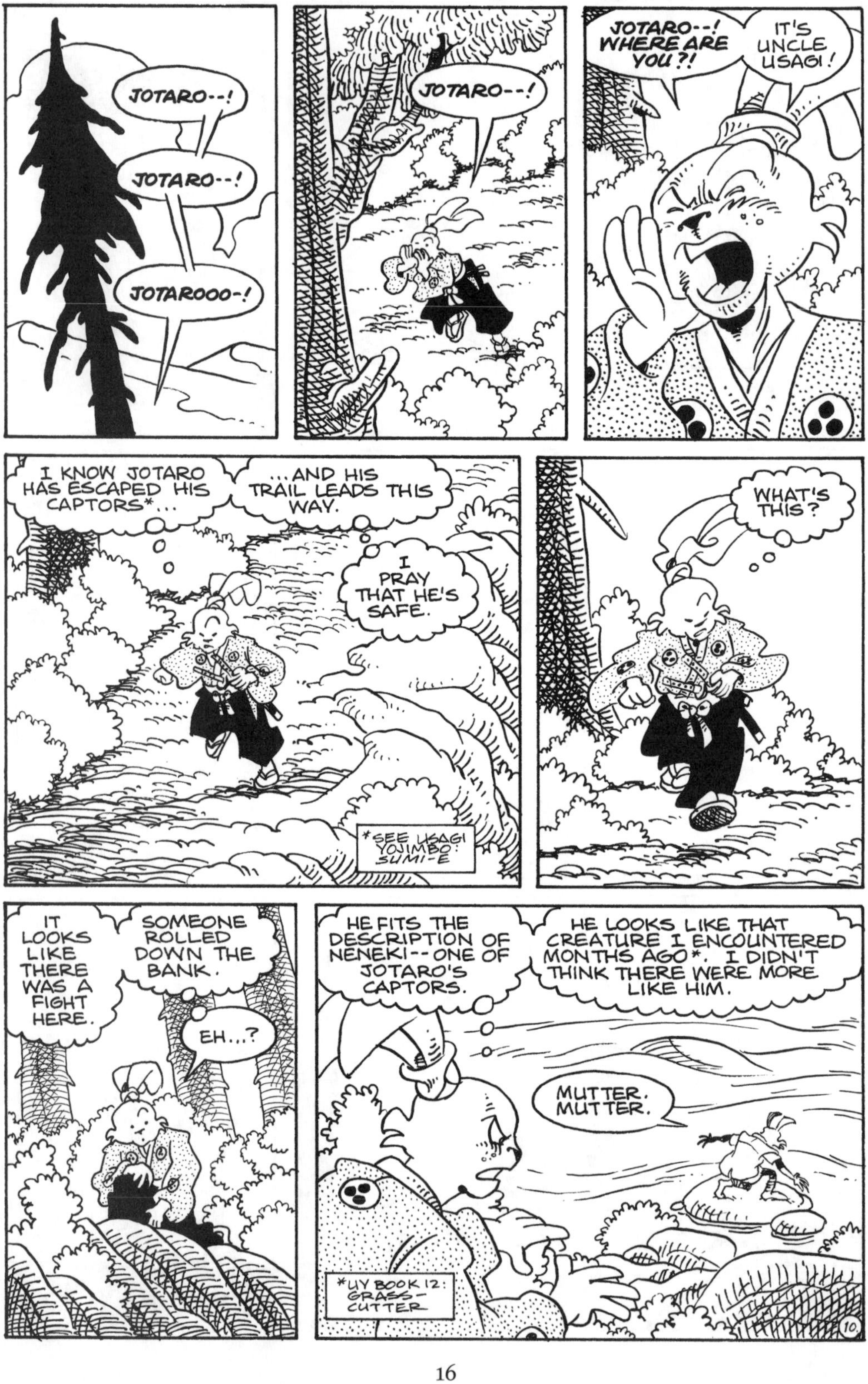
JOTARO--!
JOTARO--!
JOTAROOO-!
JOTARO--!
JOTARO--! WHERE ARE YOU?!
IT'S UNCLE USAGI!
I KNOW JOTARO HAS ESCAPED HIS CAPTORS*...
...AND HIS TRAIL LEADS THIS WAY.
I PRAY THAT HE'S SAFE.
*SEE USAGI YOJIMBO: SUMI-E
WHAT'S THIS?
IT LOOKS LIKE THERE WAS A FIGHT HERE.
SOMEONE ROLLED DOWN THE BANK.
EH...?
HE FITS THE DESCRIPTION OF NENEKI--ONE OF JOTARO'S CAPTORS.
HE LOOKS LIKE THAT CREATURE I ENCOUNTERED MONTHS AGO*. I DIDN'T THINK THERE WERE MORE LIKE HIM.
MUTTER. MUTTER.
*UY BOOK 12: GRASS-CUTTER
10

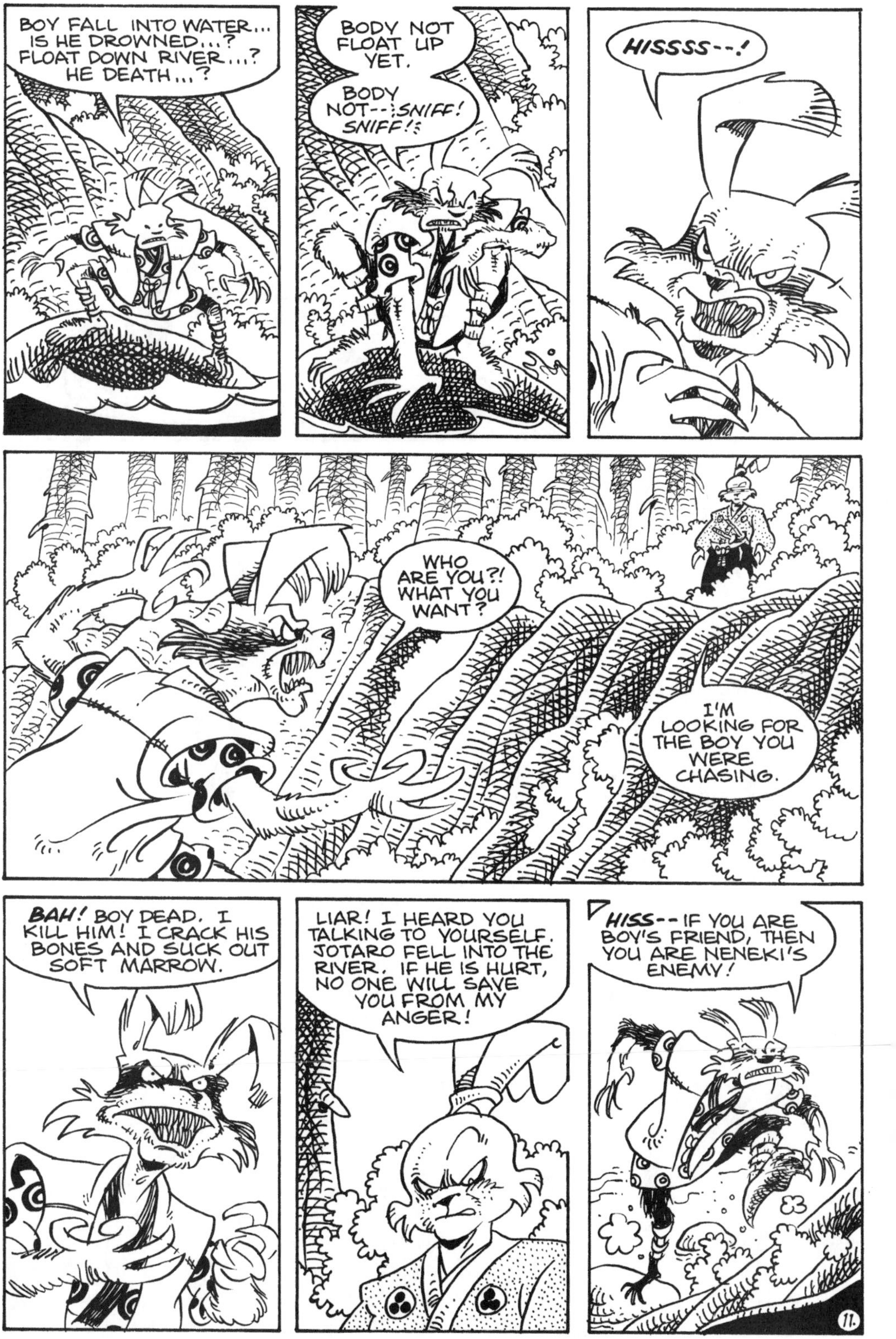
BOY FALL INTO WATER... IS HE DROWNED...? FLOAT DOWN RIVER...? HE DEATH...?
BODY NOT FLOAT UP YET.
BODY NOT--SNIFF! SNIFF!
HISSSS--!
WHO ARE YOU?! WHAT YOU WANT?
I'M LOOKING FOR THE BOY YOU WERE CHASING.
BAH! BOY DEAD. I KILL HIM! I CRACK HIS BONES AND SUCK OUT SOFT MARROW.
LIAR! I HEARD YOU TALKING TO YOURSELF. JOTARO FELL INTO THE RIVER. IF HE IS HURT, NO ONE WILL SAVE YOU FROM MY ANGER!
HISS--IF YOU ARE BOY'S FRIEND, THEN YOU ARE NENEKI'S ENEMY!
11.

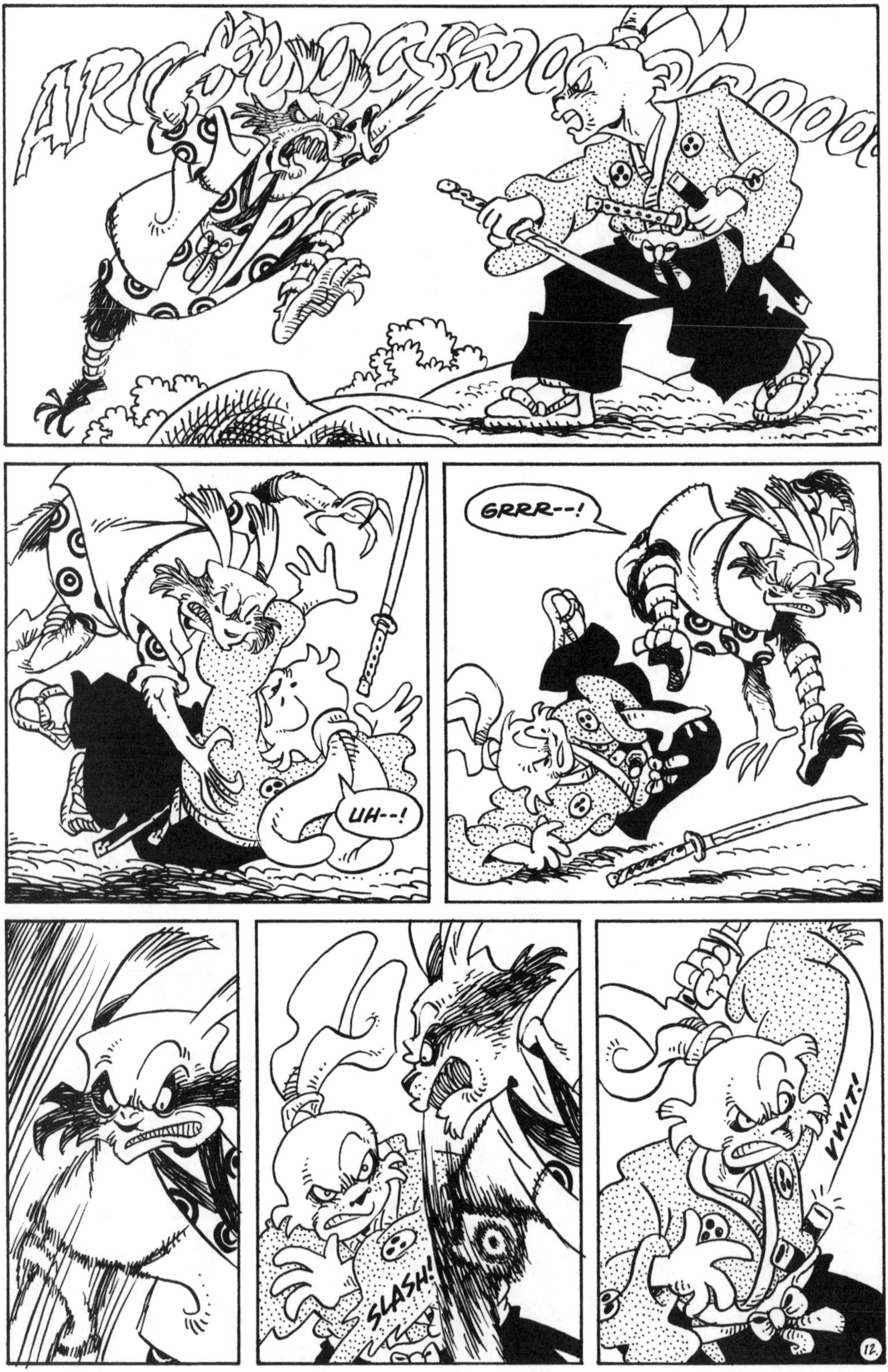
GRRR--!
UH--!
SLASH!
VWIT!

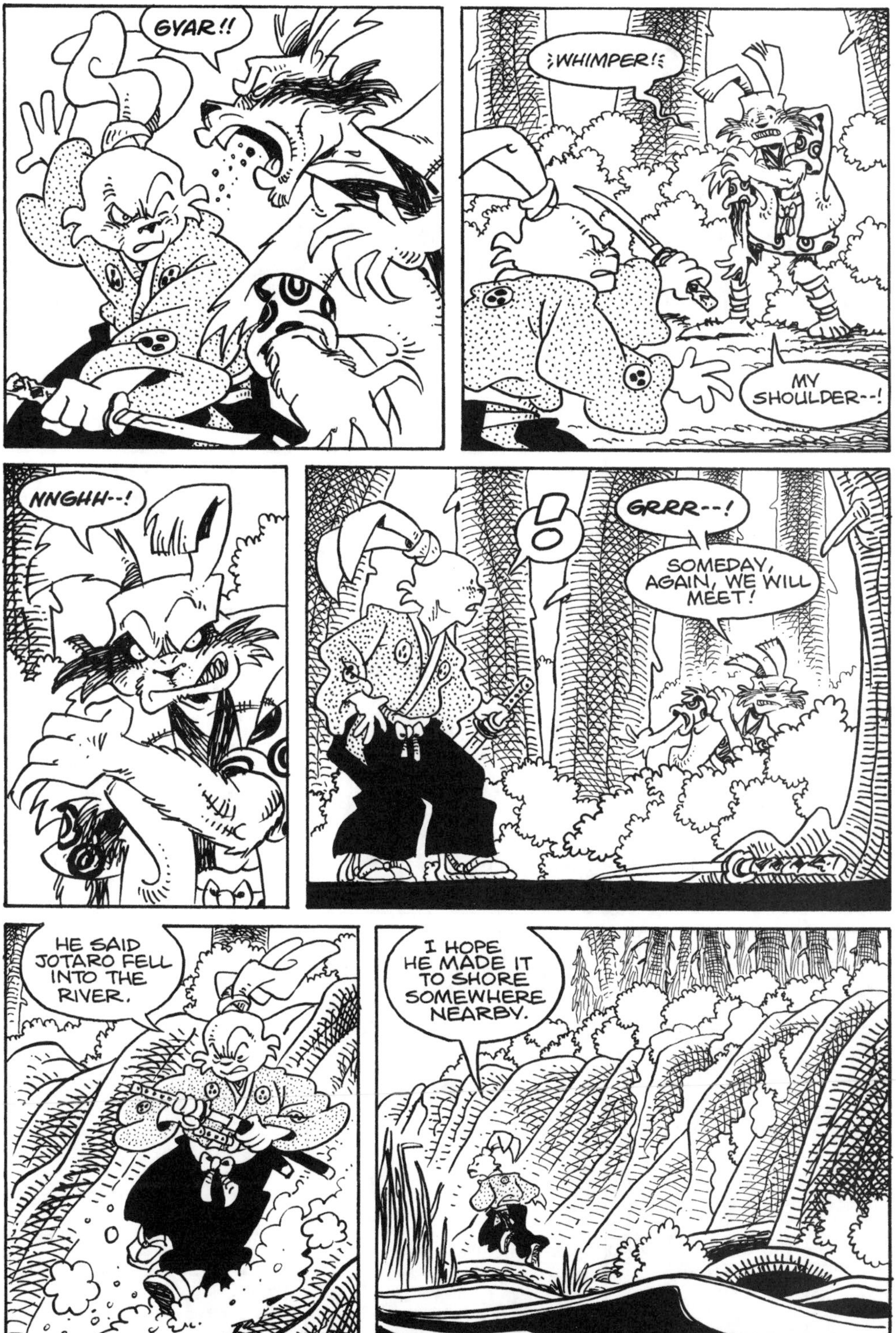
GYAR!!
WHIMPER!
MY SHOULDER--!
NNGHH--!
!
GRRR--!
SOMEDAY, AGAIN, WE WILL MEET!
HE SAID JOTARO FELL INTO THE RIVER.
I HOPE HE MADE IT TO SHORE SOMEWHERE NEARBY.
13.

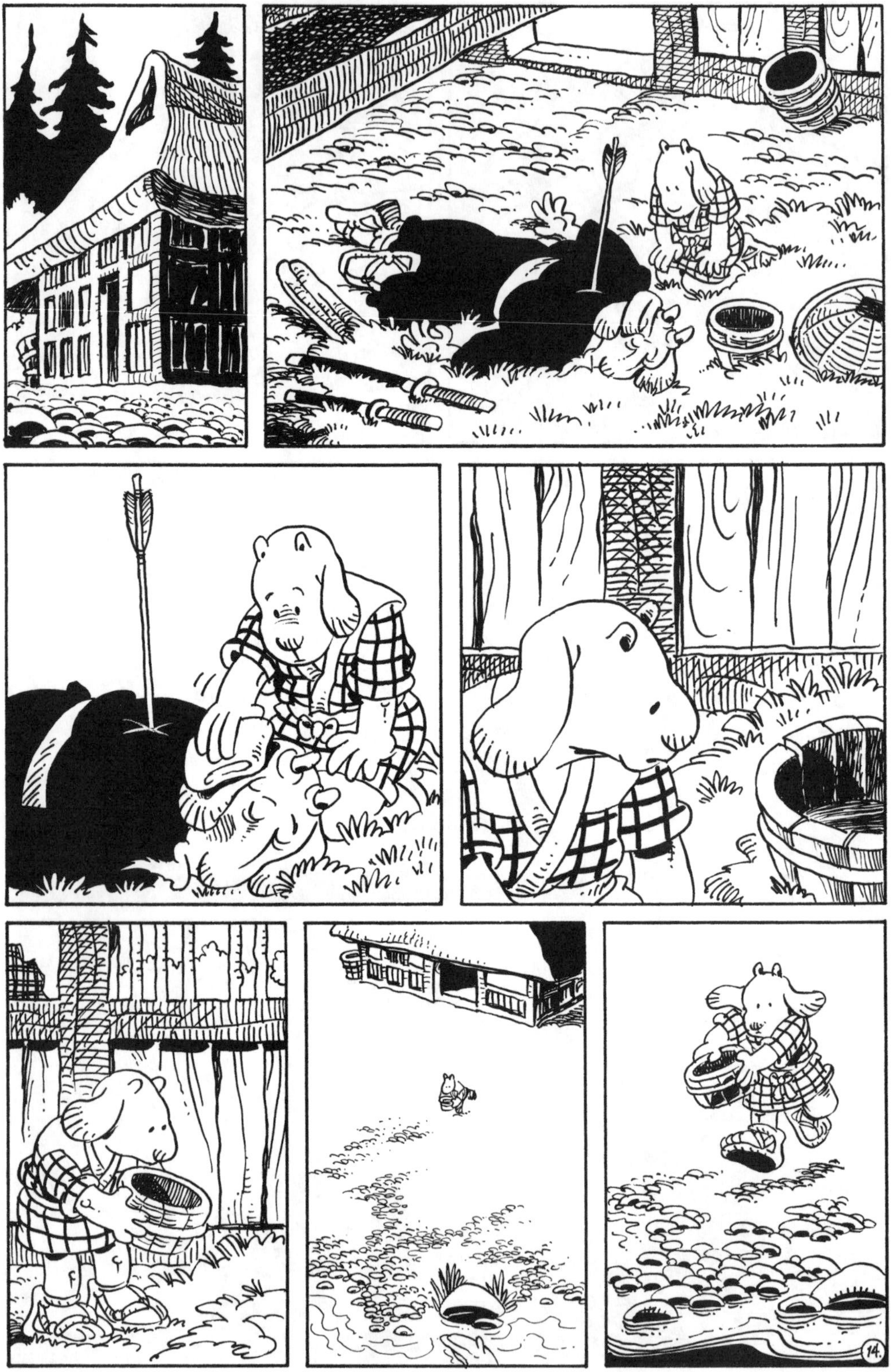
14.

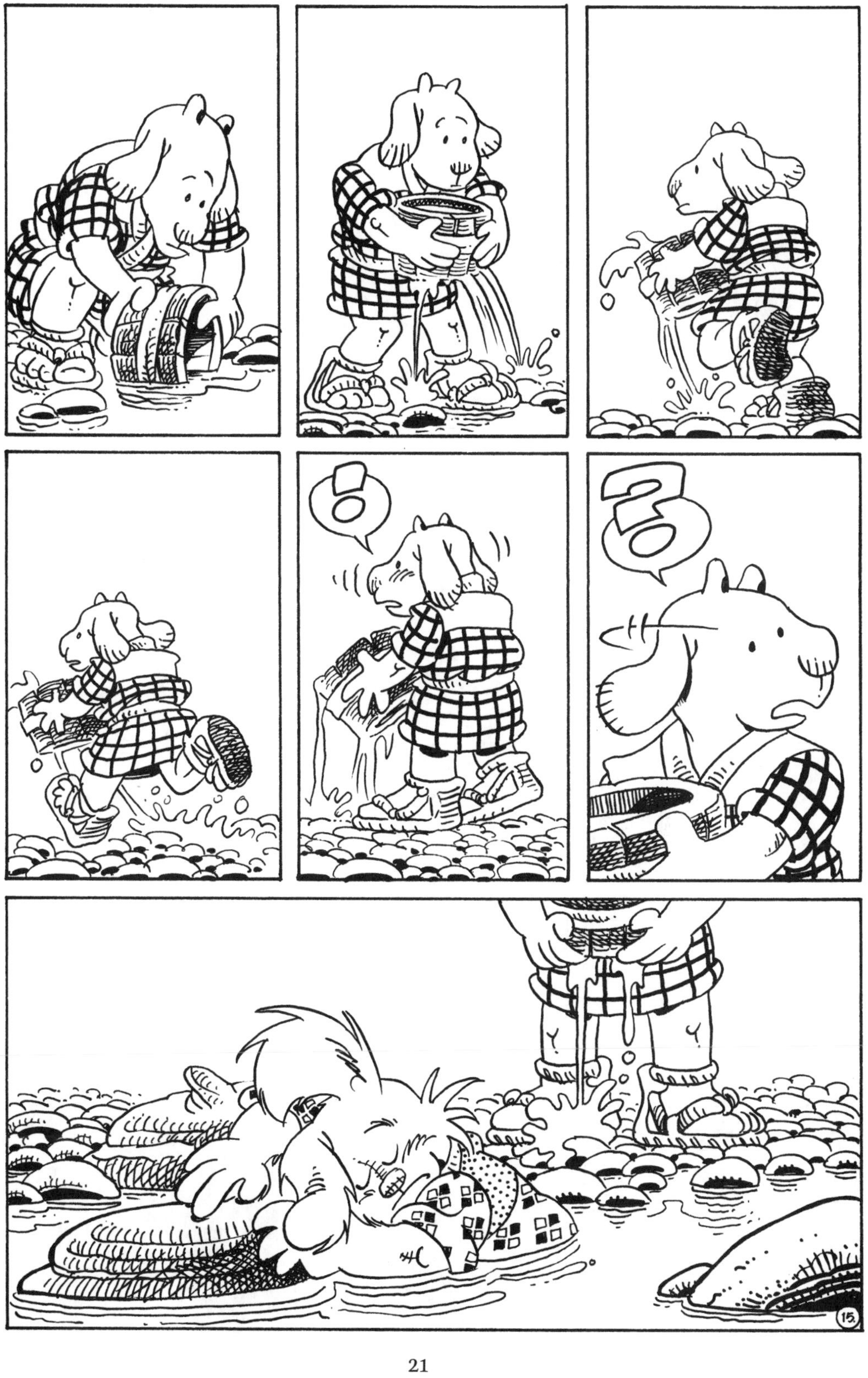
!
?
15

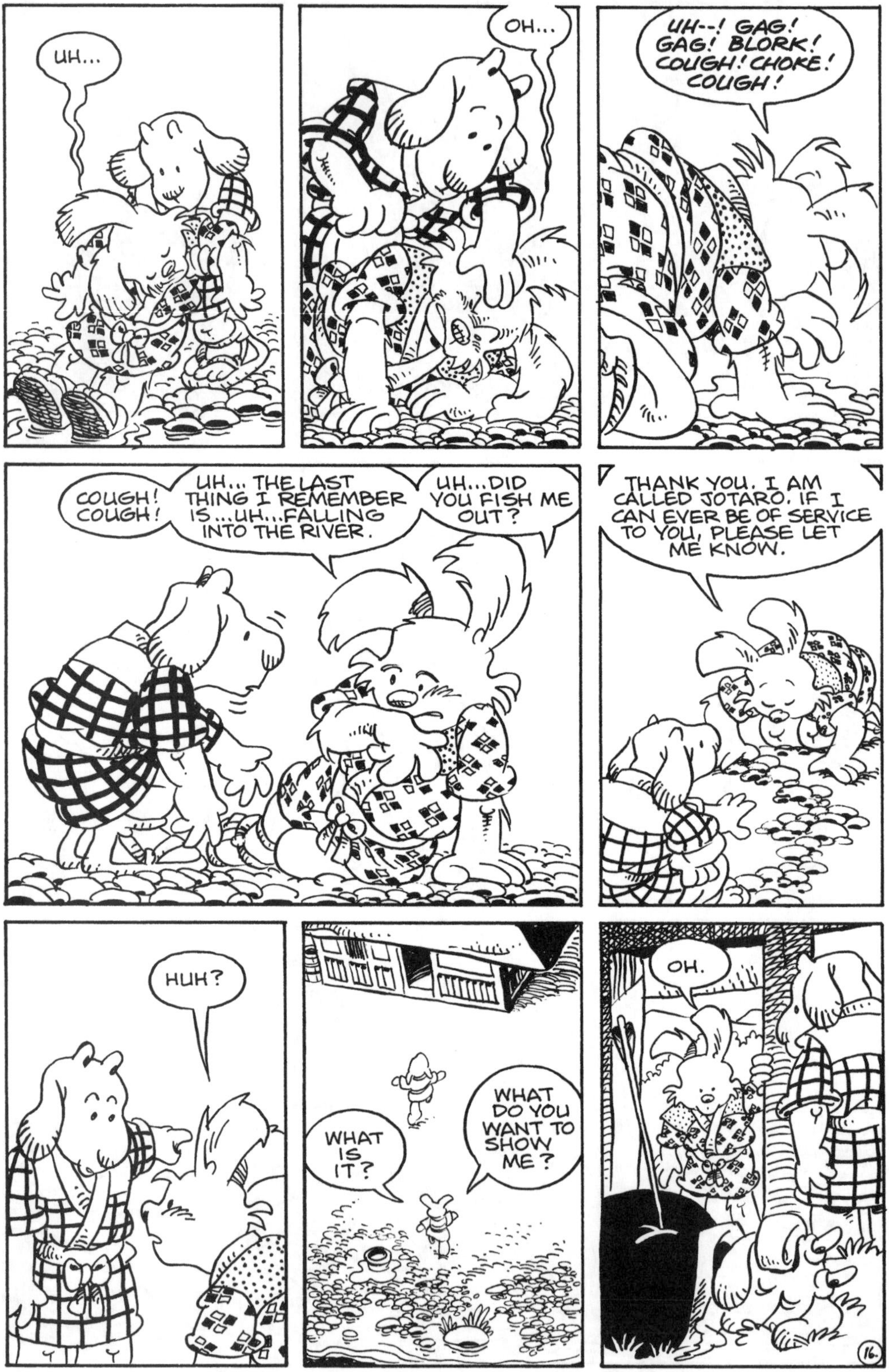
UH...
OH...
UH--! GAG! GAG! BLORK! COUGH! CHOKE! COUGH!
COUGH! COUGH!
UH... THE LAST THING I REMEMBER IS...UH...FALLING INTO THE RIVER.
UH...DID YOU FISH ME OUT?
THANK YOU. I AM CALLED JOTARO. IF I CAN EVER BE OF SERVICE TO YOU, PLEASE LET ME KNOW.
HUH?
WHAT IS IT?
WHAT DO YOU WANT TO SHOW ME?
OH.
16.

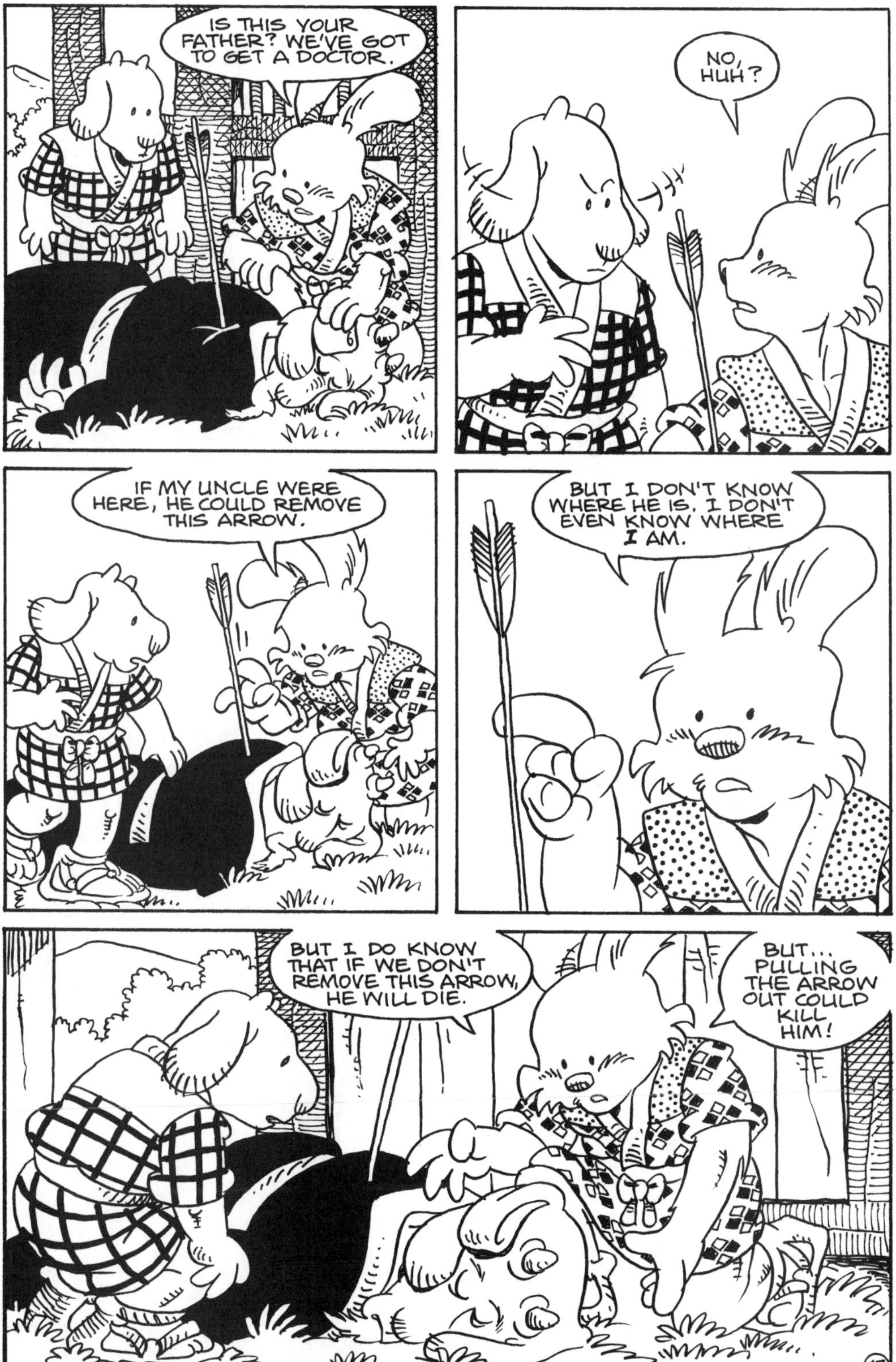
IS THIS YOUR FATHER? WE'VE GOT TO GET A DOCTOR.
NO, HUH?
IF MY UNCLE WERE HERE, HE COULD REMOVE THIS ARROW.
BUT I DON'T KNOW WHERE HE IS. I DON'T EVEN KNOW WHERE I AM.
BUT I DO KNOW THAT IF WE DON'T REMOVE THIS ARROW, HE WILL DIE.
BUT... PULLING THE ARROW OUT COULD KILL HIM!
17

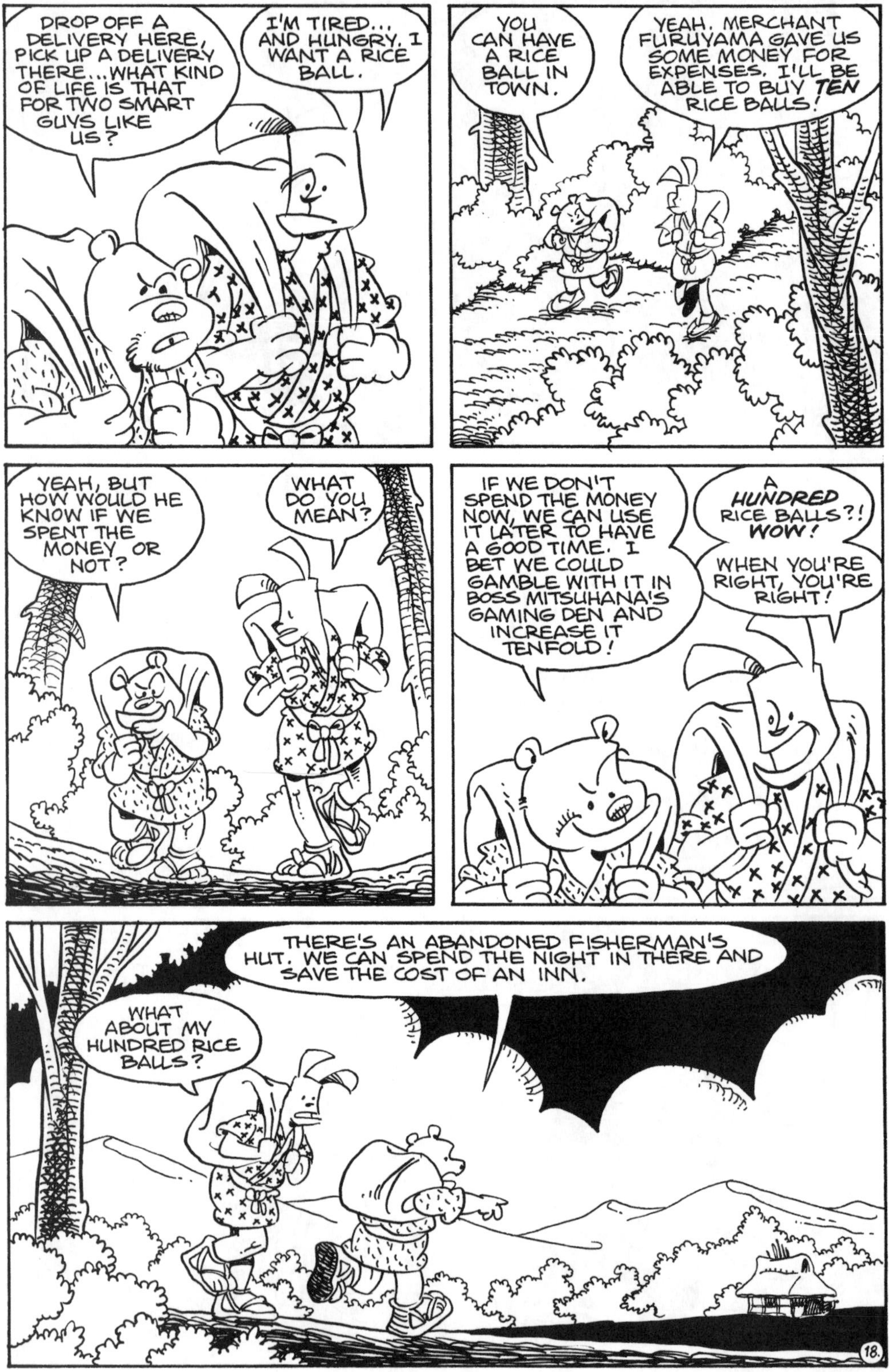
DROP OFF A DELIVERY HERE, PICK UP A DELIVERY THERE...WHAT KIND OF LIFE IS THAT FOR TWO SMART GUYS LIKE US?
I'M TIRED... AND HUNGRY. I WANT A RICE BALL.
YOU CAN HAVE A RICE BALL IN TOWN.
YEAH. MERCHANT FURUYAMA GAVE US SOME MONEY FOR EXPENSES. I'LL BE ABLE TO BUY TEN RICE BALLS!
YEAH, BUT HOW WOULD HE KNOW IF WE SPENT THE MONEY OR NOT?
WHAT DO YOU MEAN?
IF WE DON'T SPEND THE MONEY NOW, WE CAN USE IT LATER TO HAVE A GOOD TIME. I BET WE COULD GAMBLE WITH IT IN BOSS MITSUHANA'S GAMING DEN AND INCREASE IT TENFOLD!
A HUNDRED RICE BALLS?! WOW!
WHEN YOU'RE RIGHT, YOU'RE RIGHT!
THERE'S AN ABANDONED FISHERMAN'S HUT. WE CAN SPEND THE NIGHT IN THERE AND SAVE THE COST OF AN INN.
WHAT ABOUT MY HUNDRED RICE BALLS?
18.

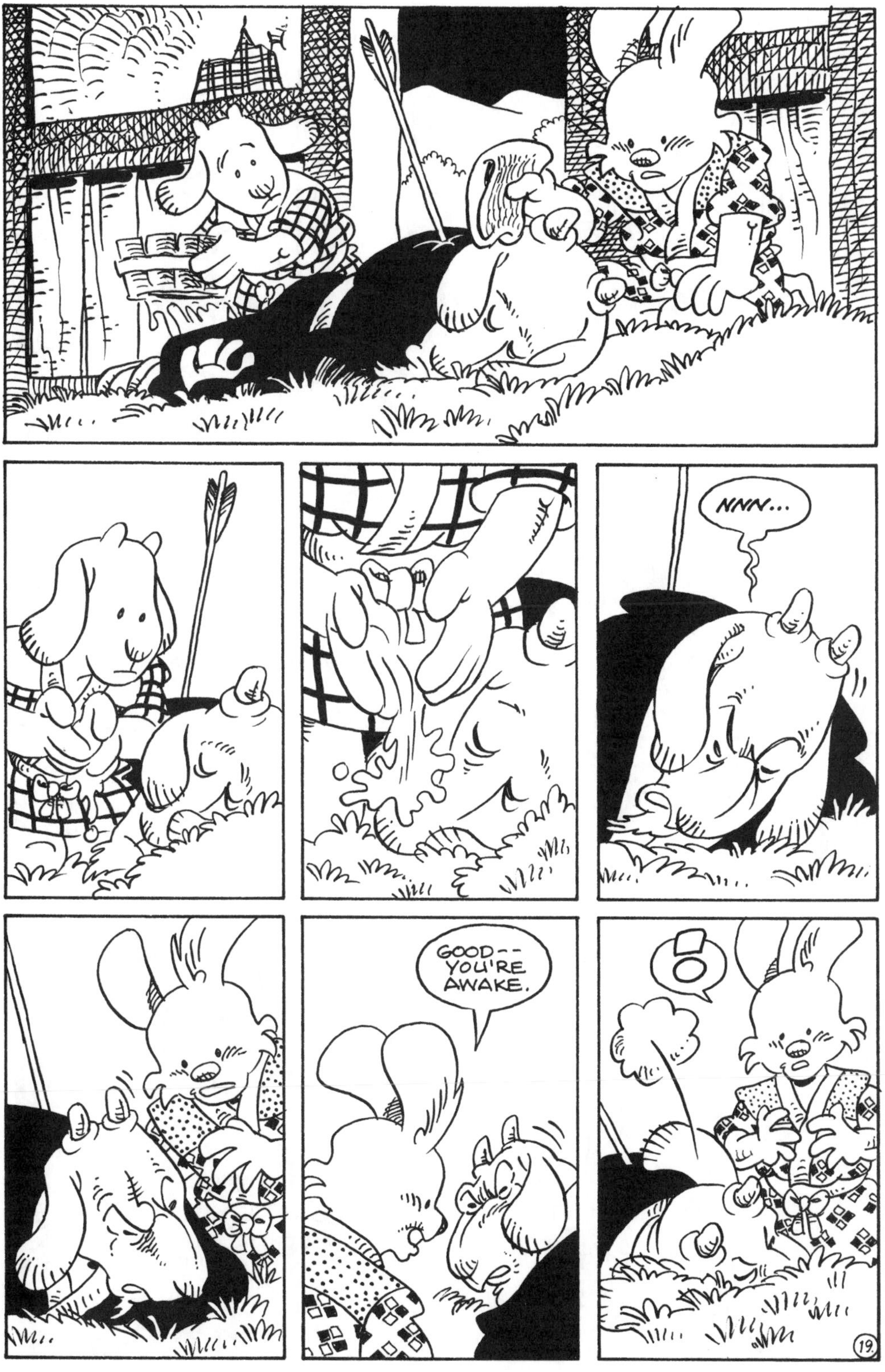
NNN...
GOOD--
YOU'RE
AWAKE.
19

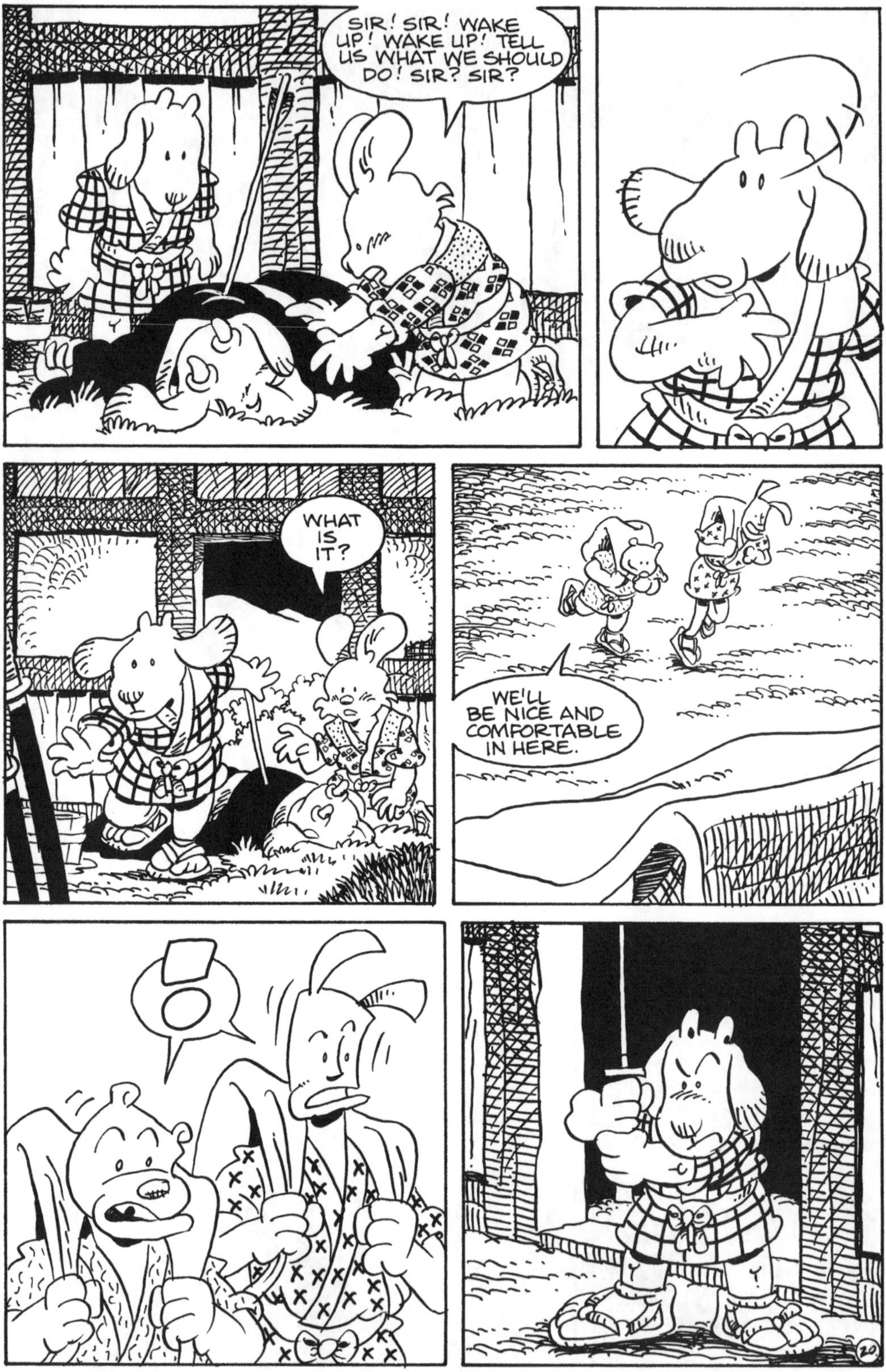

SIR! SIR! WAKE UP! WAKE UP! TELL US WHAT WE SHOULD DO! SIR? SIR?
WHAT IS IT?
WE'LL BE NICE AND COMFORTABLE IN HERE.
!
20

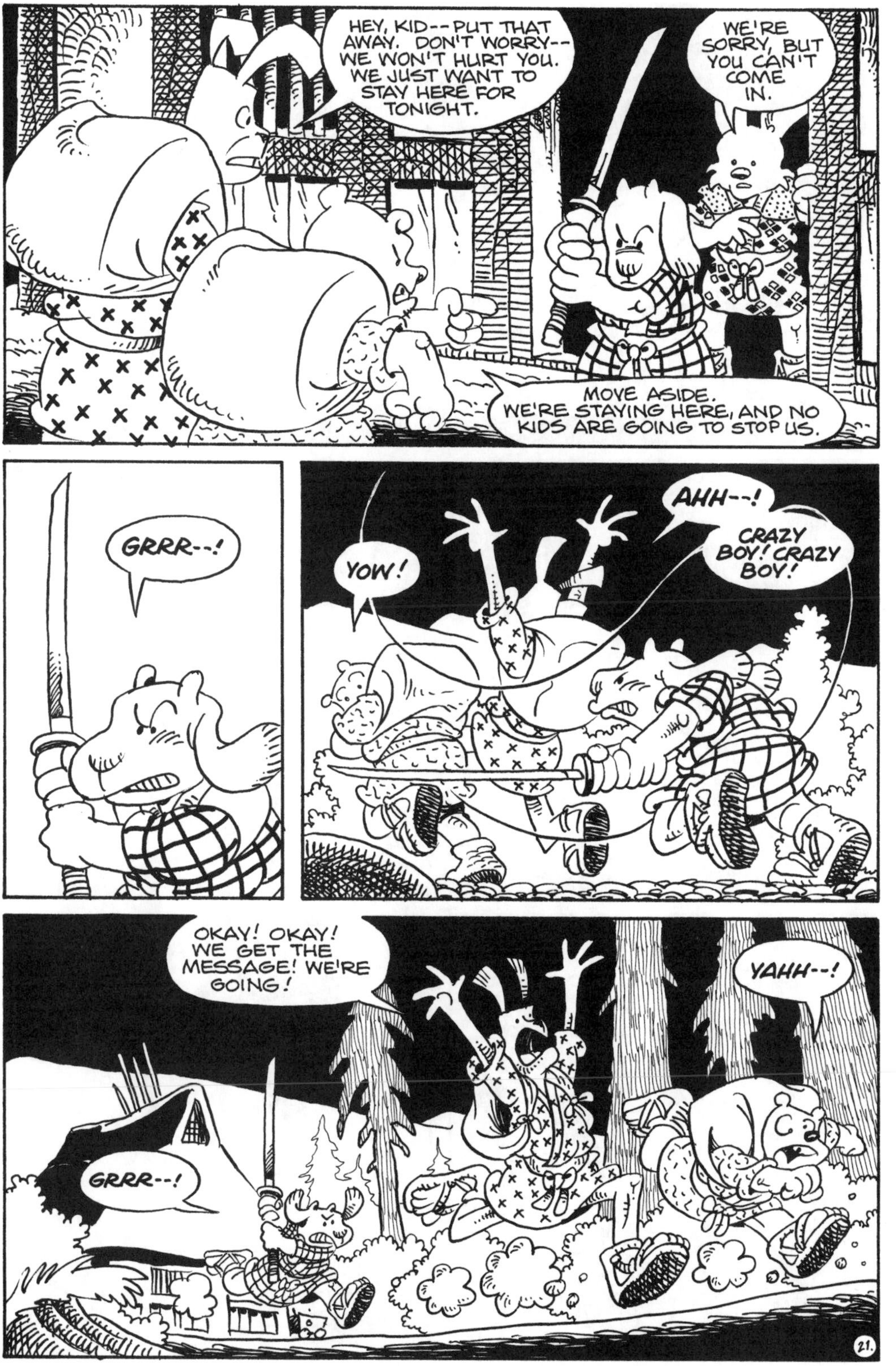
HEY, KID--PUT THAT AWAY. DON'T WORRY--WE WON'T HURT YOU. WE JUST WANT TO STAY HERE FOR TONIGHT.
WE'RE SORRY, BUT YOU CAN'T COME IN.
MOVE ASIDE. WE'RE STAYING HERE, AND NO KIDS ARE GOING TO STOP US.
GRRR--!
YOW!
AHH--!
CRAZY BOY! CRAZY BOY!
OKAY! OKAY! WE GET THE MESSAGE! WE'RE GOING!
YAHH--!
GRRR--!
21.

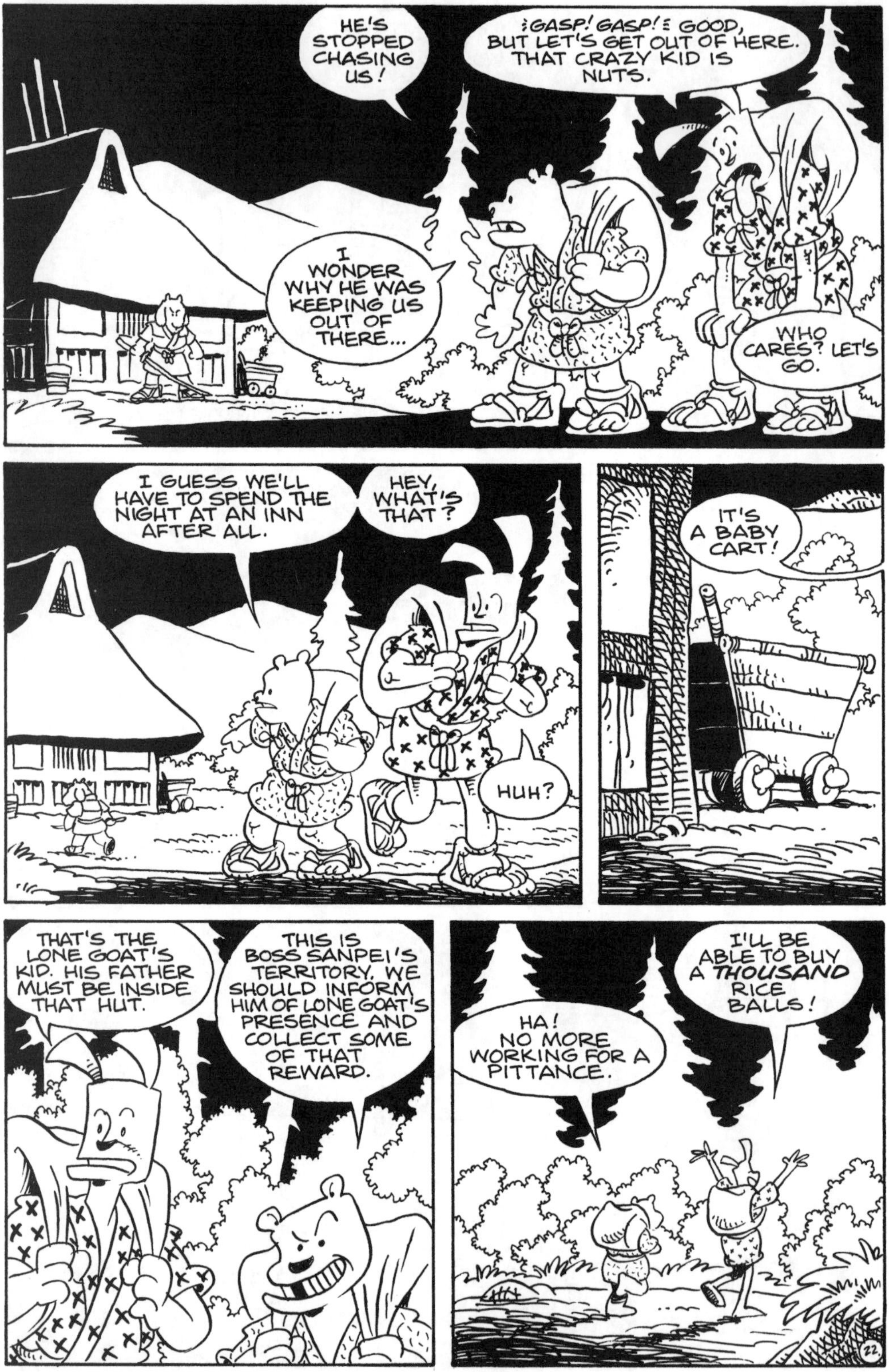
HE'S STOPPED CHASING US!
:GASP! GASP!: GOOD, BUT LET'S GET OUT OF HERE. THAT CRAZY KID IS NUTS.
I WONDER WHY HE WAS KEEPING US OUT OF THERE...
WHO CARES? LET'S GO.
I GUESS WE'LL HAVE TO SPEND THE NIGHT AT AN INN AFTER ALL.
HEY, WHAT'S THAT?
HUH?
IT'S A BABY CART!
THAT'S THE LONE GOAT'S KID. HIS FATHER MUST BE INSIDE THAT HUT.
THIS IS BOSS SANPEI'S TERRITORY. WE SHOULD INFORM HIM OF LONE GOAT'S PRESENCE AND COLLECT SOME OF THAT REWARD.
HA! NO MORE WORKING FOR A PITTANCE.
I'LL BE ABLE TO BUY A *THOUSAND* RICE BALLS!
22.

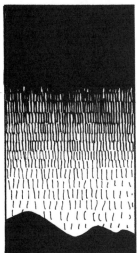

ZZZ...

NNGH...?

¡YAWN!

I WONDER WHAT THE STORY IS BEHIND THAT ARROW WOUND...

POOR LITTLE GUY. IT DOESN'T LOOK LIKE HE GOT ANY SLEEP LAST NIGHT.

I DON'T KNOW WHY HE CHASED THOSE TWO AWAY LAST NIGHT. MAYBE THEY COULD HAVE HELPED... BUT HE MUST HAVE HAD HIS REASONS.

HOW IS YOUR FATHER?

HE'S EVEN WORSE THAN YESTERDAY.

23.

29

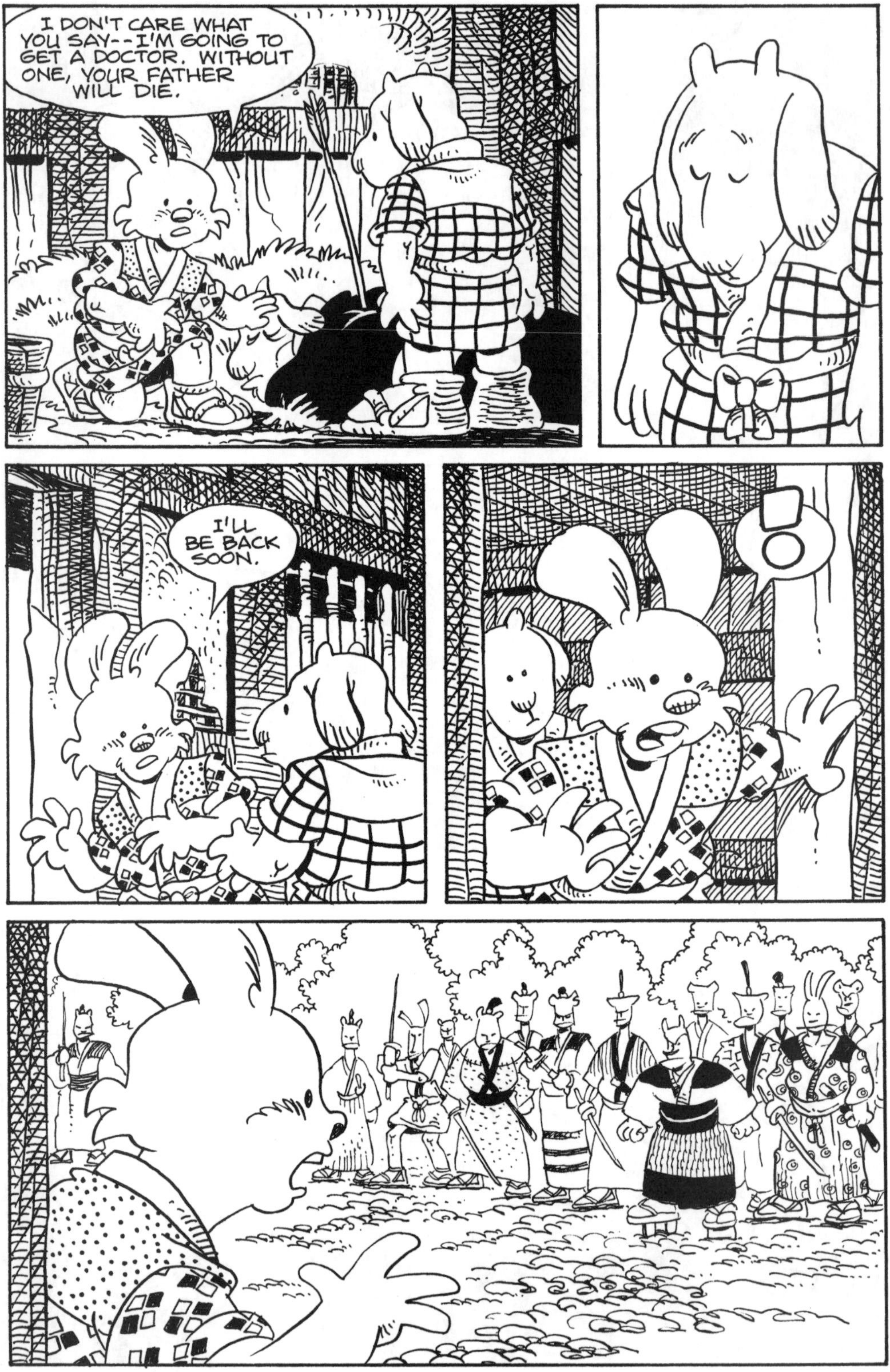
I DON'T CARE WHAT YOU SAY--I'M GOING TO GET A DOCTOR. WITHOUT ONE, YOUR FATHER WILL DIE.
I'LL BE BACK SOON.
!

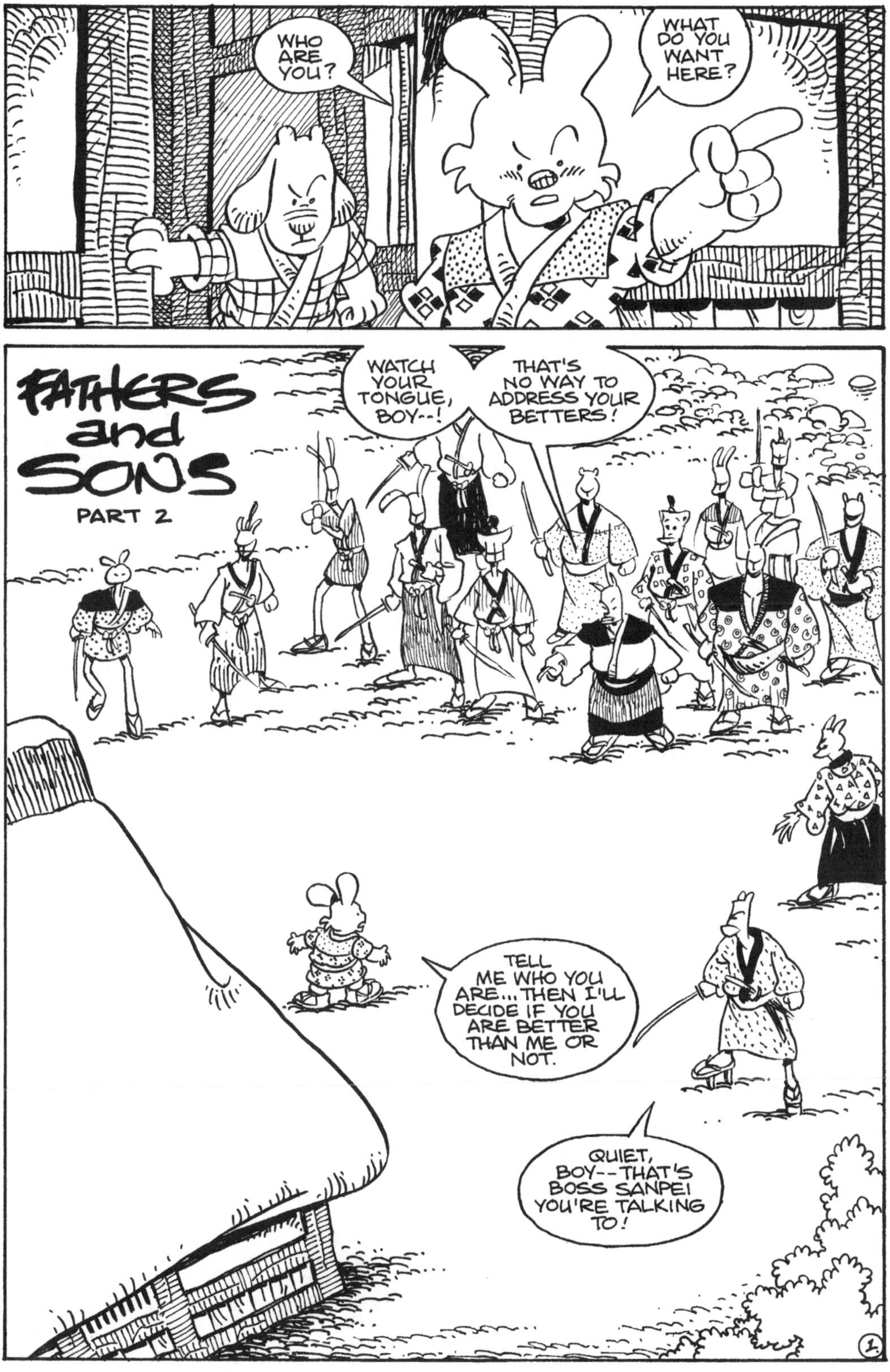
WHO ARE YOU?
WHAT DO YOU WANT HERE?
FATHERS and SONS
PART 2
WATCH YOUR TONGUE, BOY--!
THAT'S NO WAY TO ADDRESS YOUR BETTERS!
TELL ME WHO YOU ARE... THEN I'LL DECIDE IF YOU ARE BETTER THAN ME OR NOT.
QUIET, BOY--THAT'S BOSS SANPEI YOU'RE TALKING TO!
1

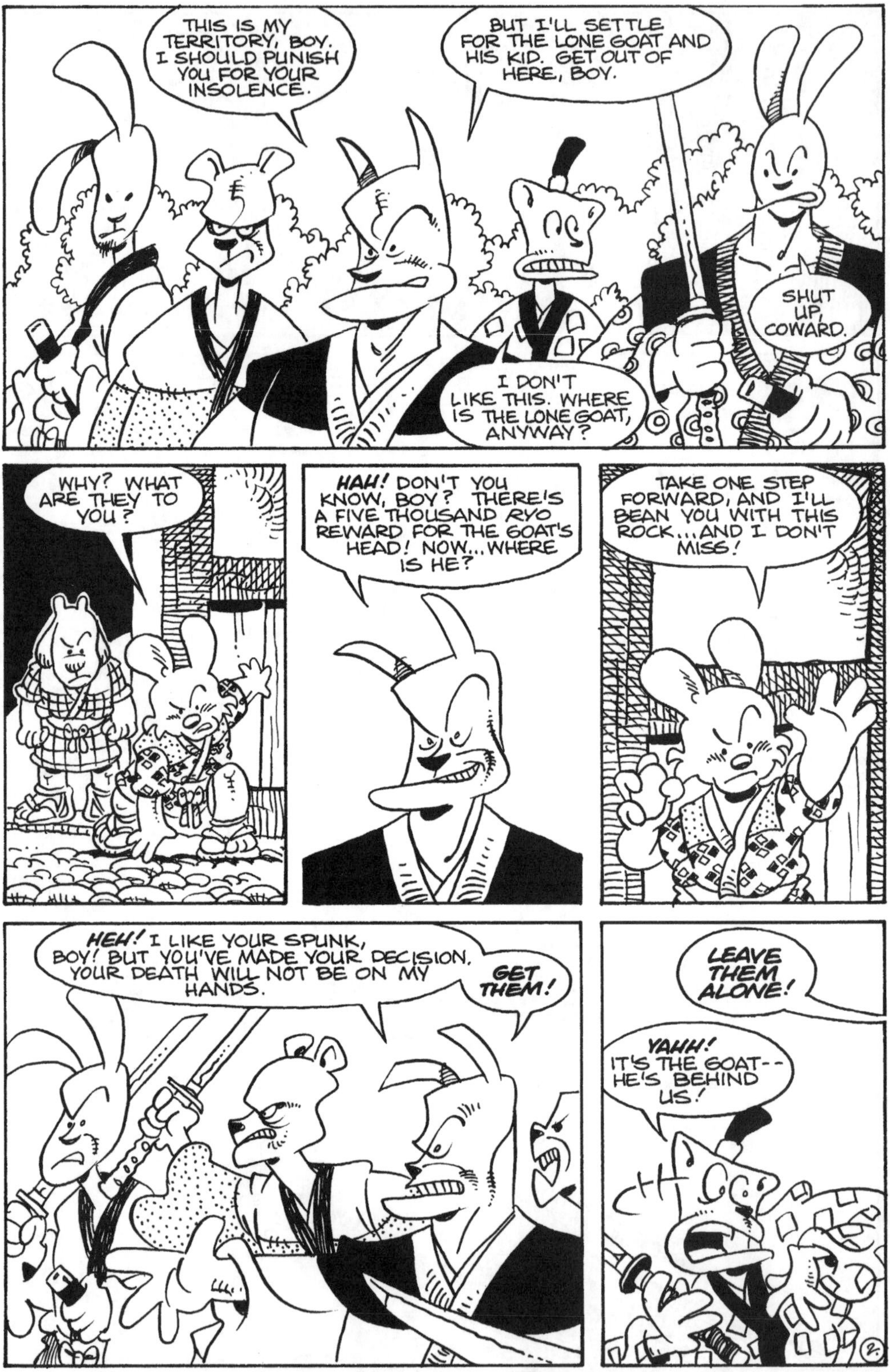
THIS IS MY TERRITORY, BOY. I SHOULD PUNISH YOU FOR YOUR INSOLENCE.
BUT I'LL SETTLE FOR THE LONE GOAT AND HIS KID. GET OUT OF HERE, BOY.
SHUT UP, COWARD.
I DON'T LIKE THIS. WHERE IS THE LONE GOAT, ANYWAY?
WHY? WHAT ARE THEY TO YOU?
HAH! DON'T YOU KNOW, BOY? THERE'S A FIVE THOUSAND RYO REWARD FOR THE GOAT'S HEAD! NOW... WHERE IS HE?
TAKE ONE STEP FORWARD, AND I'LL BEAN YOU WITH THIS ROCK... AND I DON'T MISS!
HEH! I LIKE YOUR SPUNK, BOY! BUT YOU'VE MADE YOUR DECISION. YOUR DEATH WILL NOT BE ON MY HANDS.
GET THEM!
LEAVE THEM ALONE!
YAHH! IT'S THE GOAT-- HE'S BEHIND US!
2.

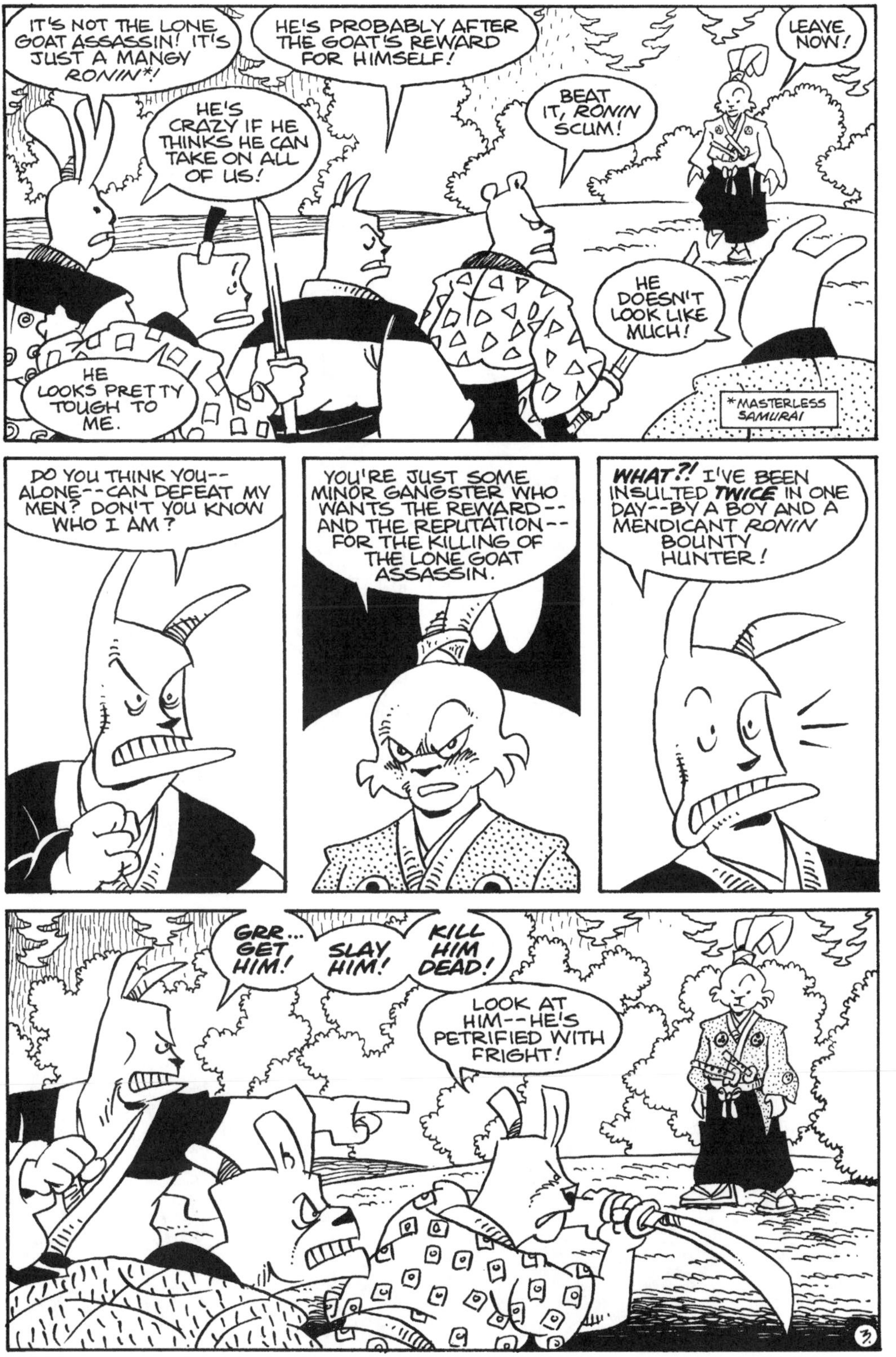
IT'S NOT THE LONE GOAT ASSASSIN! IT'S JUST A MANGY RONIN*!
HE'S PROBABLY AFTER THE GOAT'S REWARD FOR HIMSELF!
LEAVE NOW!
HE'S CRAZY IF HE THINKS HE CAN TAKE ON ALL OF US!
BEAT IT, RONIN SCUM!
HE DOESN'T LOOK LIKE MUCH!
HE LOOKS PRETTY TOUGH TO ME.
*MASTERLESS SAMURAI
DO YOU THINK YOU-- ALONE--CAN DEFEAT MY MEN? DON'T YOU KNOW WHO I AM?
YOU'RE JUST SOME MINOR GANGSTER WHO WANTS THE REWARD-- AND THE REPUTATION-- FOR THE KILLING OF THE LONE GOAT ASSASSIN.
WHAT?! I'VE BEEN INSULTED TWICE IN ONE DAY--BY A BOY AND A MENDICANT RONIN BOUNTY HUNTER!
GRR... GET HIM!
SLAY HIM!
KILL HIM DEAD!
LOOK AT HIM--HE'S PETRIFIED WITH FRIGHT!
3.

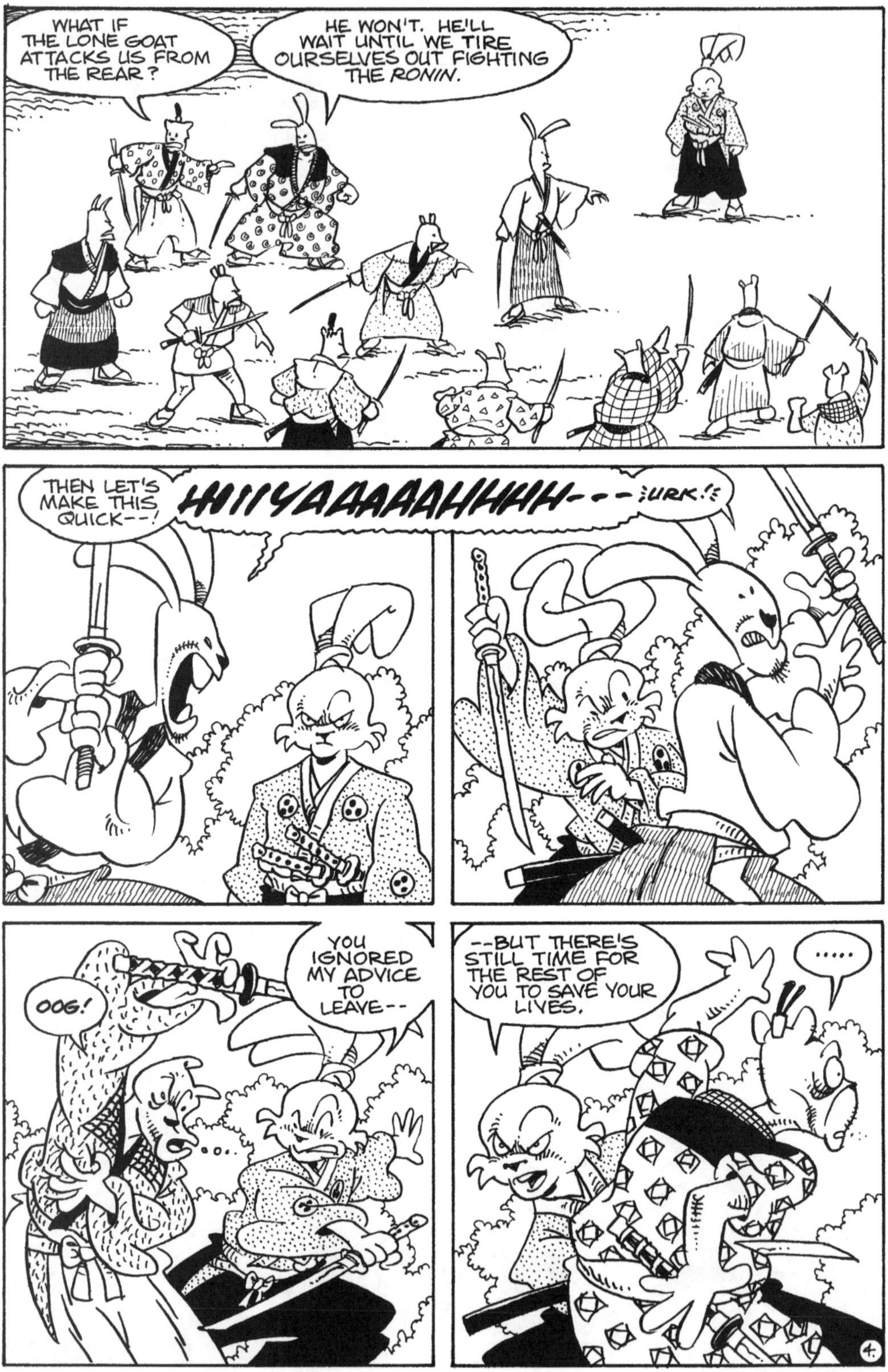
WHAT IF THE LONE GOAT ATTACKS US FROM THE REAR?
HE WON'T. HE'LL WAIT UNTIL WE TIRE OURSELVES OUT FIGHTING THE *RONIN*.
THEN LET'S MAKE THIS QUICK--!
HIIYAAAAAAHHHH---
¡URK!¡
OOG!
YOU IGNORED MY ADVICE TO LEAVE--
...
--BUT THERE'S STILL TIME FOR THE REST OF YOU TO SAVE YOUR LIVES.
.....
4.

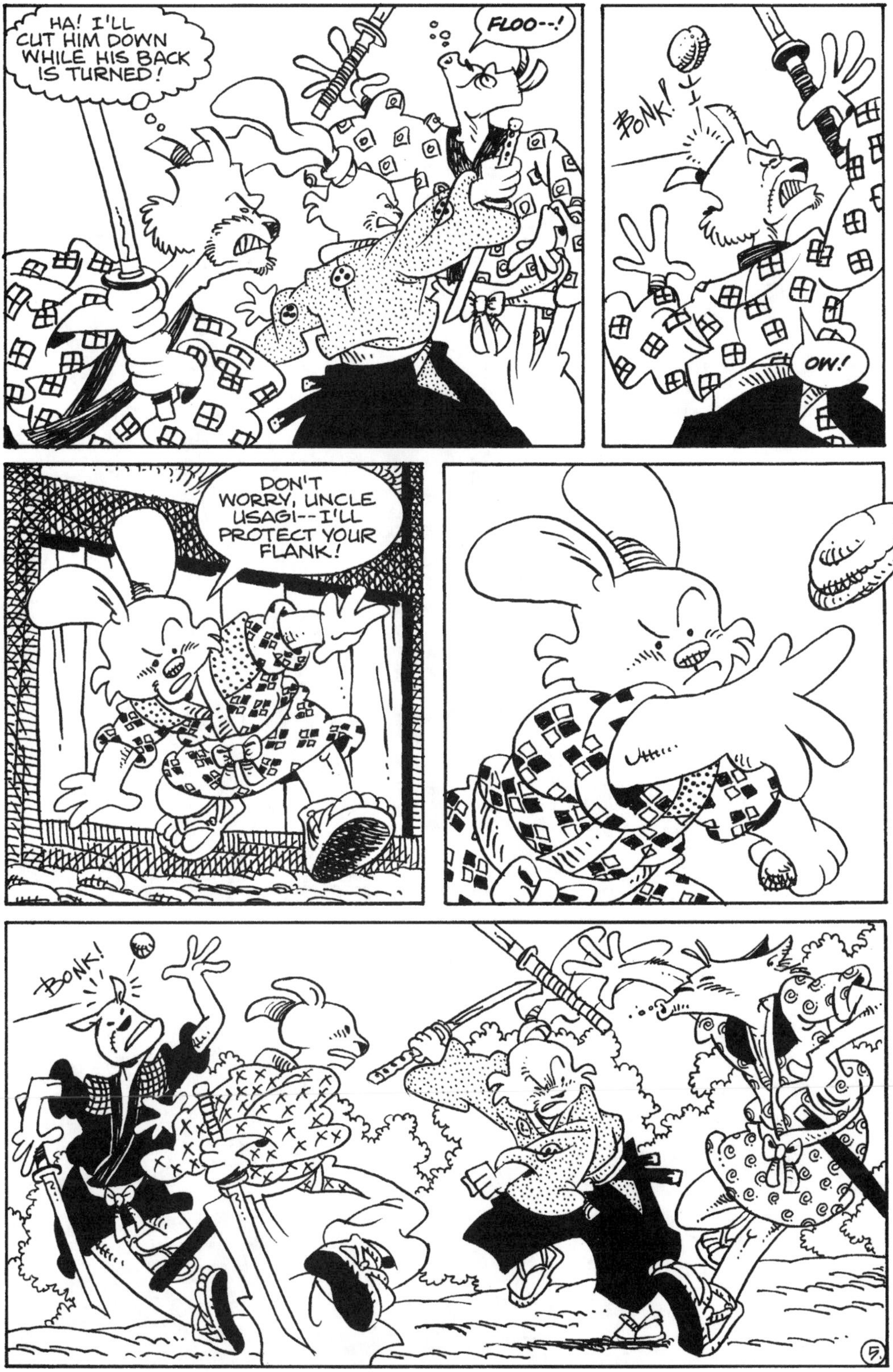
HA! I'LL CUT HIM DOWN WHILE HIS BACK IS TURNED!
FLOO--!
BONK!
OW!
DON'T WORRY, UNCLE USAGI--I'LL PROTECT YOUR FLANK!
BONK!
5

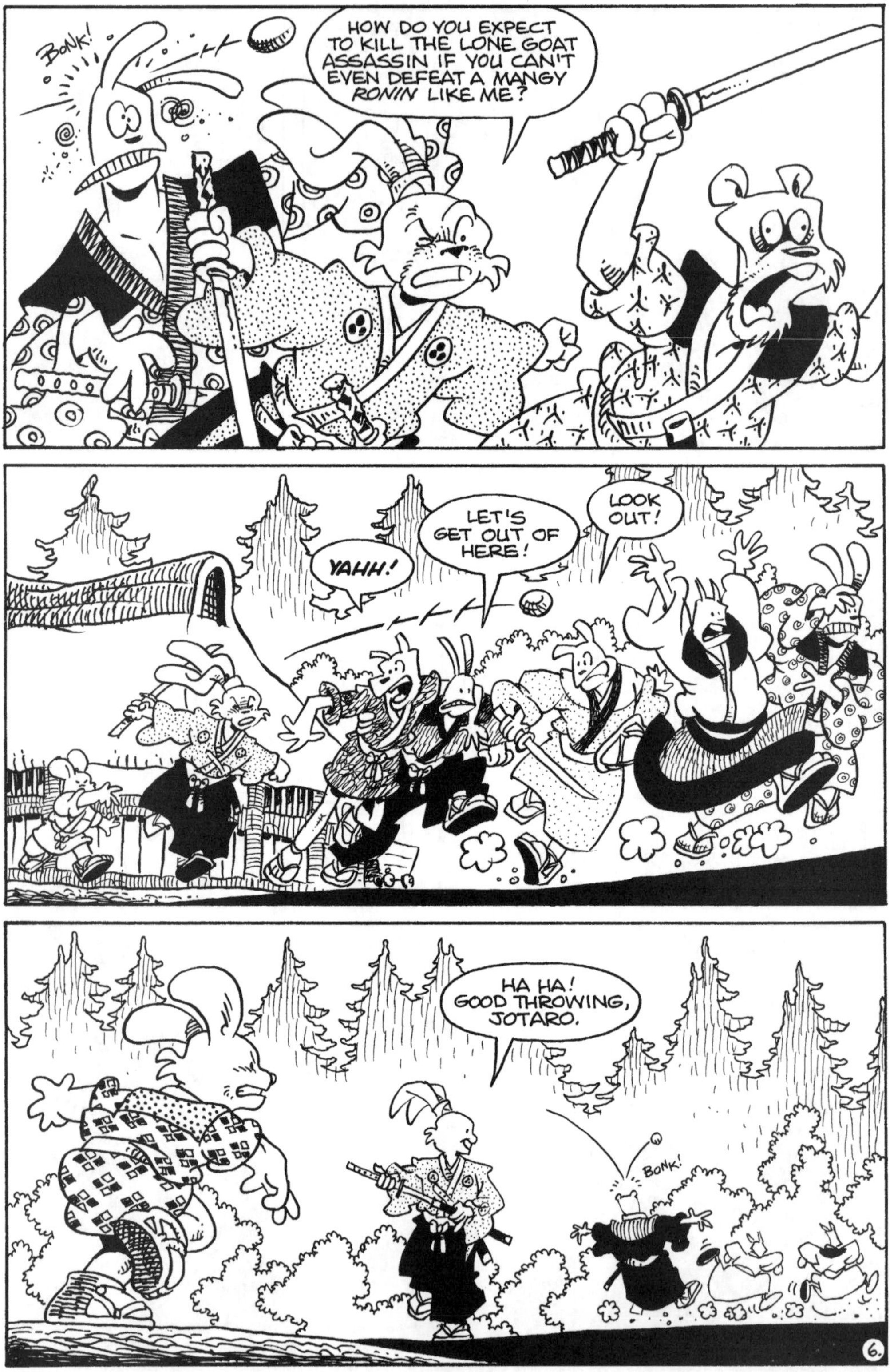
BONK!
HOW DO YOU EXPECT TO KILL THE LONE GOAT ASSASSIN IF YOU CAN'T EVEN DEFEAT A MANGY *RONIN* LIKE ME?
YAHH!
LET'S GET OUT OF HERE!
LOOK OUT!
HA HA! GOOD THROWING, JOTARO.
BONK!
6.

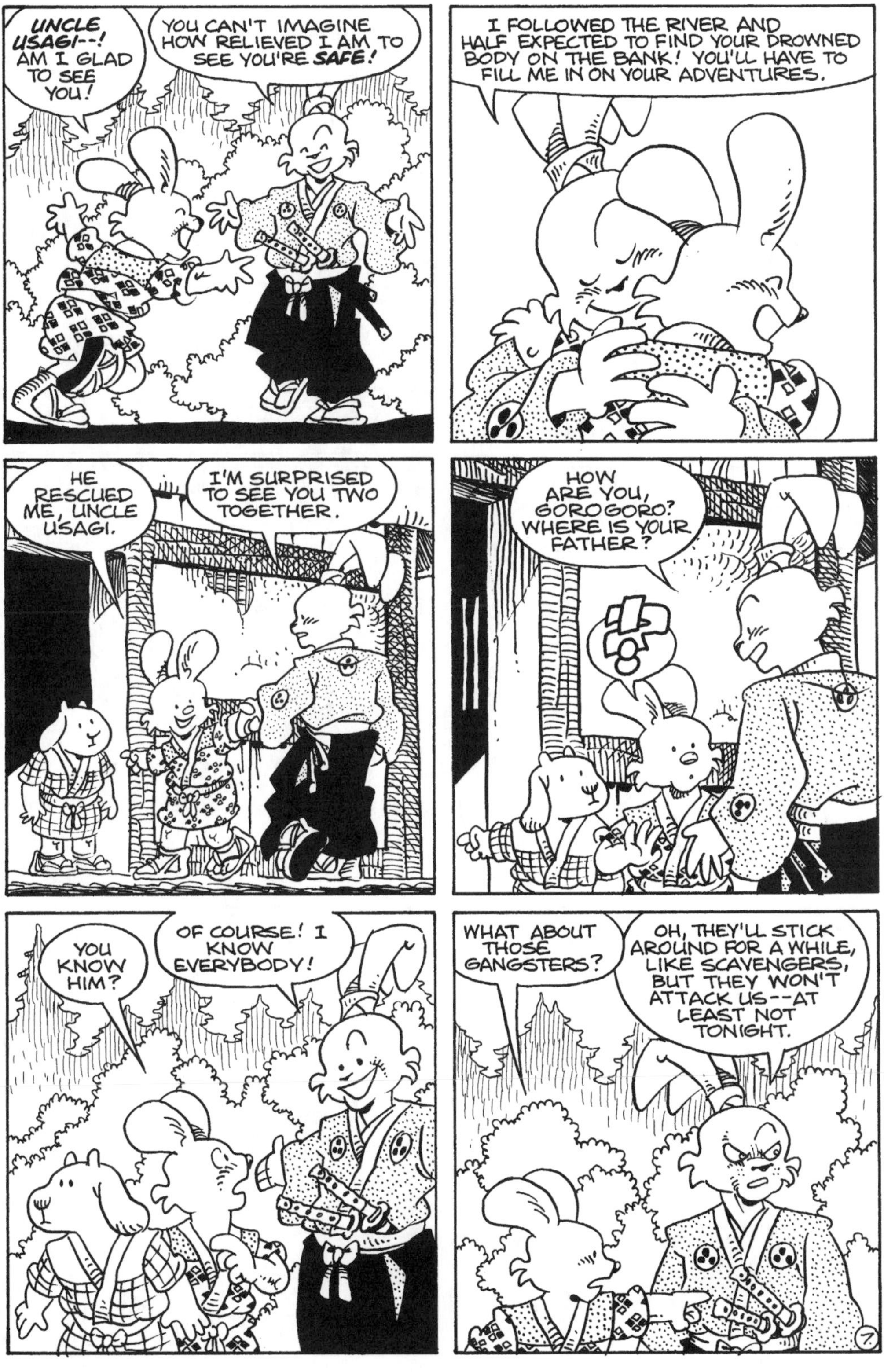
UNCLE USAGI--! AM I GLAD TO SEE YOU!
YOU CAN'T IMAGINE HOW RELIEVED I AM TO SEE YOU'RE SAFE!
I FOLLOWED THE RIVER AND HALF EXPECTED TO FIND YOUR DROWNED BODY ON THE BANK! YOU'LL HAVE TO FILL ME IN ON YOUR ADVENTURES.
HE RESCUED ME, UNCLE USAGI.
I'M SURPRISED TO SEE YOU TWO TOGETHER.
HOW ARE YOU, GOROGORO? WHERE IS YOUR FATHER?
!?
YOU KNOW HIM?
OF COURSE! I KNOW EVERYBODY!
WHAT ABOUT THOSE GANGSTERS?
OH, THEY'LL STICK AROUND FOR A WHILE, LIKE SCAVENGERS, BUT THEY WON'T ATTACK US--AT LEAST NOT TONIGHT.
7.

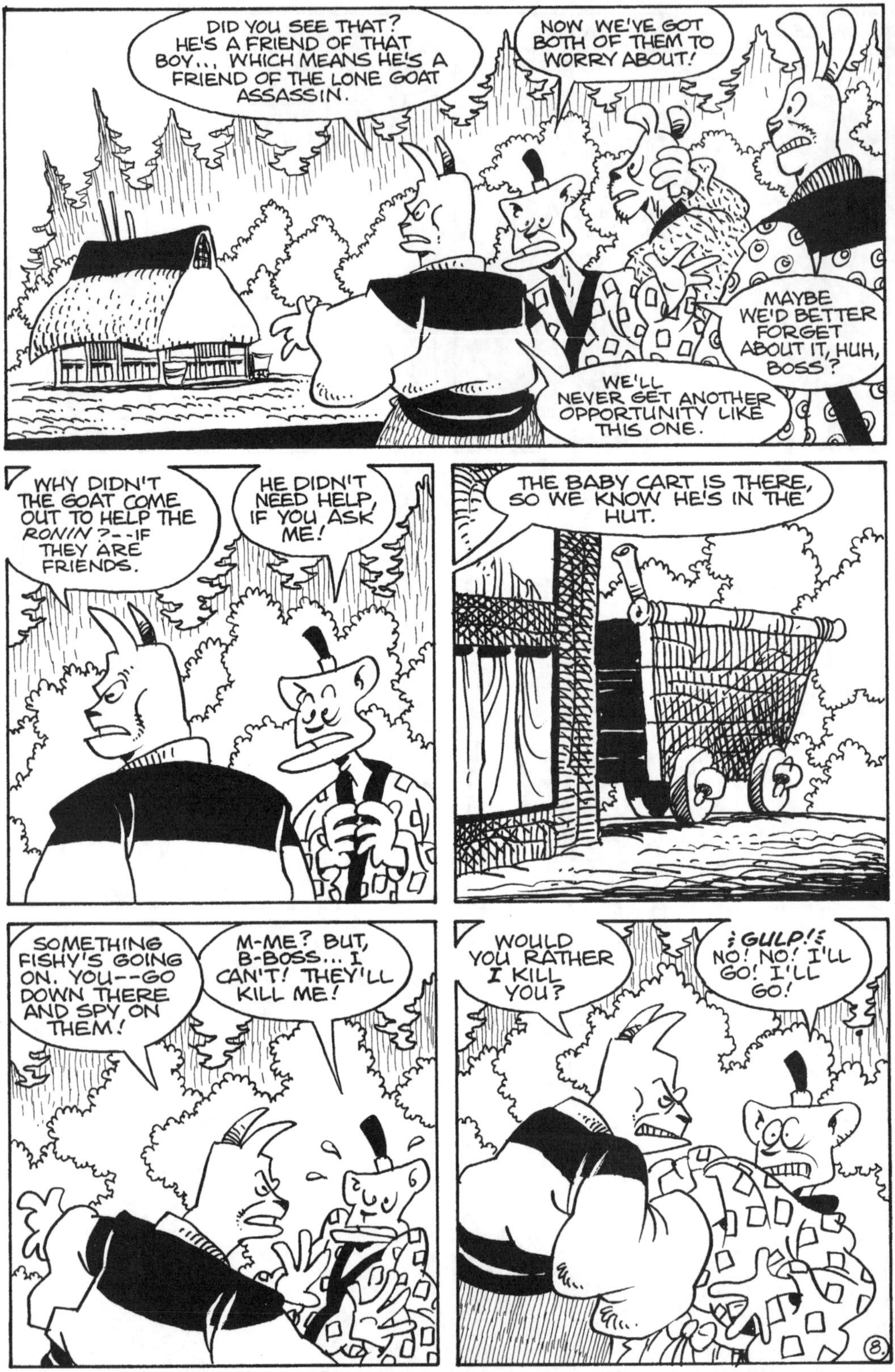
DID YOU SEE THAT? HE'S A FRIEND OF THAT BOY... WHICH MEANS HE'S A FRIEND OF THE LONE GOAT ASSASSIN.
NOW WE'VE GOT BOTH OF THEM TO WORRY ABOUT!
MAYBE WE'D BETTER FORGET ABOUT IT, HUH, BOSS?
WE'LL NEVER GET ANOTHER OPPORTUNITY LIKE THIS ONE.
WHY DIDN'T THE GOAT COME OUT TO HELP THE *RONIN*?--IF THEY ARE FRIENDS.
HE DIDN'T NEED HELP, IF YOU ASK ME!
THE BABY CART IS THERE, SO WE KNOW HE'S IN THE HUT.
SOMETHING FISHY'S GOING ON. YOU--GO DOWN THERE AND SPY ON THEM!
M-ME? BUT, B-BOSS... I CAN'T! THEY'LL KILL ME!
WOULD YOU RATHER I KILL YOU?
GULP!
NO! NO! I'LL GO! I'LL GO!
8.

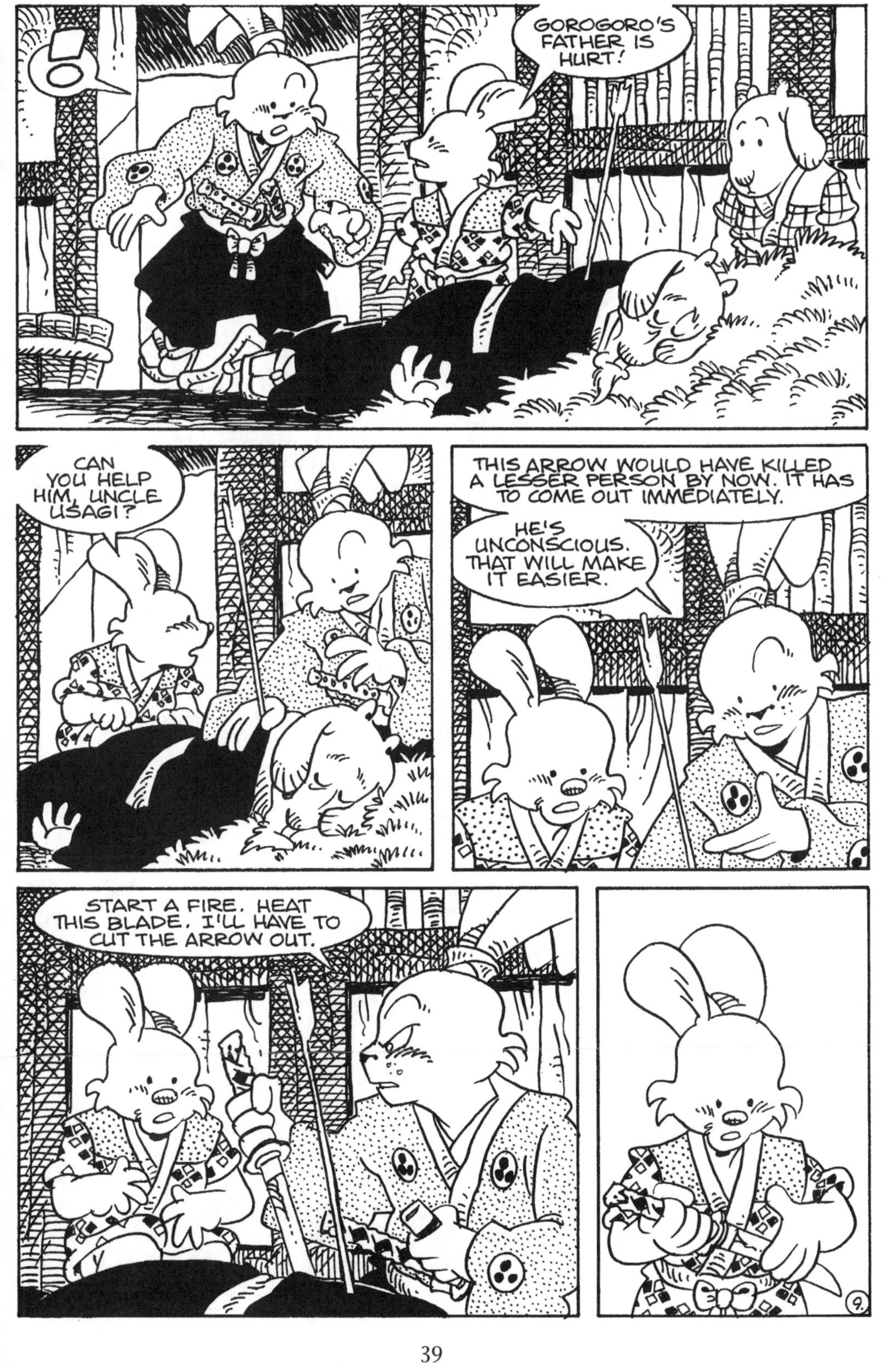
GOROGORO'S FATHER IS HURT!
CAN YOU HELP HIM, UNCLE USAGI?
THIS ARROW WOULD HAVE KILLED A LESSER PERSON BY NOW. IT HAS TO COME OUT IMMEDIATELY.
HE'S UNCONSCIOUS. THAT WILL MAKE IT EASIER.
START A FIRE. HEAT THIS BLADE. I'LL HAVE TO CUT THE ARROW OUT.

WHAT A PREDICAMENT... IF THE LONE GOAT DOESN'T KILL ME, BOSS SANPEI WILL!

SO FAR, SO GOOD.

I NEED MORE WATER-- AND GET THOSE BANDAGES READY.

OKAY, UNCLE USAGI.

WHAT'S GOING ON?

HEY, YOU-- I'LL SMASH YOU LIKE THE DIRTY VERMIN YOU ARE!

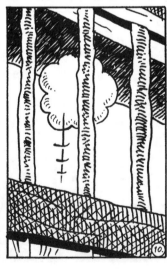

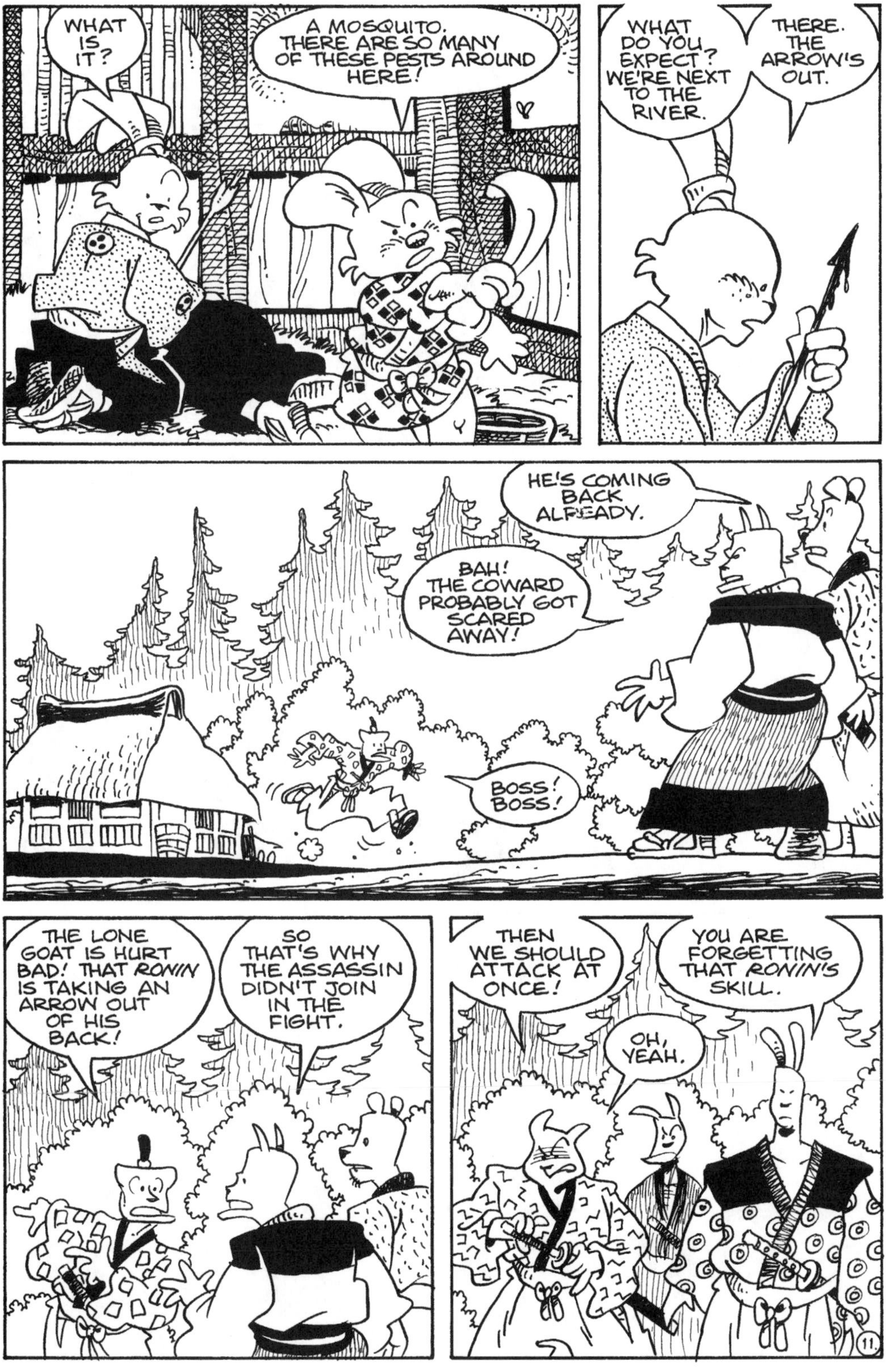
WHAT IS IT?
A MOSQUITO. THERE ARE SO MANY OF THESE PESTS AROUND HERE!
WHAT DO YOU EXPECT? WE'RE NEXT TO THE RIVER.
THERE. THE ARROW'S OUT.
HE'S COMING BACK ALREADY.
BAH! THE COWARD PROBABLY GOT SCARED AWAY!
BOSS! BOSS!
THE LONE GOAT IS HURT BAD! THAT RONIN IS TAKING AN ARROW OUT OF HIS BACK!
SO THAT'S WHY THE ASSASSIN DIDN'T JOIN IN THE FIGHT.
THEN WE SHOULD ATTACK AT ONCE!
YOU ARE FORGETTING THAT RONIN'S SKILL.
OH, YEAH.
11.

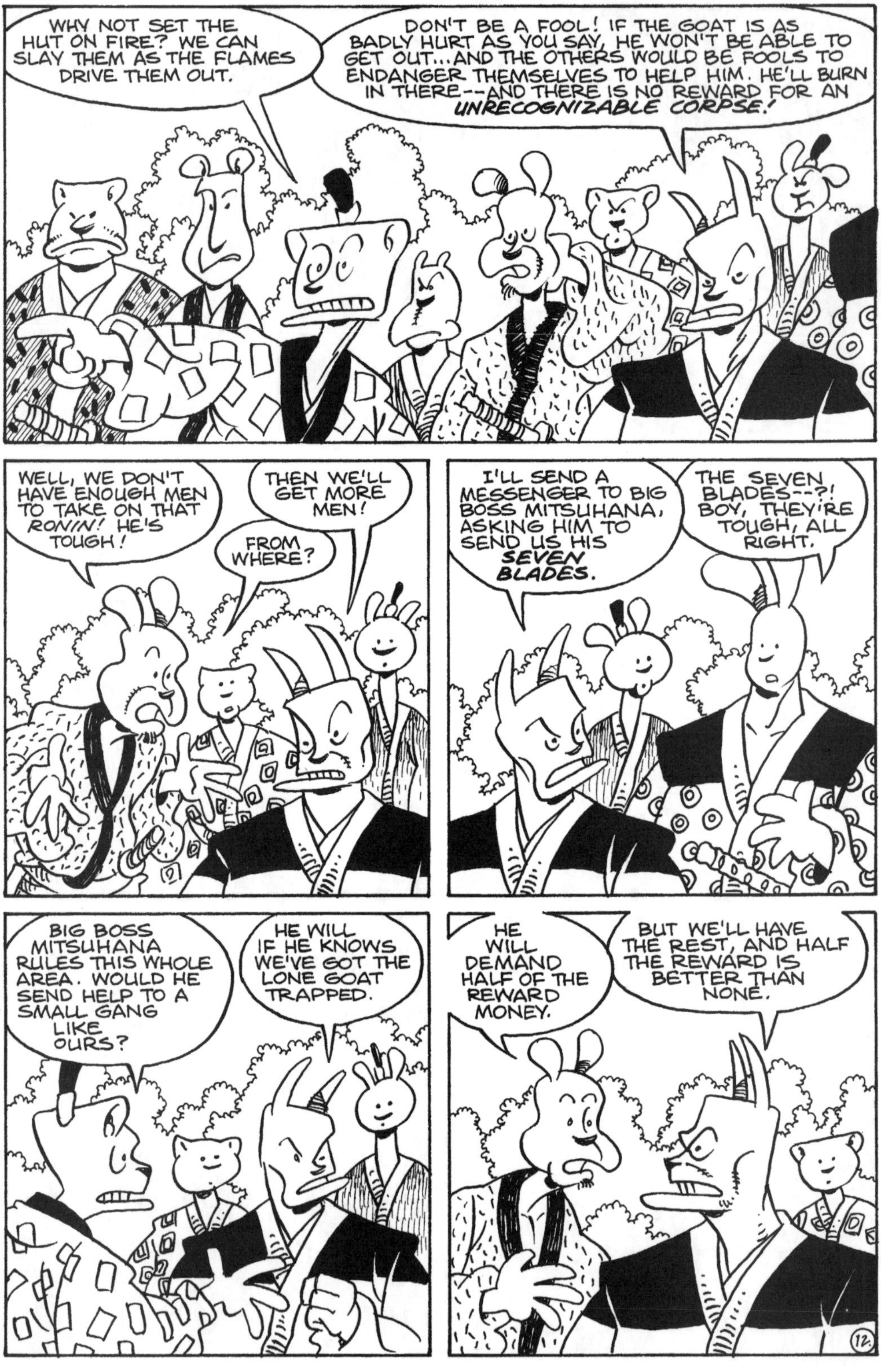
WHY NOT SET THE HUT ON FIRE? WE CAN SLAY THEM AS THE FLAMES DRIVE THEM OUT.
DON'T BE A FOOL! IF THE GOAT IS AS BADLY HURT AS YOU SAY, HE WON'T BE ABLE TO GET OUT...AND THE OTHERS WOULD BE FOOLS TO ENDANGER THEMSELVES TO HELP HIM. HE'LL BURN IN THERE--AND THERE IS NO REWARD FOR AN UNRECOGNIZABLE CORPSE!
WELL, WE DON'T HAVE ENOUGH MEN TO TAKE ON THAT RONIN! HE'S TOUGH!
FROM WHERE?
THEN WE'LL GET MORE MEN!
I'LL SEND A MESSENGER TO BIG BOSS MITSUHANA, ASKING HIM TO SEND US HIS SEVEN BLADES.
THE SEVEN BLADES--?! BOY, THEY'RE TOUGH, ALL RIGHT.
BIG BOSS MITSUHANA RULES THIS WHOLE AREA. WOULD HE SEND HELP TO A SMALL GANG LIKE OURS?
HE WILL IF HE KNOWS WE'VE GOT THE LONE GOAT TRAPPED.
HE WILL DEMAND HALF OF THE REWARD MONEY.
BUT WE'LL HAVE THE REST, AND HALF THE REWARD IS BETTER THAN NONE.
12.

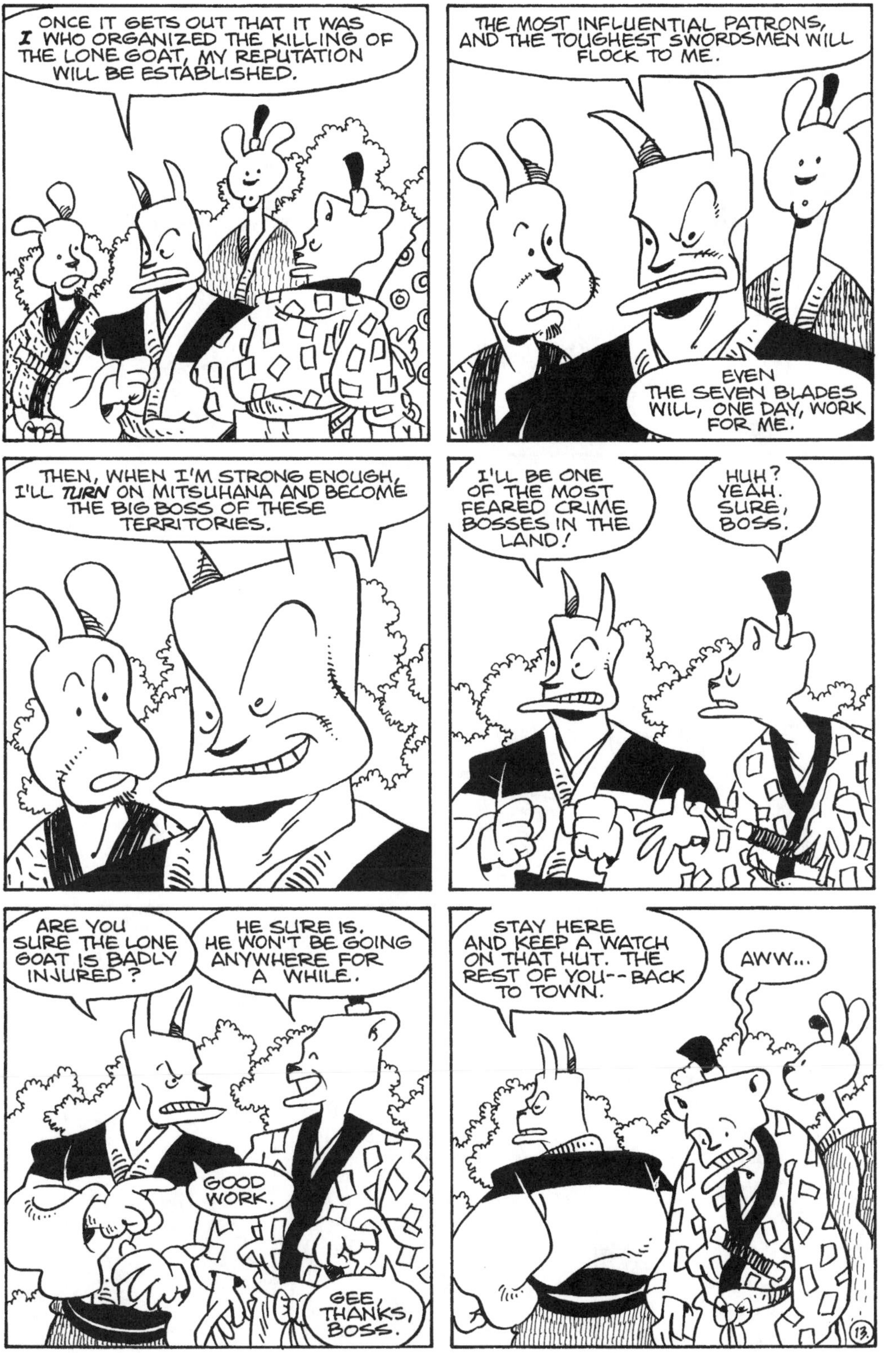
ONCE IT GETS OUT THAT IT WAS I WHO ORGANIZED THE KILLING OF THE LONE GOAT, MY REPUTATION WILL BE ESTABLISHED.
THE MOST INFLUENTIAL PATRONS, AND THE TOUGHEST SWORDSMEN WILL FLOCK TO ME.
EVEN THE SEVEN BLADES WILL, ONE DAY, WORK FOR ME.
THEN, WHEN I'M STRONG ENOUGH, I'LL TURN ON MITSUHANA AND BECOME THE BIG BOSS OF THESE TERRITORIES.
I'LL BE ONE OF THE MOST FEARED CRIME BOSSES IN THE LAND!
HUH? YEAH. SURE, BOSS.
ARE YOU SURE THE LONE GOAT IS BADLY INJURED?
HE SURE IS. HE WON'T BE GOING ANYWHERE FOR A WHILE.
GOOD WORK.
GEE, THANKS, BOSS.
STAY HERE AND KEEP A WATCH ON THAT HUT. THE REST OF YOU--BACK TO TOWN.
AWW...
13

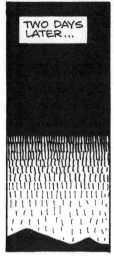

TWO DAYS LATER...

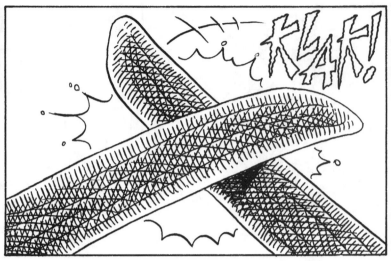

KLAK!

NGGH--!

YA HA!

HA! NOT BAD, BUT I'M BIGGER, AND FASTER, AND STRONGER, AND SMARTER THAN YOU!

UGH--! STAY STILL, YOU!

I'LL PULVERIZE YOU INTO MISO PASTE!

44

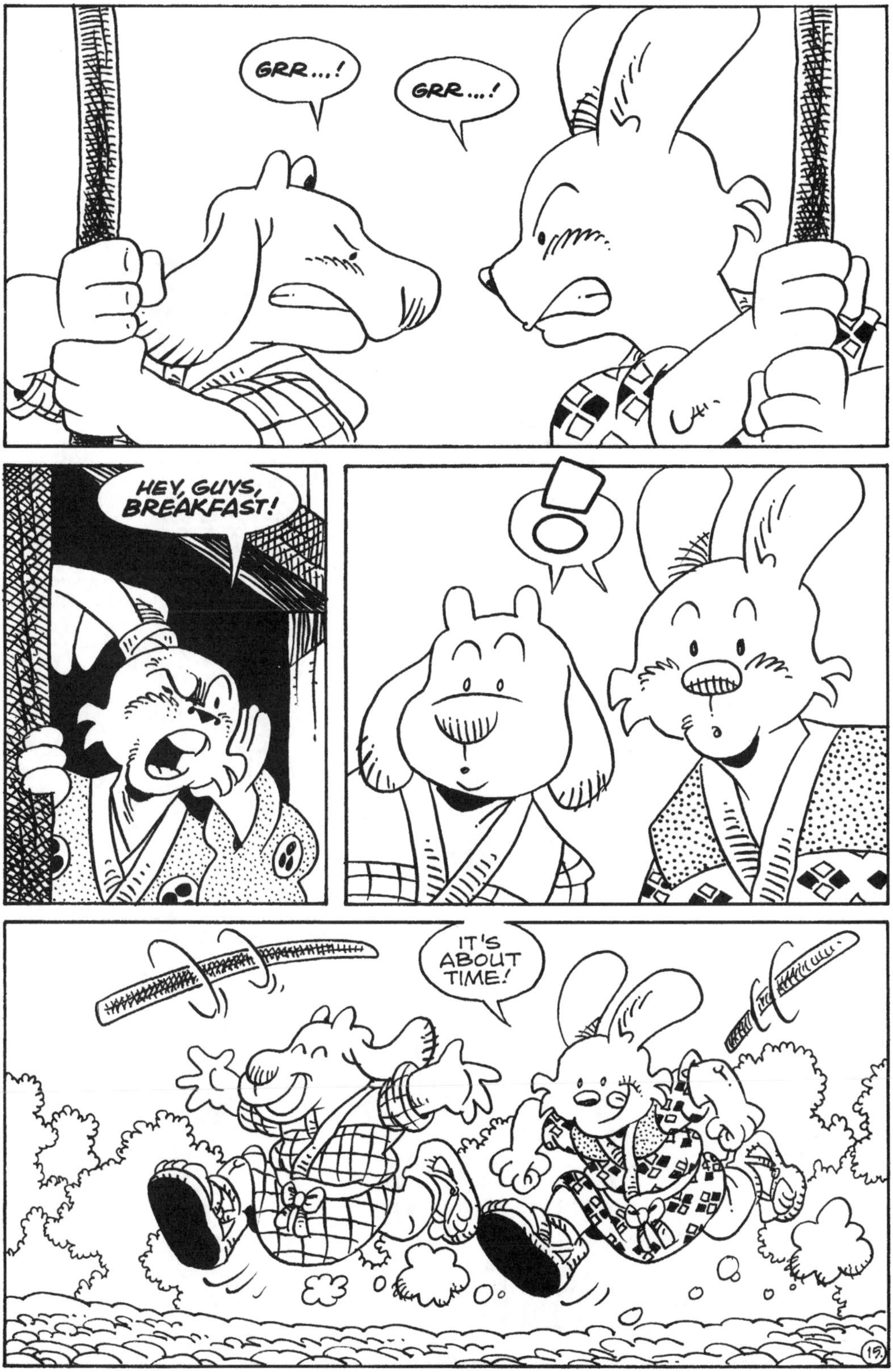
GRR...!
GRR...!
HEY, GUYS, BREAKFAST!
!
IT'S ABOUT TIME!
15.

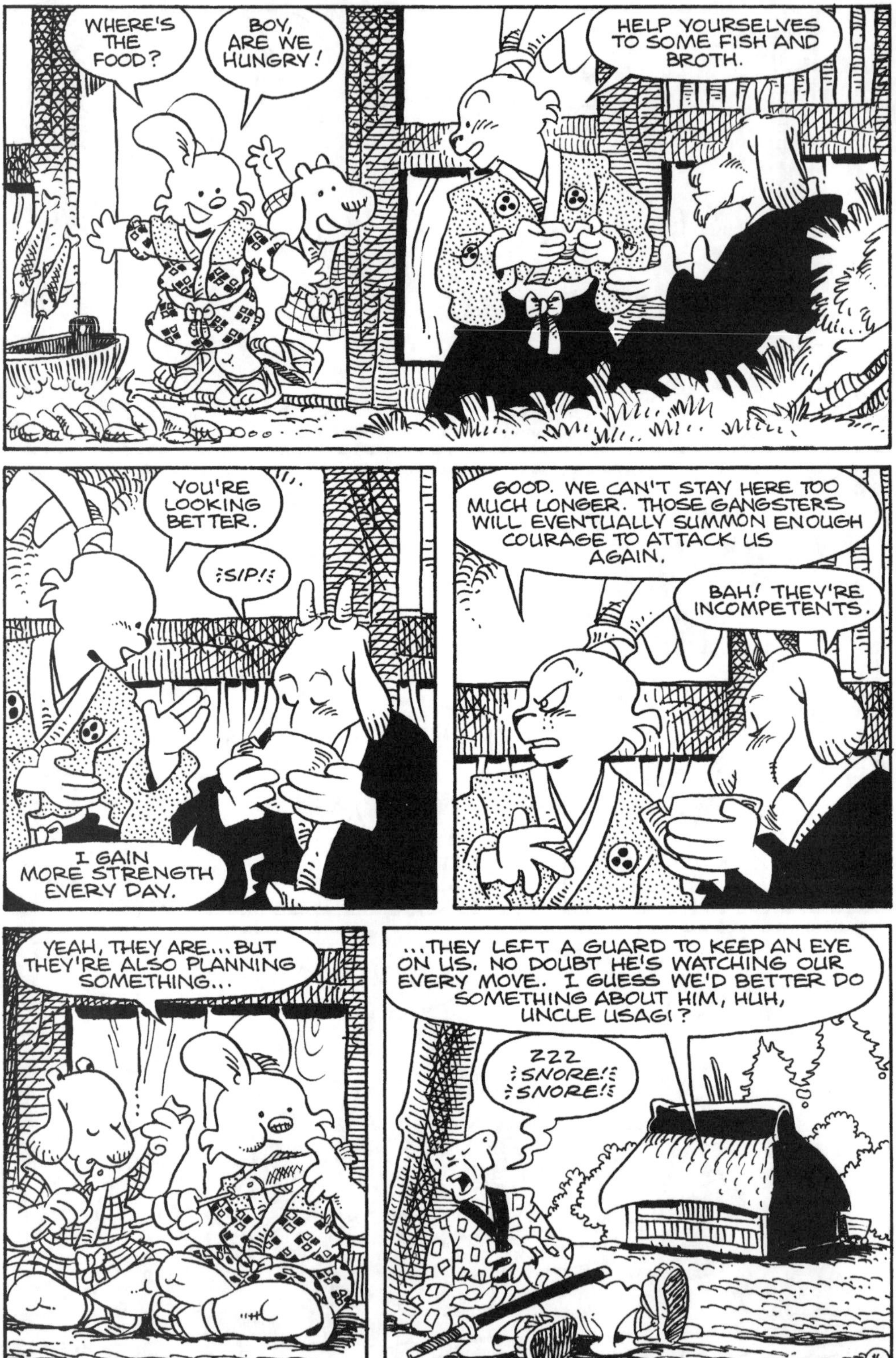
WHERE'S THE FOOD?
BOY, ARE WE HUNGRY!
HELP YOURSELVES TO SOME FISH AND BROTH.
YOU'RE LOOKING BETTER.
SIP!
I GAIN MORE STRENGTH EVERY DAY.
GOOD. WE CAN'T STAY HERE TOO MUCH LONGER. THOSE GANGSTERS WILL EVENTUALLY SUMMON ENOUGH COURAGE TO ATTACK US AGAIN.
BAH! THEY'RE INCOMPETENTS.
YEAH, THEY ARE... BUT THEY'RE ALSO PLANNING SOMETHING...
...THEY LEFT A GUARD TO KEEP AN EYE ON US. NO DOUBT HE'S WATCHING OUR EVERY MOVE. I GUESS WE'D BETTER DO SOMETHING ABOUT HIM, HUH, UNCLE USAGI?
ZZZ SNORE! SNORE!
16

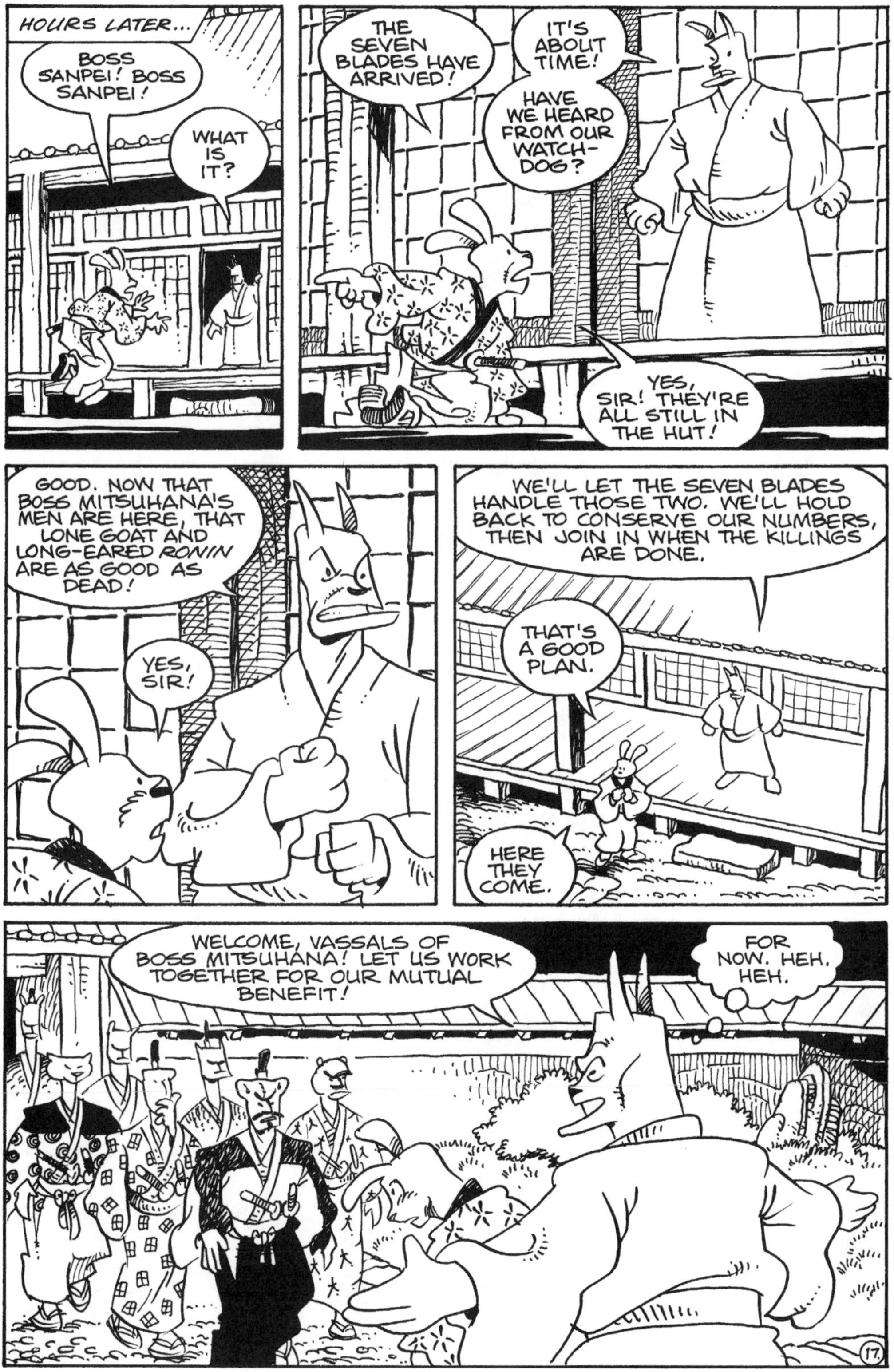
HOURS LATER...
BOSS SANPEI! BOSS SANPEI!
WHAT IS IT?
THE SEVEN BLADES HAVE ARRIVED!
IT'S ABOUT TIME!
HAVE WE HEARD FROM OUR WATCH-DOG?
YES, SIR! THEY'RE ALL STILL IN THE HUT!
GOOD. NOW THAT BOSS MITSUHANA'S MEN ARE HERE, THAT LONE GOAT AND LONG-EARED RONIN ARE AS GOOD AS DEAD!
YES, SIR!
WE'LL LET THE SEVEN BLADES HANDLE THOSE TWO. WE'LL HOLD BACK TO CONSERVE OUR NUMBERS, THEN JOIN IN WHEN THE KILLINGS ARE DONE.
THAT'S A GOOD PLAN.
HERE THEY COME.
WELCOME, VASSALS OF BOSS MITSUHANA! LET US WORK TOGETHER FOR OUR MUTUAL BENEFIT!
FOR NOW. HEH, HEH.
17

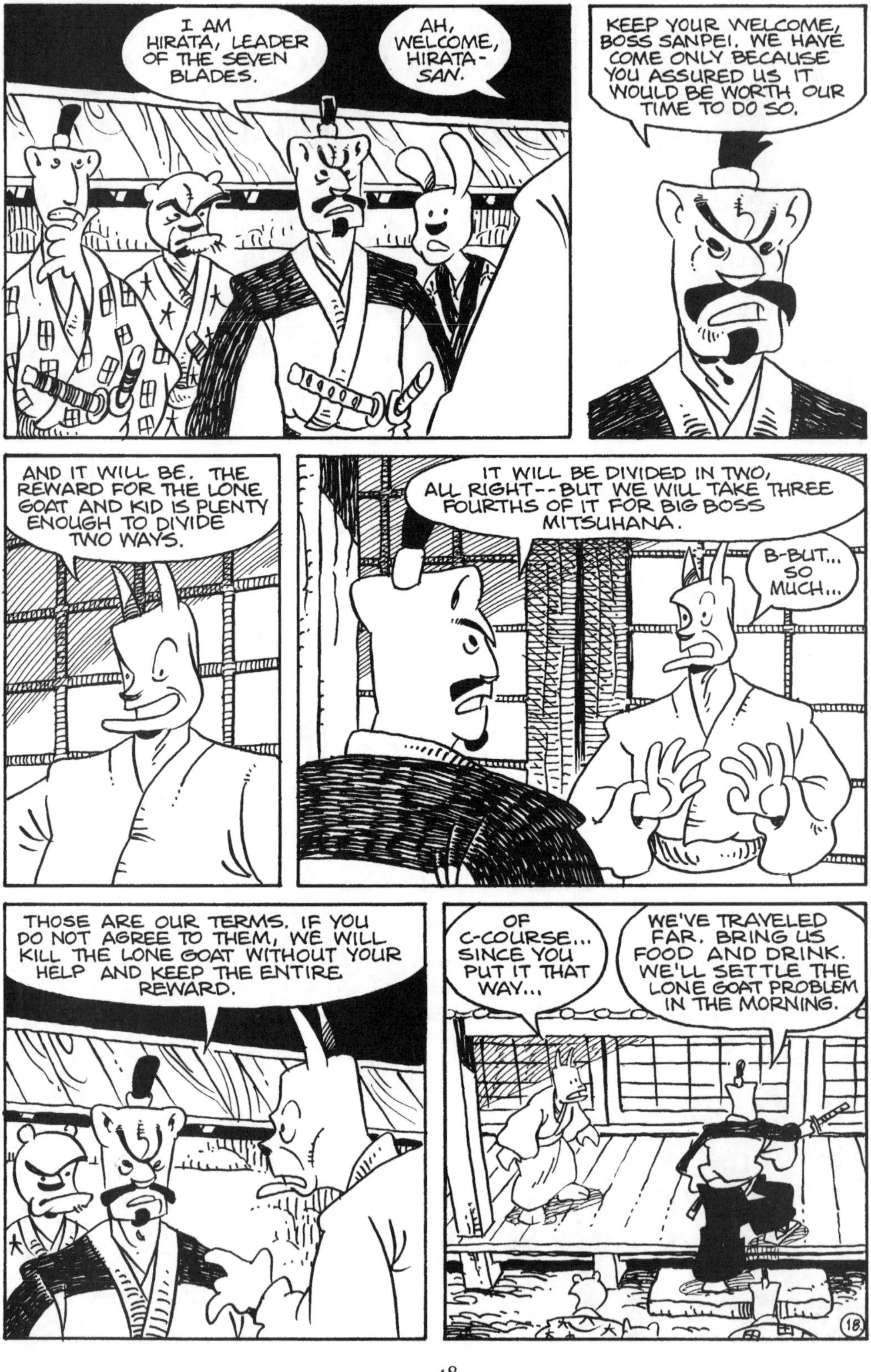
I AM HIRATA, LEADER OF THE SEVEN BLADES.
AH, WELCOME, HIRATA-SAN.
KEEP YOUR WELCOME, BOSS SANPEI. WE HAVE COME ONLY BECAUSE YOU ASSURED US IT WOULD BE WORTH OUR TIME TO DO SO.
AND IT WILL BE. THE REWARD FOR THE LONE GOAT AND KID IS PLENTY ENOUGH TO DIVIDE TWO WAYS.
IT WILL BE DIVIDED IN TWO, ALL RIGHT--BUT WE WILL TAKE THREE FOURTHS OF IT FOR BIG BOSS MITSUHANA.
B-BUT... SO MUCH...
THOSE ARE OUR TERMS. IF YOU DO NOT AGREE TO THEM, WE WILL KILL THE LONE GOAT WITHOUT YOUR HELP AND KEEP THE ENTIRE REWARD.
OF C-COURSE... SINCE YOU PUT IT THAT WAY...
WE'VE TRAVELED FAR. BRING US FOOD AND DRINK. WE'LL SETTLE THE LONE GOAT PROBLEM IN THE MORNING.
18

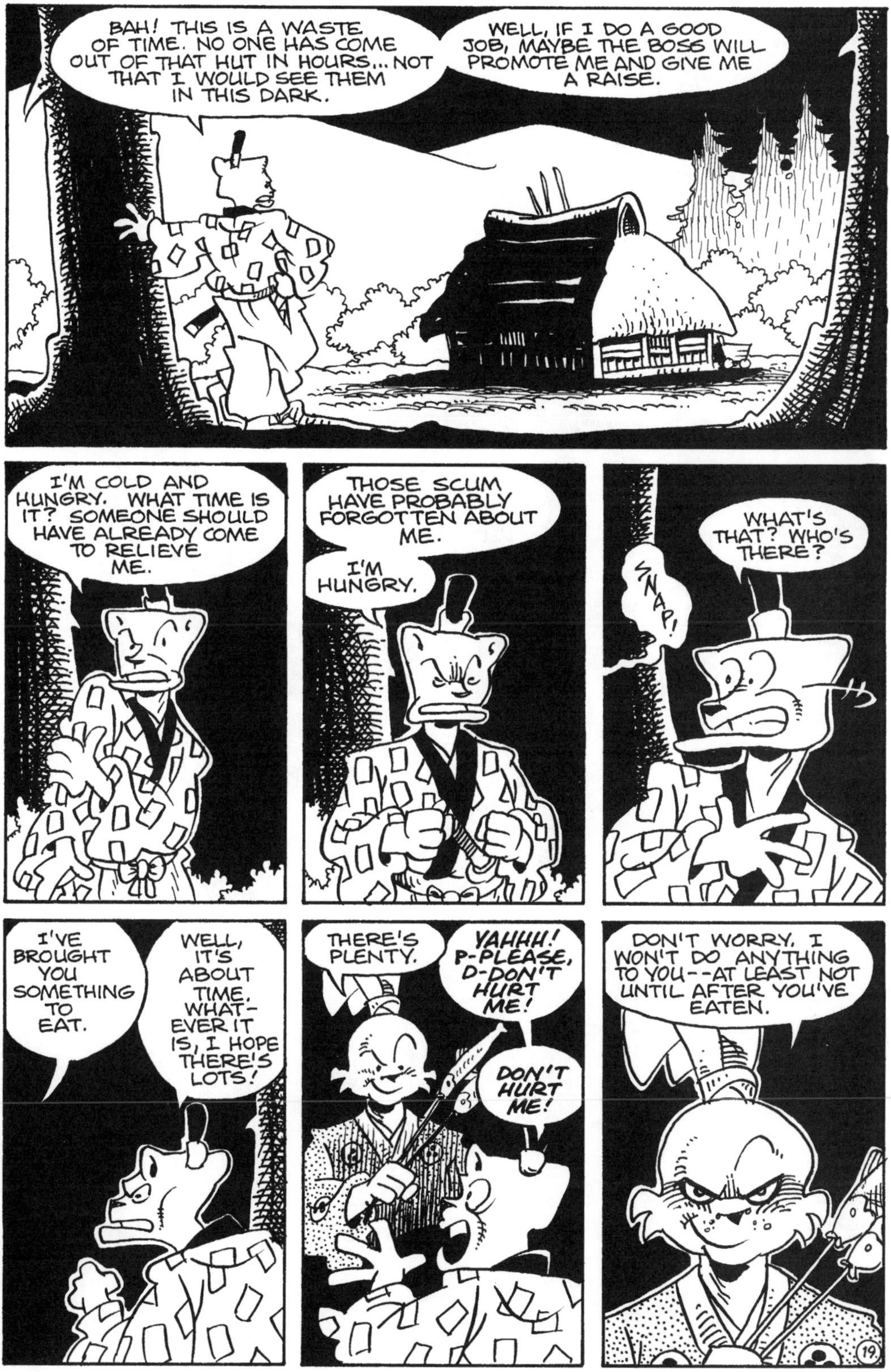
BAH! THIS IS A WASTE OF TIME. NO ONE HAS COME OUT OF THAT HUT IN HOURS... NOT THAT I WOULD SEE THEM IN THIS DARK.
WELL, IF I DO A GOOD JOB, MAYBE THE BOSS WILL PROMOTE ME AND GIVE ME A RAISE.
I'M COLD AND HUNGRY. WHAT TIME IS IT? SOMEONE SHOULD HAVE ALREADY COME TO RELIEVE ME.
THOSE SCUM HAVE PROBABLY FORGOTTEN ABOUT ME.
I'M HUNGRY.
SNAP!
WHAT'S THAT? WHO'S THERE?
I'VE BROUGHT YOU SOMETHING TO EAT.
WELL, IT'S ABOUT TIME. WHAT-EVER IT IS, I HOPE THERE'S LOTS!
THERE'S PLENTY.
YAHHH! P-PLEASE, D-DON'T HURT ME!
DON'T HURT ME!
DON'T WORRY. I WON'T DO ANYTHING TO YOU--AT LEAST NOT UNTIL AFTER YOU'VE EATEN.
19

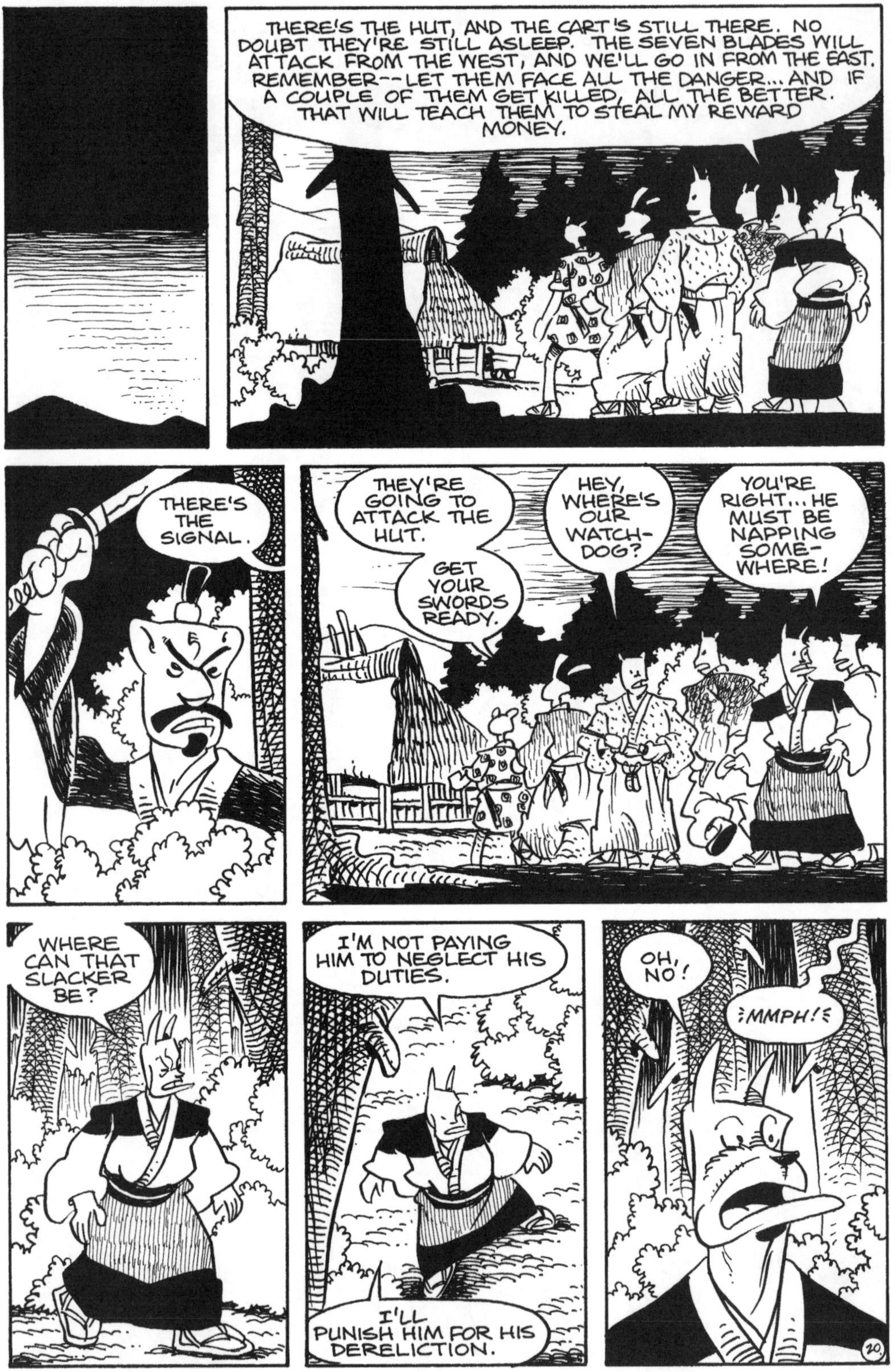
THERE'S THE HUT, AND THE CART'S STILL THERE. NO DOUBT THEY'RE STILL ASLEEP. THE SEVEN BLADES WILL ATTACK FROM THE WEST, AND WE'LL GO IN FROM THE EAST. REMEMBER-- LET THEM FACE ALL THE DANGER... AND IF A COUPLE OF THEM GET KILLED, ALL THE BETTER. THAT WILL TEACH THEM TO STEAL MY REWARD MONEY.
THERE'S THE SIGNAL.
THEY'RE GOING TO ATTACK THE HUT.
GET YOUR SWORDS READY.
HEY, WHERE'S OUR WATCH-DOG?
YOU'RE RIGHT... HE MUST BE NAPPING SOME-WHERE!
WHERE CAN THAT SLACKER BE?
I'M NOT PAYING HIM TO NEGLECT HIS DUTIES.
I'LL PUNISH HIM FOR HIS DERELICTION.
OH, NO!
MMPH!
20.

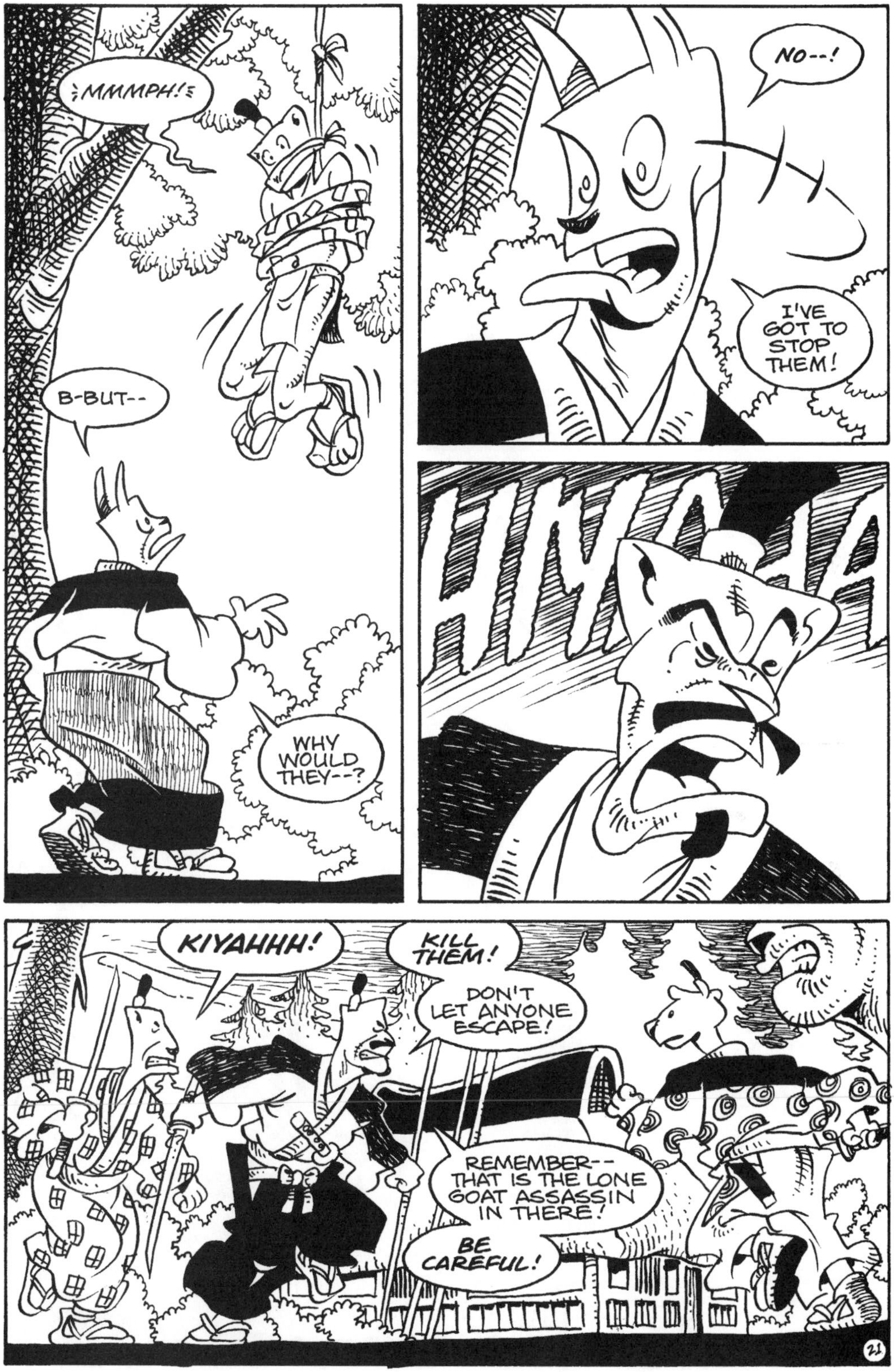
MMMPH!
B-BUT--
WHY WOULD THEY--?
NO--!
I'VE GOT TO STOP THEM!
KIYAHHH!
KILL THEM!
DON'T LET ANYONE ESCAPE!
REMEMBER-- THAT IS THE LONE GOAT ASSASSIN IN THERE!
BE CAREFUL!
21

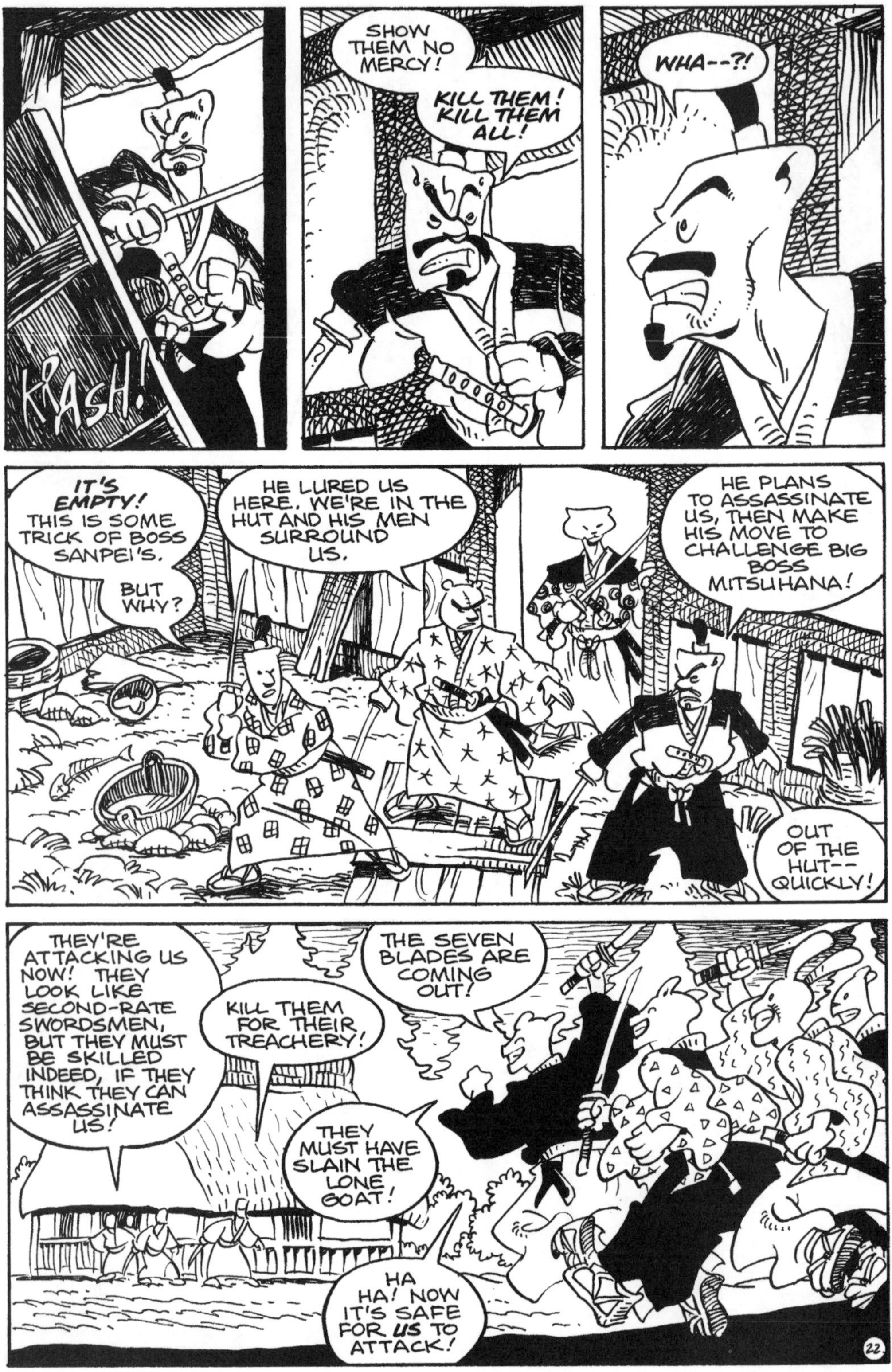
KRASH!
SHOW THEM NO MERCY!
KILL THEM! KILL THEM ALL!
WHA--?!
IT'S EMPTY! THIS IS SOME TRICK OF BOSS SANPEI'S.
BUT WHY?
HE LURED US HERE. WE'RE IN THE HUT AND HIS MEN SURROUND US.
HE PLANS TO ASSASSINATE US, THEN MAKE HIS MOVE TO CHALLENGE BIG BOSS MITSUHANA!
OUT OF THE HUT-- QUICKLY!
THEY'RE ATTACKING US NOW! THEY LOOK LIKE SECOND-RATE SWORDSMEN, BUT THEY MUST BE SKILLED INDEED, IF THEY THINK THEY CAN ASSASSINATE US!
KILL THEM FOR THEIR TREACHERY!
THE SEVEN BLADES ARE COMING OUT!
THEY MUST HAVE SLAIN THE LONE GOAT!
HA HA! NOW IT'S SAFE FOR US TO ATTACK!
22.

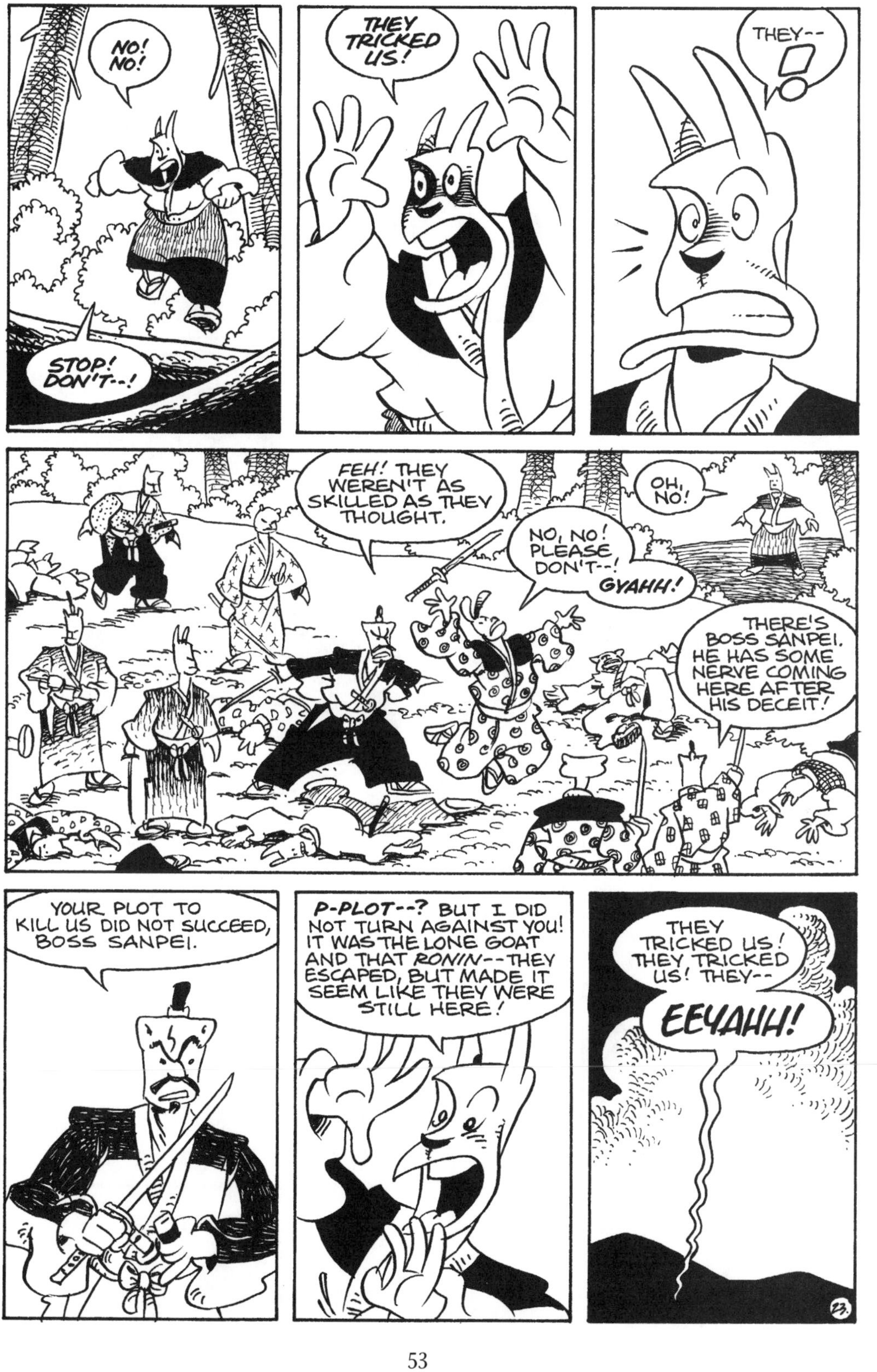
NO! NO!
STOP! DON'T--!
THEY TRICKED US!
THEY--
FEH! THEY WEREN'T AS SKILLED AS THEY THOUGHT.
NO, NO! PLEASE DON'T--! GYAHH!
OH, NO!
THERE'S BOSS SANPEI. HE HAS SOME NERVE COMING HERE AFTER HIS DECEIT!
YOUR PLOT TO KILL US DID NOT SUCCEED, BOSS SANPEI.
P-PLOT--? BUT I DID NOT TURN AGAINST YOU! IT WAS THE LONE GOAT AND THAT RONIN--THEY ESCAPED, BUT MADE IT SEEM LIKE THEY WERE STILL HERE!
THEY TRICKED US! THEY TRICKED US! THEY--
EEYAHH!
23.

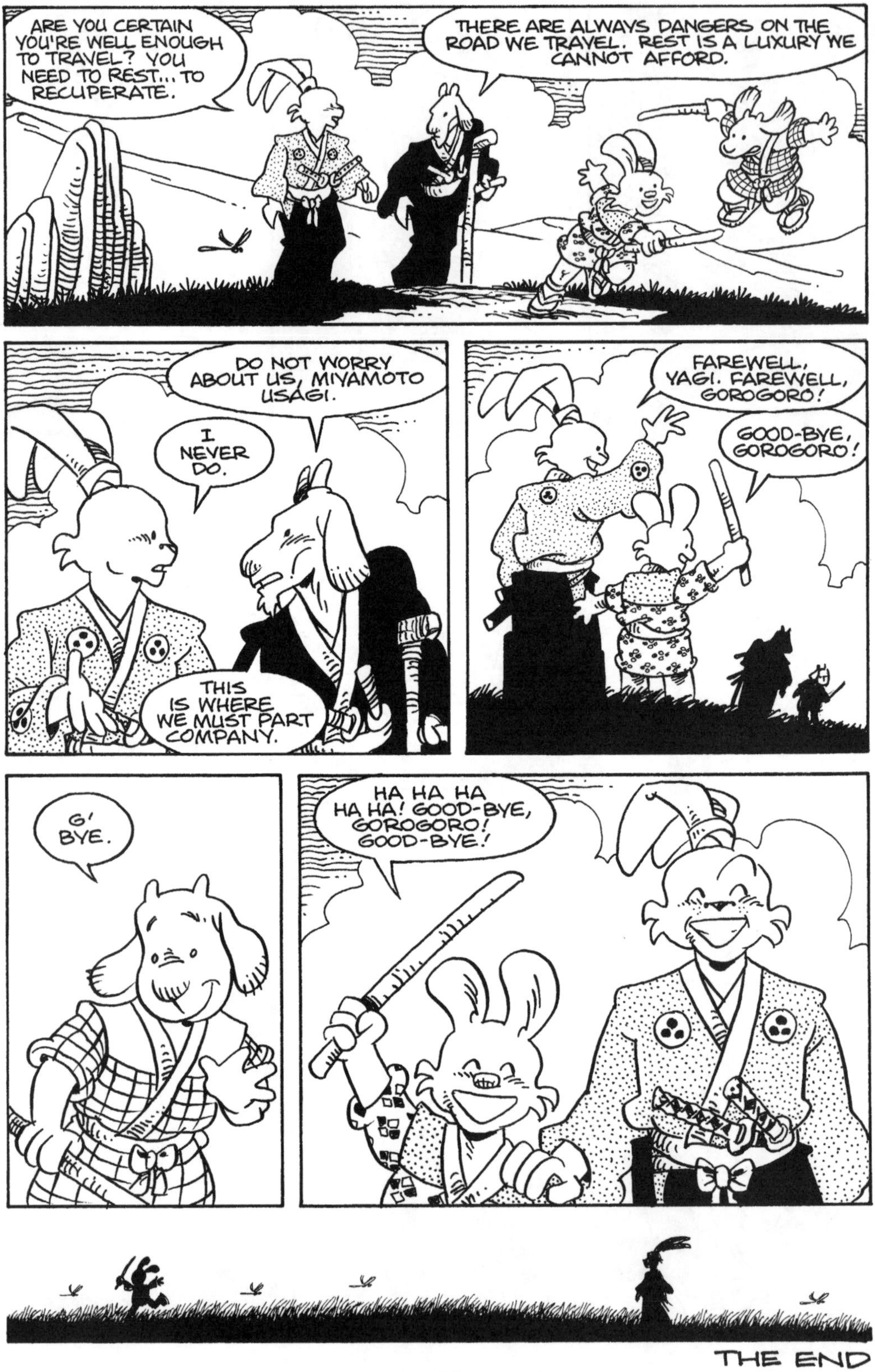
ARE YOU CERTAIN YOU'RE WELL ENOUGH TO TRAVEL? YOU NEED TO REST... TO RECUPERATE.
THERE ARE ALWAYS DANGERS ON THE ROAD WE TRAVEL. REST IS A LUXURY WE CANNOT AFFORD.
DO NOT WORRY ABOUT US, MIYAMOTO USAGI.
I NEVER DO.
THIS IS WHERE WE MUST PART COMPANY.
FAREWELL, YAGI. FAREWELL, GOROGORO!
GOOD-BYE, GOROGORO!
G' BYE.
HA HA HA HA HA! GOOD-BYE, GOROGORO! GOOD-BYE!

THE END

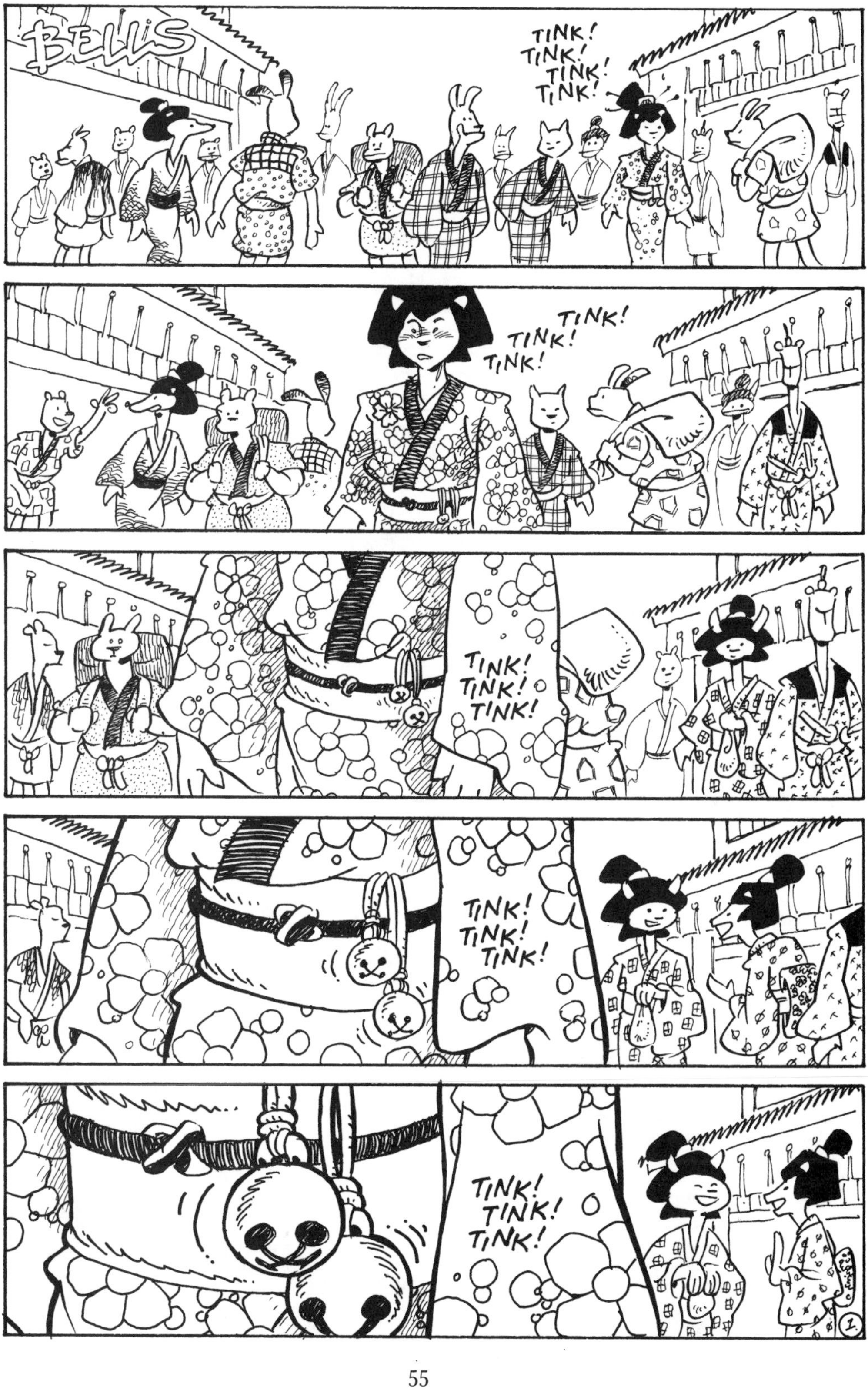

BELLS
TINK!
TINK!
TINK!
TINK!
TINK!
TINK!
TINK!
TINK!
TINK!
TINK!
TINK!
TINK!
TINK!
TINK!
TINK!
TINK!

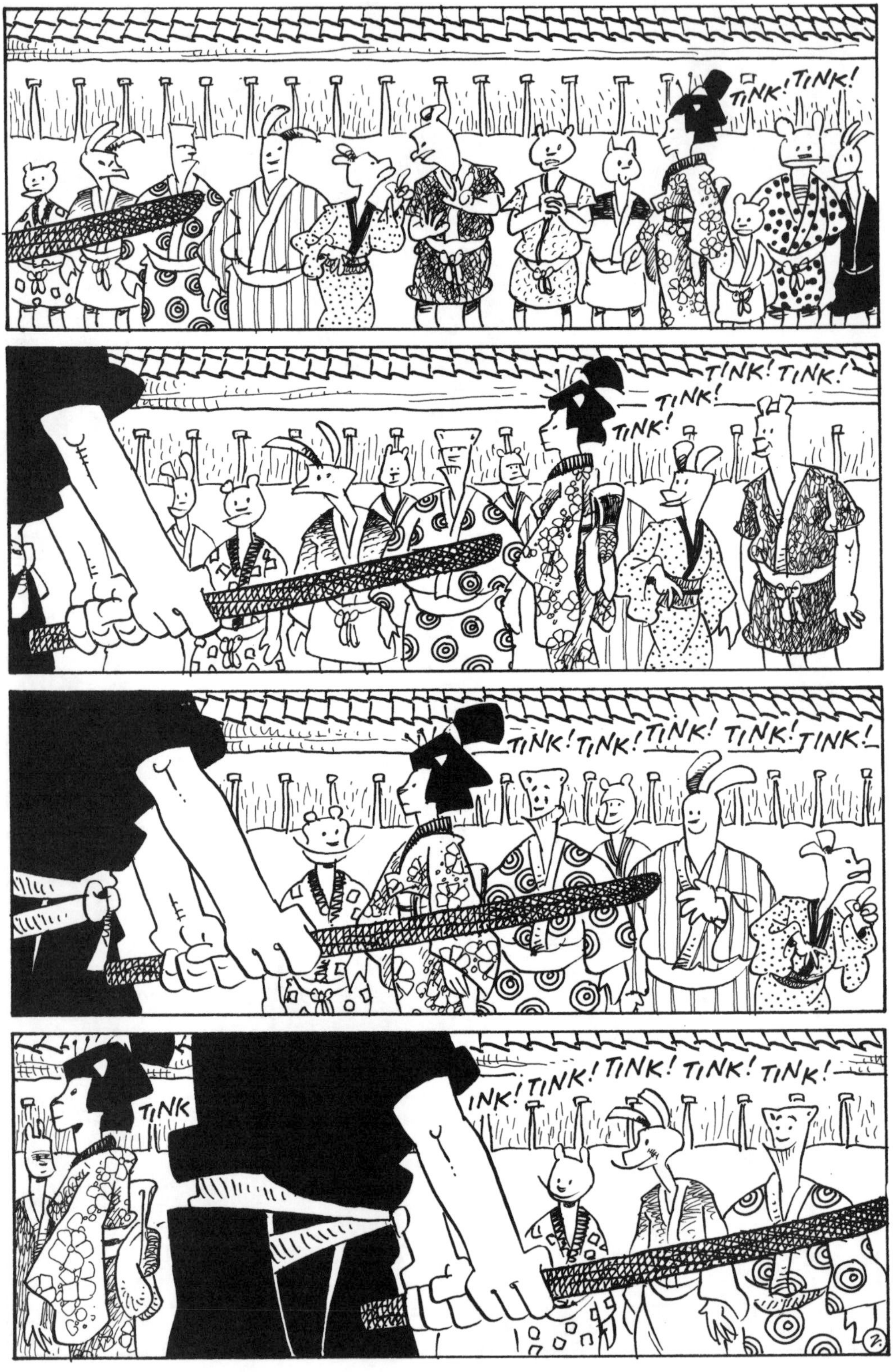
TINK! TINK!
TINK! TINK!
TINK!
TINK!
TINK! TINK! TINK! TINK! TINK!
TINK
INK! TINK! TINK! TINK! TINK!

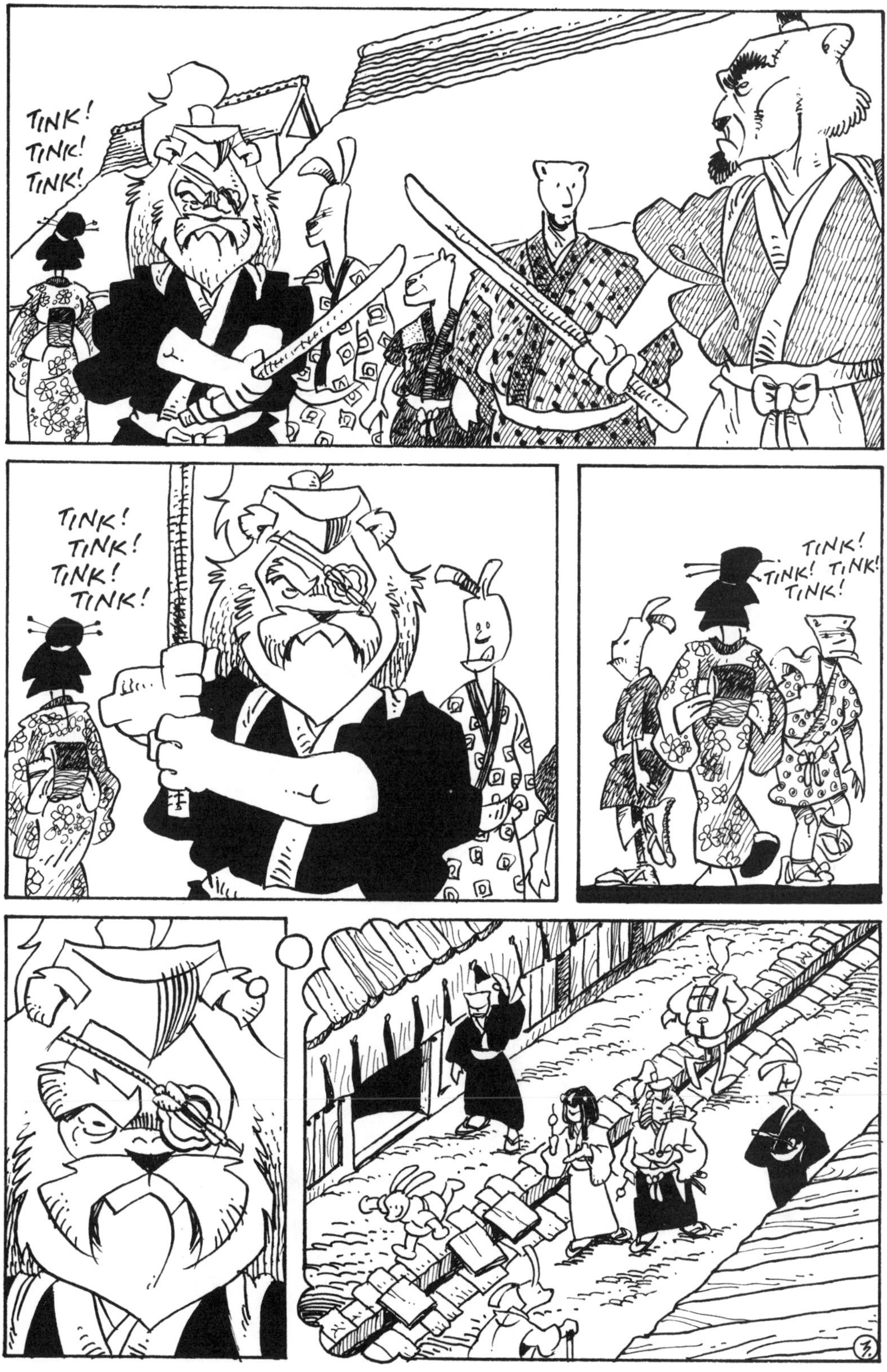
TINK!
TINK!
TINK!
TINK!
TINK!
TINK!
TINK!
TINK!
TINK! TINK!
TINK!

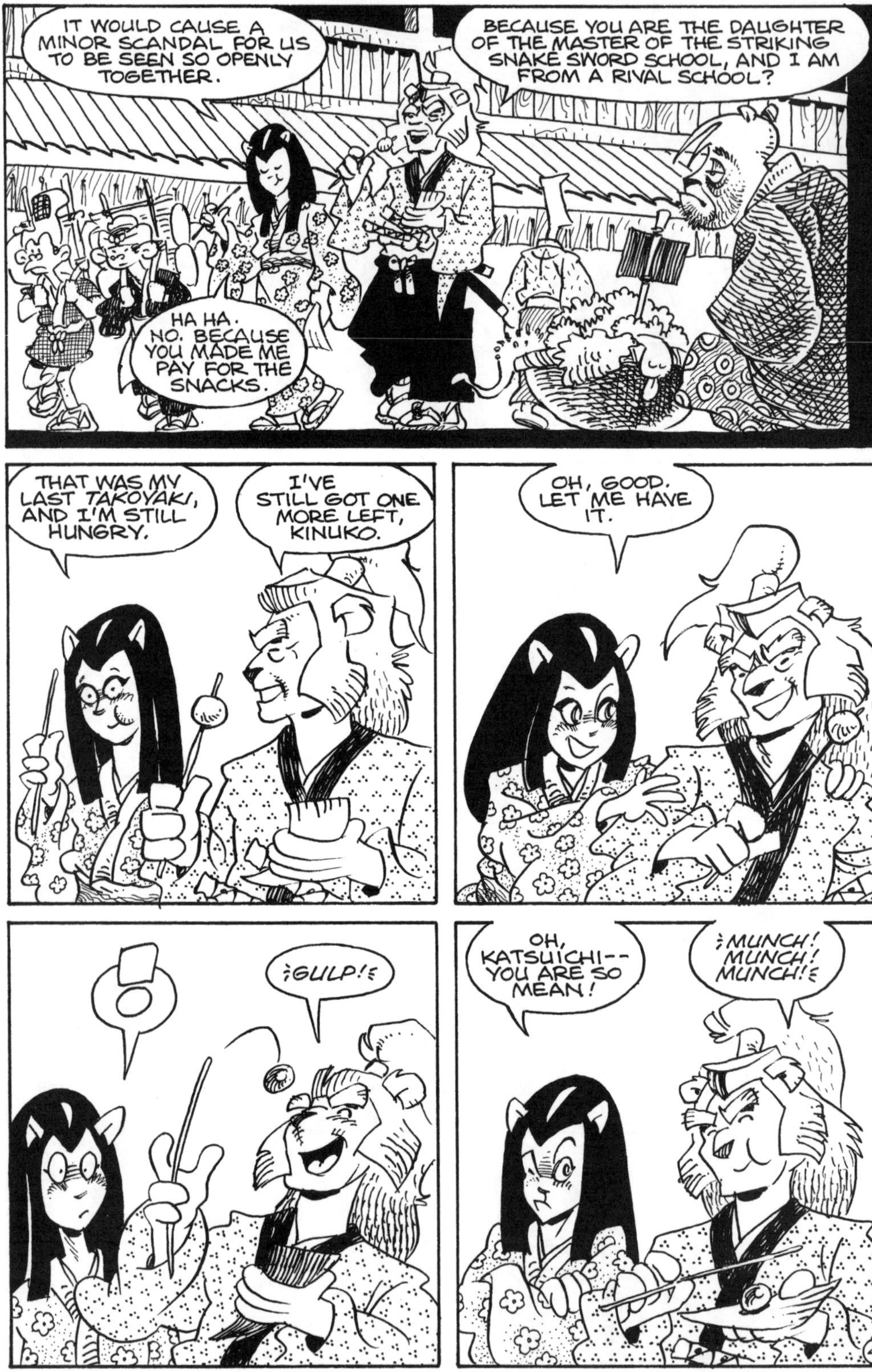
IT WOULD CAUSE A MINOR SCANDAL FOR US TO BE SEEN SO OPENLY TOGETHER.
BECAUSE YOU ARE THE DAUGHTER OF THE MASTER OF THE STRIKING SNAKE SWORD SCHOOL, AND I AM FROM A RIVAL SCHOOL?
HA HA. NO. BECAUSE YOU MADE ME PAY FOR THE SNACKS.
THAT WAS MY LAST *TAKOYAKI*, AND I'M STILL HUNGRY.
I'VE STILL GOT ONE MORE LEFT, KINUKO.
OH, GOOD. LET ME HAVE IT.
GULP!
OH, KATSUICHI-- YOU ARE SO MEAN!
MUNCH! MUNCH! MUNCH!
4

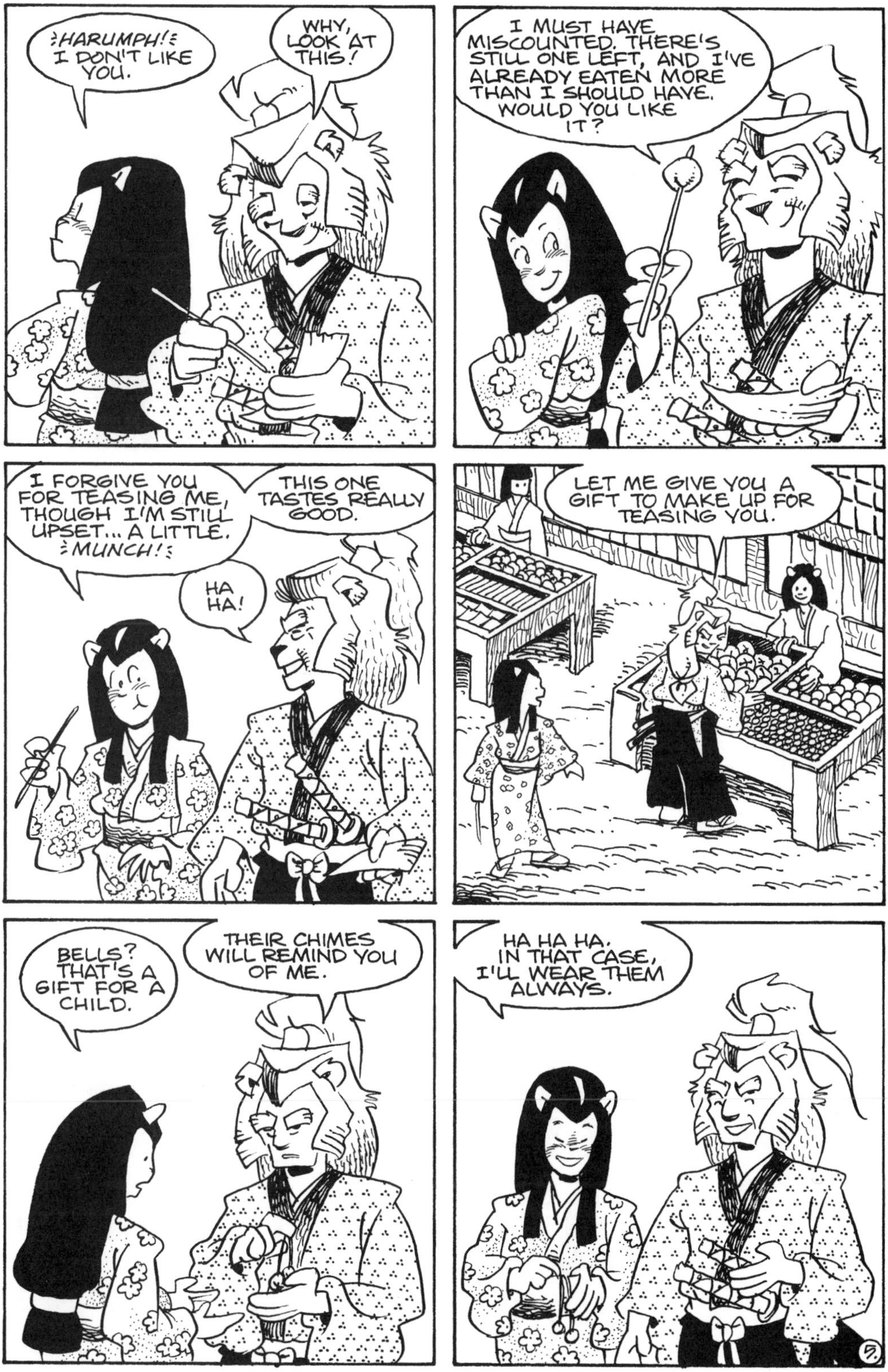
HARUMPH! I DON'T LIKE YOU.
WHY, LOOK AT THIS!
I MUST HAVE MISCOUNTED. THERE'S STILL ONE LEFT, AND I'VE ALREADY EATEN MORE THAN I SHOULD HAVE. WOULD YOU LIKE IT?
I FORGIVE YOU FOR TEASING ME, THOUGH I'M STILL UPSET... A LITTLE. MUNCH!
THIS ONE TASTES REALLY GOOD.
HA HA!
LET ME GIVE YOU A GIFT TO MAKE UP FOR TEASING YOU.
BELLS? THAT'S A GIFT FOR A CHILD.
THEIR CHIMES WILL REMIND YOU OF ME.
HA HA HA. IN THAT CASE, I'LL WEAR THEM ALWAYS.

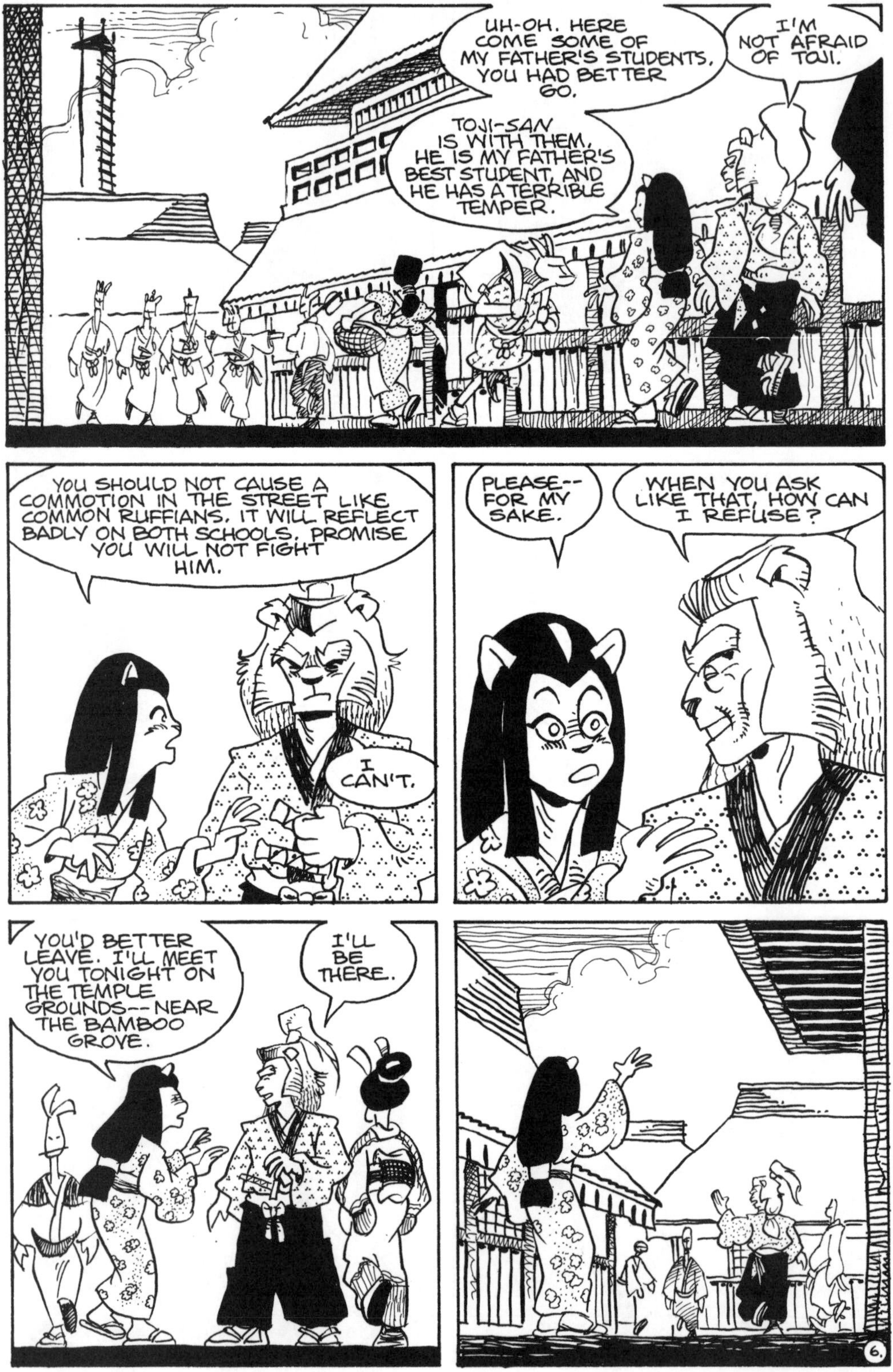
UH-OH. HERE COME SOME OF MY FATHER'S STUDENTS. YOU HAD BETTER GO.
TOJI-SAN IS WITH THEM. HE IS MY FATHER'S BEST STUDENT, AND HE HAS A TERRIBLE TEMPER.
I'M NOT AFRAID OF TOJI.
YOU SHOULD NOT CAUSE A COMMOTION IN THE STREET LIKE COMMON RUFFIANS. IT WILL REFLECT BADLY ON BOTH SCHOOLS. PROMISE YOU WILL NOT FIGHT HIM.
I CAN'T.
PLEASE-- FOR MY SAKE.
WHEN YOU ASK LIKE THAT, HOW CAN I REFUSE?
YOU'D BETTER LEAVE. I'LL MEET YOU TONIGHT ON THE TEMPLE GROUNDS-- NEAR THE BAMBOO GROVE.
I'LL BE THERE.
6.

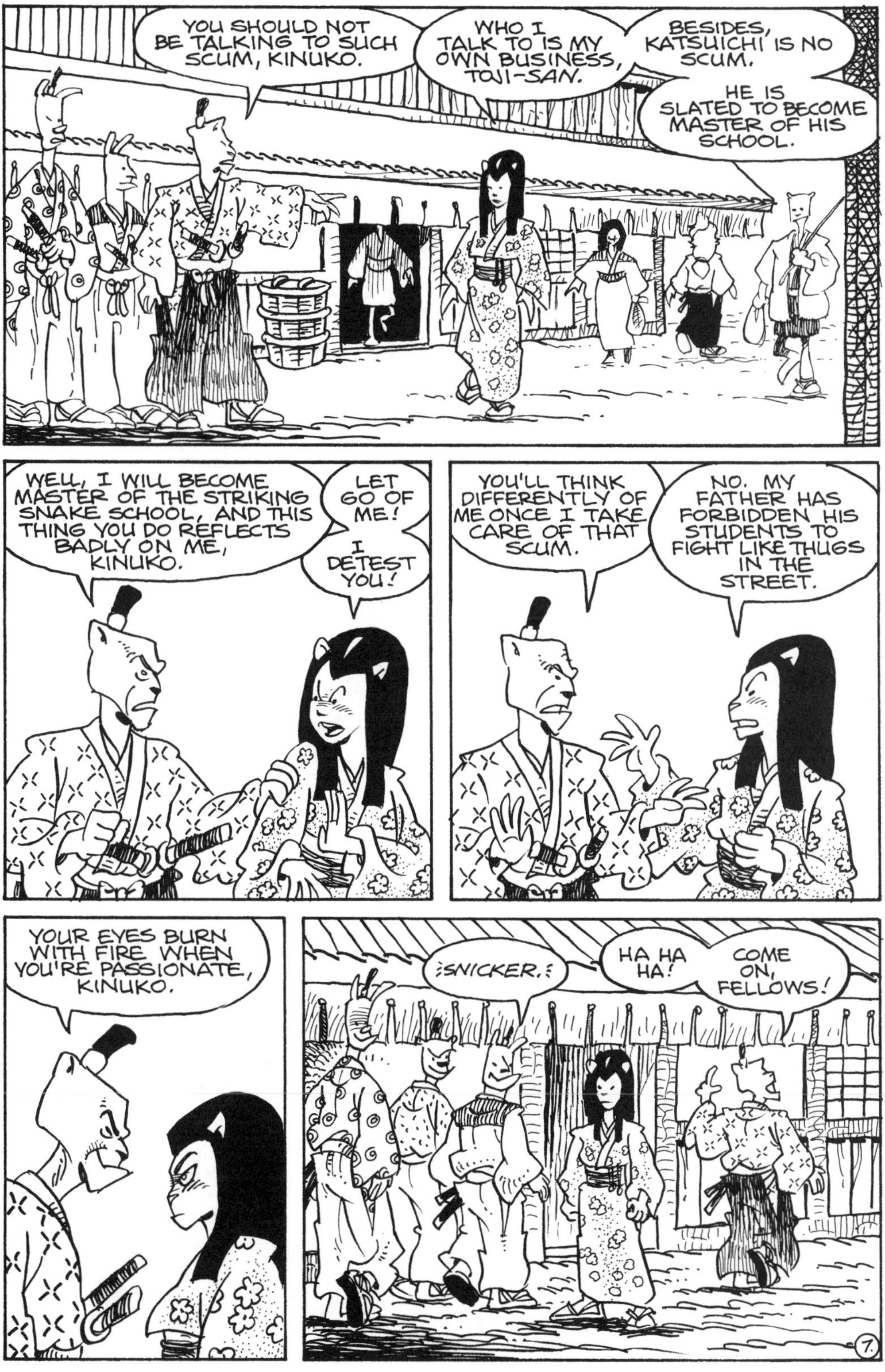
YOU SHOULD NOT BE TALKING TO SUCH SCUM, KINUKO.
WHO I TALK TO IS MY OWN BUSINESS, TOJI-SAN.
BESIDES, KATSUICHI IS NO SCUM.
HE IS SLATED TO BECOME MASTER OF HIS SCHOOL.
WELL, I WILL BECOME MASTER OF THE STRIKING SNAKE SCHOOL, AND THIS THING YOU DO REFLECTS BADLY ON ME, KINUKO.
LET GO OF ME!
I DETEST YOU!
YOU'LL THINK DIFFERENTLY OF ME ONCE I TAKE CARE OF THAT SCUM.
NO. MY FATHER HAS FORBIDDEN HIS STUDENTS TO FIGHT LIKE THUGS IN THE STREET.
YOUR EYES BURN WITH FIRE WHEN YOU'RE PASSIONATE, KINUKO.
SNICKER.
HA HA HA!
COME ON, FELLOWS!
7.

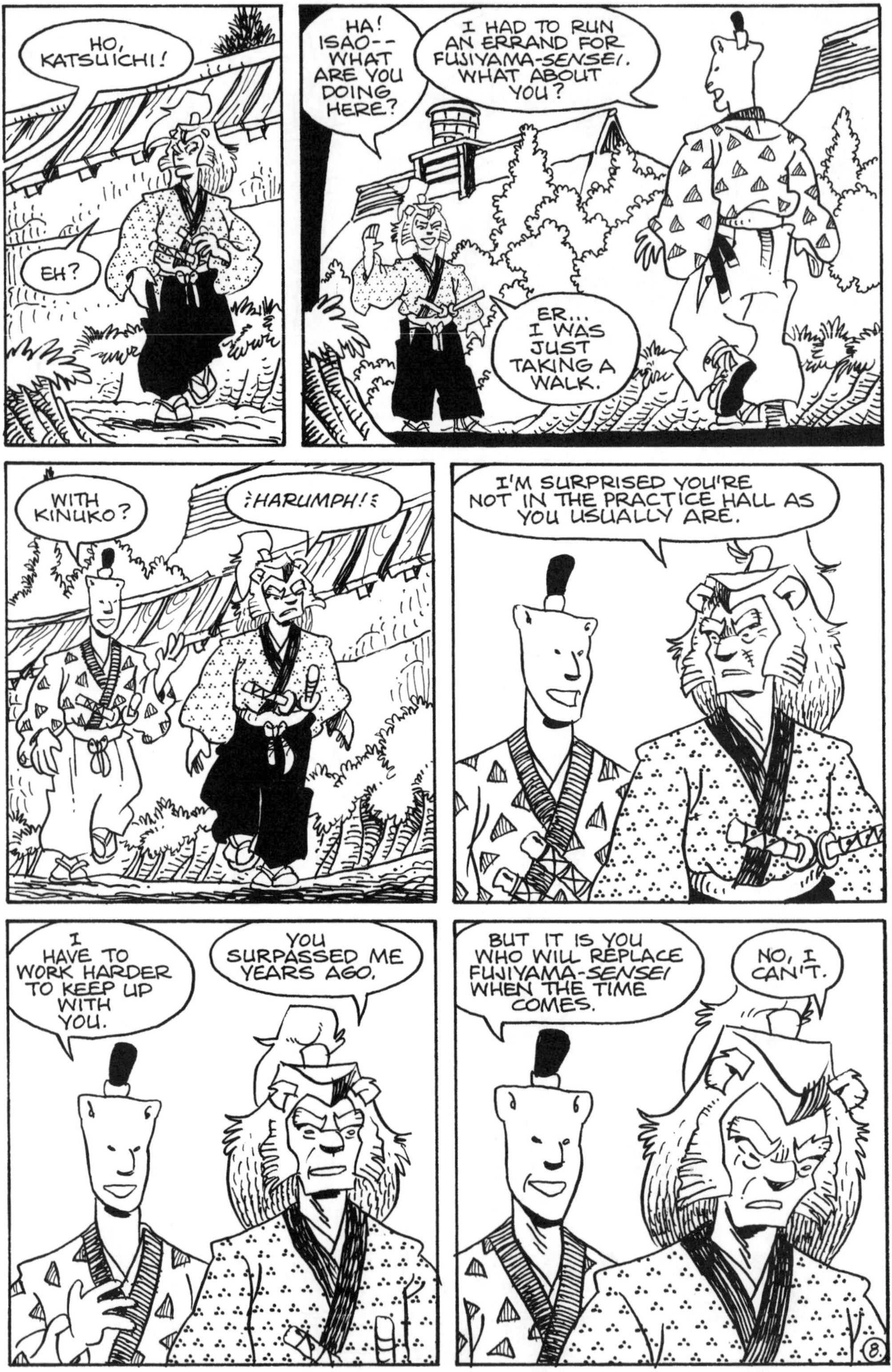
HO, KATSUICHI!
EH?
HA! ISAO-- WHAT ARE YOU DOING HERE?
I HAD TO RUN AN ERRAND FOR FUJIYAMA-SENSEI. WHAT ABOUT YOU?
ER... I WAS JUST TAKING A WALK.
WITH KINUKO?
HARUMPH!
I'M SURPRISED YOU'RE NOT IN THE PRACTICE HALL AS YOU USUALLY ARE.
I HAVE TO WORK HARDER TO KEEP UP WITH YOU.
YOU SURPASSED ME YEARS AGO.
BUT IT IS YOU WHO WILL REPLACE FUJIYAMA-SENSEI WHEN THE TIME COMES.
NO, I CAN'T.
8

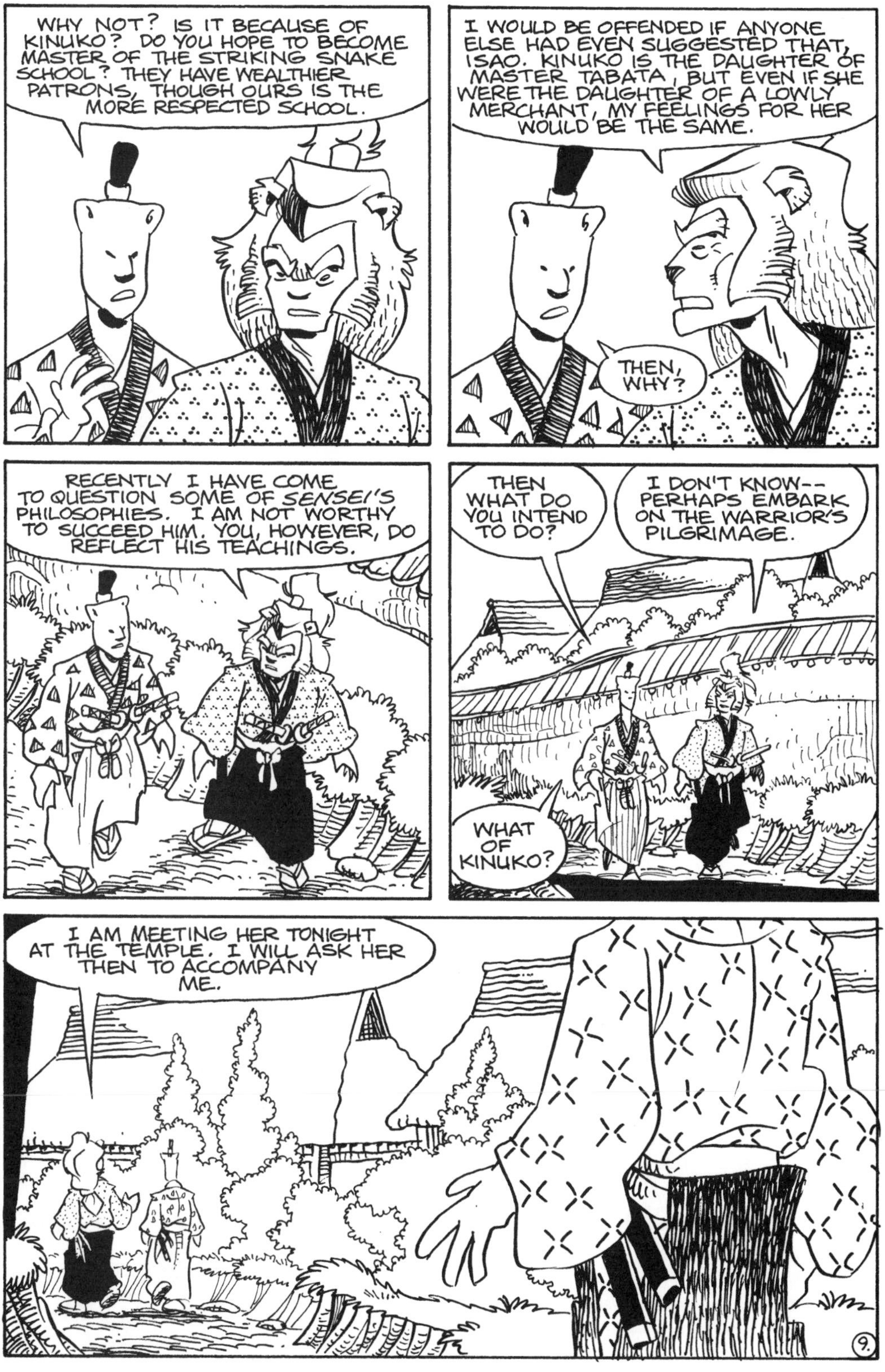
WHY NOT? IS IT BECAUSE OF KINUKO? DO YOU HOPE TO BECOME MASTER OF THE STRIKING SNAKE SCHOOL? THEY HAVE WEALTHIER PATRONS, THOUGH OURS IS THE MORE RESPECTED SCHOOL.
I WOULD BE OFFENDED IF ANYONE ELSE HAD EVEN SUGGESTED THAT, ISAO. KINUKO IS THE DAUGHTER OF MASTER TABATA, BUT EVEN IF SHE WERE THE DAUGHTER OF A LOWLY MERCHANT, MY FEELINGS FOR HER WOULD BE THE SAME.
THEN, WHY?
RECENTLY I HAVE COME TO QUESTION SOME OF SENSEI'S PHILOSOPHIES. I AM NOT WORTHY TO SUCCEED HIM. YOU, HOWEVER, DO REFLECT HIS TEACHINGS.
THEN WHAT DO YOU INTEND TO DO?
I DON'T KNOW-- PERHAPS EMBARK ON THE WARRIOR'S PILGRIMAGE.
WHAT OF KINUKO?
I AM MEETING HER TONIGHT AT THE TEMPLE. I WILL ASK HER THEN TO ACCOMPANY ME.
9.

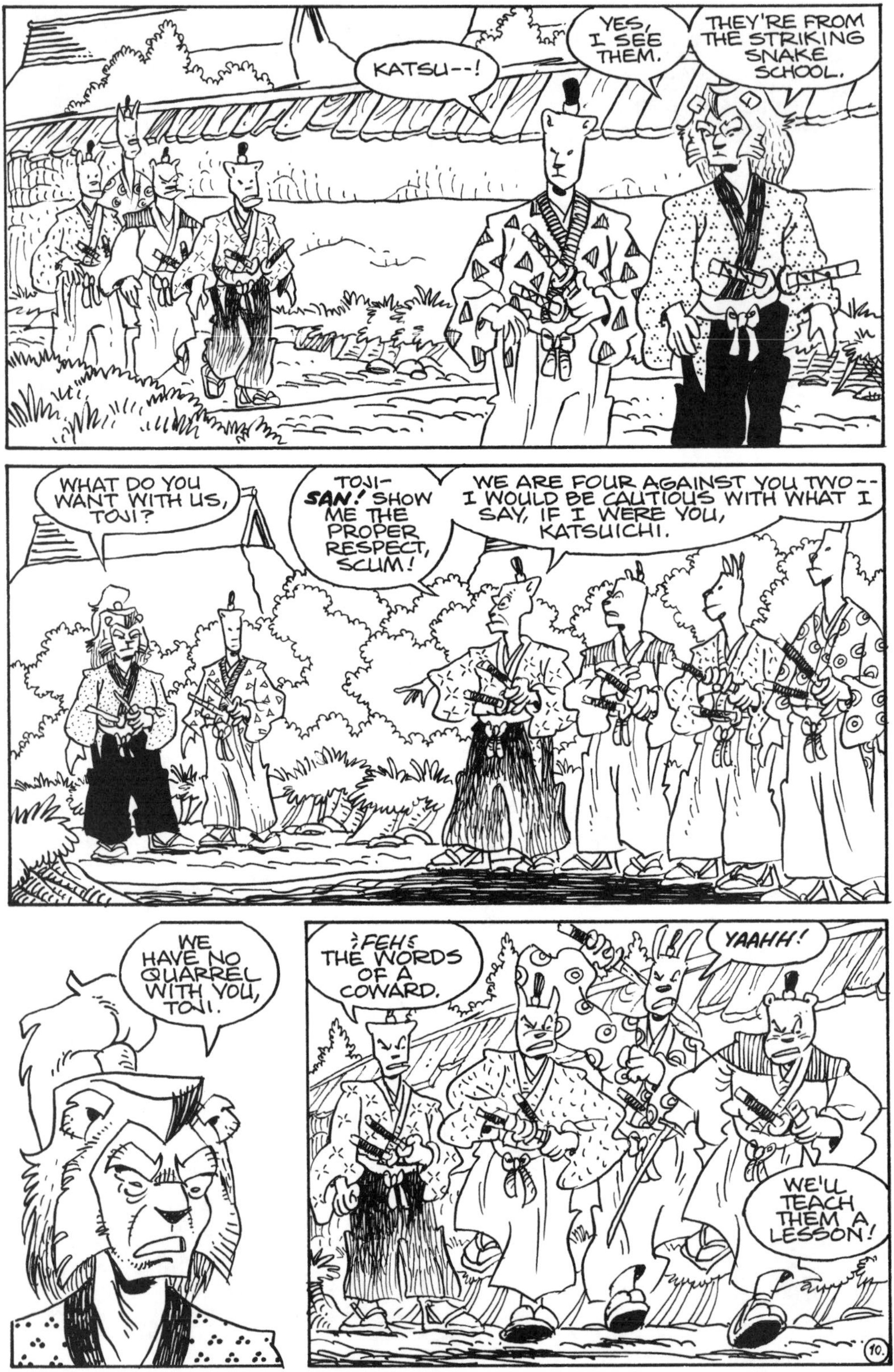
KATSU--!
YES, I SEE THEM.
THEY'RE FROM THE STRIKING SNAKE SCHOOL.
WHAT DO YOU WANT WITH US, TOJI?
TOJI-SAN! SHOW ME THE PROPER RESPECT, SCUM!
WE ARE FOUR AGAINST YOU TWO-- I WOULD BE CAUTIOUS WITH WHAT I SAY, IF I WERE YOU, KATSUICHI.
WE HAVE NO QUARREL WITH YOU, TOJI.
FEH THE WORDS OF A COWARD.
YAAHH!
WE'LL TEACH THEM A LESSON!
10.

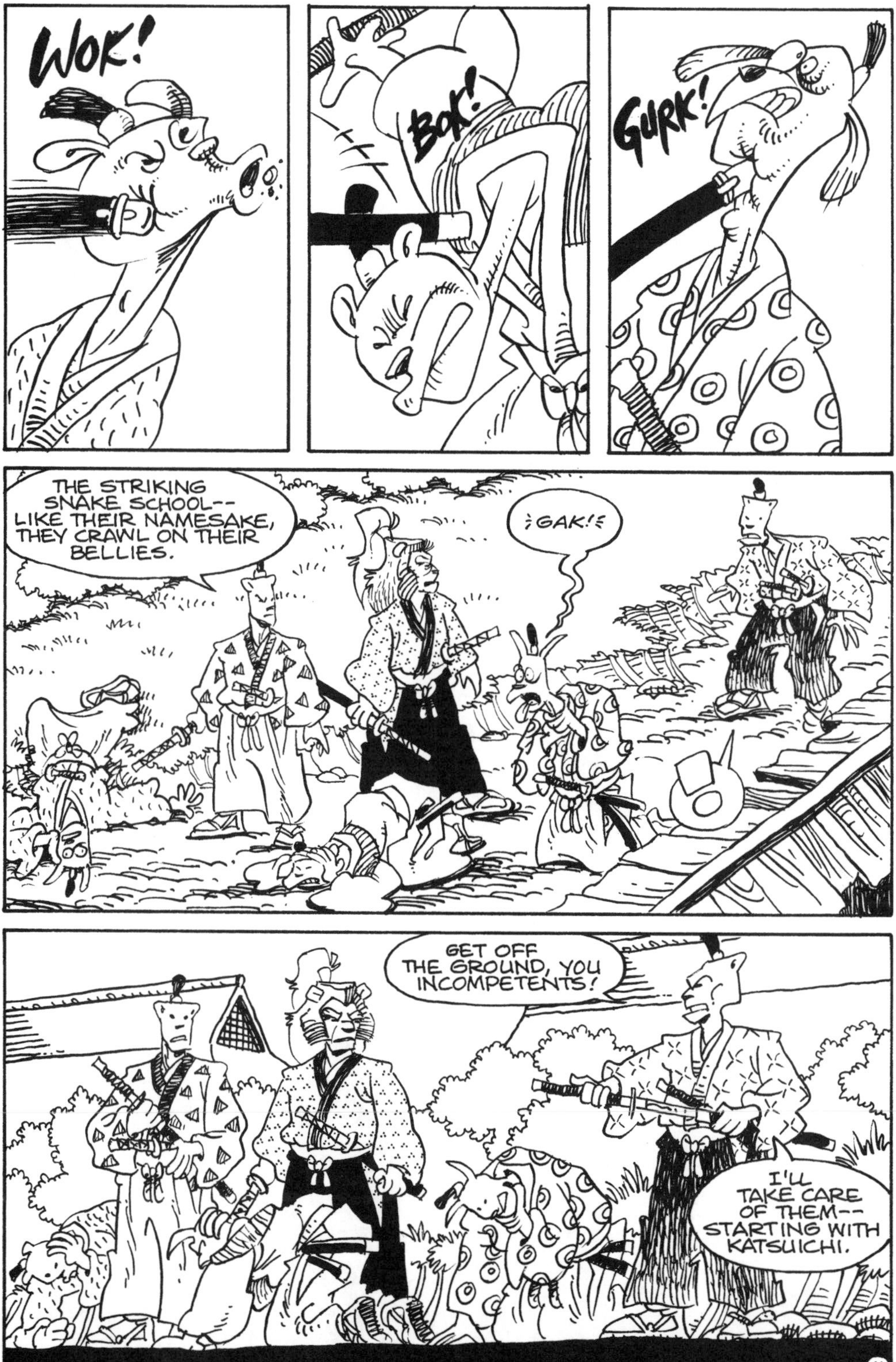
WOK!
BOK!
GURK!
THE STRIKING SNAKE SCHOOL-- LIKE THEIR NAMESAKE, THEY CRAWL ON THEIR BELLIES.
GAK!
GET OFF THE GROUND, YOU INCOMPETENTS!
I'LL TAKE CARE OF THEM-- STARTING WITH KATSUICHI.
11.

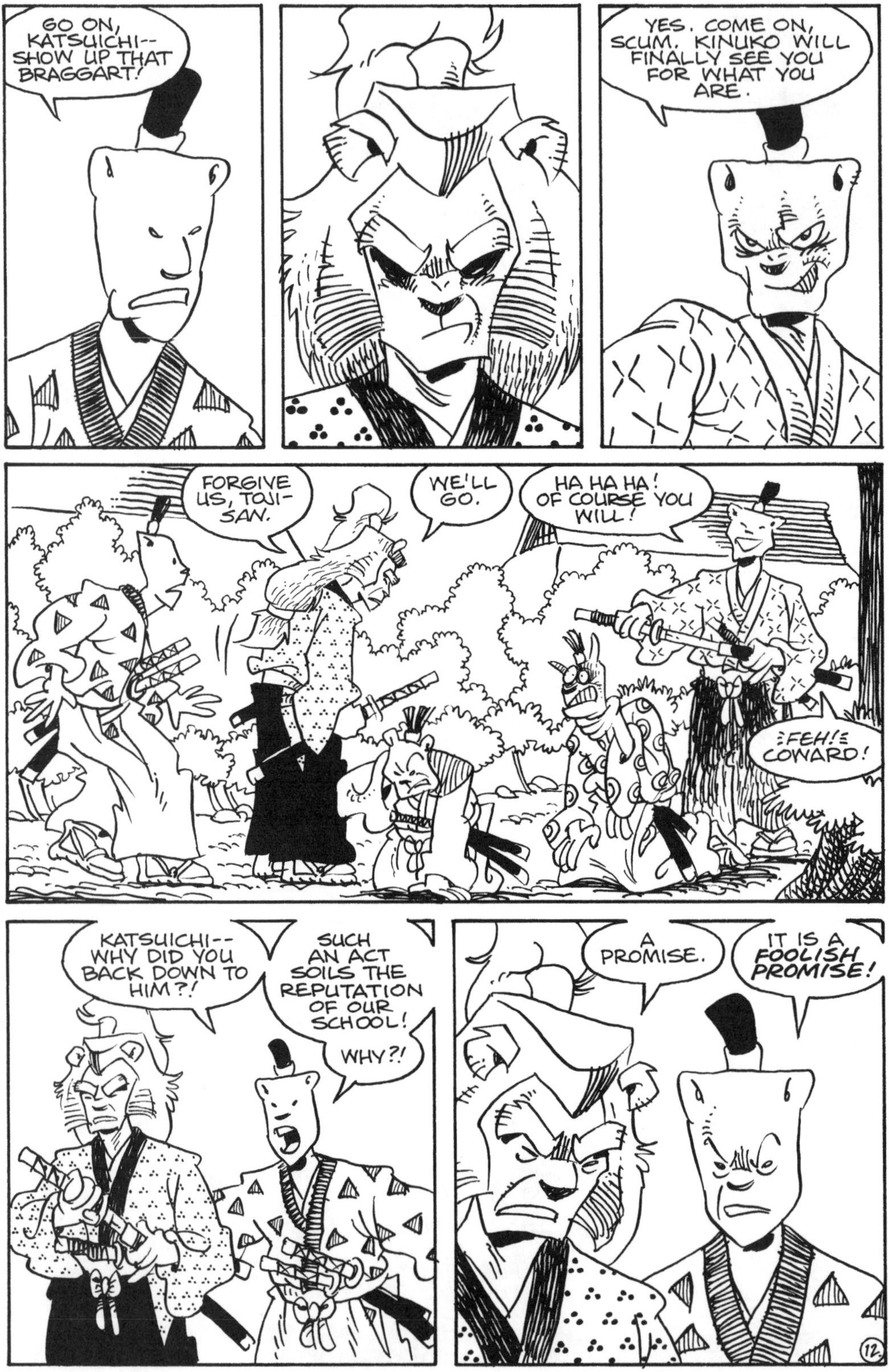
GO ON, KATSUICHI-- SHOW UP THAT BRAGGART!
YES. COME ON, SCUM. KINUKO WILL FINALLY SEE YOU FOR WHAT YOU ARE.
FORGIVE US, TOJI-SAN.
WE'LL GO.
HA HA HA! OF COURSE YOU WILL!
FEH! COWARD!
KATSUICHI-- WHY DID YOU BACK DOWN TO HIM?!
SUCH AN ACT SOILS THE REPUTATION OF OUR SCHOOL!
WHY?!
A PROMISE.
IT IS A FOOLISH PROMISE!
12

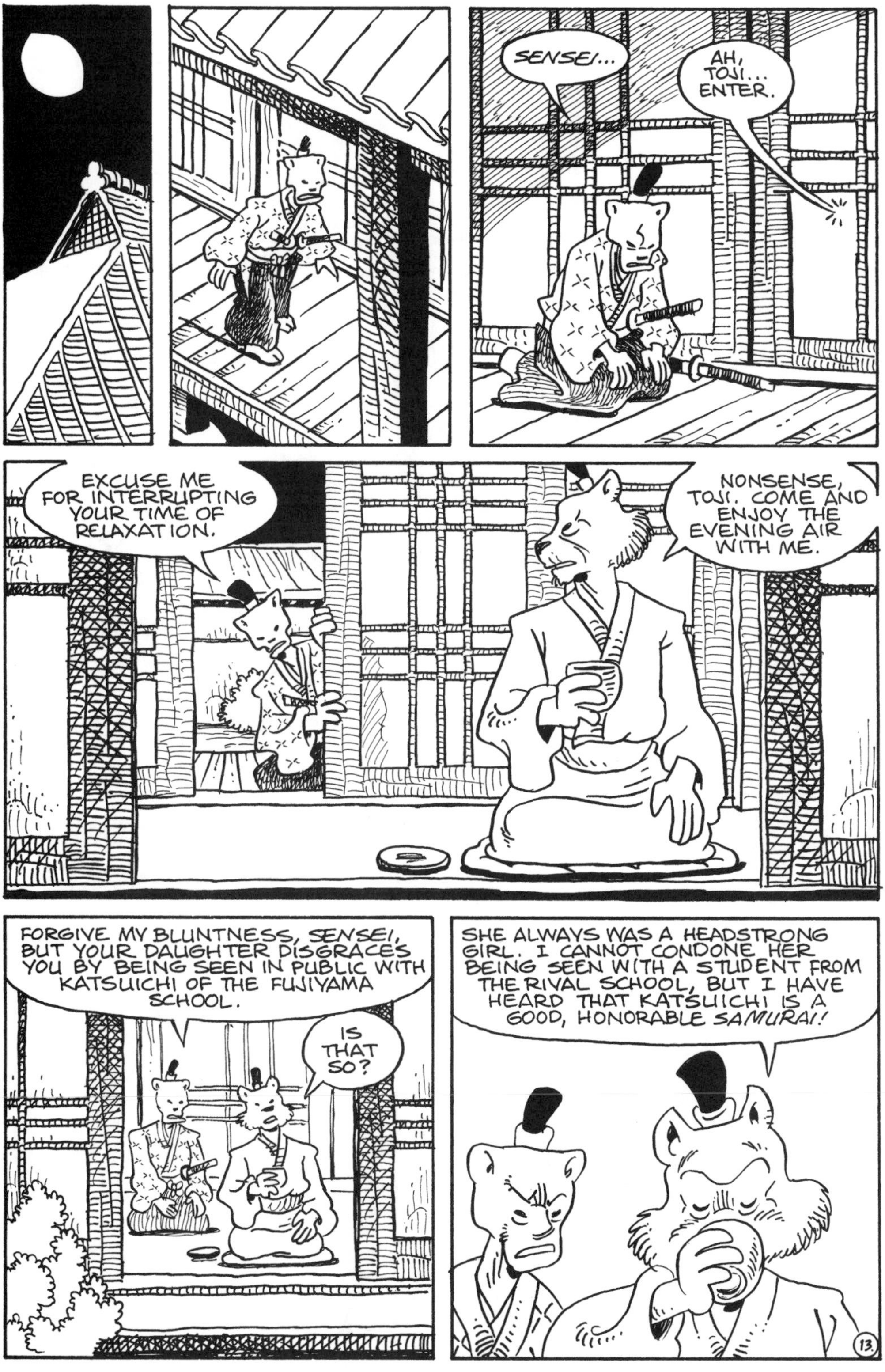
SENSEI...
AH, TOJI... ENTER.
EXCUSE ME FOR INTERRUPTING YOUR TIME OF RELAXATION.
NONSENSE, TOJI. COME AND ENJOY THE EVENING AIR WITH ME.
FORGIVE MY BLUNTNESS, SENSEI, BUT YOUR DAUGHTER DISGRACES YOU BY BEING SEEN IN PUBLIC WITH KATSUICHI OF THE FUJIYAMA SCHOOL.
IS THAT SO?
SHE ALWAYS WAS A HEADSTRONG GIRL. I CANNOT CONDONE HER BEING SEEN WITH A STUDENT FROM THE RIVAL SCHOOL, BUT I HAVE HEARD THAT KATSUICHI IS A GOOD, HONORABLE *SAMURAI*!
13.

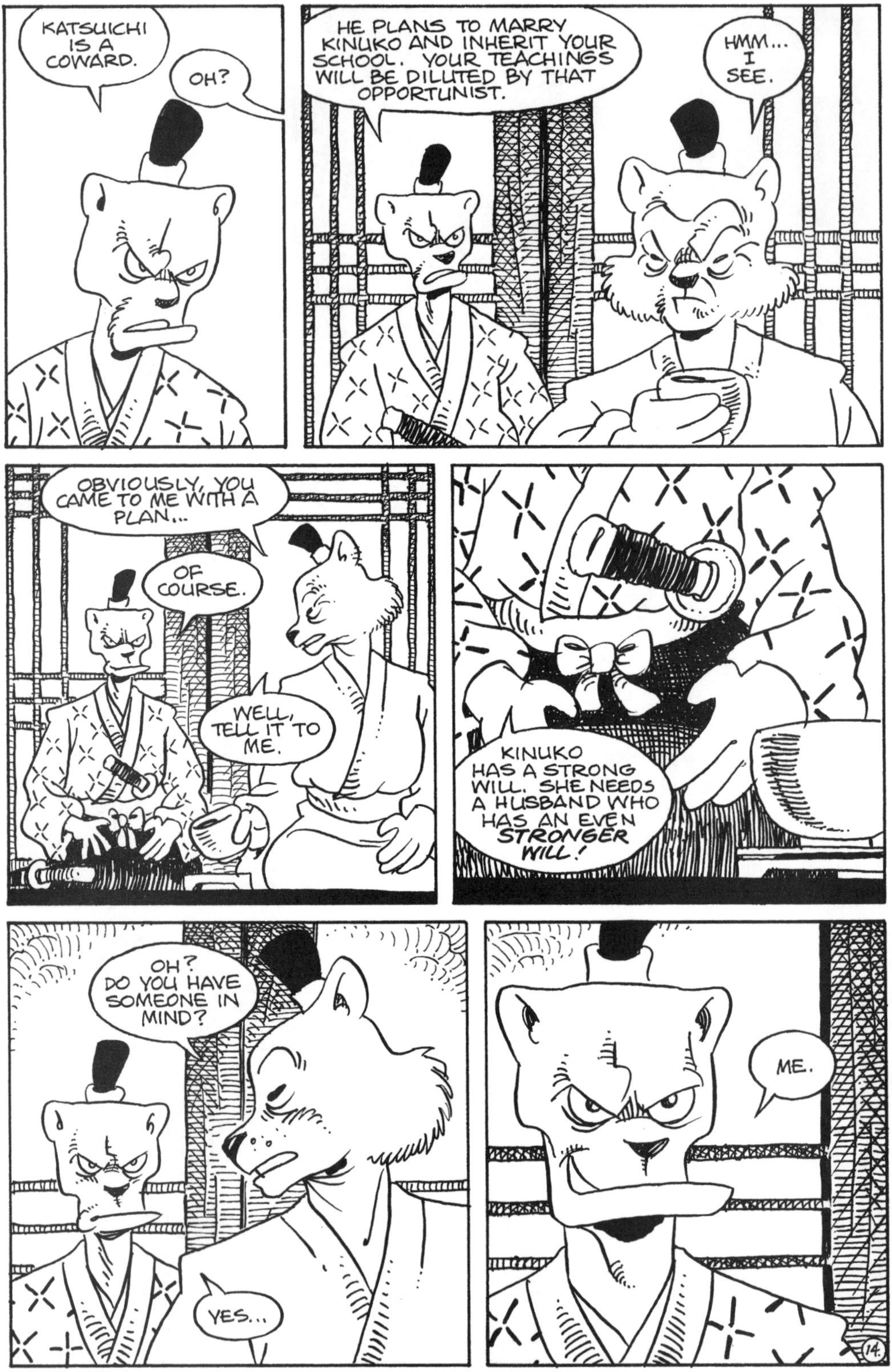
KATSUICHI IS A COWARD.
OH?
HE PLANS TO MARRY KINUKO AND INHERIT YOUR SCHOOL. YOUR TEACHINGS WILL BE DILUTED BY THAT OPPORTUNIST.
HMM... I SEE.
OBVIOUSLY, YOU CAME TO ME WITH A PLAN...
OF COURSE.
WELL, TELL IT TO ME.
KINUKO HAS A STRONG WILL. SHE NEEDS A HUSBAND WHO HAS AN EVEN STRONGER WILL!
OH? DO YOU HAVE SOMEONE IN MIND?
YES...
ME.
14.

TINK!
TINK!
TINK!

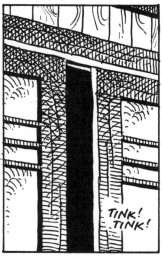

TINK!
TINK!

TINK!
TINK!

TINK! TINK!
TINK!

TINK!
TINK!
TINK!

YOU REALLY ARE A DISGRACE.

OH--!

A DECENT WOMAN DOES NOT WALK THE STREETS AT THIS TIME OF NIGHT.

ESPECIALLY WEARING BELLS, AS IF PLYING HER TRADE LIKE A COMMON NIGHT HAWK*

TOJI--! HOW DARE YOU FOLLOW ME?!

* PROSTITUTE

15.

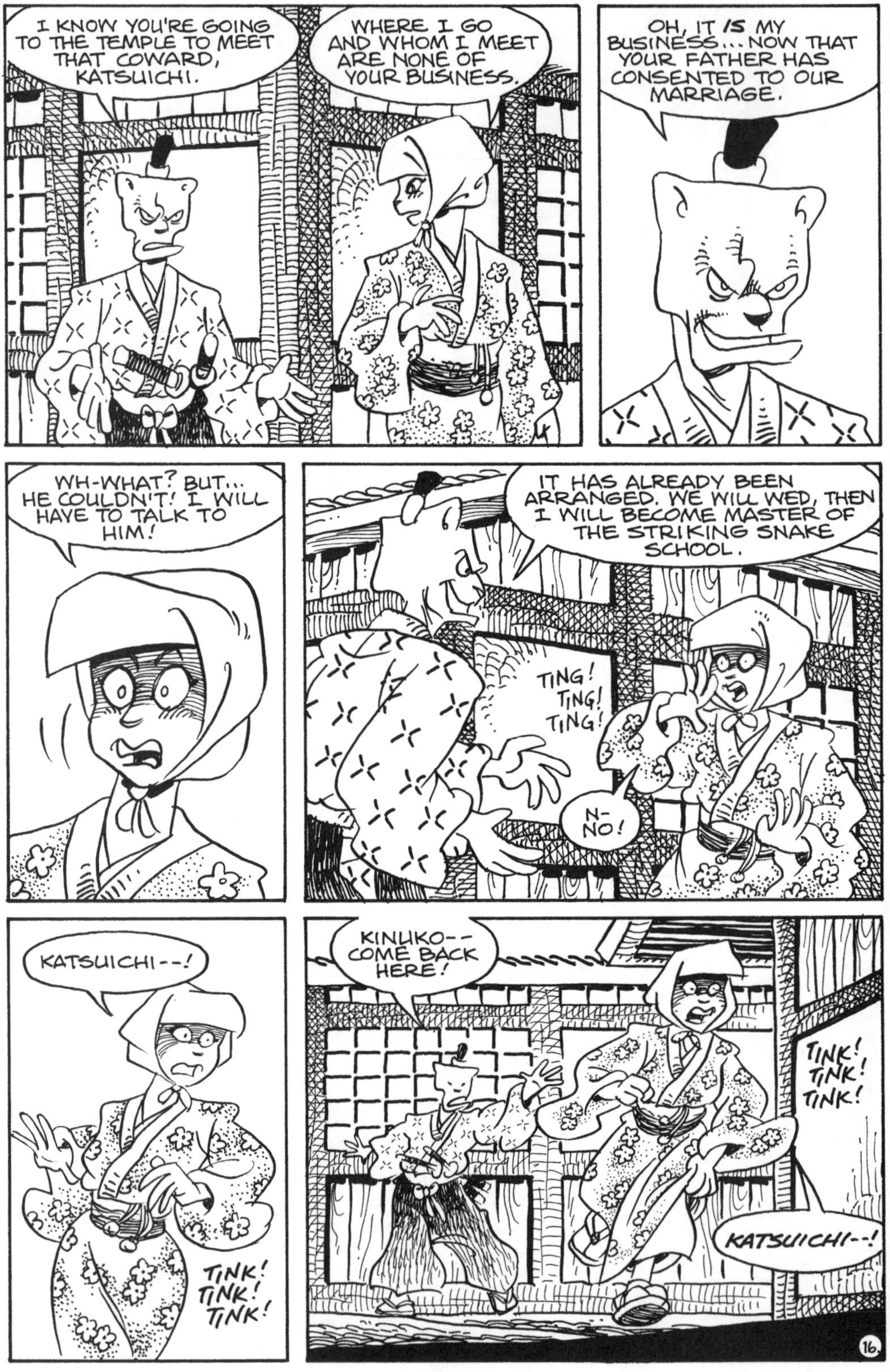
I KNOW YOU'RE GOING TO THE TEMPLE TO MEET THAT COWARD, KATSUICHI.
WHERE I GO AND WHOM I MEET ARE NONE OF YOUR BUSINESS.
OH, IT IS MY BUSINESS... NOW THAT YOUR FATHER HAS CONSENTED TO OUR MARRIAGE.
WH-WHAT? BUT... HE COULDN'T! I WILL HAVE TO TALK TO HIM!
IT HAS ALREADY BEEN ARRANGED. WE WILL WED, THEN I WILL BECOME MASTER OF THE STRIKING SNAKE SCHOOL.
TING! TING! TING!
N-NO!
KATSUICHI--!
TINK! TINK! TINK!
KINUKO--COME BACK HERE!
TINK! TINK! TINK!
KATSUICHI--!
16.

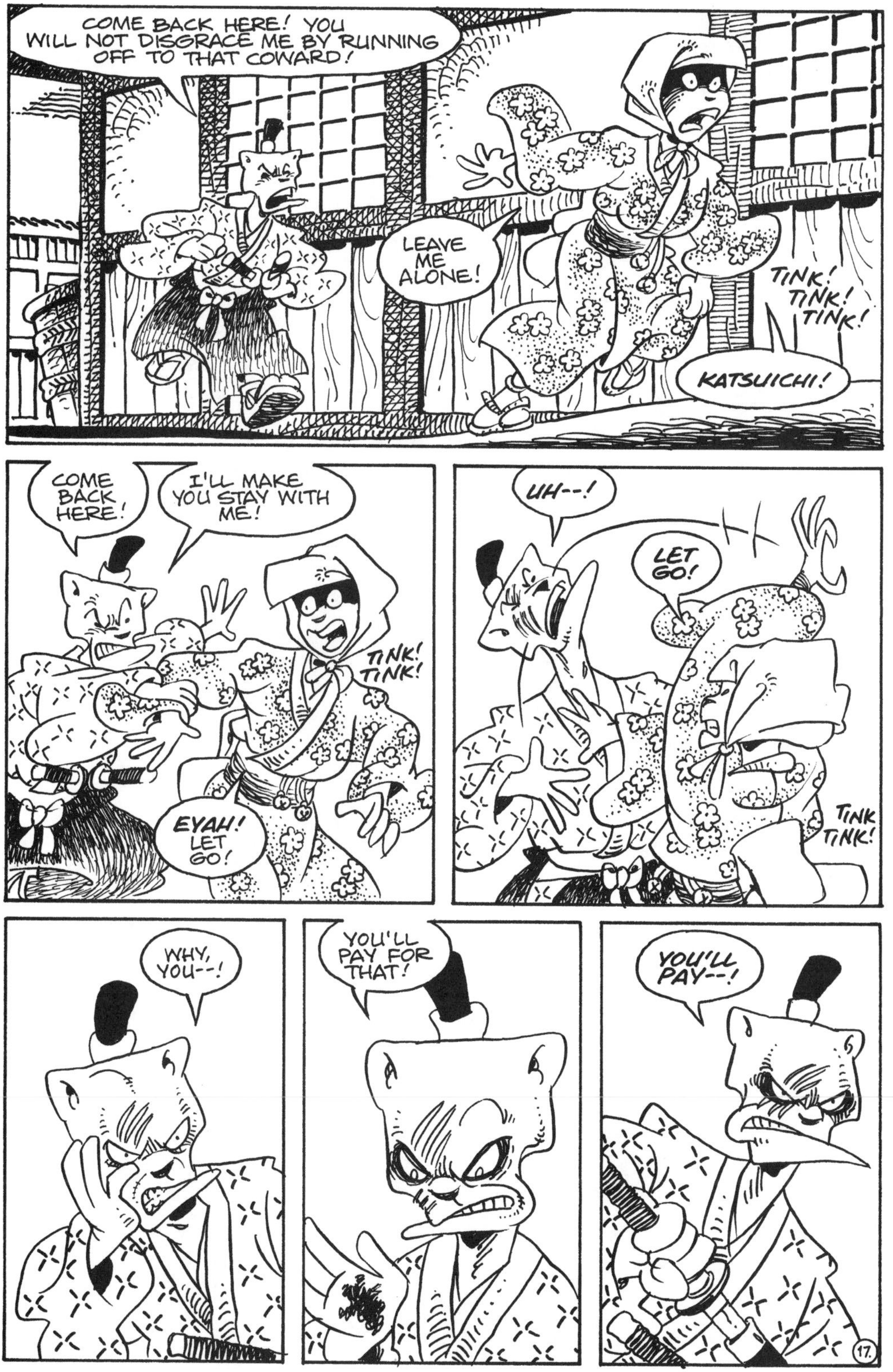
COME BACK HERE! YOU WILL NOT DISGRACE ME BY RUNNING OFF TO THAT COWARD!
LEAVE ME ALONE!
TINK! TINK! TINK!
KATSUICHI!
COME BACK HERE!
I'LL MAKE YOU STAY WITH ME!
TINK! TINK!
EYAH! LET GO!
UH--!
LET GO!
TINK TINK!
WHY, YOU--!
YOU'LL PAY FOR THAT!
YOU'LL PAY--!
17.

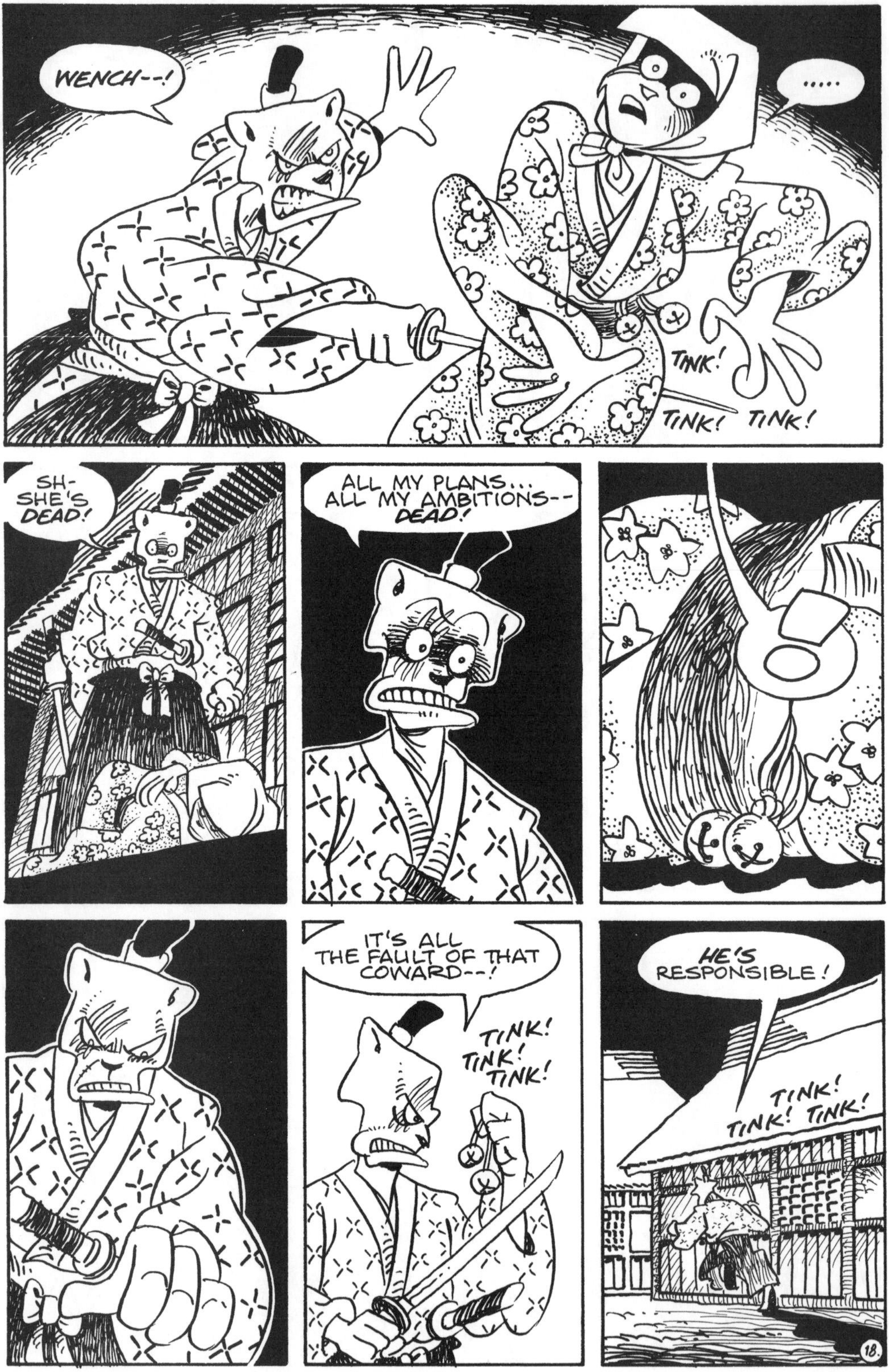
WENCH--!
.....
TINK!
TINK! TINK!
SH- SHE'S DEAD!
ALL MY PLANS... ALL MY AMBITIONS-- DEAD!
IT'S ALL THE FAULT OF THAT COWARD--!
TINK! TINK! TINK!
HE'S RESPONSIBLE!
TINK! TINK! TINK!
18.

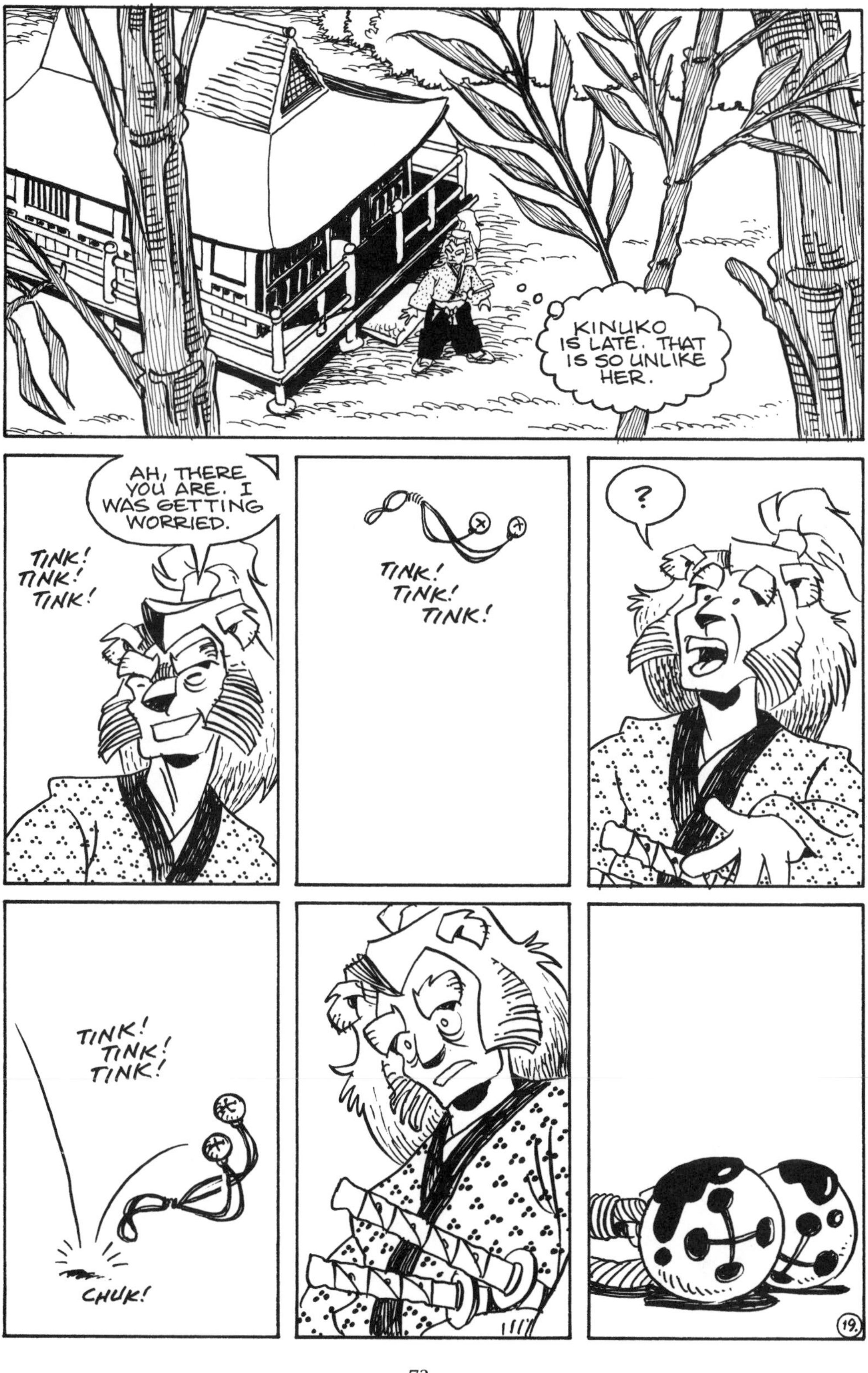
KINUKO IS LATE. THAT IS SO UNLIKE HER.
AH, THERE YOU ARE. I WAS GETTING WORRIED.
TINK! TINK! TINK!
TINK! TINK! TINK!
?
TINK! TINK! TINK!
CHUK!
19.

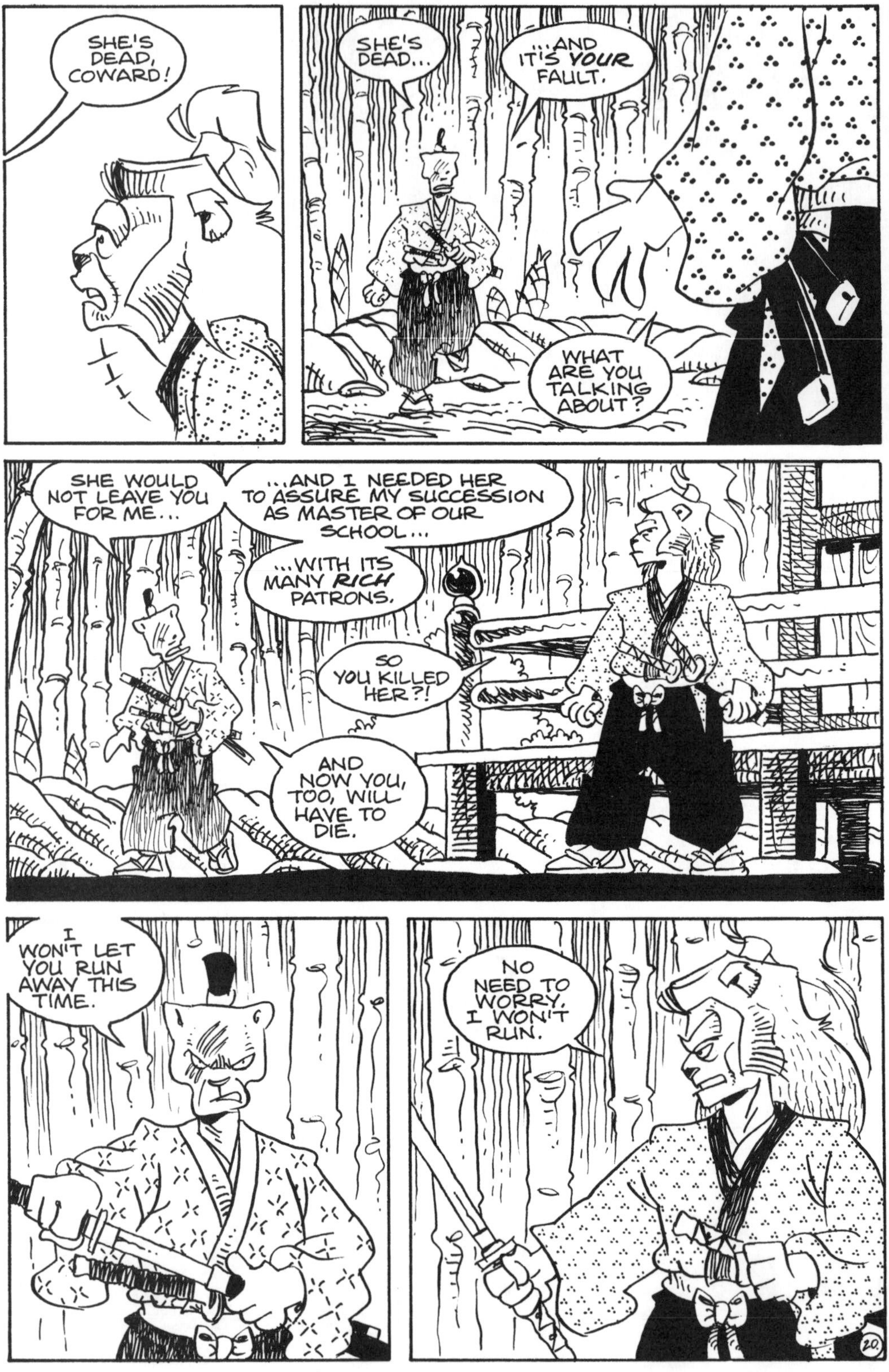
SHE'S DEAD, COWARD!
SHE'S DEAD...
...AND IT'S YOUR FAULT.
WHAT ARE YOU TALKING ABOUT?
SHE WOULD NOT LEAVE YOU FOR ME...
...AND I NEEDED HER TO ASSURE MY SUCCESSION AS MASTER OF OUR SCHOOL...
...WITH ITS MANY RICH PATRONS.
SO YOU KILLED HER?!
AND NOW YOU, TOO, WILL HAVE TO DIE.
I WON'T LET YOU RUN AWAY THIS TIME.
NO NEED TO WORRY. I WON'T RUN.
20

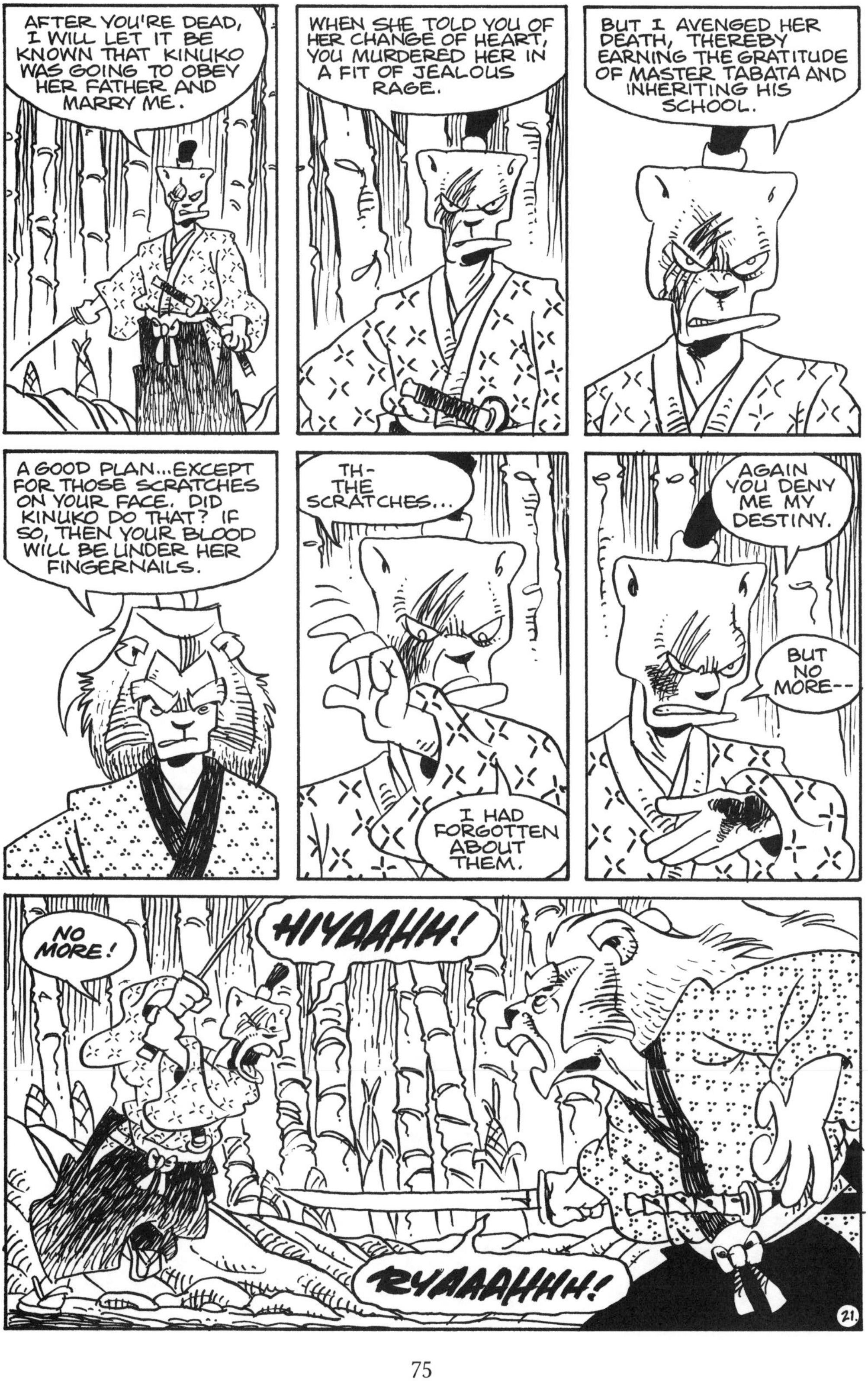
AFTER YOU'RE DEAD, I WILL LET IT BE KNOWN THAT KINUKO WAS GOING TO OBEY HER FATHER AND MARRY ME.
WHEN SHE TOLD YOU OF HER CHANGE OF HEART, YOU MURDERED HER IN A FIT OF JEALOUS RAGE.
BUT I AVENGED HER DEATH, THEREBY EARNING THE GRATITUDE OF MASTER TABATA AND INHERITING HIS SCHOOL.
A GOOD PLAN...EXCEPT FOR THOSE SCRATCHES ON YOUR FACE. DID KINUKO DO THAT? IF SO, THEN YOUR BLOOD WILL BE UNDER HER FINGERNAILS.
TH- THE SCRATCHES...
I HAD FORGOTTEN ABOUT THEM.
AGAIN YOU DENY ME MY DESTINY.
BUT NO MORE--
NO MORE!
HIYAAHH!
RYAAAHHH!
21.

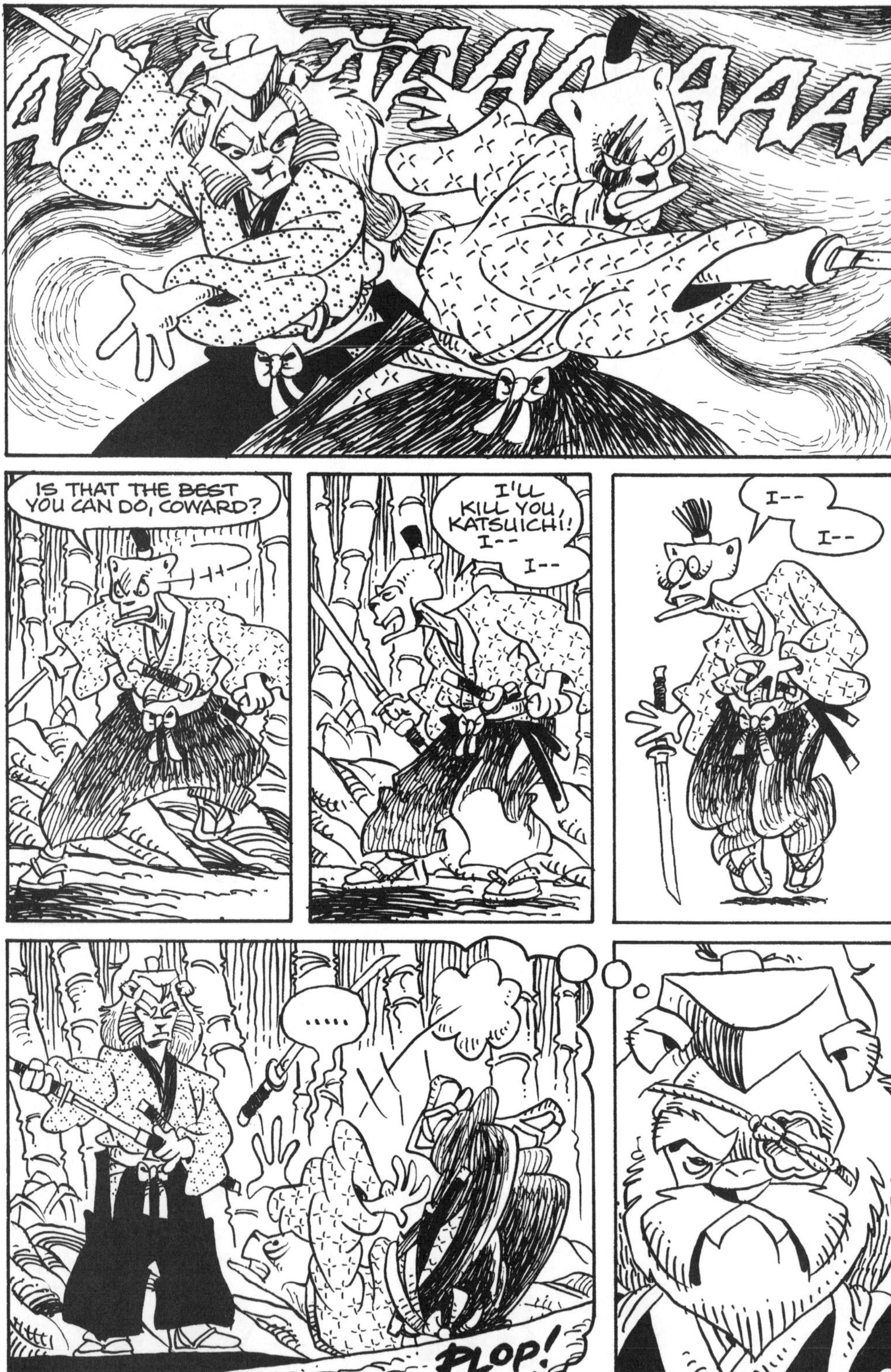
AAAAAAAAAA
IS THAT THE BEST YOU CAN DO, COWARD?
I'LL KILL YOU, KATSUICHI! I--
I--
I--
I--
.....
PLOP!
22.

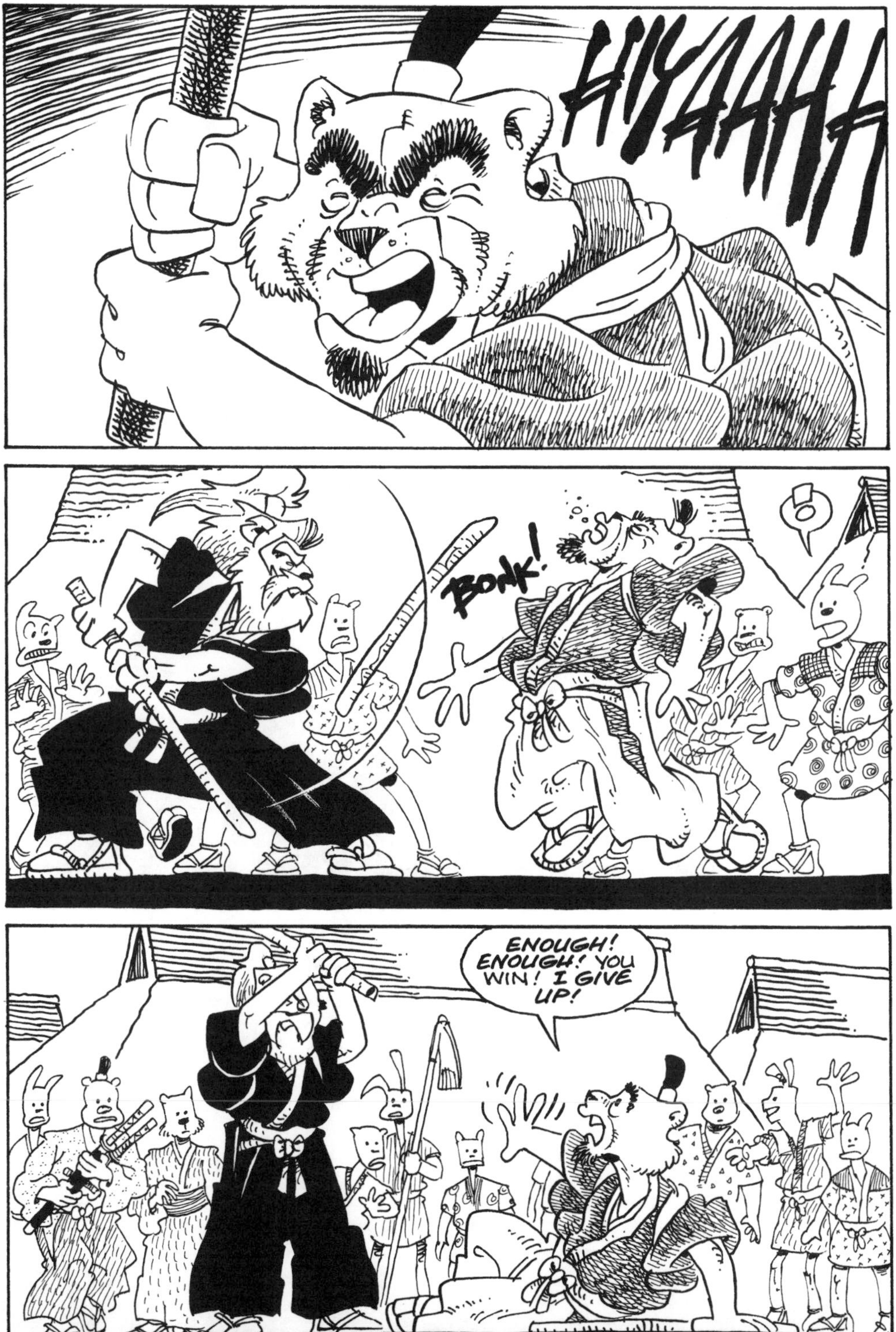
HIYAAHH
BONK!
ENOUGH! ENOUGH! YOU WIN! I GIVE UP!
23.

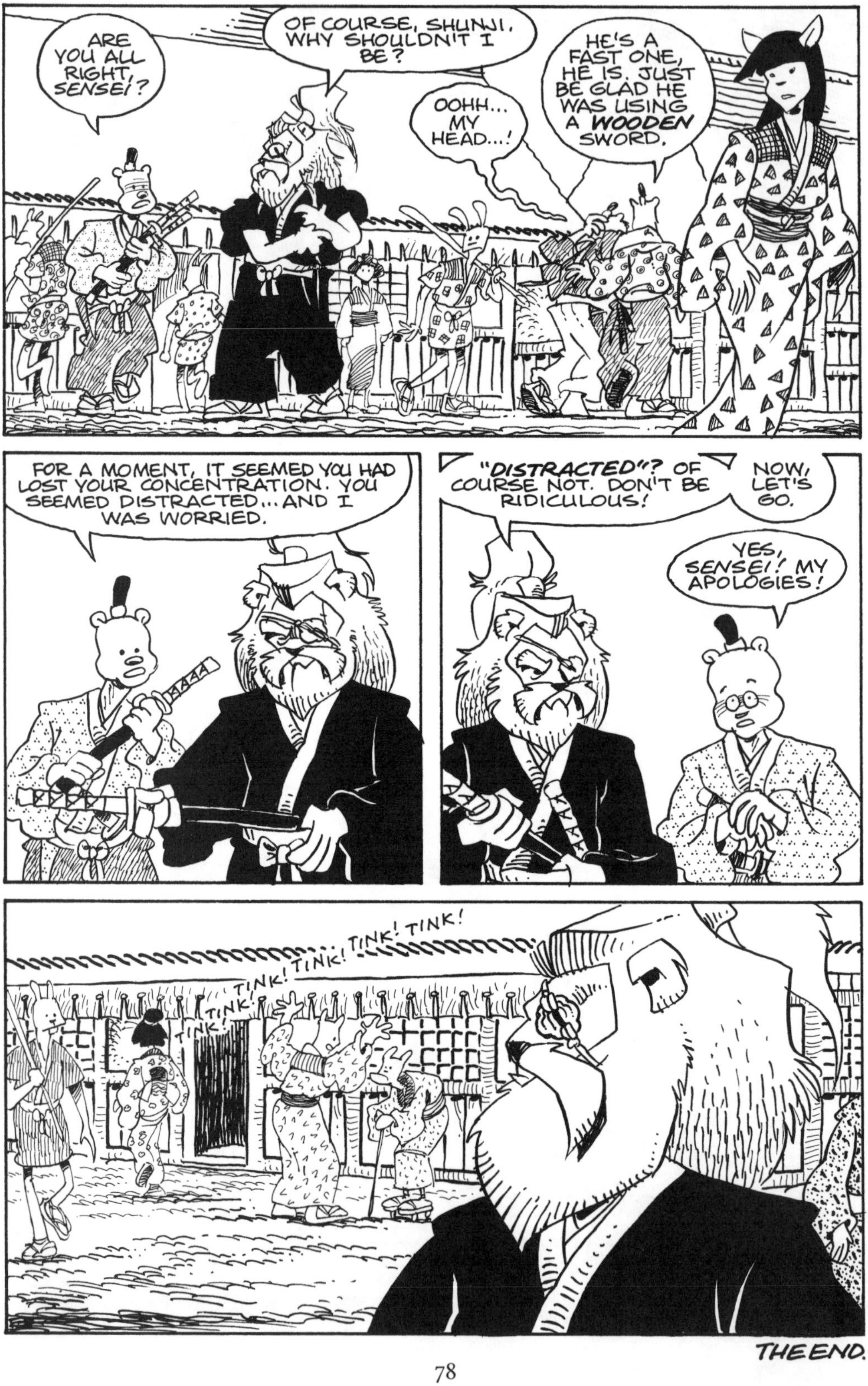
ARE YOU ALL RIGHT, SENSEI?
OF COURSE, SHUNJI. WHY SHOULDN'T I BE?
OOHH... MY HEAD...!
HE'S A FAST ONE, HE IS. JUST BE GLAD HE WAS USING A **WOODEN** SWORD.
FOR A MOMENT, IT SEEMED YOU HAD LOST YOUR CONCENTRATION. YOU SEEMED DISTRACTED... AND I WAS WORRIED.
"*DISTRACTED*"? OF COURSE NOT. DON'T BE RIDICULOUS!
NOW, LET'S GO.
YES, SENSEI! MY APOLOGIES!
TINK! TINK! TINK! TINK! TINK! TINK!

THE END.

KILL THE GEISHU LORD!

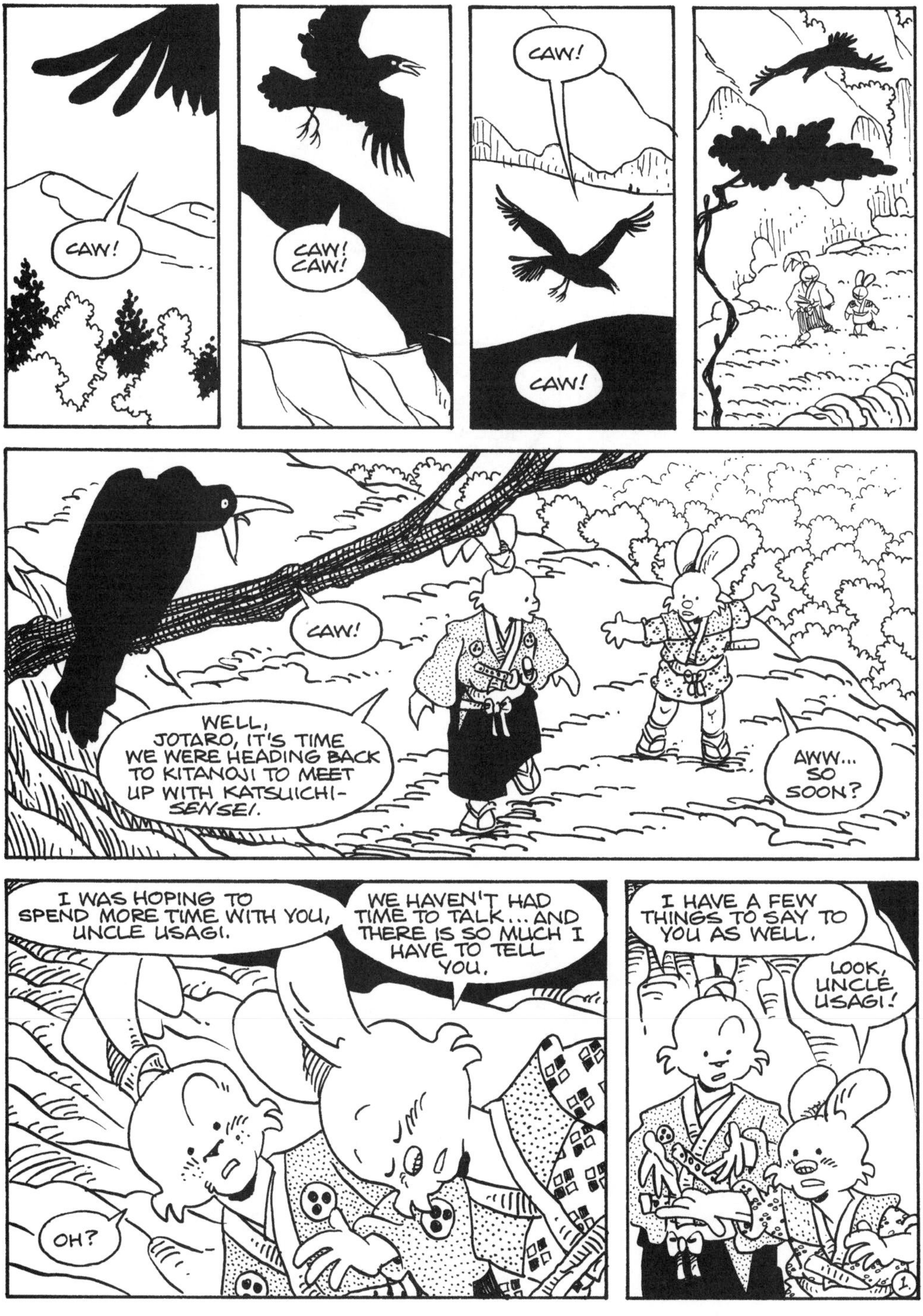
CAW!
CAW! CAW!
CAW!
CAW!
CAW!
WELL, JOTARO, IT'S TIME WE WERE HEADING BACK TO KITANOJI TO MEET UP WITH KATSUICHI-SENSEI.
AWW... SO SOON?
I WAS HOPING TO SPEND MORE TIME WITH YOU, UNCLE USAGI.
WE HAVEN'T HAD TIME TO TALK... AND THERE IS SO MUCH I HAVE TO TELL YOU.
OH?
I HAVE A FEW THINGS TO SAY TO YOU AS WELL.
LOOK, UNCLE USAGI!
1.

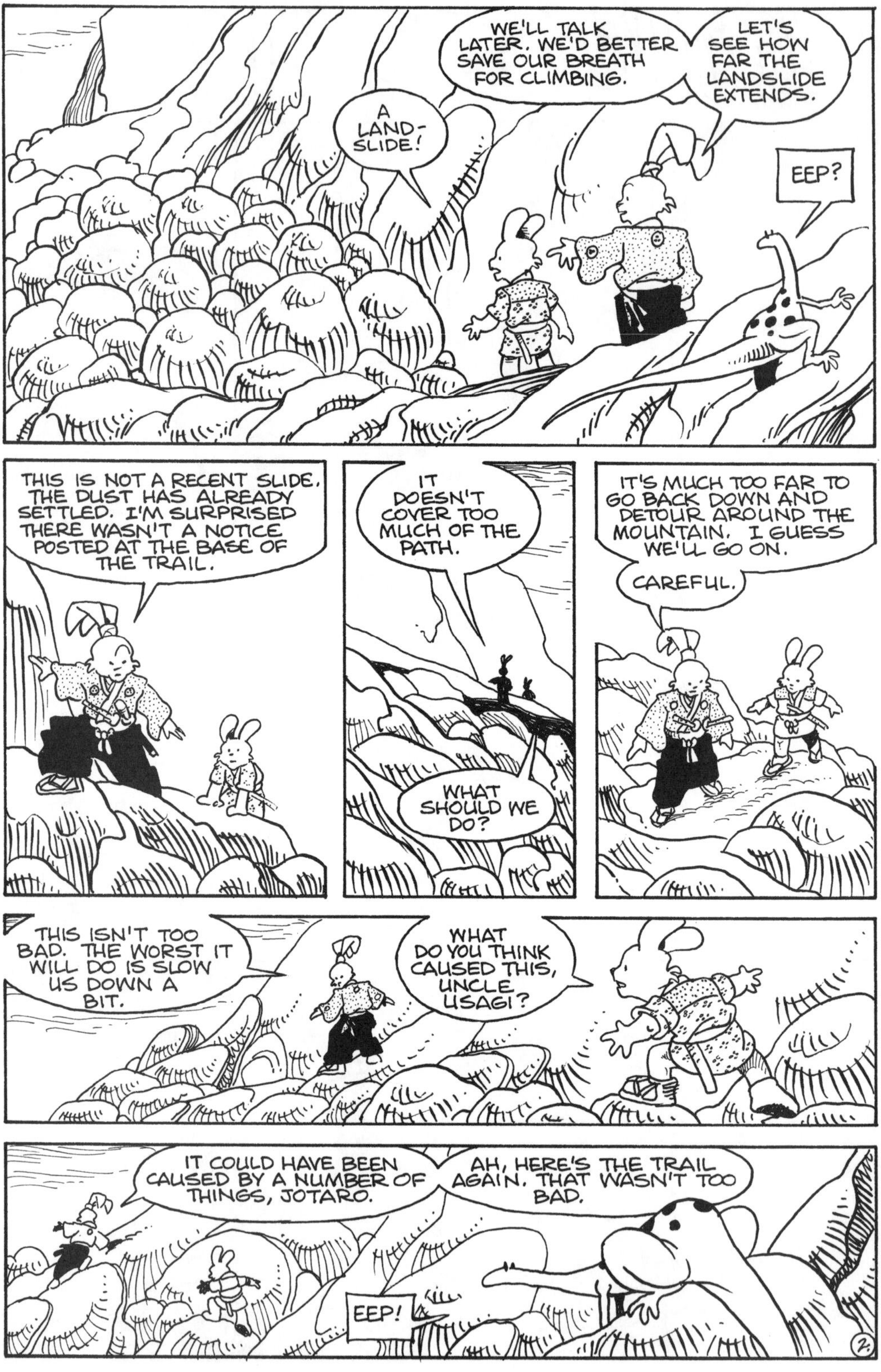
A LAND-SLIDE!
WE'LL TALK LATER. WE'D BETTER SAVE OUR BREATH FOR CLIMBING.
LET'S SEE HOW FAR THE LANDSLIDE EXTENDS.
EEP?
THIS IS NOT A RECENT SLIDE. THE DUST HAS ALREADY SETTLED. I'M SURPRISED THERE WASN'T A NOTICE POSTED AT THE BASE OF THE TRAIL.
IT DOESN'T COVER TOO MUCH OF THE PATH.
WHAT SHOULD WE DO?
IT'S MUCH TOO FAR TO GO BACK DOWN AND DETOUR AROUND THE MOUNTAIN. I GUESS WE'LL GO ON.
CAREFUL.
THIS ISN'T TOO BAD. THE WORST IT WILL DO IS SLOW US DOWN A BIT.
WHAT DO YOU THINK CAUSED THIS, UNCLE USAGI?
IT COULD HAVE BEEN CAUSED BY A NUMBER OF THINGS, JOTARO.
AH, HERE'S THE TRAIL AGAIN. THAT WASN'T TOO BAD.
EEP!
2.

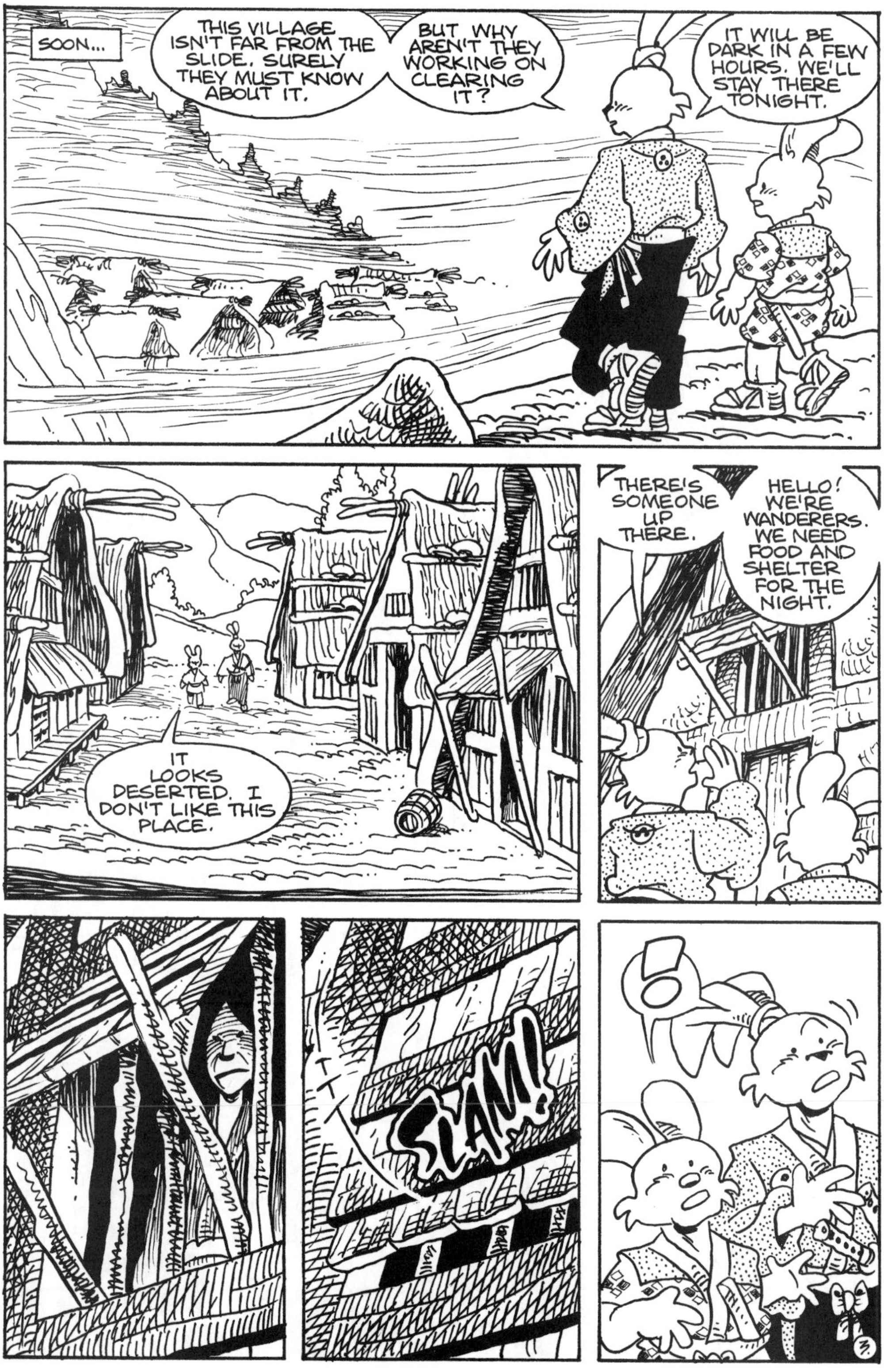
SOON...
THIS VILLAGE ISN'T FAR FROM THE SLIDE. SURELY THEY MUST KNOW ABOUT IT.
BUT WHY AREN'T THEY WORKING ON CLEARING IT?
IT WILL BE DARK IN A FEW HOURS. WE'LL STAY THERE TONIGHT.
IT LOOKS DESERTED. I DON'T LIKE THIS PLACE.
THERE'S SOMEONE UP THERE.
HELLO! WE'RE WANDERERS. WE NEED FOOD AND SHELTER FOR THE NIGHT.
SLAM!
!

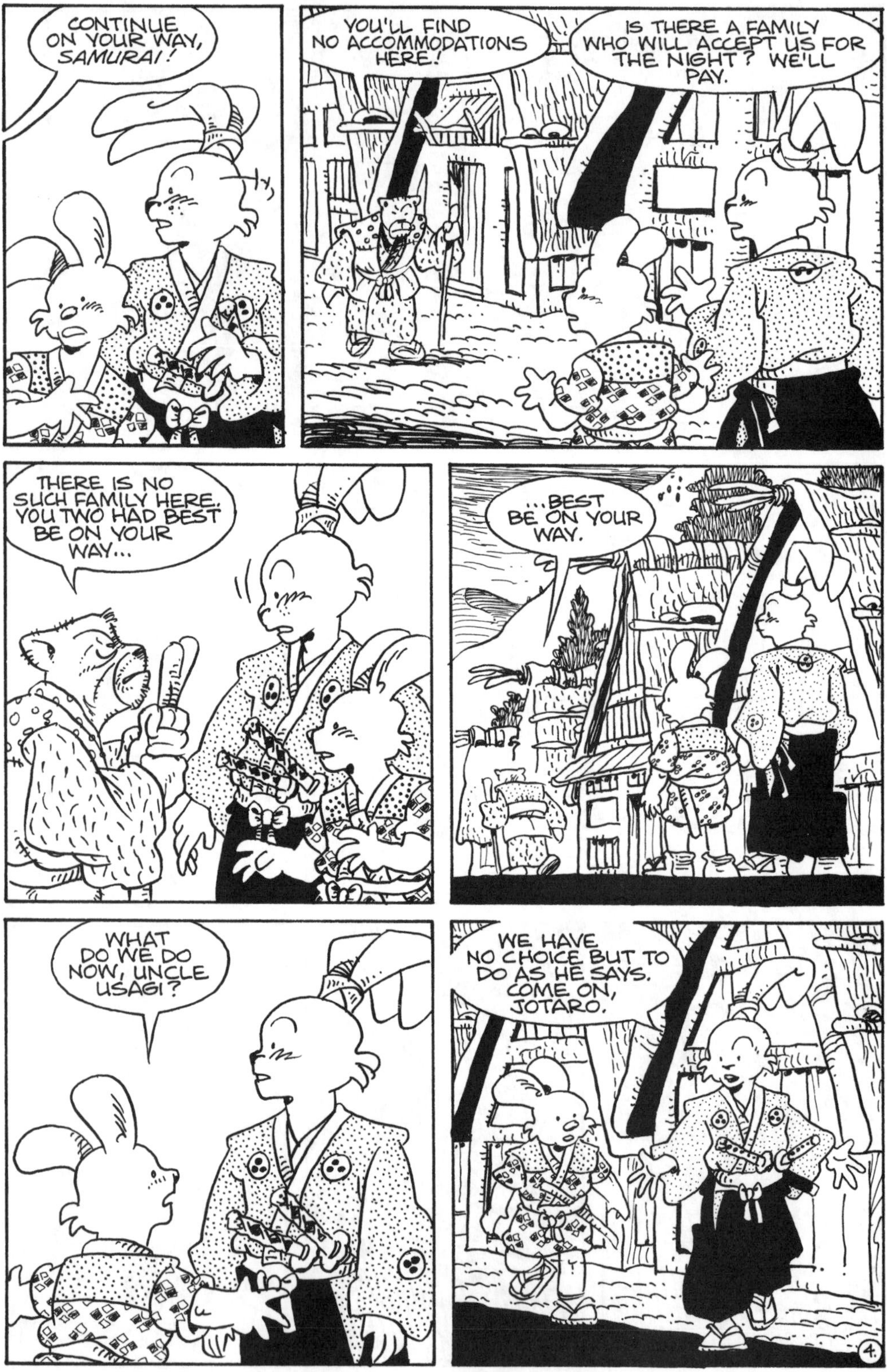
CONTINUE ON YOUR WAY, SAMURAI!
YOU'LL FIND NO ACCOMMODATIONS HERE!
IS THERE A FAMILY WHO WILL ACCEPT US FOR THE NIGHT? WE'LL PAY.
THERE IS NO SUCH FAMILY HERE. YOU TWO HAD BEST BE ON YOUR WAY...
...BEST BE ON YOUR WAY.
WHAT DO WE DO NOW, UNCLE USAGI?
WE HAVE NO CHOICE BUT TO DO AS HE SAYS. COME ON, JOTARO.
4.

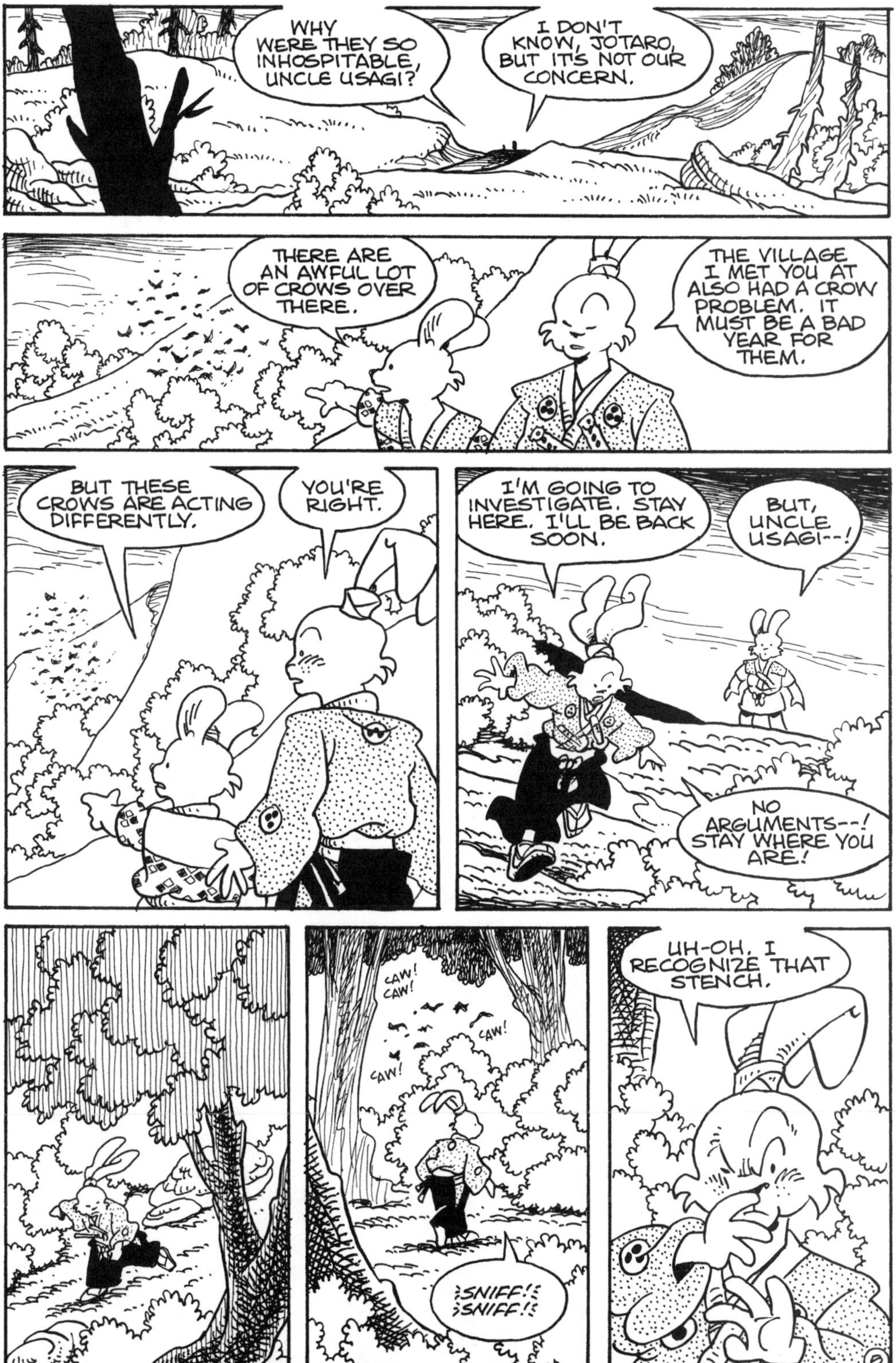
WHY WERE THEY SO INHOSPITABLE, UNCLE USAGI?
I DON'T KNOW, JOTARO, BUT IT'S NOT OUR CONCERN.
THERE ARE AN AWFUL LOT OF CROWS OVER THERE.
THE VILLAGE I MET YOU AT ALSO HAD A CROW PROBLEM. IT MUST BE A BAD YEAR FOR THEM.
BUT THESE CROWS ARE ACTING DIFFERENTLY.
YOU'RE RIGHT.
I'M GOING TO INVESTIGATE. STAY HERE. I'LL BE BACK SOON.
BUT, UNCLE USAGI--!
NO ARGUMENTS--! STAY WHERE YOU ARE!
CAW! CAW!
CAW!
CAW!
SNIFF! SNIFF!
UH-OH. I RECOGNIZE THAT STENCH.

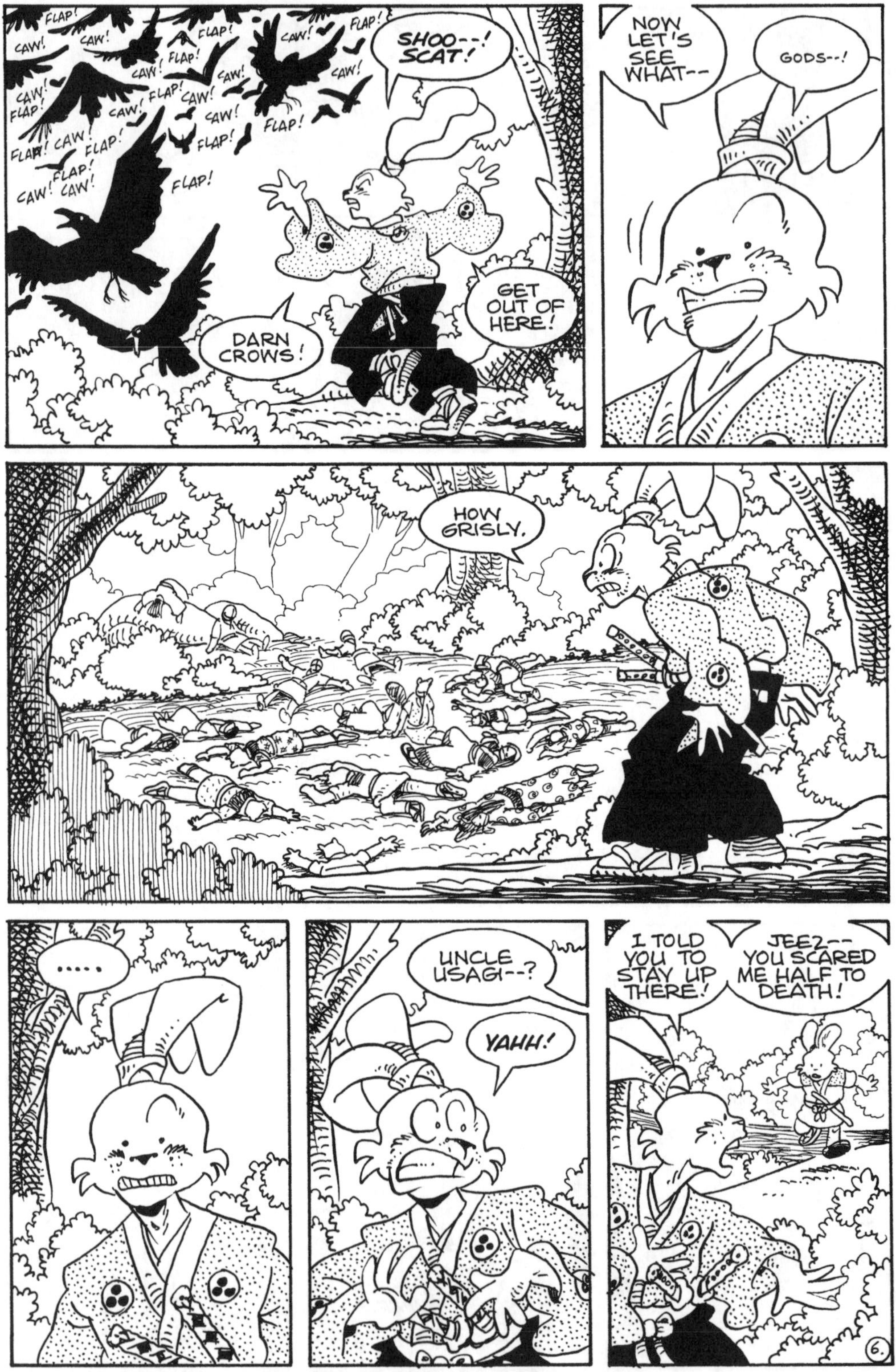
FLAP! CAW! CAW! FLAP! FLAP! CAW! FLAP! CAW! FLAP! CAW! CAW! FLAP! CAW! CAW! CAW! FLAP! CAW! FLAP! FLAP! FLAP! CAW! FLAP! CAW! CAW! FLAP! FLAP!
SHOO--! SCAT!
DARN CROWS!
GET OUT OF HERE!
NOW LET'S SEE WHAT--
GODS--!
HOW GRISLY.
.....
UNCLE USAGI--?
YAHH!
I TOLD YOU TO STAY UP THERE!
JEEZ-- YOU SCARED ME HALF TO DEATH!
6.

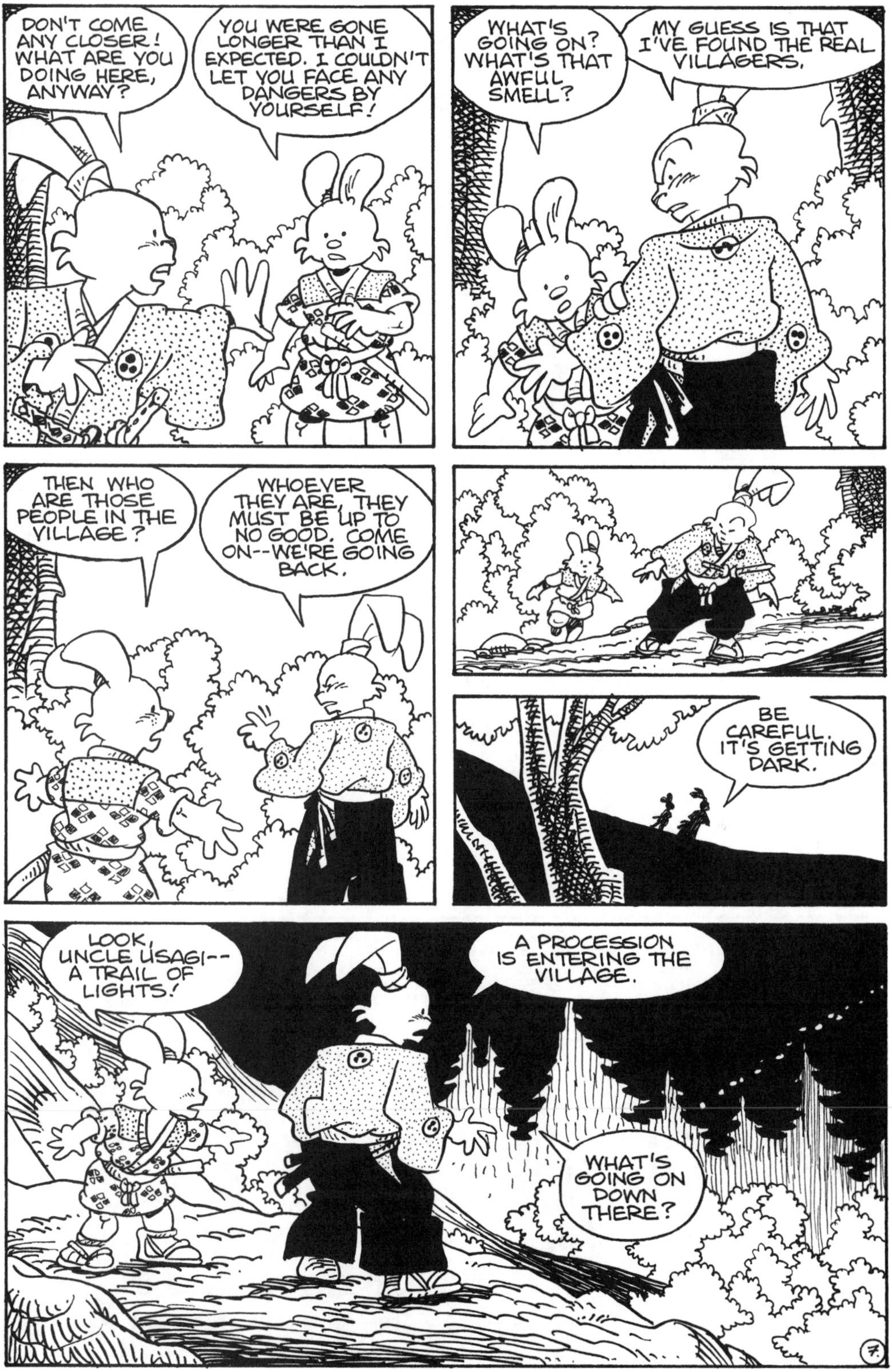
DON'T COME ANY CLOSER! WHAT ARE YOU DOING HERE, ANYWAY?
YOU WERE GONE LONGER THAN I EXPECTED. I COULDN'T LET YOU FACE ANY DANGERS BY YOURSELF!
WHAT'S GOING ON? WHAT'S THAT AWFUL SMELL?
MY GUESS IS THAT I'VE FOUND THE REAL VILLAGERS.
THEN WHO ARE THOSE PEOPLE IN THE VILLAGE?
WHOEVER THEY ARE, THEY MUST BE UP TO NO GOOD. COME ON--WE'RE GOING BACK.
BE CAREFUL. IT'S GETTING DARK.
LOOK, UNCLE USAGI--A TRAIL OF LIGHTS!
A PROCESSION IS ENTERING THE VILLAGE.
WHAT'S GOING ON DOWN THERE?
7

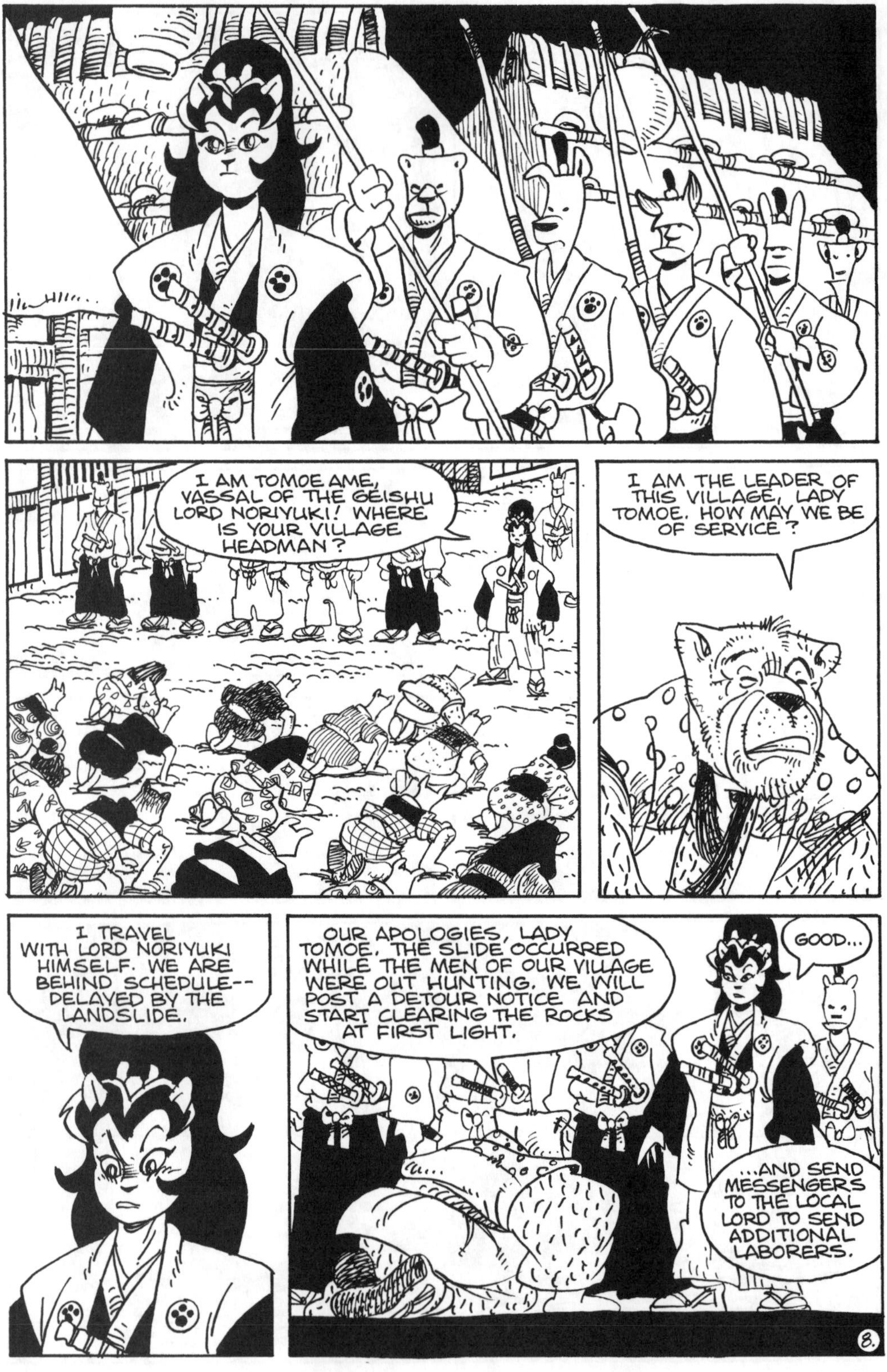
I AM TOMOE AME, VASSAL OF THE GEISHU LORD NORIYUKI! WHERE IS YOUR VILLAGE HEADMAN?
I AM THE LEADER OF THIS VILLAGE, LADY TOMOE. HOW MAY WE BE OF SERVICE?
I TRAVEL WITH LORD NORIYUKI HIMSELF. WE ARE BEHIND SCHEDULE-- DELAYED BY THE LANDSLIDE.
OUR APOLOGIES, LADY TOMOE. THE SLIDE OCCURRED WHILE THE MEN OF OUR VILLAGE WERE OUT HUNTING. WE WILL POST A DETOUR NOTICE AND START CLEARING THE ROCKS AT FIRST LIGHT.
...AND SEND MESSENGERS TO THE LOCAL LORD TO SEND ADDITIONAL LABORERS.
GOOD...
8.

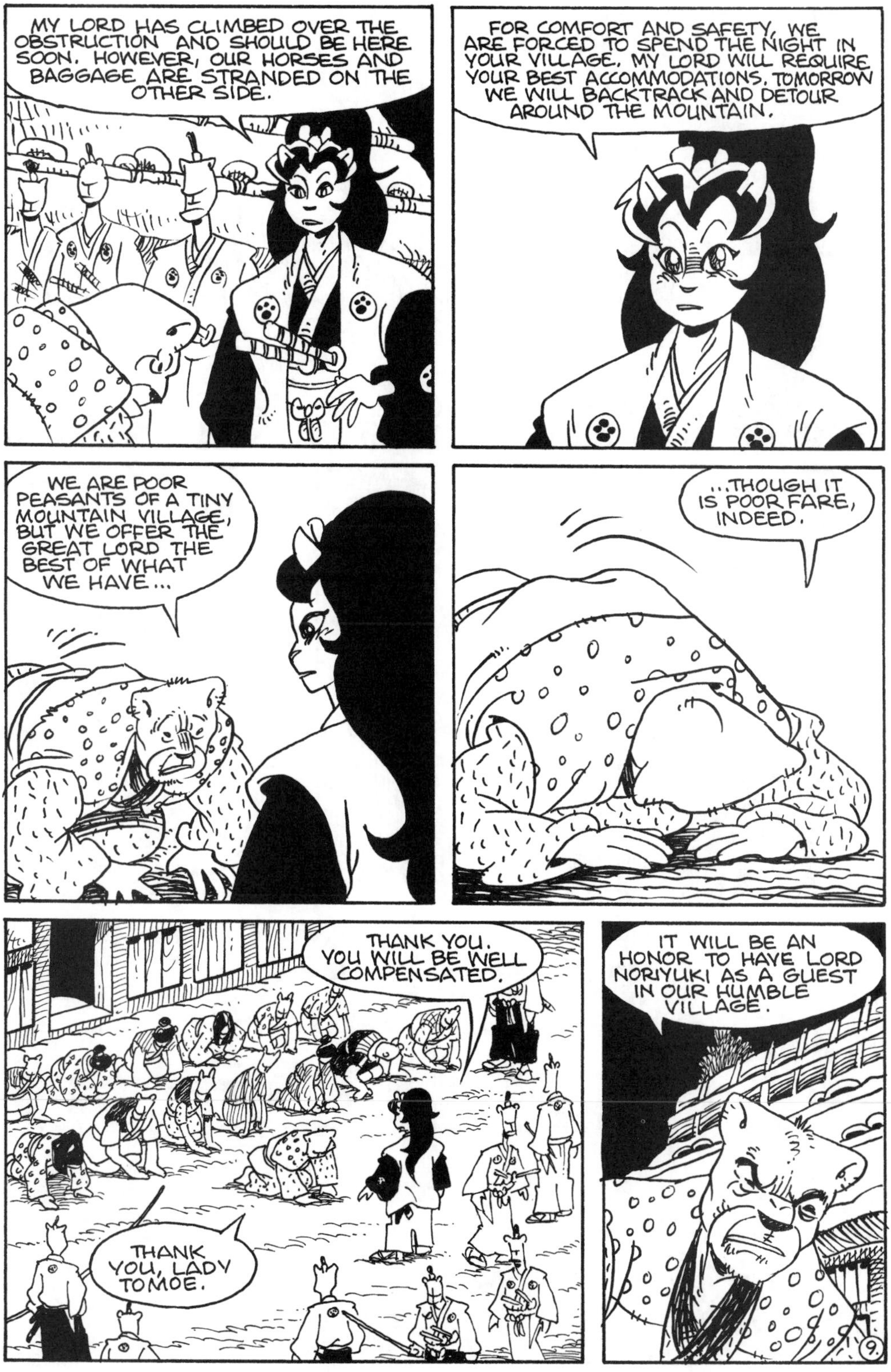
MY LORD HAS CLIMBED OVER THE OBSTRUCTION AND SHOULD BE HERE SOON. HOWEVER, OUR HORSES AND BAGGAGE ARE STRANDED ON THE OTHER SIDE.
FOR COMFORT AND SAFETY, WE ARE FORCED TO SPEND THE NIGHT IN YOUR VILLAGE. MY LORD WILL REQUIRE YOUR BEST ACCOMMODATIONS. TOMORROW WE WILL BACKTRACK AND DETOUR AROUND THE MOUNTAIN.
WE ARE POOR PEASANTS OF A TINY MOUNTAIN VILLAGE, BUT WE OFFER THE GREAT LORD THE BEST OF WHAT WE HAVE...
...THOUGH IT IS POOR FARE, INDEED.
THANK YOU. YOU WILL BE WELL COMPENSATED.
THANK YOU, LADY TOMOE.
IT WILL BE AN HONOR TO HAVE LORD NORIYUKI AS A GUEST IN OUR HUMBLE VILLAGE.
9.

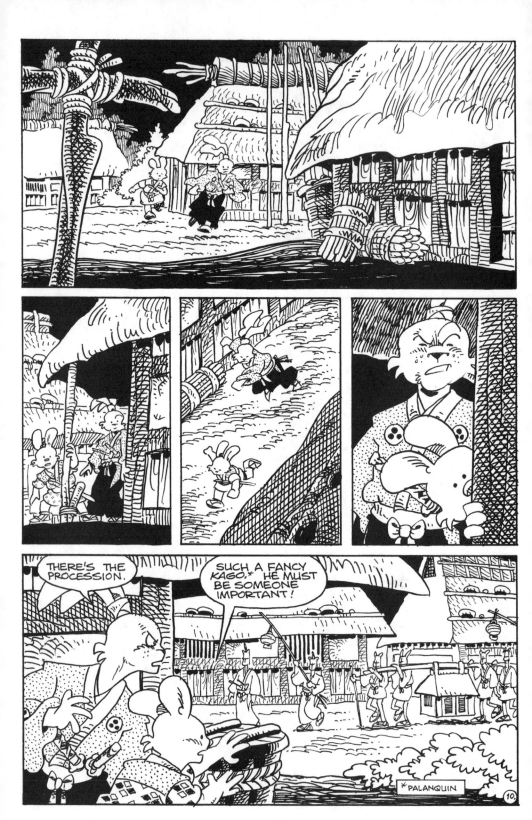

THERE'S THE PROCESSION.

SUCH A FANCY KAGO,* HE MUST BE SOMEONE IMPORTANT!

*PALANQUIN

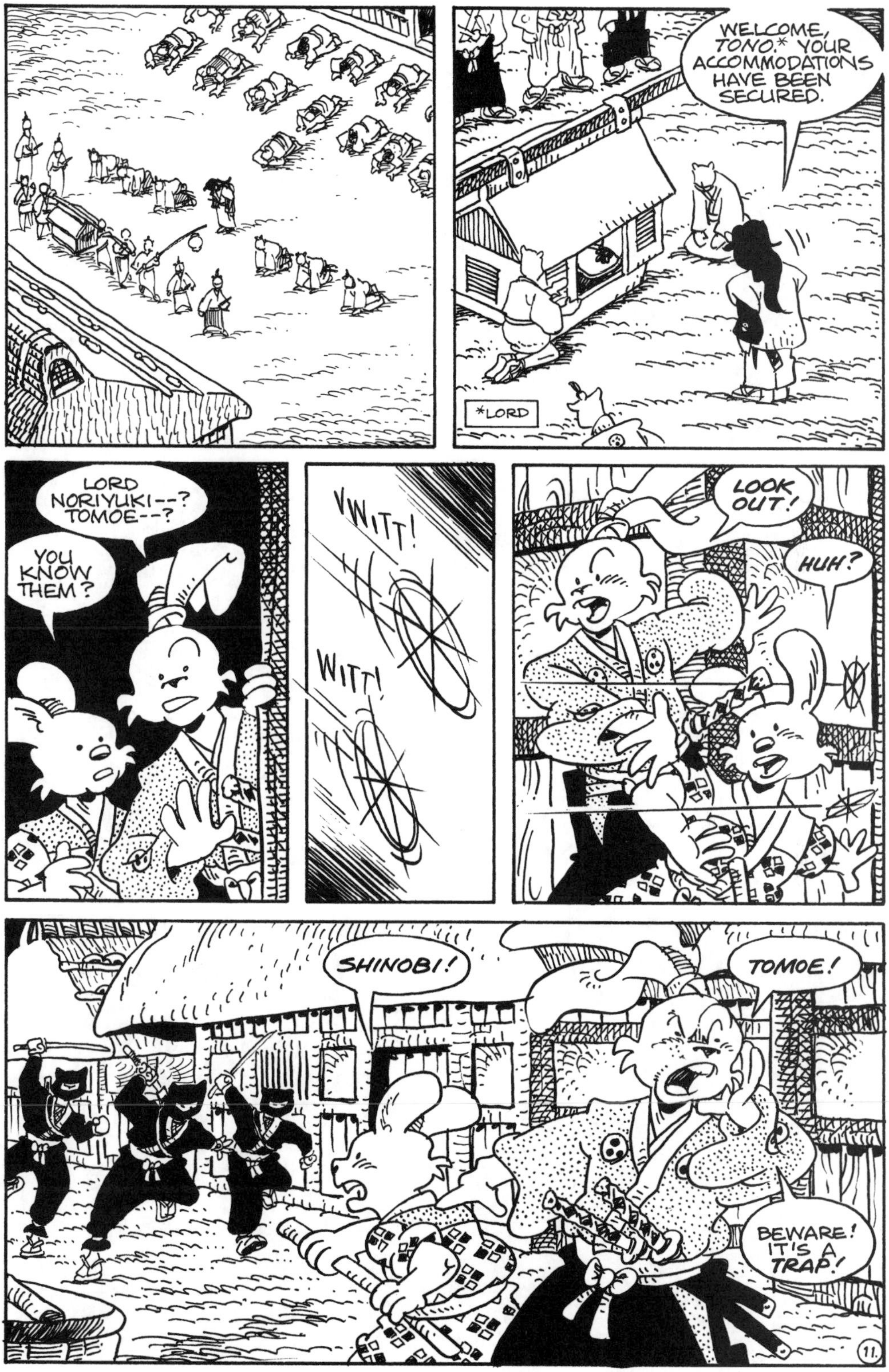
WELCOME, TONO.* YOUR ACCOMMODATIONS HAVE BEEN SECURED.
*LORD
LORD NORIYUKI--? TOMOE--?
YOU KNOW THEM?
VWITT!
WITT!
LOOK OUT!
HUH?
SHINOBI!
TOMOE!
BEWARE! IT'S A TRAP!
11.

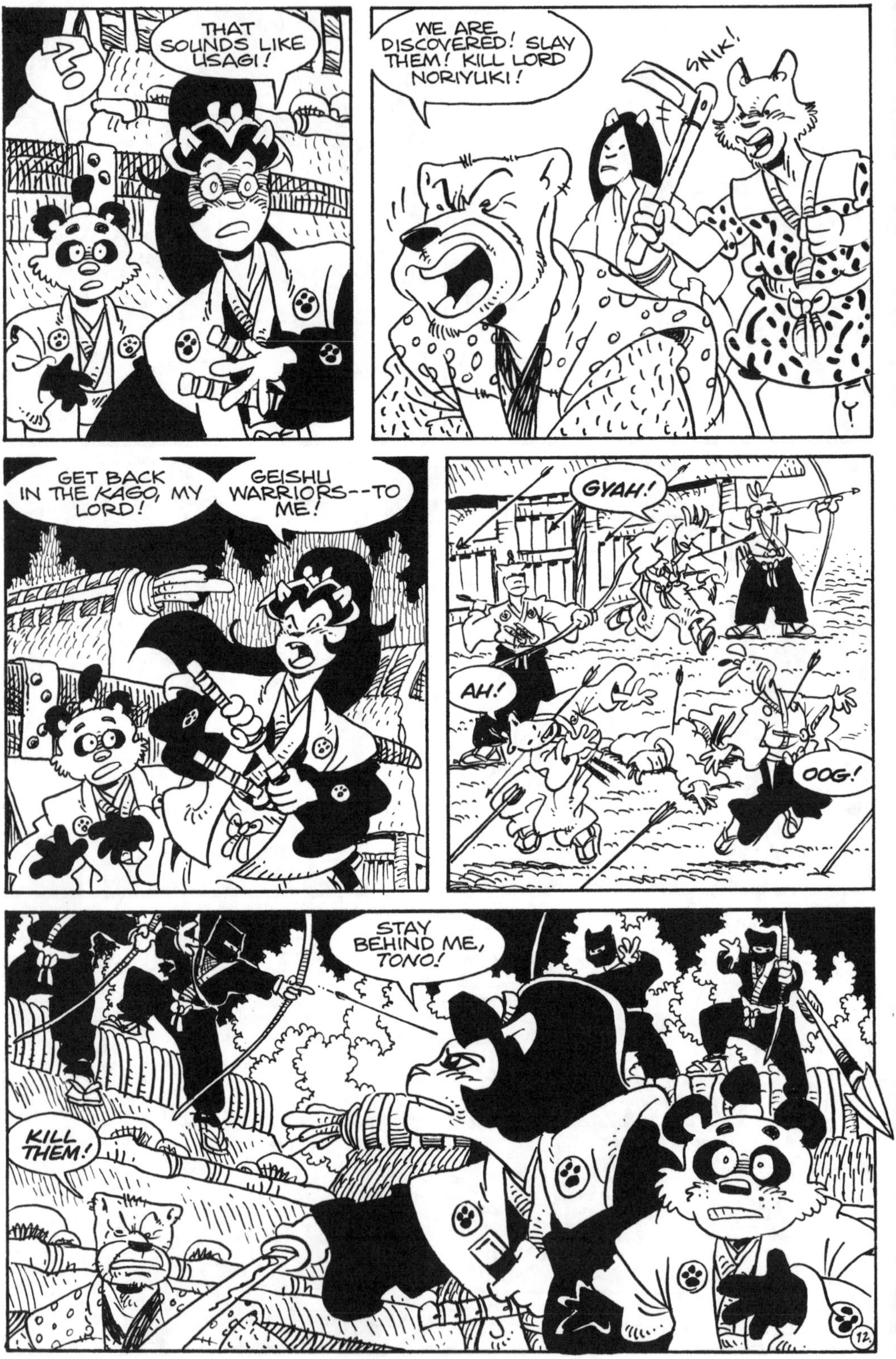
?
THAT SOUNDS LIKE USAGI!
WE ARE DISCOVERED! SLAY THEM! KILL LORD NORIYUKI!
SNIK!
GET BACK IN THE KAGO, MY LORD!
GEISHU WARRIORS--TO ME!
GYAH!
AH!
OOG!
STAY BEHIND ME, TONO!
KILL THEM!
12.

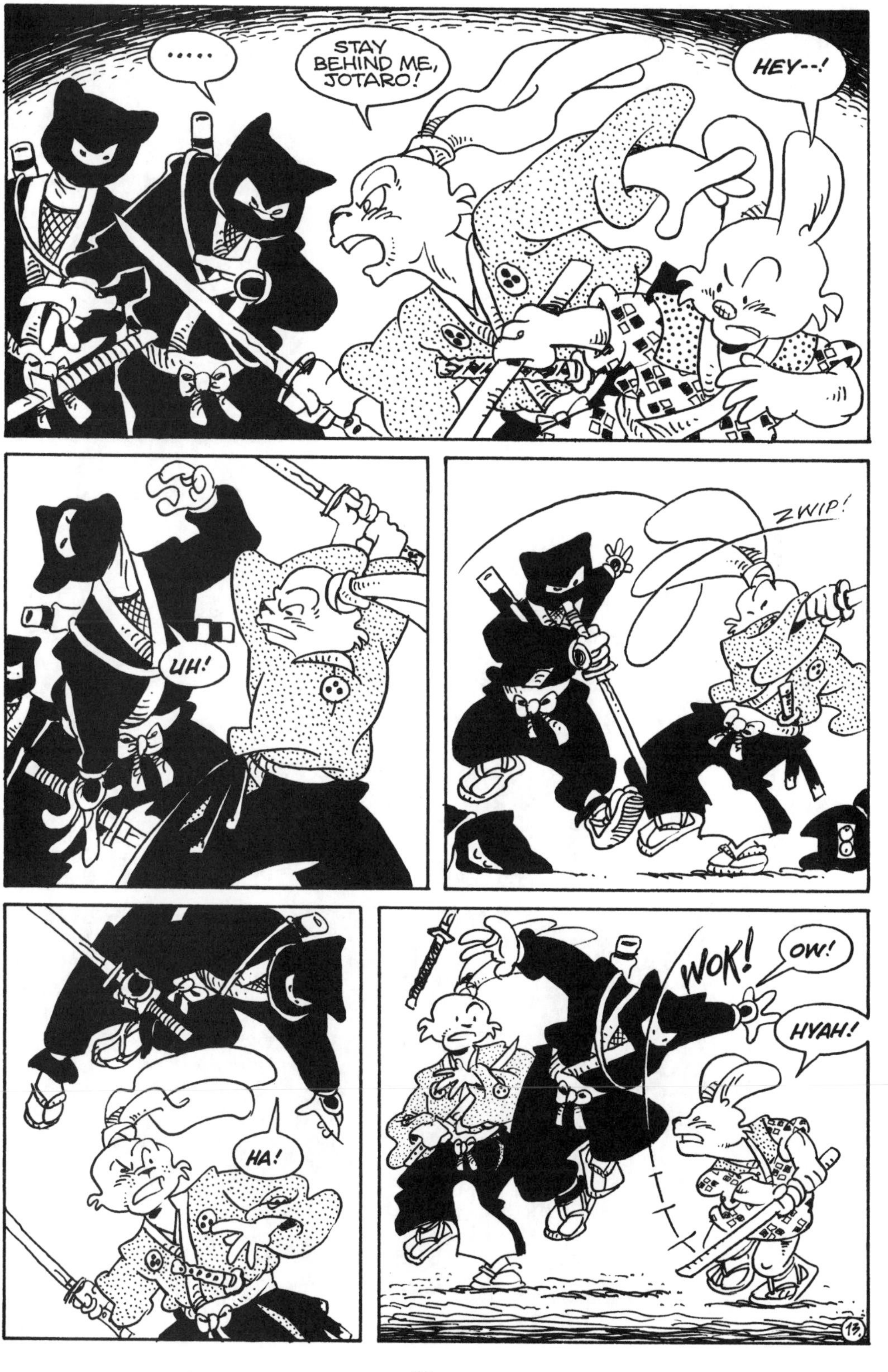

.....
STAY BEHIND ME, JOTARO!
HEY--!
UH!
ZWIP!
HA!
WOK!
OW!
HYAH!
13.

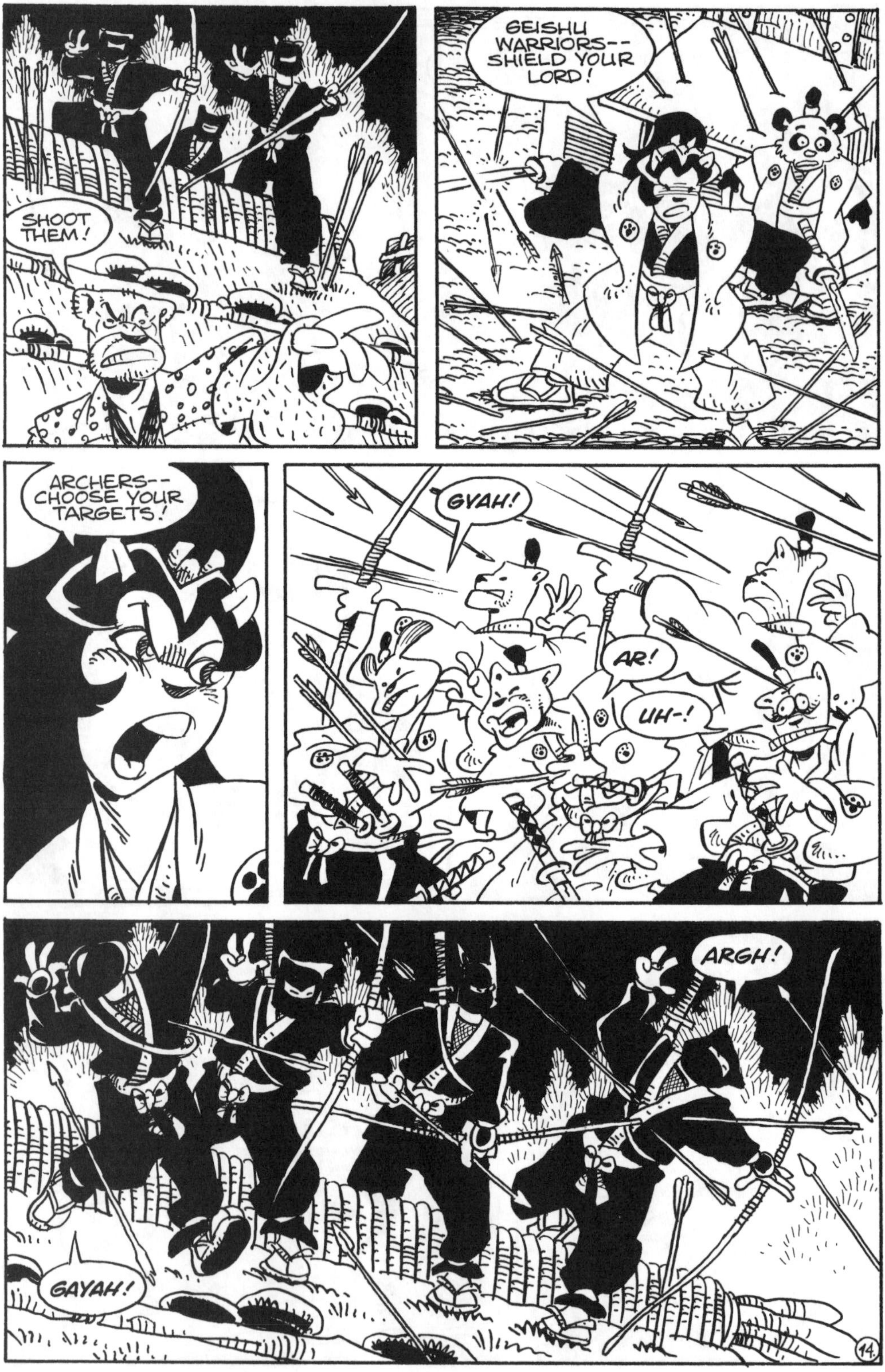
SHOOT THEM!
GEISHU WARRIORS-- SHIELD YOUR LORD!
ARCHERS-- CHOOSE YOUR TARGETS!
GYAH!
AR!
UH-!
ARGH!
GAYAH!
14.

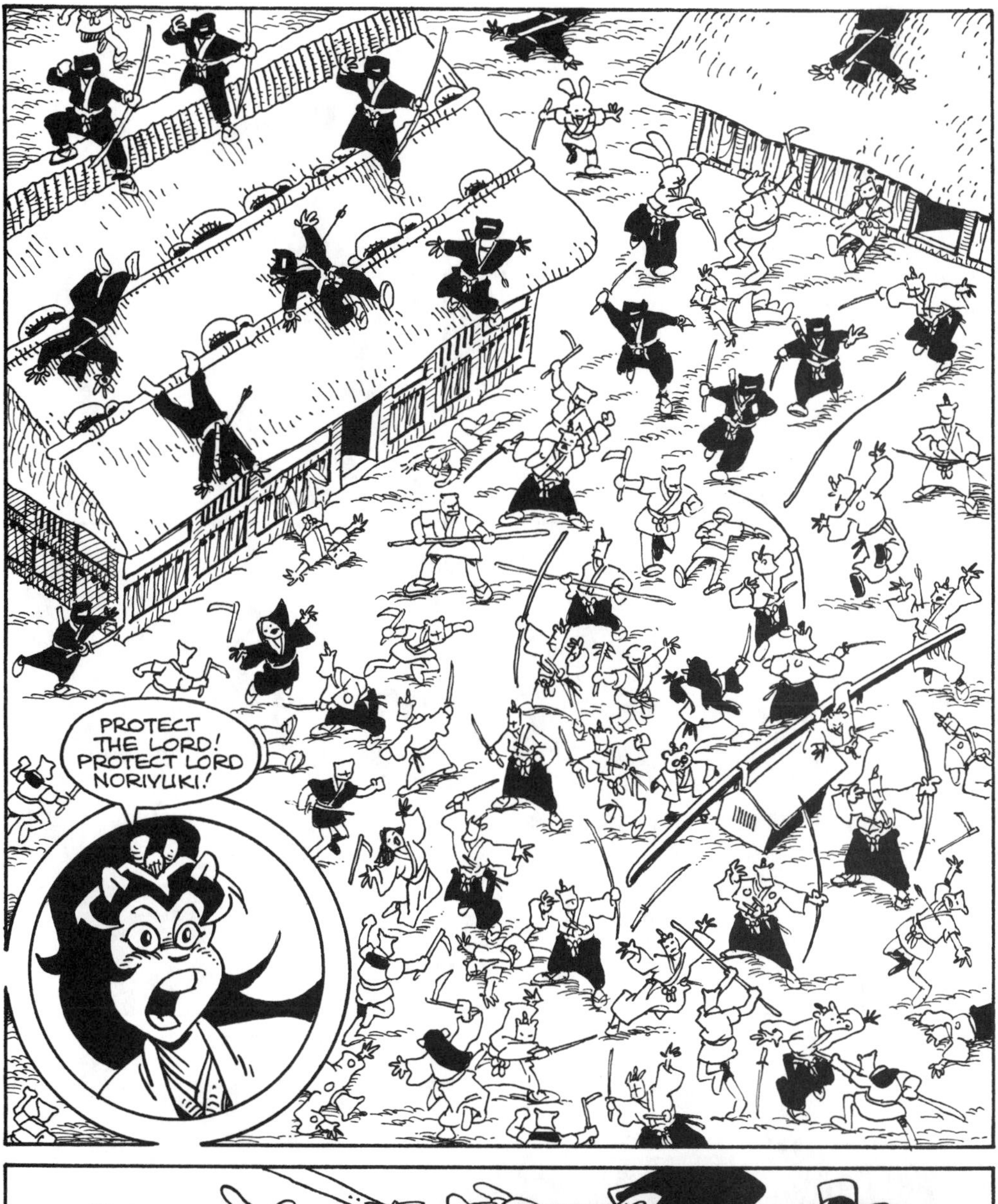
PROTECT THE LORD! PROTECT LORD NORIYUKI!

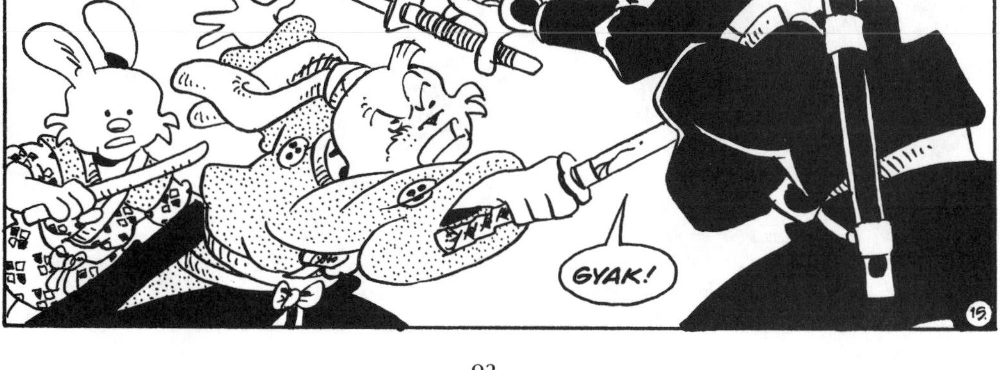
GYAK!
15

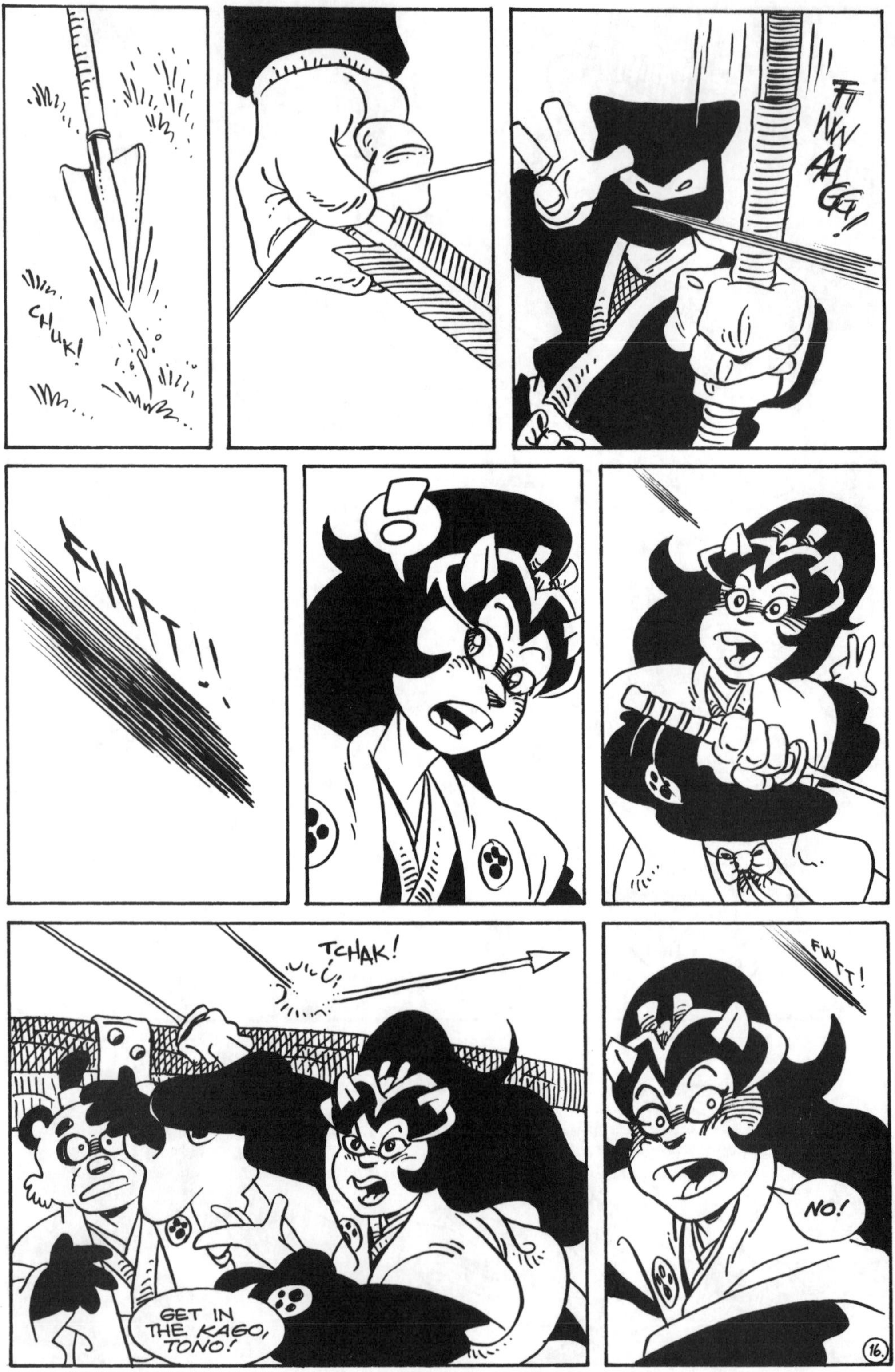
CHUK!
FTWWAAGG!
FWTTT!!
!
TCHAK!
GET IN THE KAGO, TONO!
FWTT!
NO!
16.

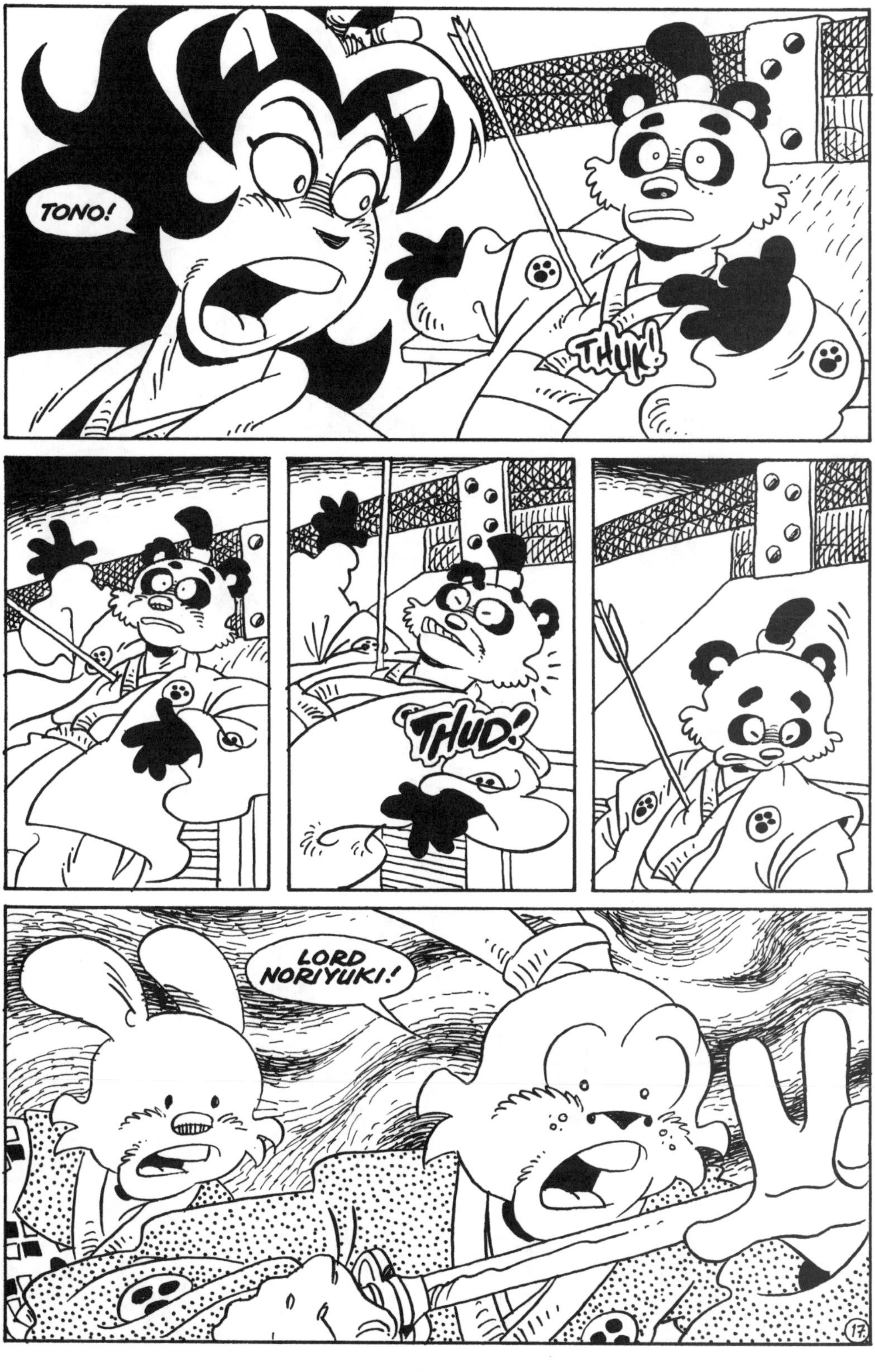
TONO!
THUK!
THUD!
LORD NORIYUKI!
17

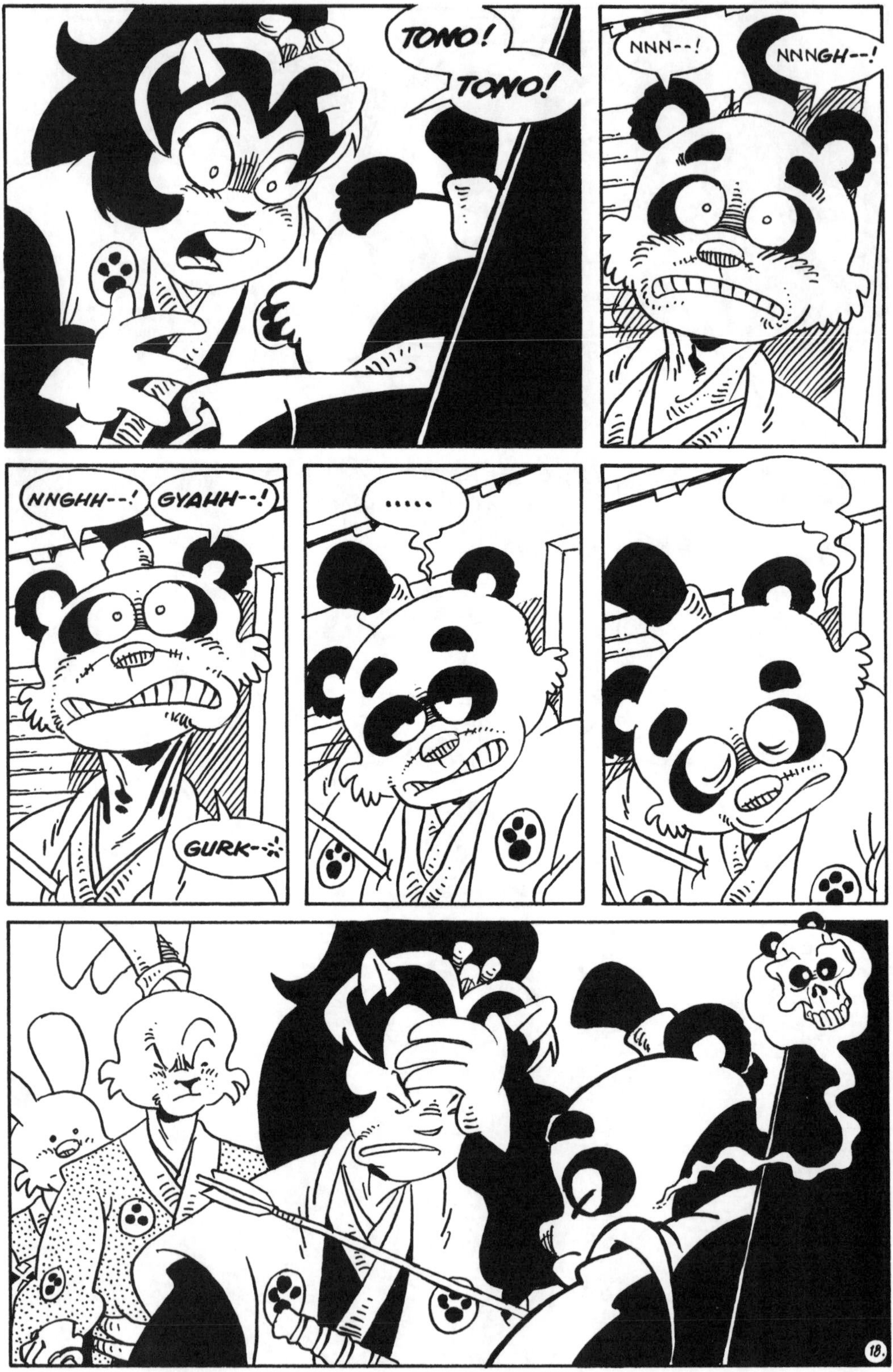

TONO!
TONO!
NNN--!
NNNGH--!
NNGHH--!
GYAHH--!
GURK--
.....
18.

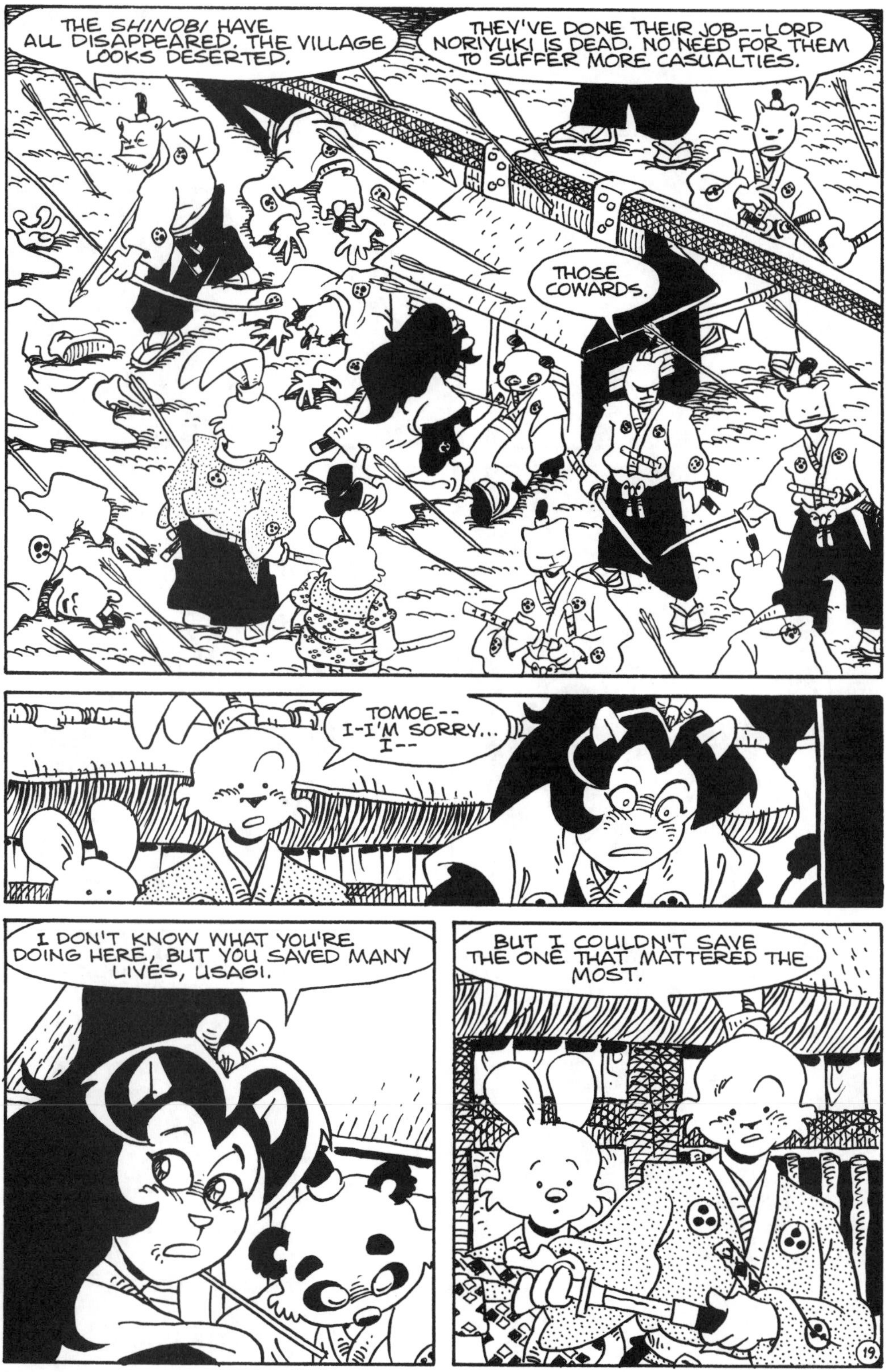
THE SHINOBI HAVE ALL DISAPPEARED. THE VILLAGE LOOKS DESERTED.
THEY'VE DONE THEIR JOB--LORD NORIYUKI IS DEAD. NO NEED FOR THEM TO SUFFER MORE CASUALTIES.
THOSE COWARDS.
TOMOE-- I-I'M SORRY... I--
I DON'T KNOW WHAT YOU'RE DOING HERE, BUT YOU SAVED MANY LIVES, USAGI.
BUT I COULDN'T SAVE THE ONE THAT MATTERED THE MOST.
19.

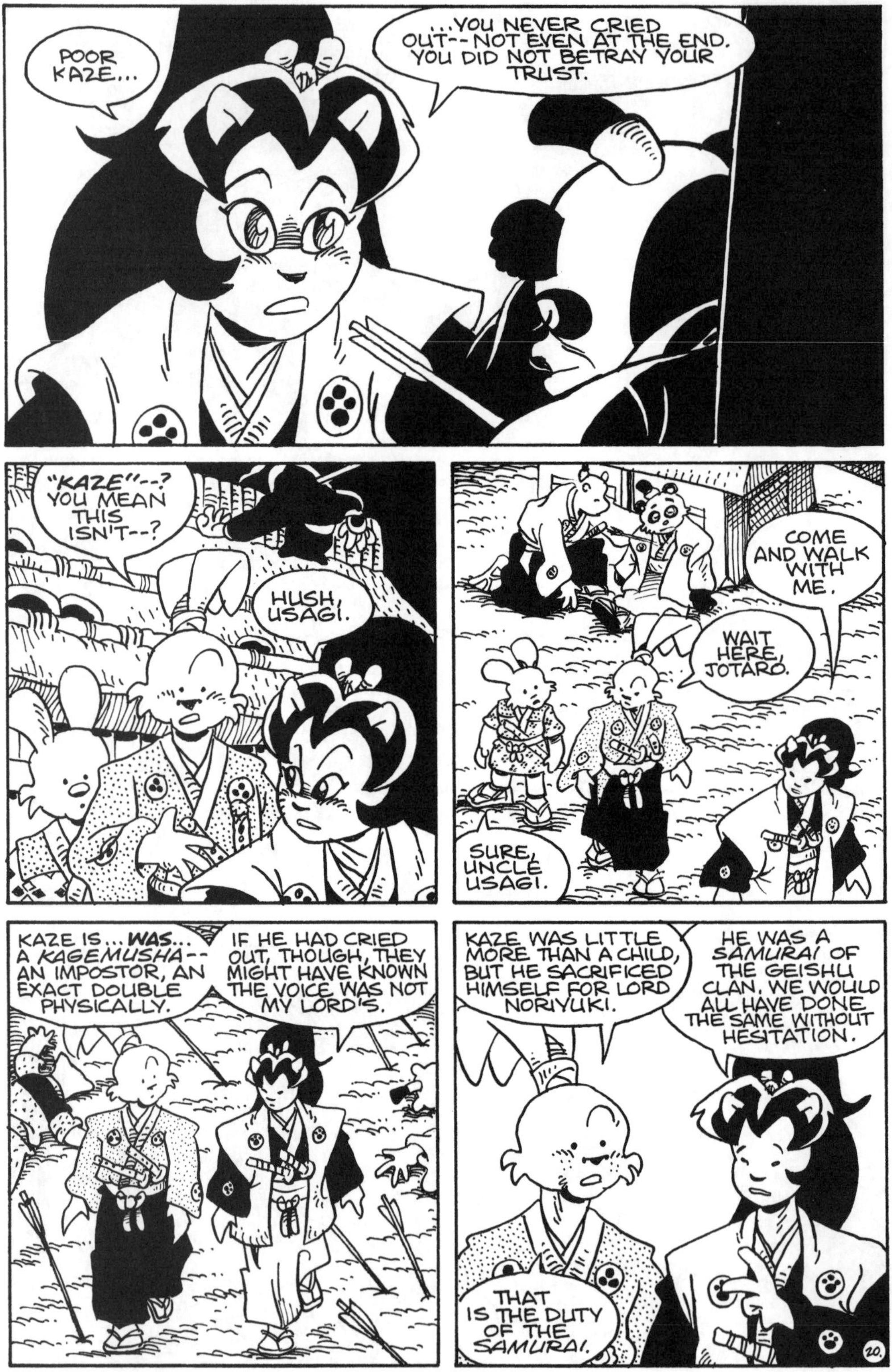
POOR KAZE...
...YOU NEVER CRIED OUT--NOT EVEN AT THE END. YOU DID NOT BETRAY YOUR TRUST.
"KAZE"--? YOU MEAN THIS ISN'T--?
HUSH, USAGI.
COME AND WALK WITH ME.
WAIT HERE, JOTARO.
SURE, UNCLE USAGI.
KAZE IS ... WAS... A KAGEMUSHA--AN IMPOSTOR, AN EXACT DOUBLE PHYSICALLY.
IF HE HAD CRIED OUT, THOUGH, THEY MIGHT HAVE KNOWN THE VOICE WAS NOT MY LORD'S.
KAZE WAS LITTLE MORE THAN A CHILD, BUT HE SACRIFICED HIMSELF FOR LORD NORIYUKI.
HE WAS A SAMURAI OF THE GEISHU CLAN. WE WOULD ALL HAVE DONE THE SAME WITHOUT HESITATION.
THAT IS THE DUTY OF THE SAMURAI.
20.

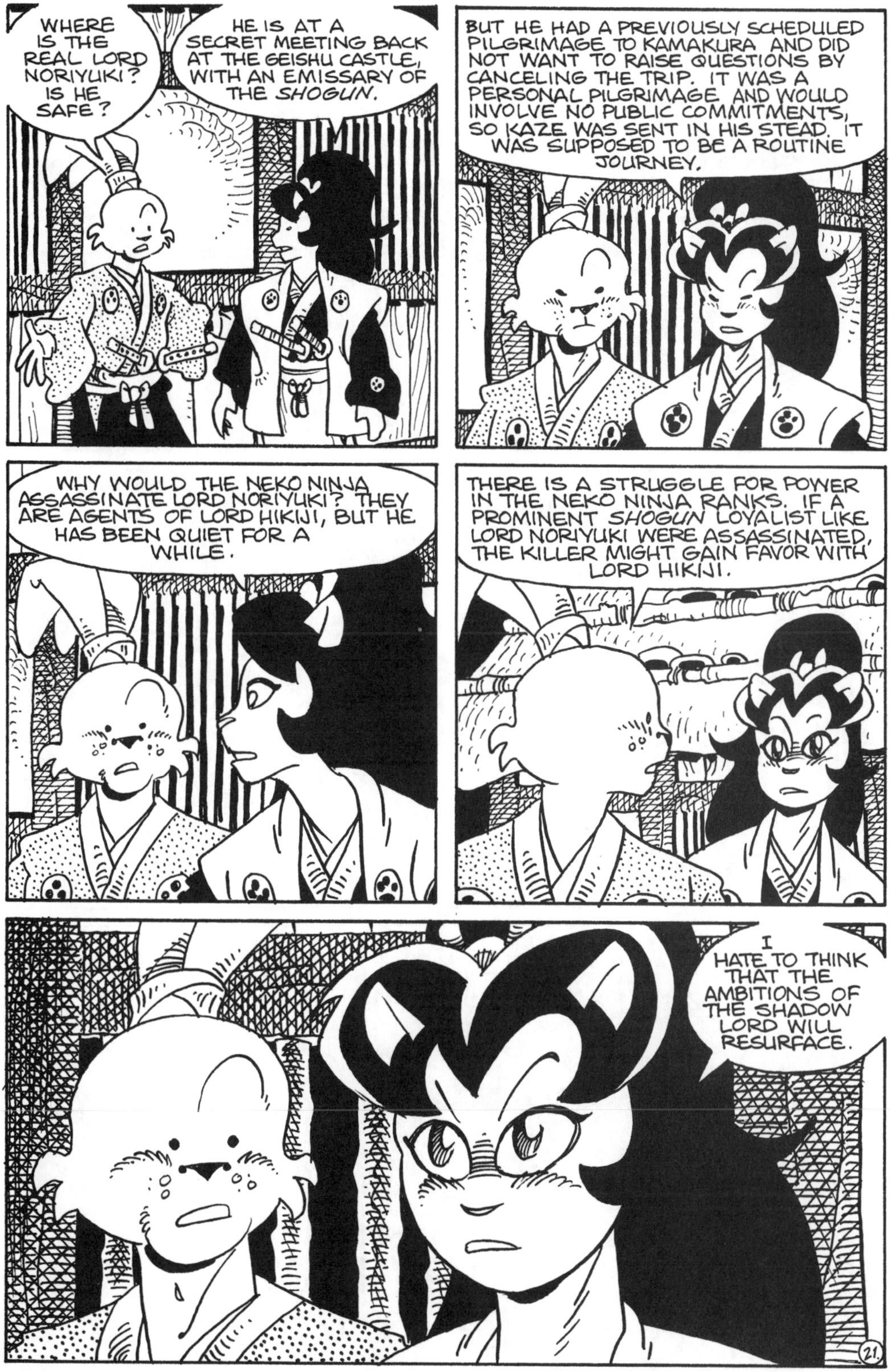
WHERE IS THE REAL LORD NORIYUKI? IS HE SAFE?
HE IS AT A SECRET MEETING BACK AT THE GEISHU CASTLE, WITH AN EMISSARY OF THE SHOGUN.
BUT HE HAD A PREVIOUSLY SCHEDULED PILGRIMAGE TO KAMAKURA AND DID NOT WANT TO RAISE QUESTIONS BY CANCELING THE TRIP. IT WAS A PERSONAL PILGRIMAGE AND WOULD INVOLVE NO PUBLIC COMMITMENTS, SO KAZE WAS SENT IN HIS STEAD. IT WAS SUPPOSED TO BE A ROUTINE JOURNEY.
WHY WOULD THE NEKO NINJA ASSASSINATE LORD NORIYUKI? THEY ARE AGENTS OF LORD HIKIJI, BUT HE HAS BEEN QUIET FOR A WHILE.
THERE IS A STRUGGLE FOR POWER IN THE NEKO NINJA RANKS. IF A PROMINENT SHOGUN LOYALIST LIKE LORD NORIYUKI WERE ASSASSINATED, THE KILLER MIGHT GAIN FAVOR WITH LORD HIKIJI.
I HATE TO THINK THAT THE AMBITIONS OF THE SHADOW LORD WILL RESURFACE.
21.

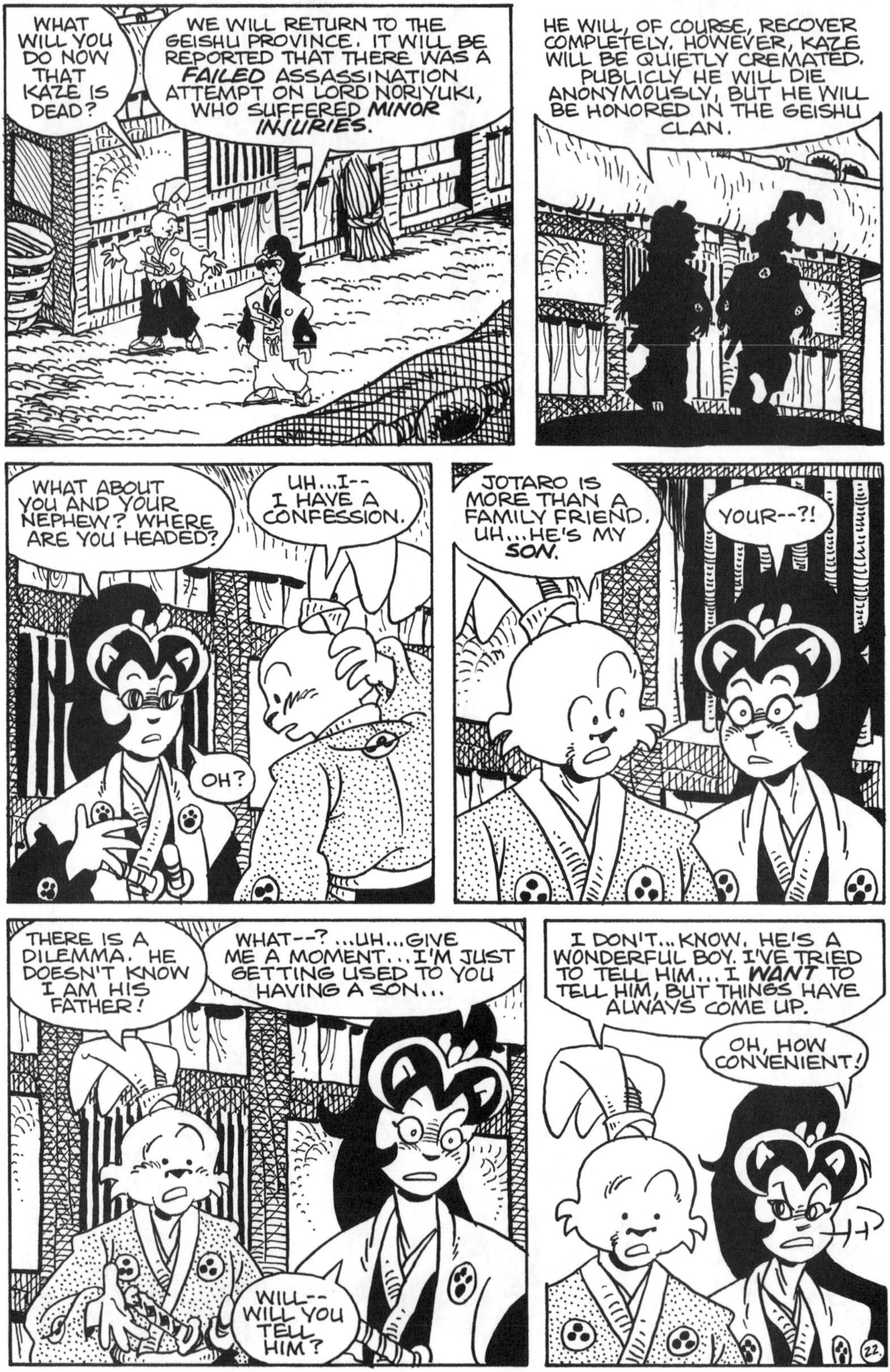
WHAT WILL YOU DO NOW THAT KAZE IS DEAD?
WE WILL RETURN TO THE GEISHU PROVINCE. IT WILL BE REPORTED THAT THERE WAS A *FAILED* ASSASSINATION ATTEMPT ON LORD NORIYUKI, WHO SUFFERED *MINOR INJURIES*.
HE WILL, OF COURSE, RECOVER COMPLETELY. HOWEVER, KAZE WILL BE QUIETLY CREMATED. PUBLICLY HE WILL DIE ANONYMOUSLY, BUT HE WILL BE HONORED IN THE GEISHU CLAN.
WHAT ABOUT YOU AND YOUR NEPHEW? WHERE ARE YOU HEADED?
UH...I-- I HAVE A CONFESSION.
OH?
JOTARO IS MORE THAN A FAMILY FRIEND. UH...HE'S MY *SON*.
YOUR--?!
THERE IS A DILEMMA. HE DOESN'T KNOW I AM HIS FATHER!
WHAT--? ...UH...GIVE ME A MOMENT...I'M JUST GETTING USED TO YOU HAVING A SON...
WILL-- WILL YOU TELL HIM?
I DON'T...KNOW. HE'S A WONDERFUL BOY. I'VE TRIED TO TELL HIM... I *WANT* TO TELL HIM, BUT THINGS HAVE ALWAYS COME UP.
OH, HOW CONVENIENT!
22.

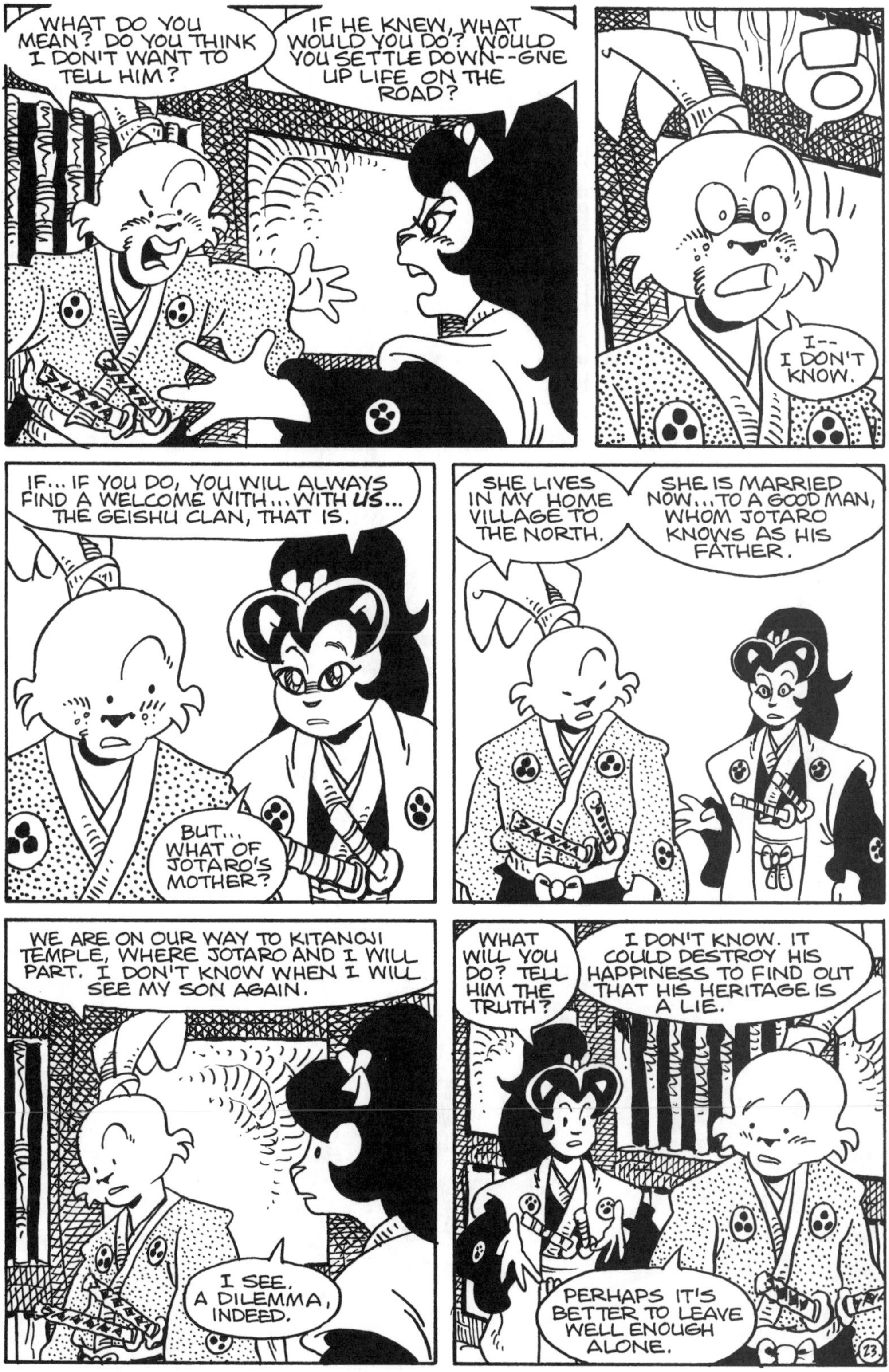
WHAT DO YOU MEAN? DO YOU THINK I DON'T WANT TO TELL HIM?
IF HE KNEW, WHAT WOULD YOU DO? WOULD YOU SETTLE DOWN--GIVE UP LIFE ON THE ROAD?
I-- I DON'T KNOW.
IF... IF YOU DO, YOU WILL ALWAYS FIND A WELCOME WITH... WITH US... THE GEISHU CLAN, THAT IS.
BUT... WHAT OF JOTARO'S MOTHER?
SHE LIVES IN MY HOME VILLAGE TO THE NORTH.
SHE IS MARRIED NOW... TO A GOOD MAN, WHOM JOTARO KNOWS AS HIS FATHER.
WE ARE ON OUR WAY TO KITANOJI TEMPLE, WHERE JOTARO AND I WILL PART. I DON'T KNOW WHEN I WILL SEE MY SON AGAIN.
I SEE. A DILEMMA, INDEED.
WHAT WILL YOU DO? TELL HIM THE TRUTH?
I DON'T KNOW. IT COULD DESTROY HIS HAPPINESS TO FIND OUT THAT HIS HERITAGE IS A LIE.
PERHAPS IT'S BETTER TO LEAVE WELL ENOUGH ALONE.
23.

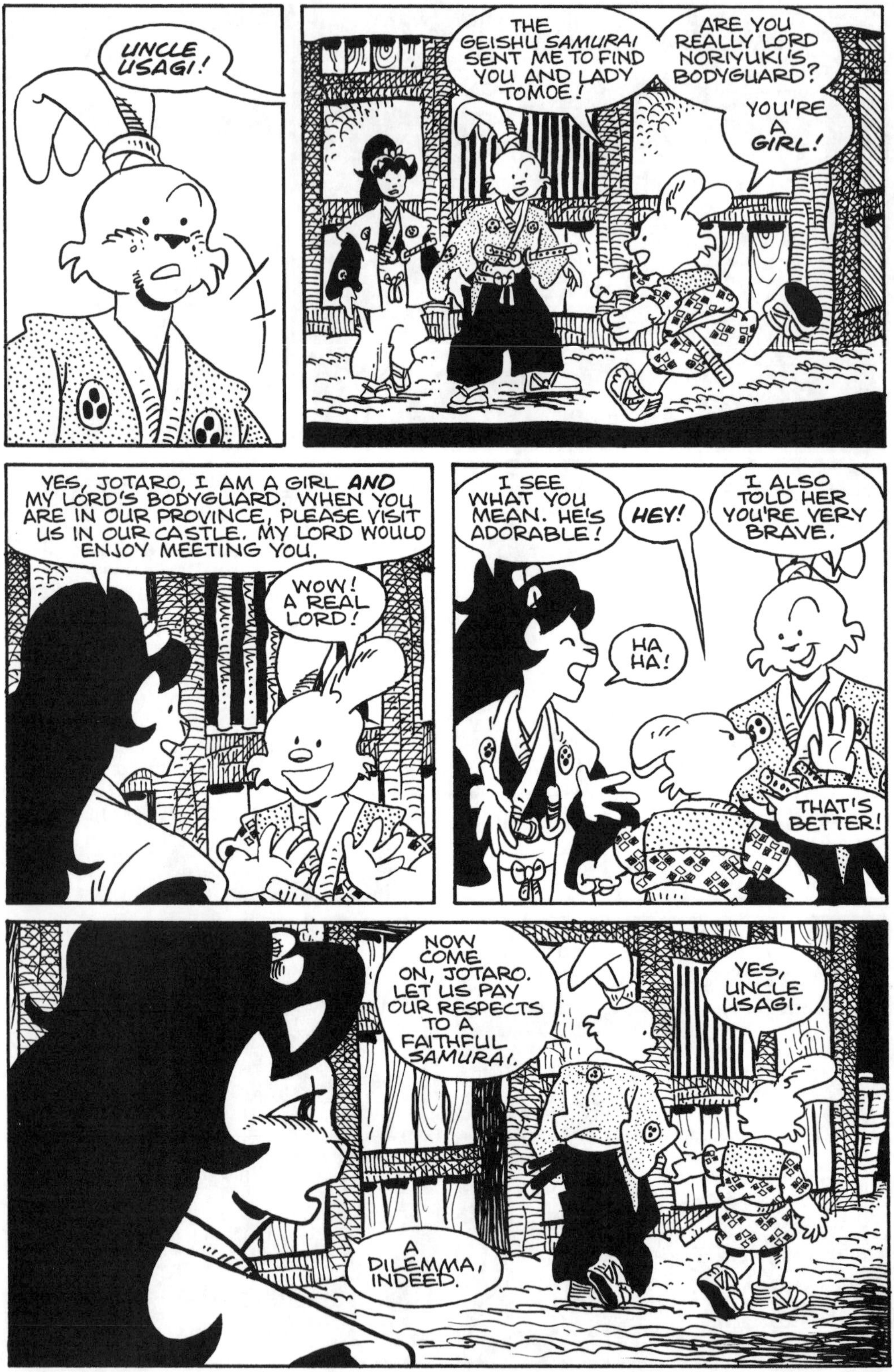
UNCLE USAGI!
THE GEISHU SAMURAI SENT ME TO FIND YOU AND LADY TOMOE!
ARE YOU REALLY LORD NORIYUKI'S BODYGUARD?
YOU'RE A GIRL!
YES, JOTARO, I AM A GIRL AND MY LORD'S BODYGUARD. WHEN YOU ARE IN OUR PROVINCE, PLEASE VISIT US IN OUR CASTLE. MY LORD WOULD ENJOY MEETING YOU.
WOW! A REAL LORD!
I SEE WHAT YOU MEAN. HE'S ADORABLE!
HEY!
I ALSO TOLD HER YOU'RE VERY BRAVE.
HA HA!
THAT'S BETTER!
NOW COME ON, JOTARO. LET US PAY OUR RESPECTS TO A FAITHFUL SAMURAI.
YES, UNCLE USAGI.
A DILEMMA, INDEED.

THE END.

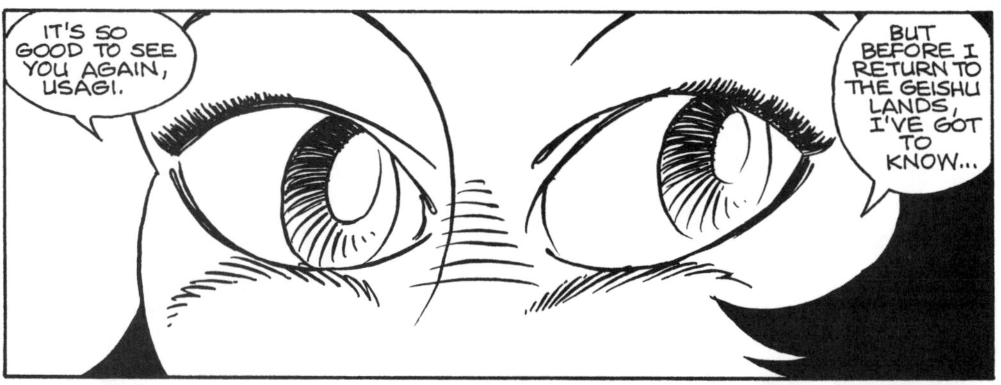
IT'S SO GOOD TO SEE YOU AGAIN, USAGI.
BUT BEFORE I RETURN TO THE GEISHU LANDS, I'VE GOT TO KNOW...

THE PRIDE of the SAMURAI

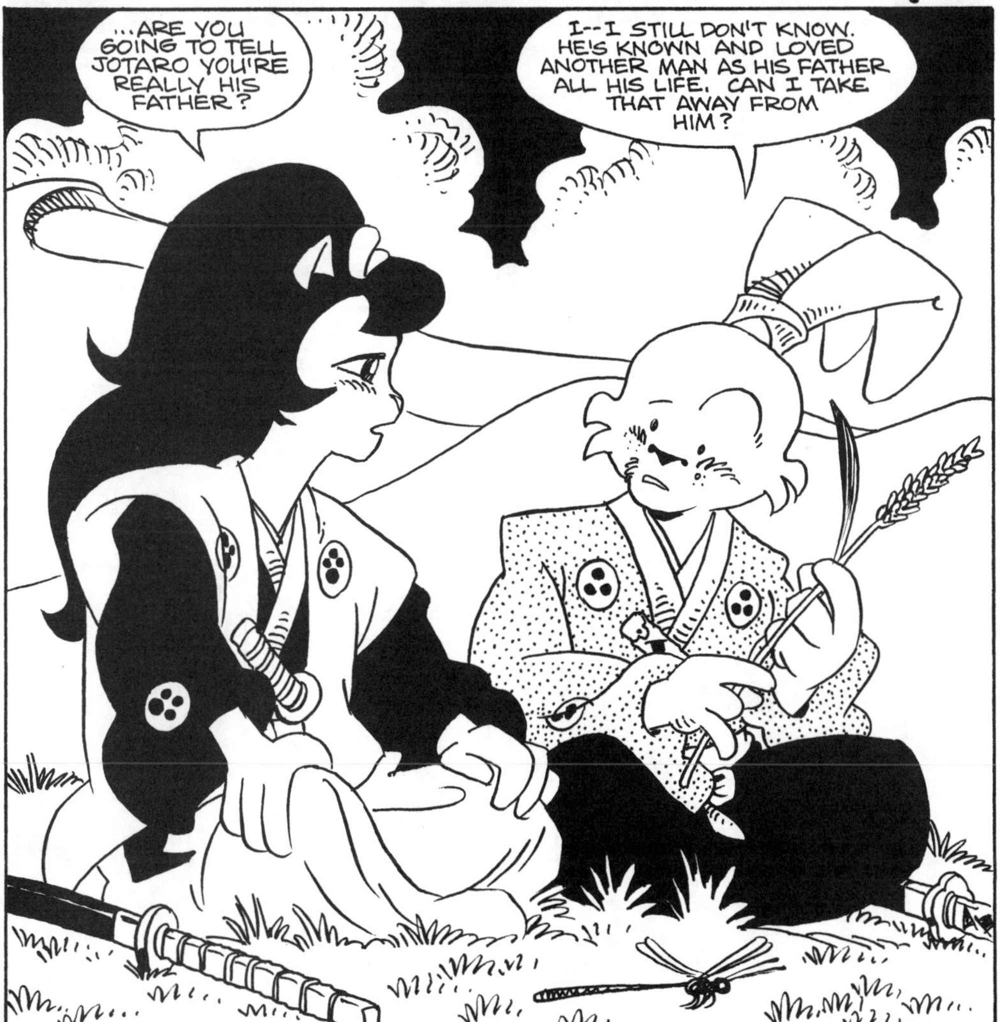
...ARE YOU GOING TO TELL JOTARO YOU'RE REALLY HIS FATHER?
I--I STILL DON'T KNOW. HE'S KNOWN AND LOVED ANOTHER MAN AS HIS FATHER ALL HIS LIFE. CAN I TAKE THAT AWAY FROM HIM?
1.

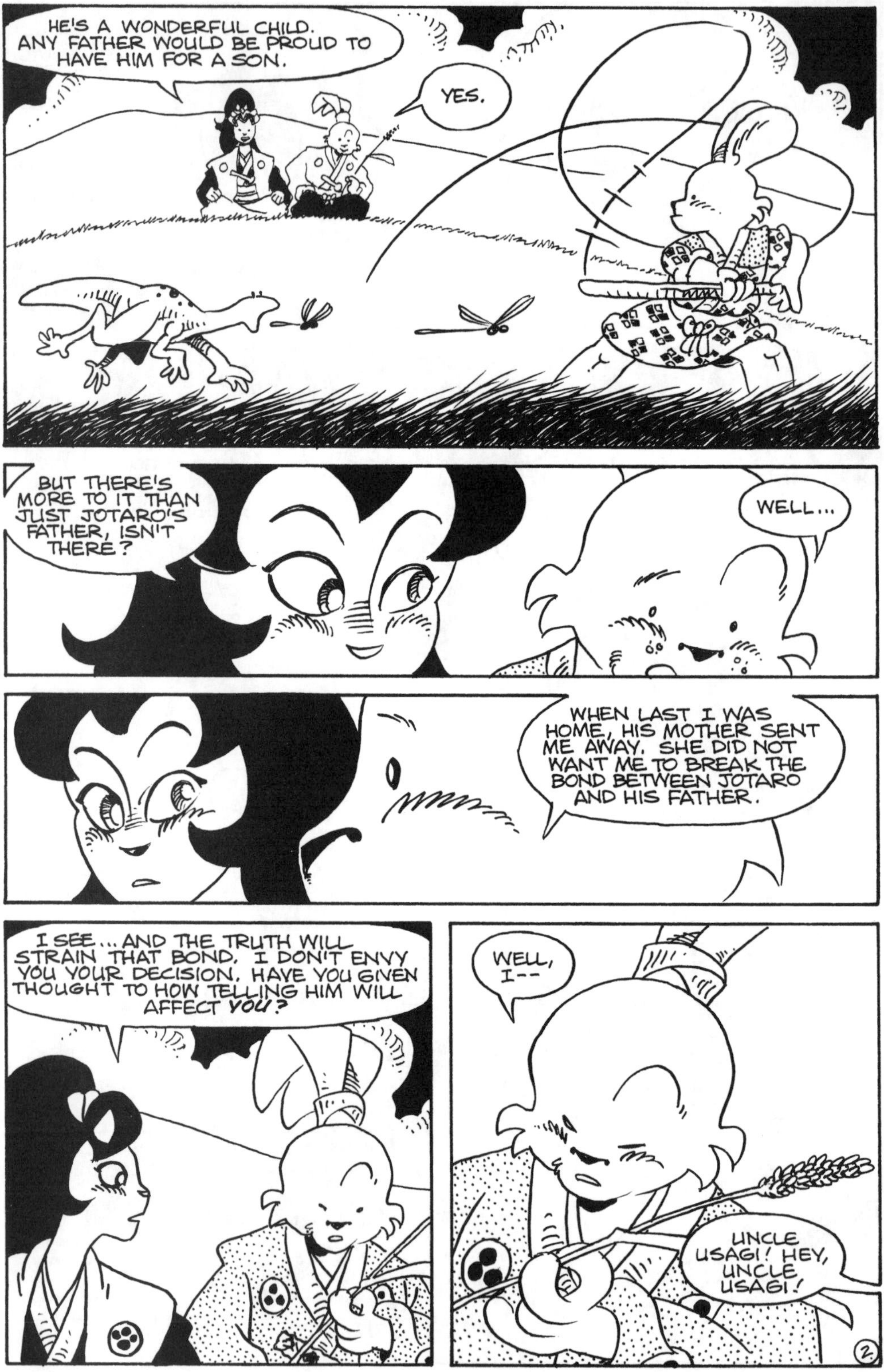
HE'S A WONDERFUL CHILD. ANY FATHER WOULD BE PROUD TO HAVE HIM FOR A SON.
YES.
BUT THERE'S MORE TO IT THAN JUST JOTARO'S FATHER, ISN'T THERE?
WELL...
WHEN LAST I WAS HOME, HIS MOTHER SENT ME AWAY. SHE DID NOT WANT ME TO BREAK THE BOND BETWEEN JOTARO AND HIS FATHER.
I SEE... AND THE TRUTH WILL STRAIN THAT BOND. I DON'T ENVY YOU YOUR DECISION. HAVE YOU GIVEN THOUGHT TO HOW TELLING HIM WILL AFFECT *YOU*?
WELL, I--
UNCLE USAGI! HEY, UNCLE USAGI!
2

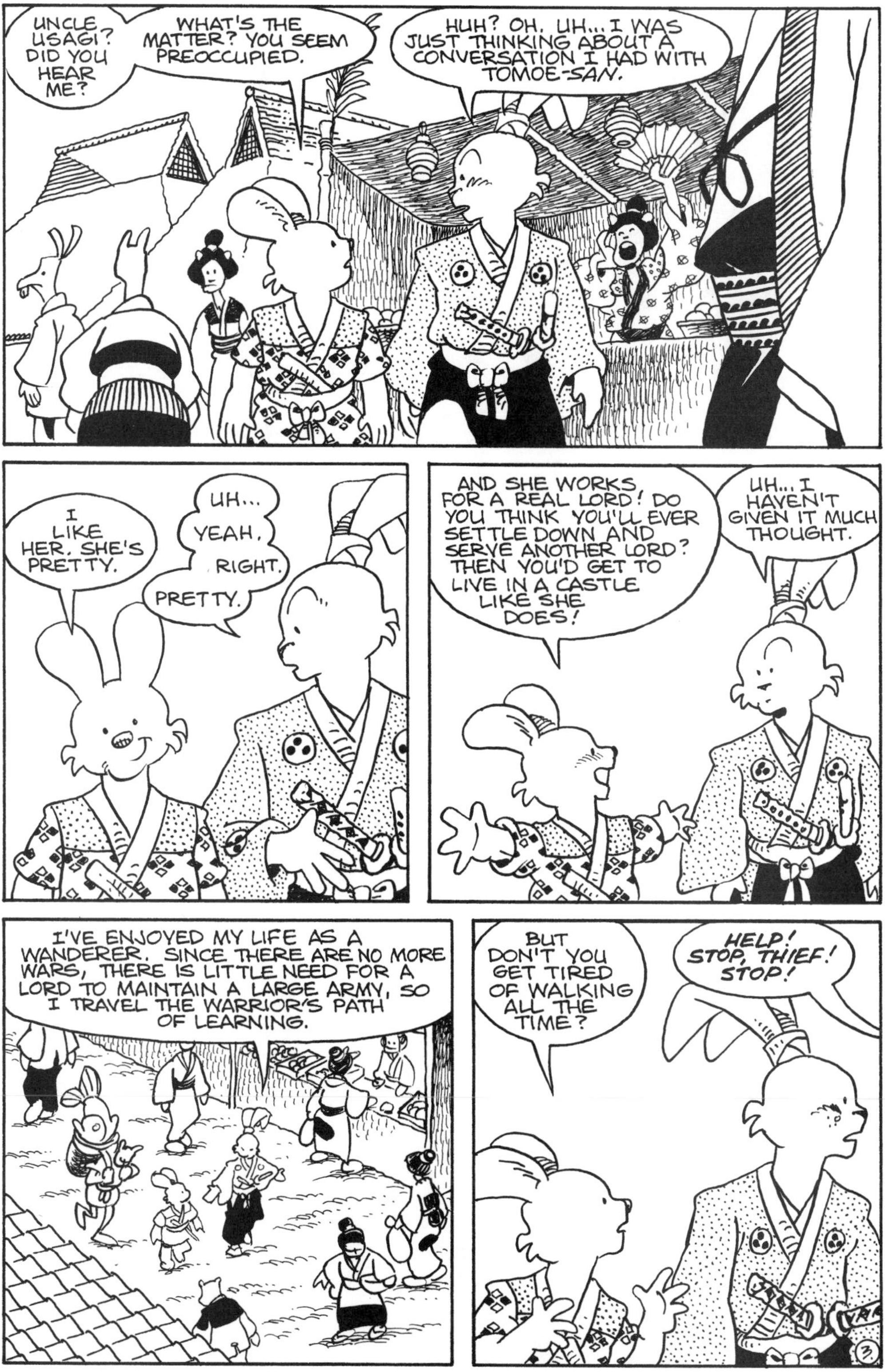
UNCLE USAGI? DID YOU HEAR ME?
WHAT'S THE MATTER? YOU SEEM PREOCCUPIED.
HUH? OH. UH... I WAS JUST THINKING ABOUT A CONVERSATION I HAD WITH TOMOE-SAN.
I LIKE HER. SHE'S PRETTY.
UH... YEAH, RIGHT. PRETTY.
AND SHE WORKS FOR A REAL LORD! DO YOU THINK YOU'LL EVER SETTLE DOWN AND SERVE ANOTHER LORD? THEN YOU'D GET TO LIVE IN A CASTLE LIKE SHE DOES!
UH... I HAVEN'T GIVEN IT MUCH THOUGHT.
I'VE ENJOYED MY LIFE AS A WANDERER. SINCE THERE ARE NO MORE WARS, THERE IS LITTLE NEED FOR A LORD TO MAINTAIN A LARGE ARMY, SO I TRAVEL THE WARRIOR'S PATH OF LEARNING.
BUT DON'T YOU GET TIRED OF WALKING ALL THE TIME?
HELP! STOP, THIEF! STOP!
3.

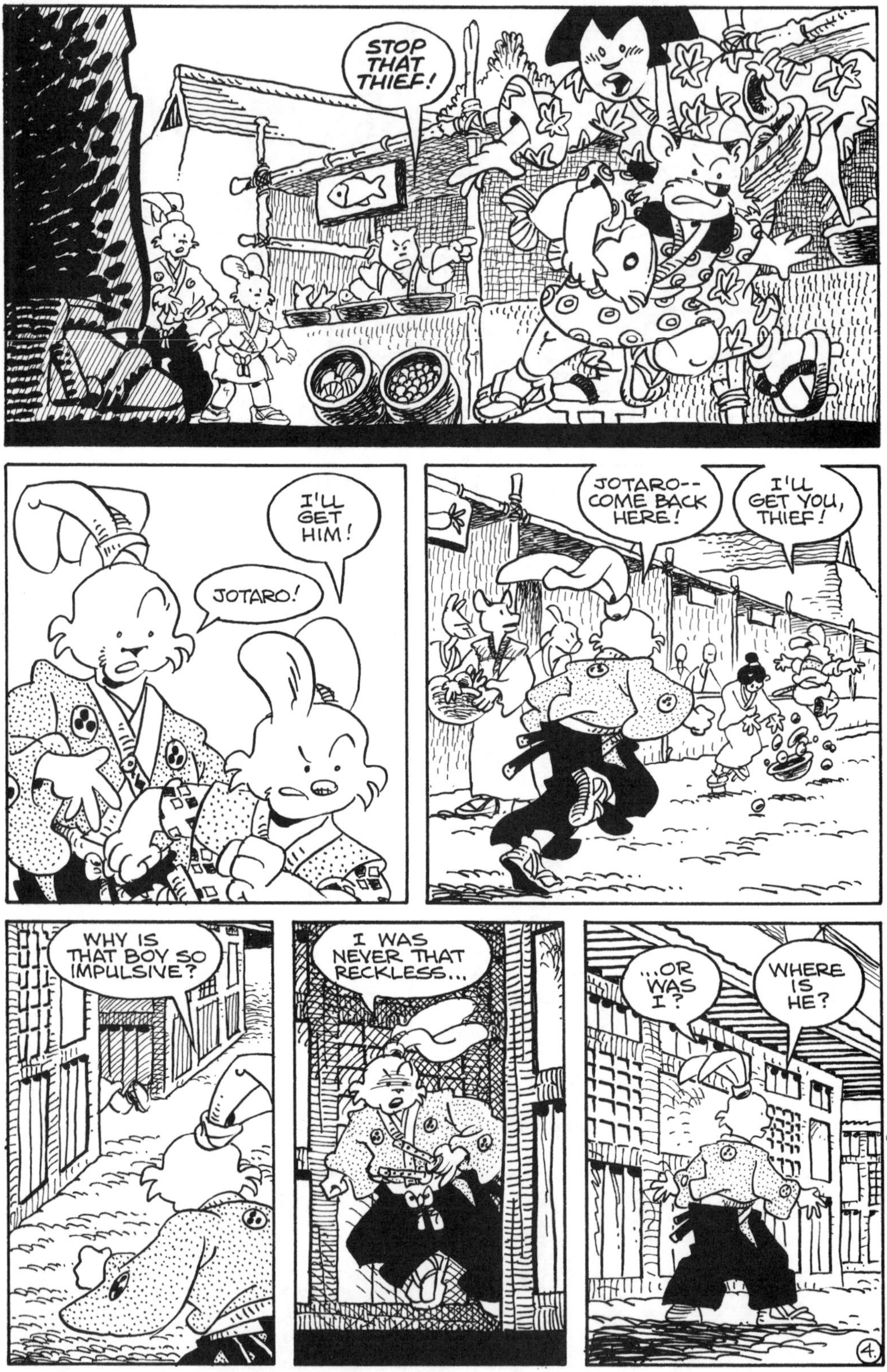
STOP THAT THIEF!
I'LL GET HIM!
JOTARO!
JOTARO-- COME BACK HERE!
I'LL GET YOU, THIEF!
WHY IS THAT BOY SO IMPULSIVE?
I WAS NEVER THAT RECKLESS...
...OR WAS I?
WHERE IS HE?
4

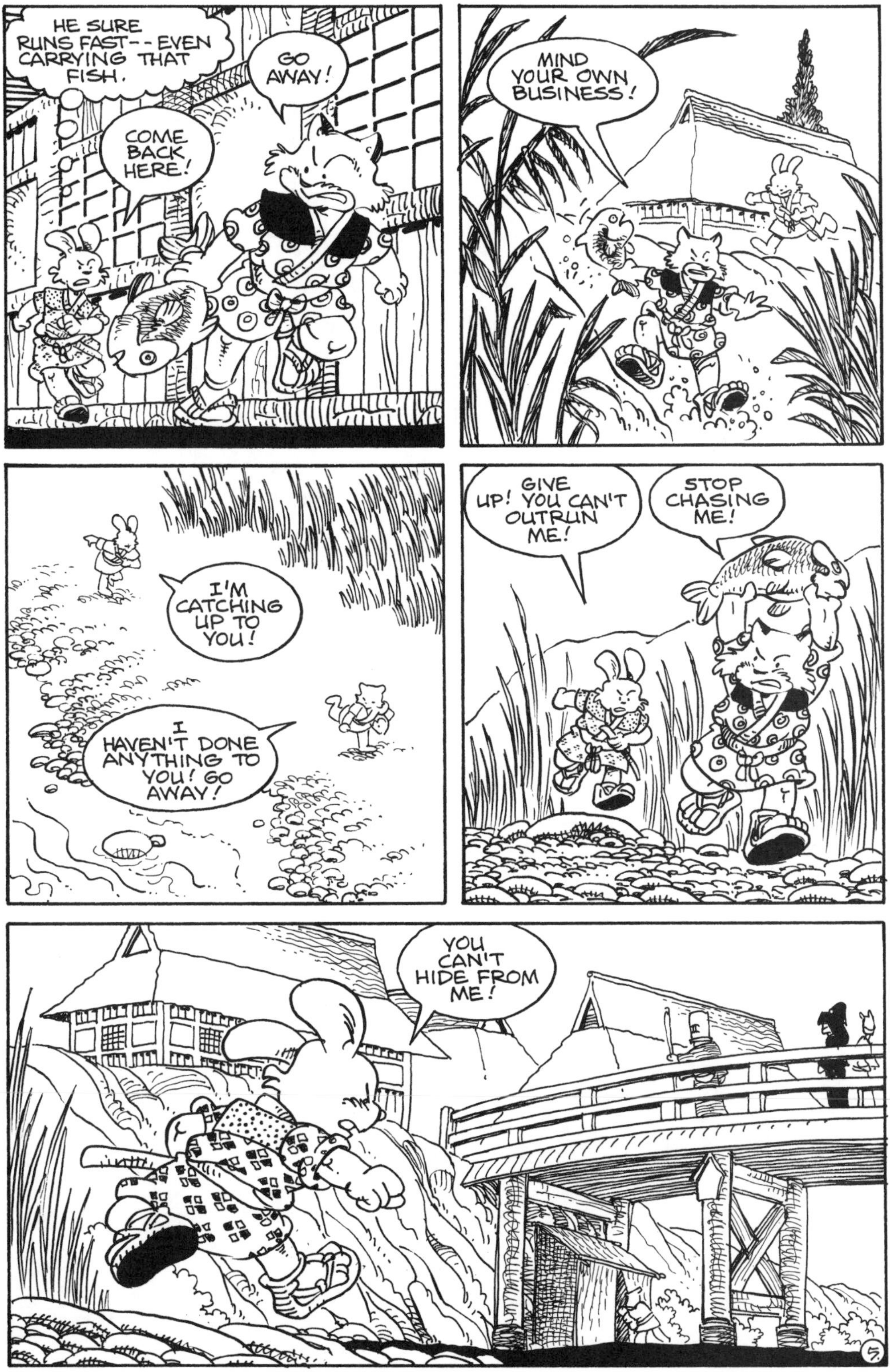
HE SURE RUNS FAST--EVEN CARRYING THAT FISH.
GO AWAY!
COME BACK HERE!
MIND YOUR OWN BUSINESS!
I'M CATCHING UP TO YOU!
I HAVEN'T DONE ANYTHING TO YOU! GO AWAY!
GIVE UP! YOU CAN'T OUTRUN ME!
STOP CHASING ME!
YOU CAN'T HIDE FROM ME!
5.

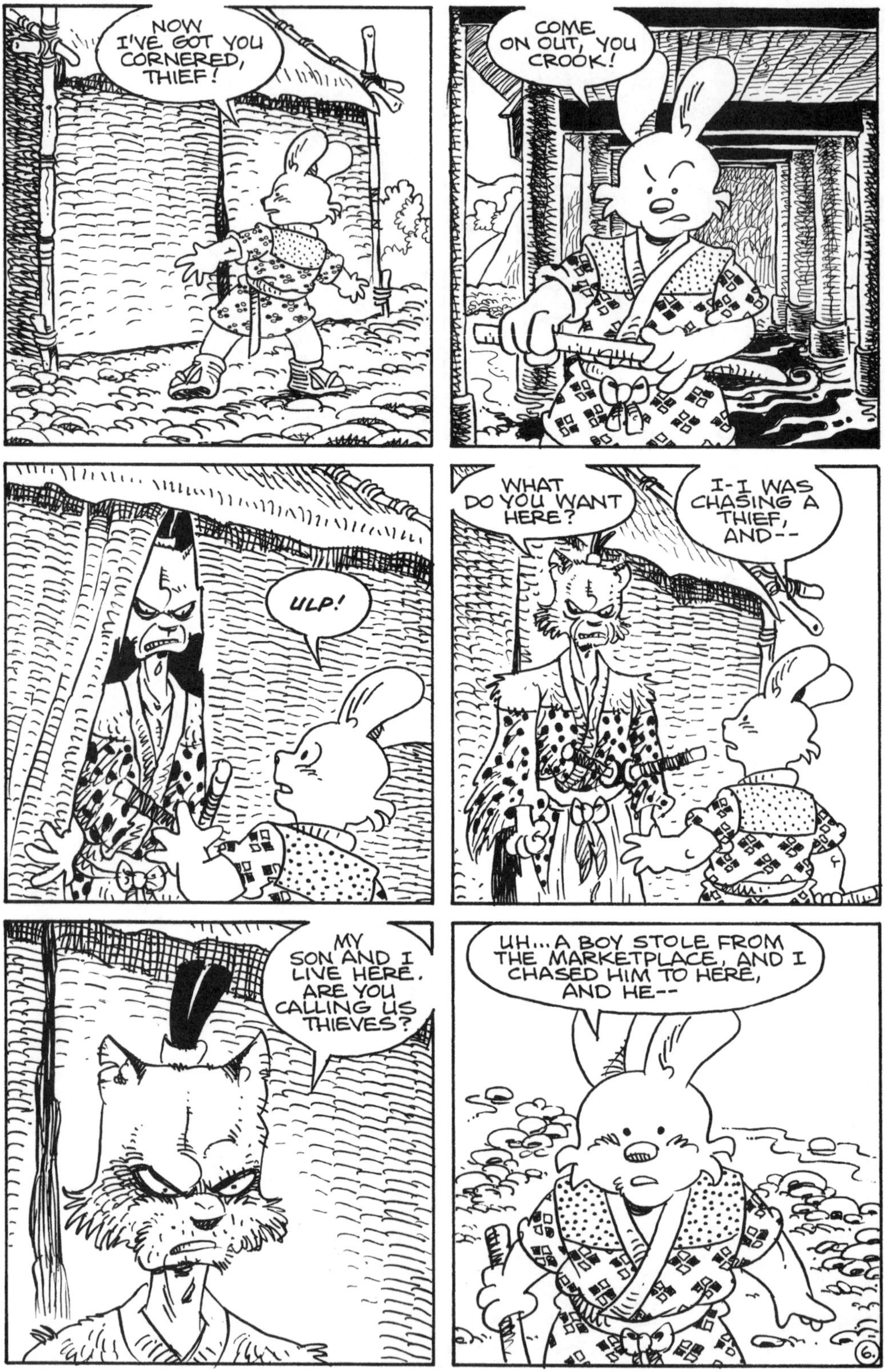

NOW I'VE GOT YOU CORNERED, THIEF!
COME ON OUT, YOU CROOK!
ULP!
WHAT DO YOU WANT HERE?
I-I WAS CHASING A THIEF, AND--
MY SON AND I LIVE HERE. ARE YOU CALLING US THIEVES?
UH...A BOY STOLE FROM THE MARKETPLACE, AND I CHASED HIM TO HERE, AND HE--
6.

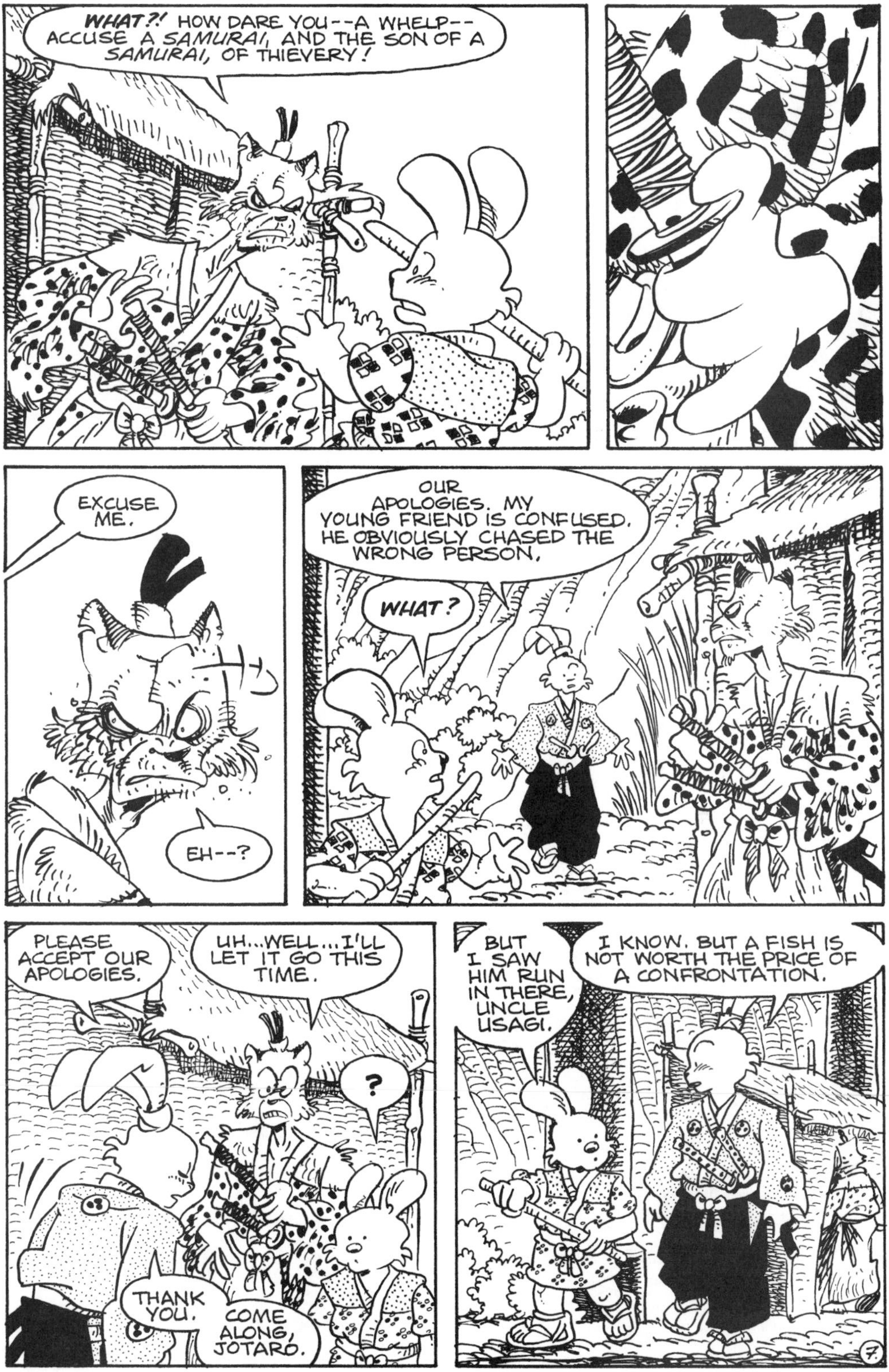
WHAT?! HOW DARE YOU--A WHELP--ACCUSE A SAMURAI, AND THE SON OF A SAMURAI, OF THIEVERY!
EXCUSE ME.
EH--?
OUR APOLOGIES. MY YOUNG FRIEND IS CONFUSED. HE OBVIOUSLY CHASED THE WRONG PERSON.
WHAT?
PLEASE ACCEPT OUR APOLOGIES.
UH...WELL...I'LL LET IT GO THIS TIME.
?
THANK YOU.
COME ALONG, JOTARO.
BUT I SAW HIM RUN IN THERE, UNCLE USAGI.
I KNOW. BUT A FISH IS NOT WORTH THE PRICE OF A CONFRONTATION.
7

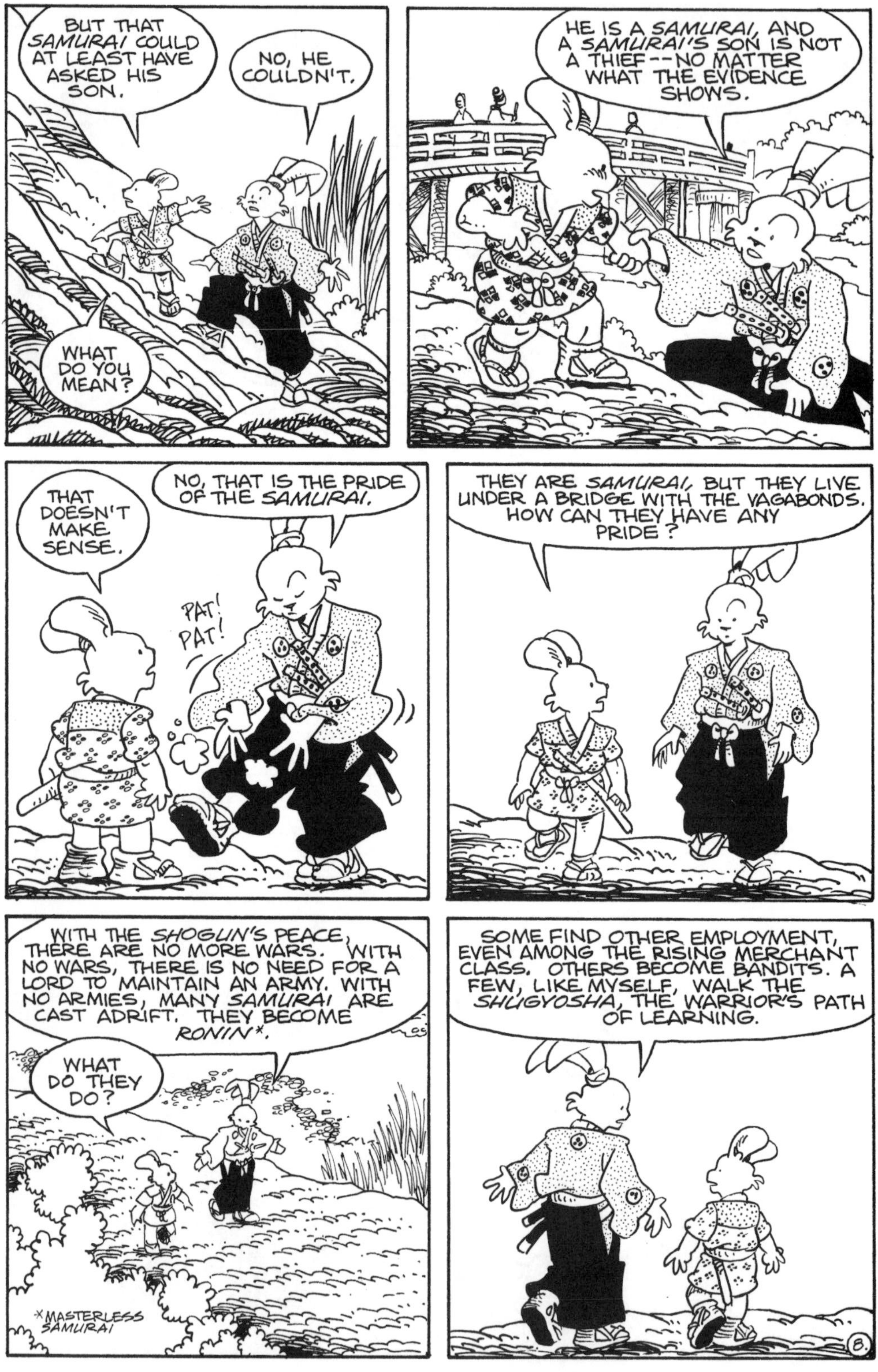
BUT THAT SAMURAI COULD AT LEAST HAVE ASKED HIS SON.
NO, HE COULDN'T.
WHAT DO YOU MEAN?
HE IS A SAMURAI, AND A SAMURAI'S SON IS NOT A THIEF--NO MATTER WHAT THE EVIDENCE SHOWS.
THAT DOESN'T MAKE SENSE.
NO, THAT IS THE PRIDE OF THE SAMURAI.
PAT! PAT!
THEY ARE SAMURAI, BUT THEY LIVE UNDER A BRIDGE WITH THE VAGABONDS. HOW CAN THEY HAVE ANY PRIDE?
WITH THE SHOGUN'S PEACE, THERE ARE NO MORE WARS. WITH NO WARS, THERE IS NO NEED FOR A LORD TO MAINTAIN AN ARMY. WITH NO ARMIES, MANY SAMURAI ARE CAST ADRIFT. THEY BECOME RONIN*.
WHAT DO THEY DO?
*MASTERLESS SAMURAI
SOME FIND OTHER EMPLOYMENT, EVEN AMONG THE RISING MERCHANT CLASS. OTHERS BECOME BANDITS. A FEW, LIKE MYSELF, WALK THE SHUGYOSHA, THE WARRIOR'S PATH OF LEARNING.
8.

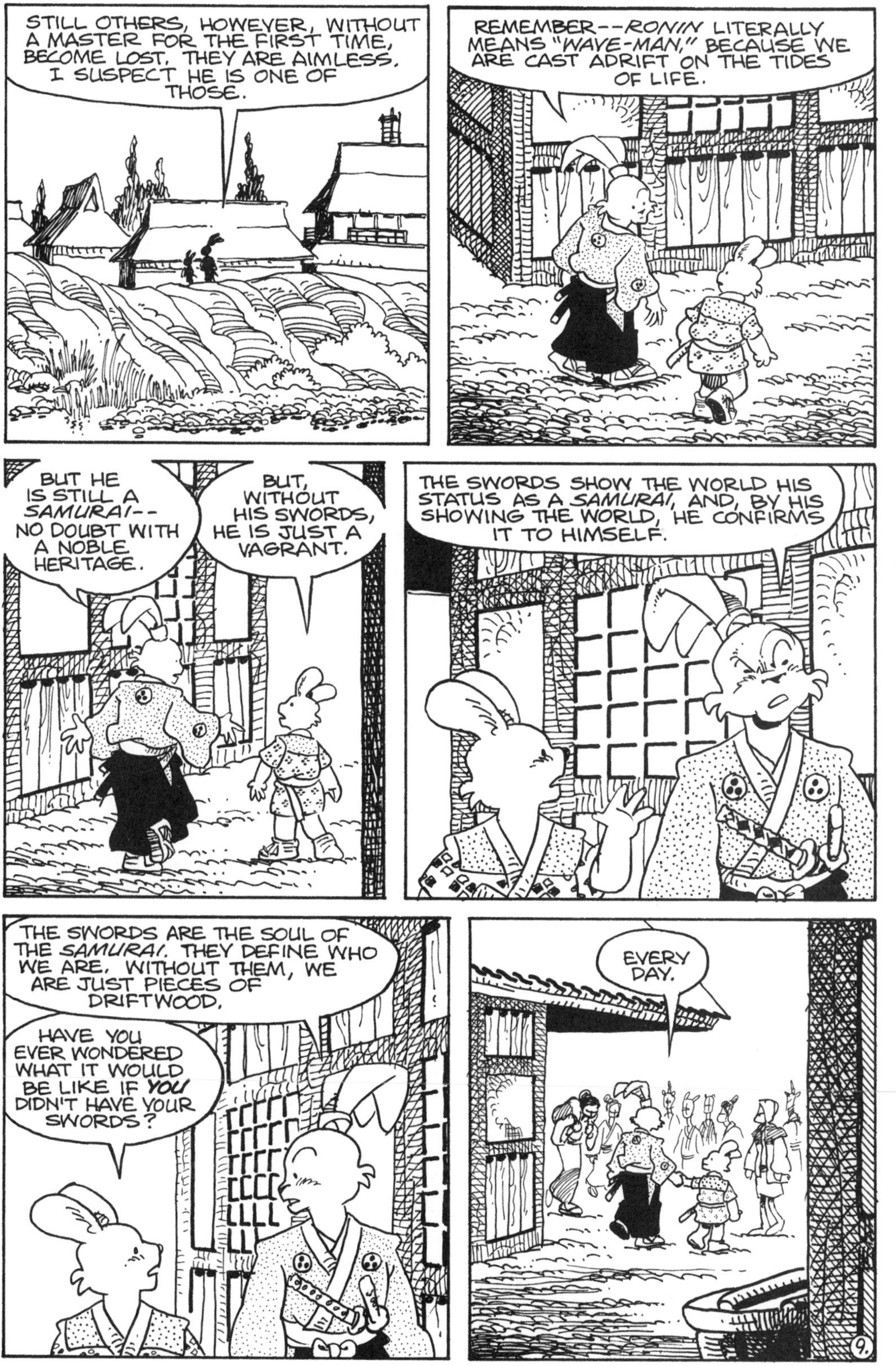
STILL OTHERS, HOWEVER, WITHOUT A MASTER FOR THE FIRST TIME, BECOME LOST. THEY ARE AIMLESS. I SUSPECT HE IS ONE OF THOSE.
REMEMBER--RONIN LITERALLY MEANS "WAVE-MAN," BECAUSE WE ARE CAST ADRIFT ON THE TIDES OF LIFE.
BUT HE IS STILL A SAMURAI-- NO DOUBT WITH A NOBLE HERITAGE.
BUT, WITHOUT HIS SWORDS, HE IS JUST A VAGRANT.
THE SWORDS SHOW THE WORLD HIS STATUS AS A SAMURAI, AND, BY HIS SHOWING THE WORLD, HE CONFIRMS IT TO HIMSELF.
THE SWORDS ARE THE SOUL OF THE SAMURAI. THEY DEFINE WHO WE ARE. WITHOUT THEM, WE ARE JUST PIECES OF DRIFTWOOD.
HAVE YOU EVER WONDERED WHAT IT WOULD BE LIKE IF YOU DIDN'T HAVE YOUR SWORDS?
EVERY DAY.
9.

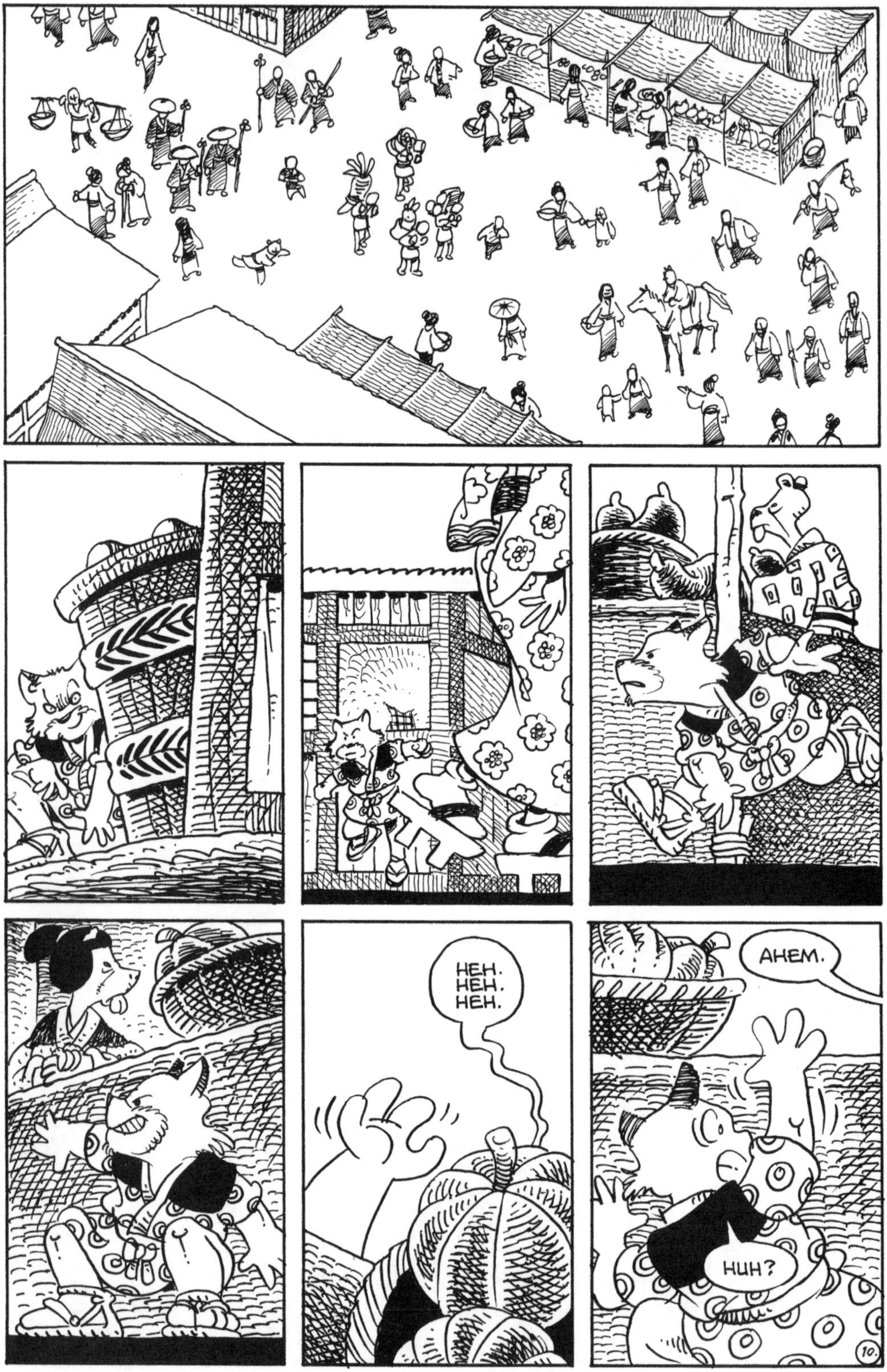
HEH.
HEH.
HEH.
AHEM.
HUH?
10.

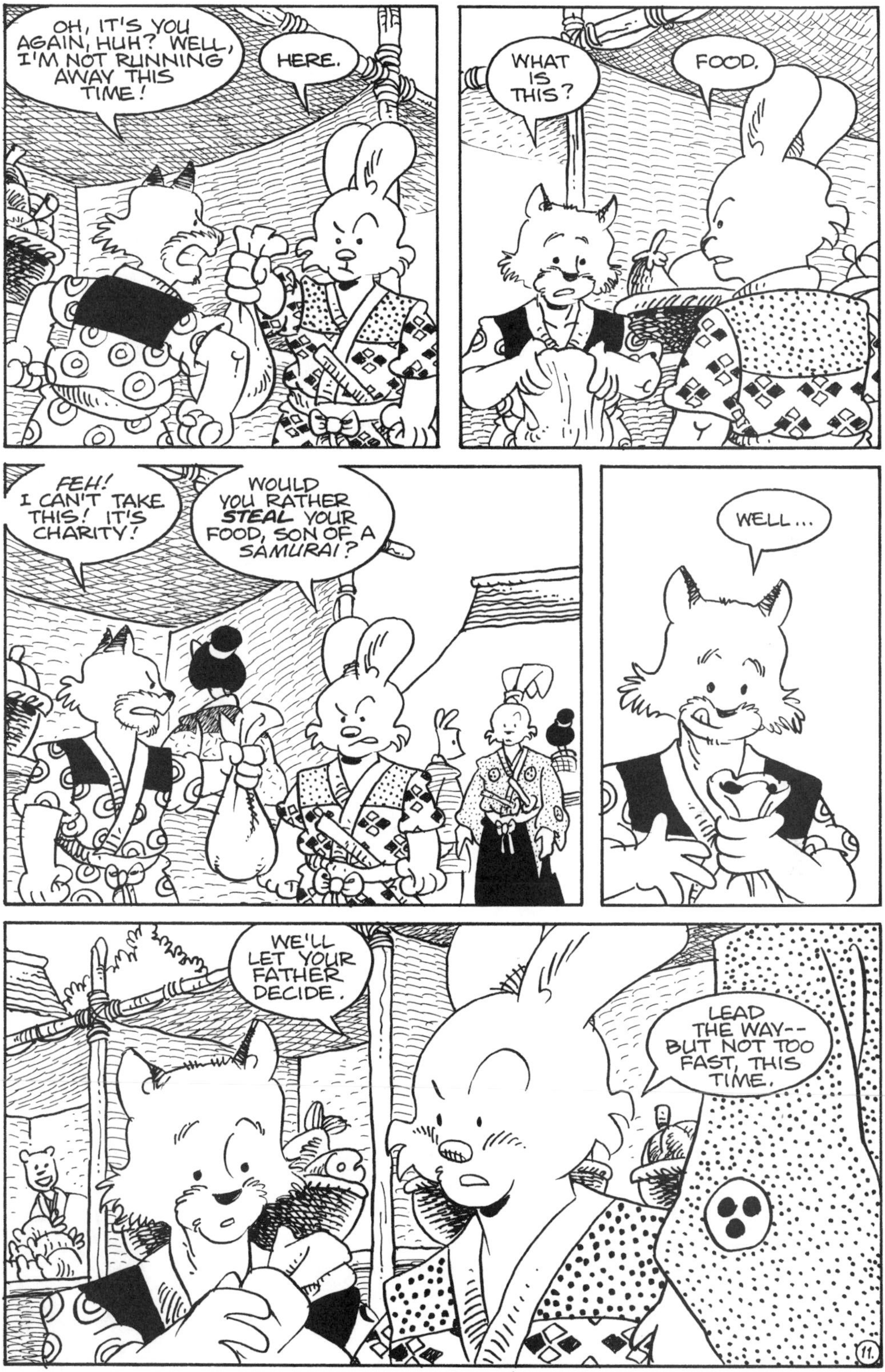
OH, IT'S YOU AGAIN, HUH? WELL, I'M NOT RUNNING AWAY THIS TIME!
HERE.
WHAT IS THIS?
FOOD.
FEH! I CAN'T TAKE THIS! IT'S CHARITY!
WOULD YOU RATHER STEAL YOUR FOOD, SON OF A SAMURAI?
WELL...
WE'LL LET YOUR FATHER DECIDE.
LEAD THE WAY-- BUT NOT TOO FAST, THIS TIME.
11.

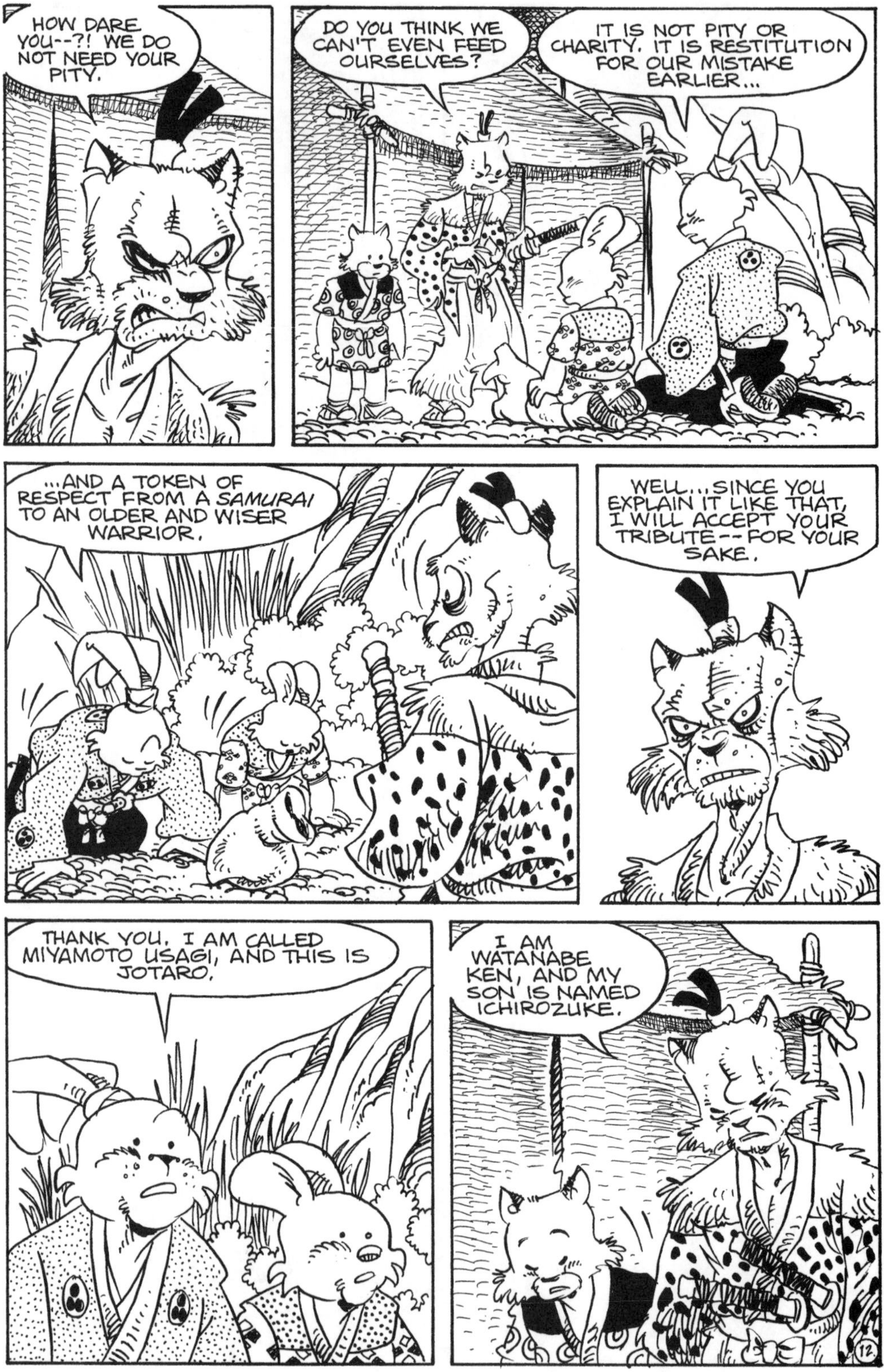
HOW DARE YOU--?! WE DO NOT NEED YOUR PITY.
DO YOU THINK WE CAN'T EVEN FEED OURSELVES?
IT IS NOT PITY OR CHARITY. IT IS RESTITUTION FOR OUR MISTAKE EARLIER...
...AND A TOKEN OF RESPECT FROM A *SAMURAI* TO AN OLDER AND WISER WARRIOR.
WELL...SINCE YOU EXPLAIN IT LIKE THAT, I WILL ACCEPT YOUR TRIBUTE--FOR YOUR SAKE.
THANK YOU. I AM CALLED MIYAMOTO USAGI, AND THIS IS JOTARO.
I AM WATANABE KEN, AND MY SON IS NAMED ICHIROZUKE.
12

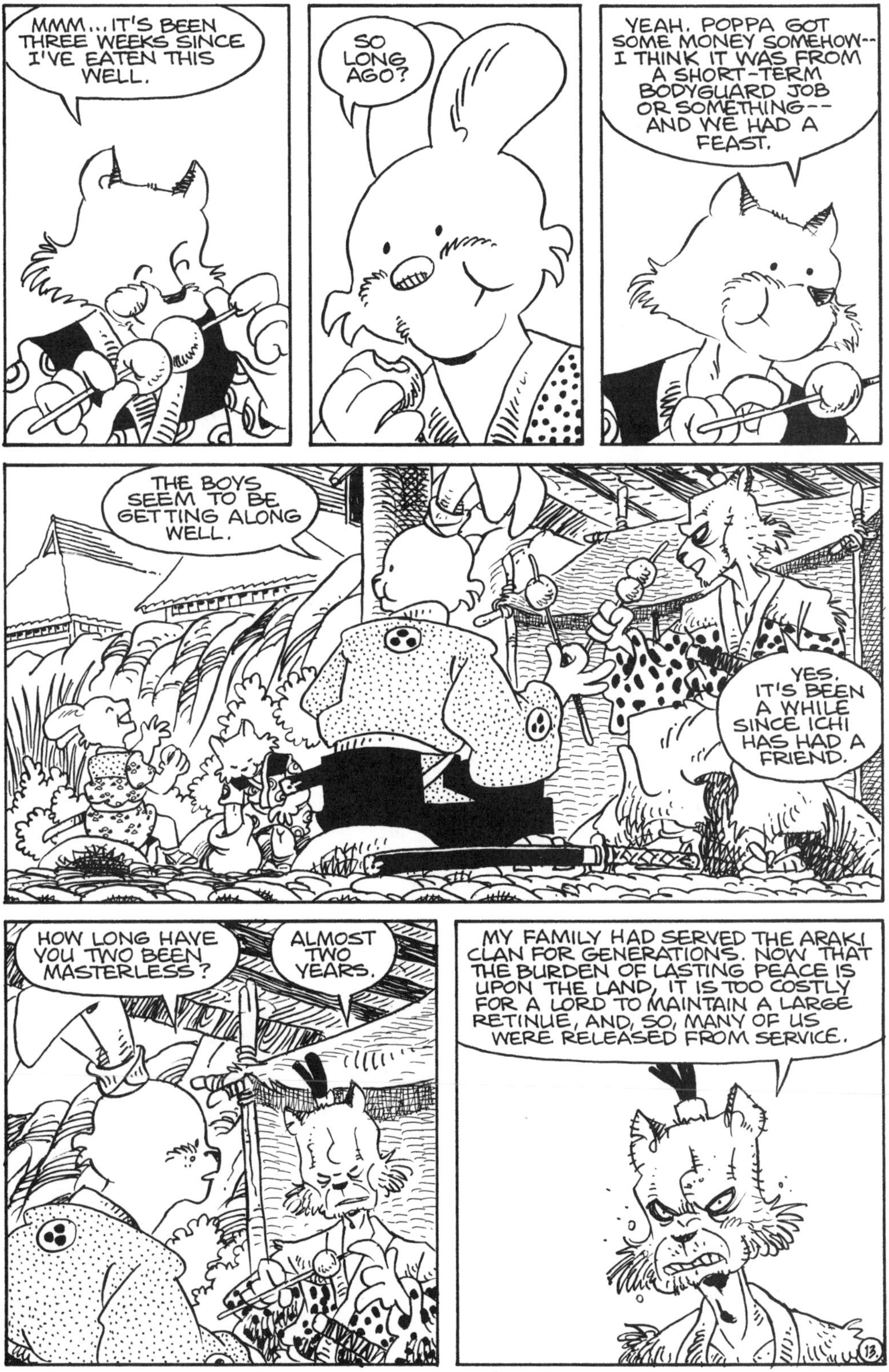
MMM... IT'S BEEN THREE WEEKS SINCE I'VE EATEN THIS WELL.
SO LONG AGO?
YEAH. POPPA GOT SOME MONEY SOMEHOW-- I THINK IT WAS FROM A SHORT-TERM BODYGUARD JOB OR SOMETHING-- AND WE HAD A FEAST.
THE BOYS SEEM TO BE GETTING ALONG WELL.
YES. IT'S BEEN A WHILE SINCE ICHI HAS HAD A FRIEND.
HOW LONG HAVE YOU TWO BEEN MASTERLESS?
ALMOST TWO YEARS.
MY FAMILY HAD SERVED THE ARAKI CLAN FOR GENERATIONS. NOW THAT THE BURDEN OF LASTING PEACE IS UPON THE LAND, IT IS TOO COSTLY FOR A LORD TO MAINTAIN A LARGE RETINUE, AND, SO, MANY OF US WERE RELEASED FROM SERVICE.
13.

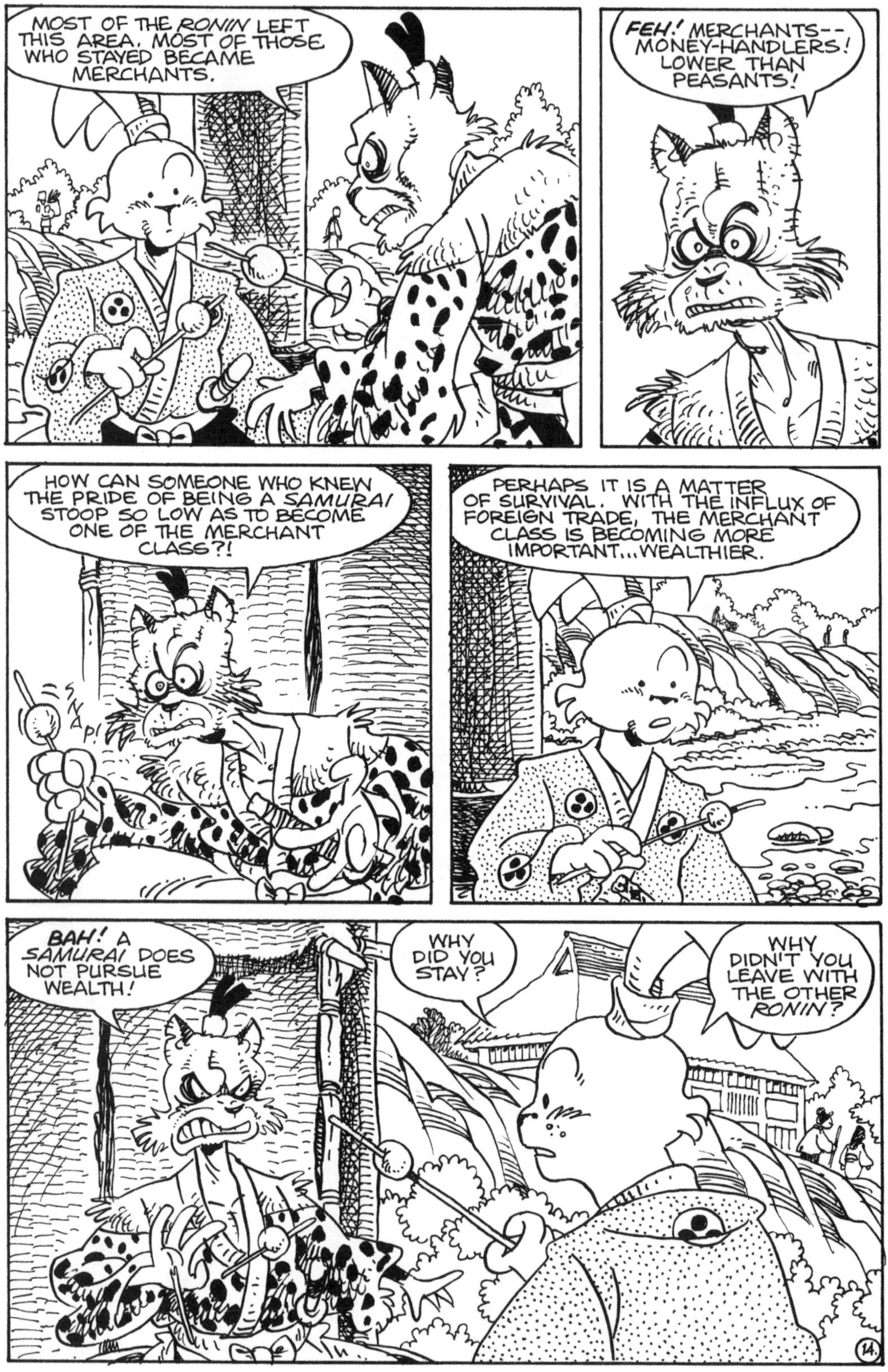
MOST OF THE RONIN LEFT THIS AREA. MOST OF THOSE WHO STAYED BECAME MERCHANTS.
FEH! MERCHANTS-- MONEY-HANDLERS! LOWER THAN PEASANTS!
HOW CAN SOMEONE WHO KNEW THE PRIDE OF BEING A SAMURAI STOOP SO LOW AS TO BECOME ONE OF THE MERCHANT CLASS?!
SNAP!
PERHAPS IT IS A MATTER OF SURVIVAL. WITH THE INFLUX OF FOREIGN TRADE, THE MERCHANT CLASS IS BECOMING MORE IMPORTANT...WEALTHIER.
BAH! A SAMURAI DOES NOT PURSUE WEALTH!
WHY DID YOU STAY?
WHY DIDN'T YOU LEAVE WITH THE OTHER RONIN?
14.

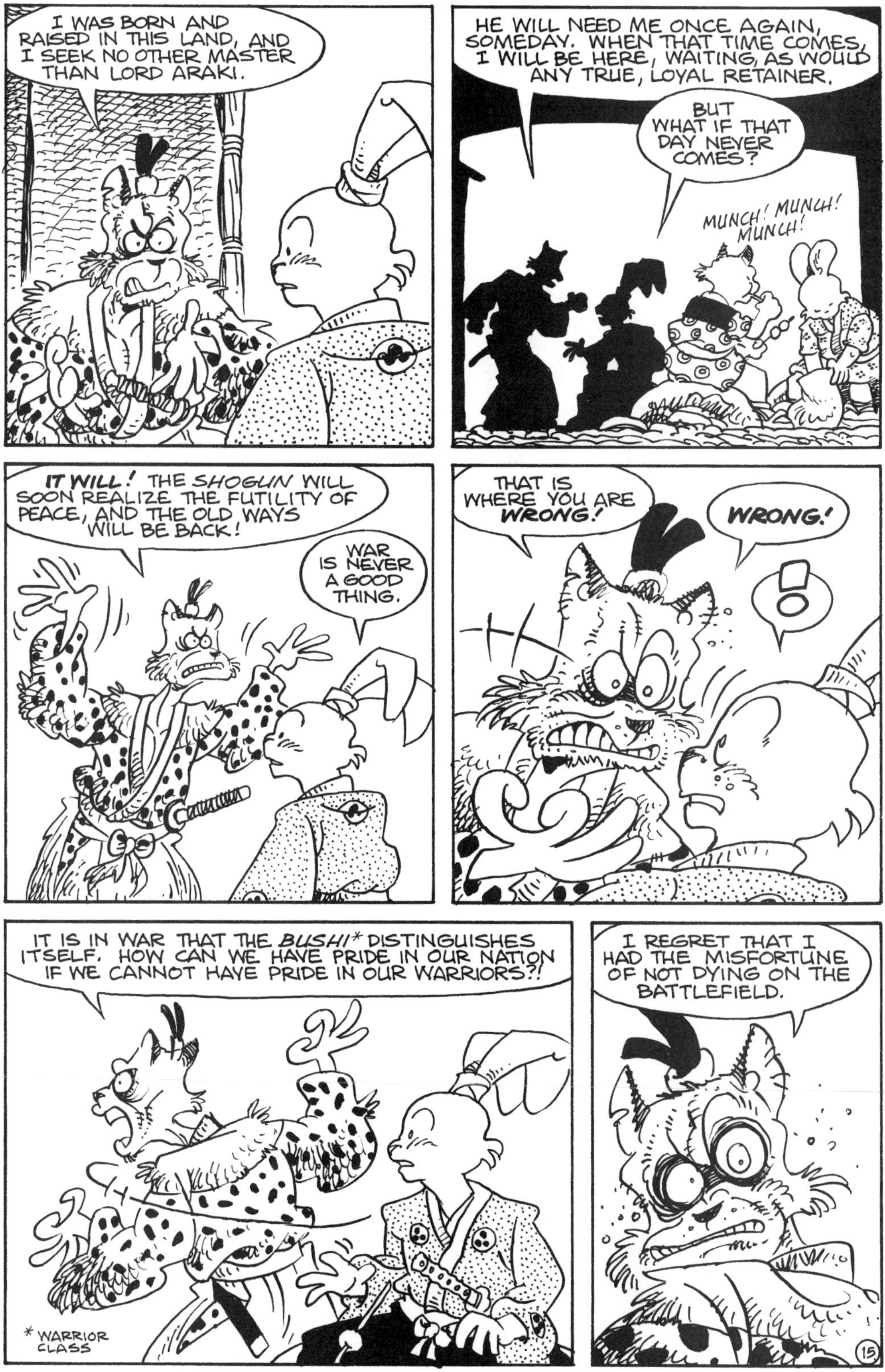
I WAS BORN AND RAISED IN THIS LAND, AND I SEEK NO OTHER MASTER THAN LORD ARAKI.
HE WILL NEED ME ONCE AGAIN, SOMEDAY. WHEN THAT TIME COMES, I WILL BE HERE, WAITING, AS WOULD ANY TRUE, LOYAL RETAINER.
BUT WHAT IF THAT DAY NEVER COMES?
MUNCH! MUNCH! MUNCH!
IT WILL! THE SHOGUN WILL SOON REALIZE THE FUTILITY OF PEACE, AND THE OLD WAYS WILL BE BACK!
WAR IS NEVER A GOOD THING.
THAT IS WHERE YOU ARE WRONG!
WRONG!
!
IT IS IN WAR THAT THE BUSHI* DISTINGUISHES ITSELF. HOW CAN WE HAVE PRIDE IN OUR NATION IF WE CANNOT HAVE PRIDE IN OUR WARRIORS?!
*WARRIOR CLASS
I REGRET THAT I HAD THE MISFORTUNE OF NOT DYING ON THE BATTLEFIELD.
15

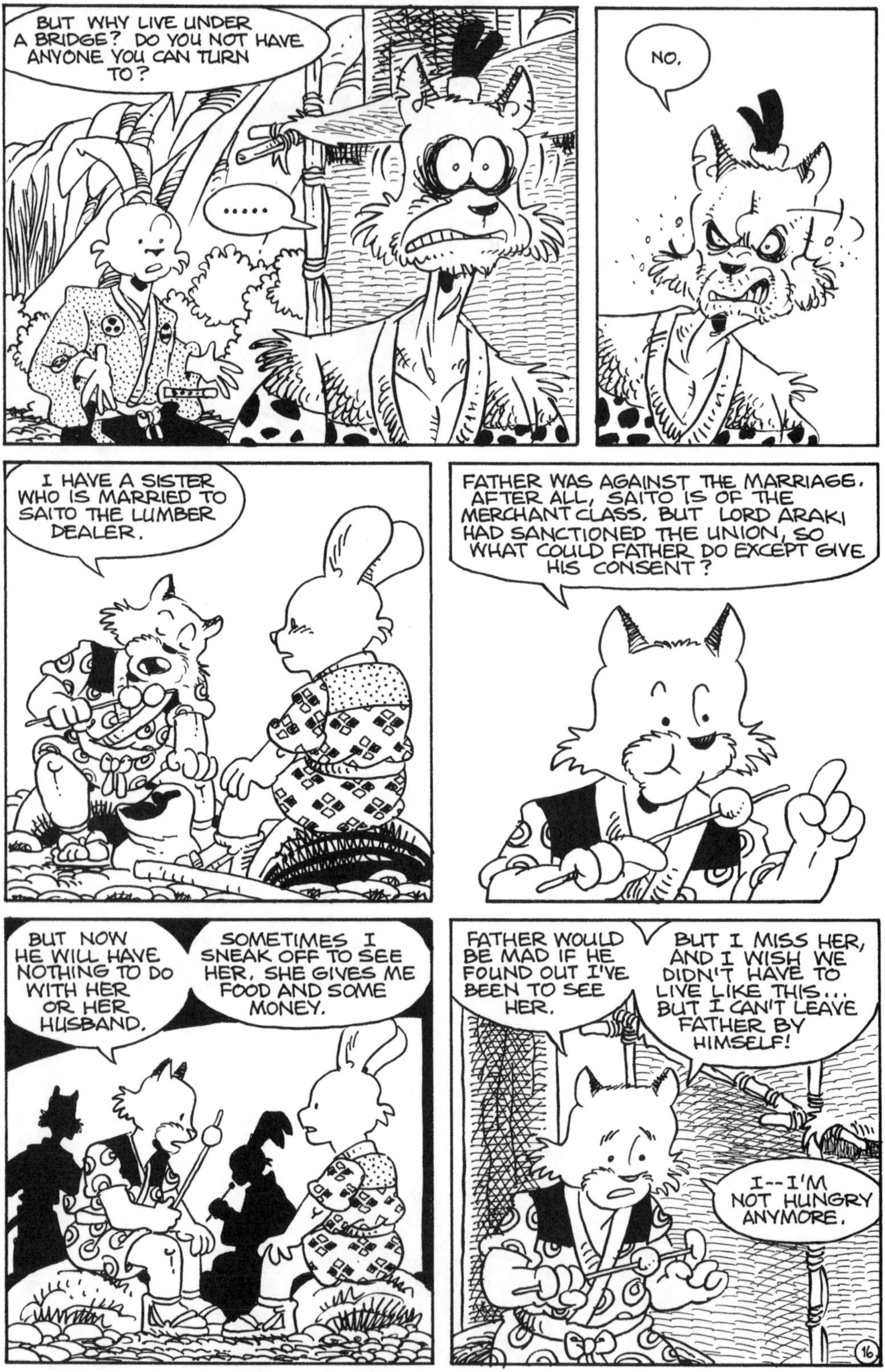
BUT WHY LIVE UNDER A BRIDGE? DO YOU NOT HAVE ANYONE YOU CAN TURN TO?
.....
NO.
I HAVE A SISTER WHO IS MARRIED TO SAITO THE LUMBER DEALER.
FATHER WAS AGAINST THE MARRIAGE. AFTER ALL, SAITO IS OF THE MERCHANT CLASS. BUT LORD ARAKI HAD SANCTIONED THE UNION, SO WHAT COULD FATHER DO EXCEPT GIVE HIS CONSENT?
BUT NOW HE WILL HAVE NOTHING TO DO WITH HER OR HER HUSBAND.
SOMETIMES I SNEAK OFF TO SEE HER. SHE GIVES ME FOOD AND SOME MONEY.
FATHER WOULD BE MAD IF HE FOUND OUT I'VE BEEN TO SEE HER.
BUT I MISS HER, AND I WISH WE DIDN'T HAVE TO LIVE LIKE THIS... BUT I CAN'T LEAVE FATHER BY HIMSELF!
I--I'M NOT HUNGRY ANYMORE.
16

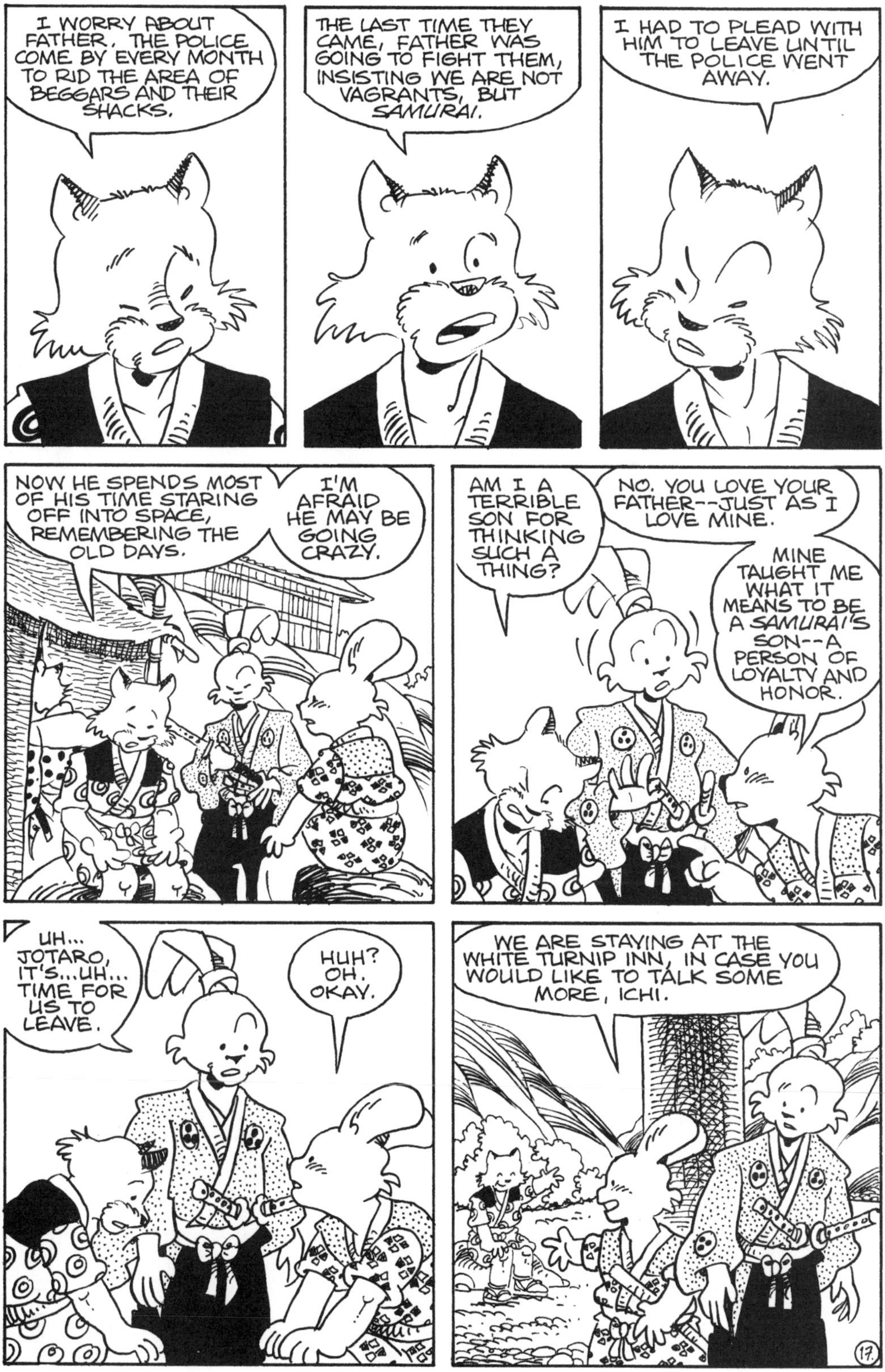
I WORRY ABOUT FATHER. THE POLICE COME BY EVERY MONTH TO RID THE AREA OF BEGGARS AND THEIR SHACKS.
THE LAST TIME THEY CAME, FATHER WAS GOING TO FIGHT THEM, INSISTING WE ARE NOT VAGRANTS, BUT SAMURAI.
I HAD TO PLEAD WITH HIM TO LEAVE UNTIL THE POLICE WENT AWAY.
NOW HE SPENDS MOST OF HIS TIME STARING OFF INTO SPACE, REMEMBERING THE OLD DAYS.
I'M AFRAID HE MAY BE GOING CRAZY.
AM I A TERRIBLE SON FOR THINKING SUCH A THING?
NO. YOU LOVE YOUR FATHER--JUST AS I LOVE MINE.
MINE TAUGHT ME WHAT IT MEANS TO BE A SAMURAI'S SON--A PERSON OF LOYALTY AND HONOR.
UH... JOTARO, IT'S...UH... TIME FOR US TO LEAVE.
HUH? OH. OKAY.
WE ARE STAYING AT THE WHITE TURNIP INN, IN CASE YOU WOULD LIKE TO TALK SOME MORE, ICHI.
17.

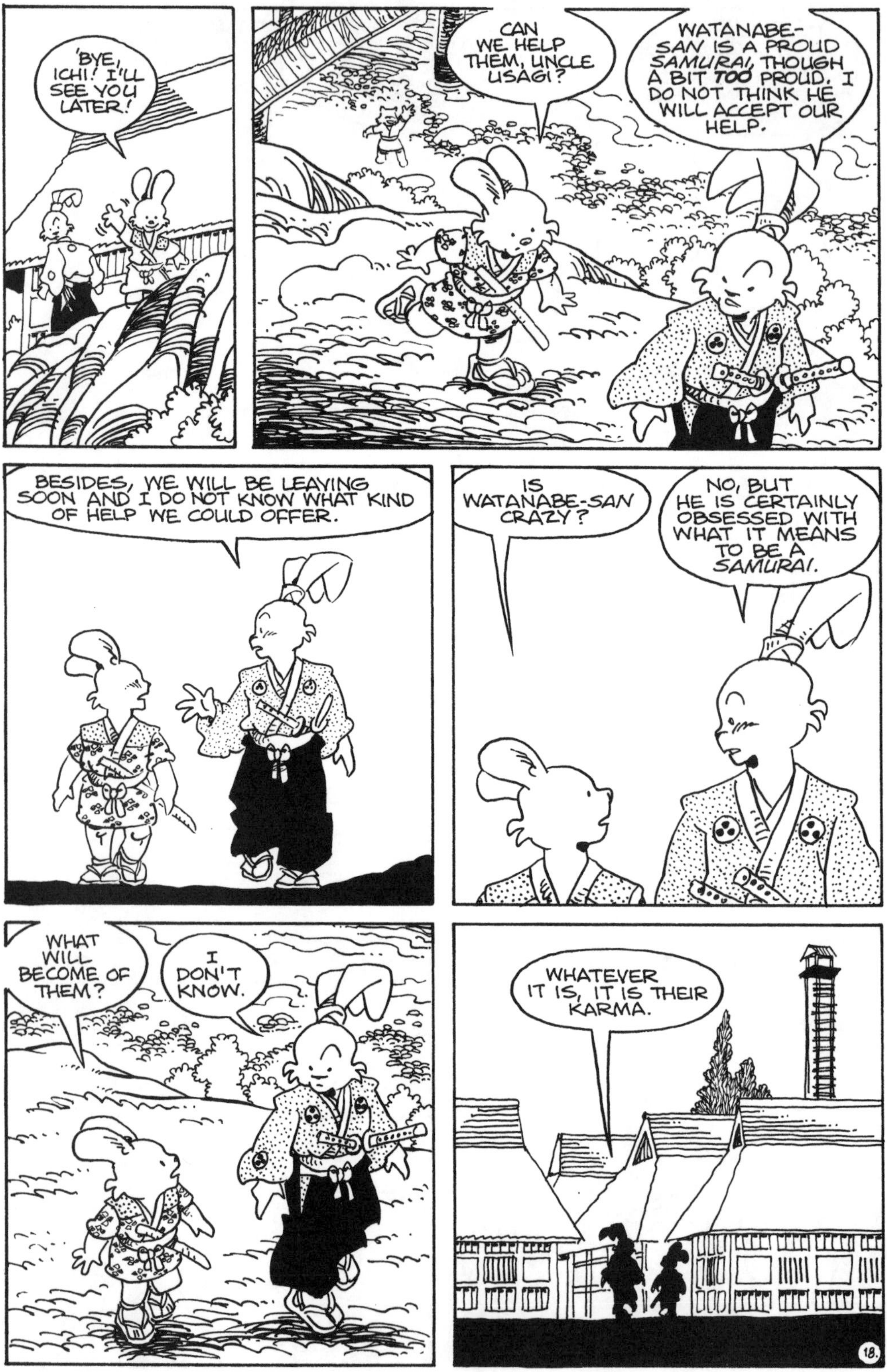
'BYE, ICHI! I'LL SEE YOU LATER!
CAN WE HELP THEM, UNCLE USAGI?
WATANABE-SAN IS A PROUD SAMURAI, THOUGH A BIT TOO PROUD. I DO NOT THINK HE WILL ACCEPT OUR HELP.
BESIDES, WE WILL BE LEAVING SOON AND I DO NOT KNOW WHAT KIND OF HELP WE COULD OFFER.
IS WATANABE-SAN CRAZY?
NO, BUT HE IS CERTAINLY OBSESSED WITH WHAT IT MEANS TO BE A SAMURAI.
WHAT WILL BECOME OF THEM?
I DON'T KNOW.
WHATEVER IT IS, IT IS THEIR KARMA.
18.

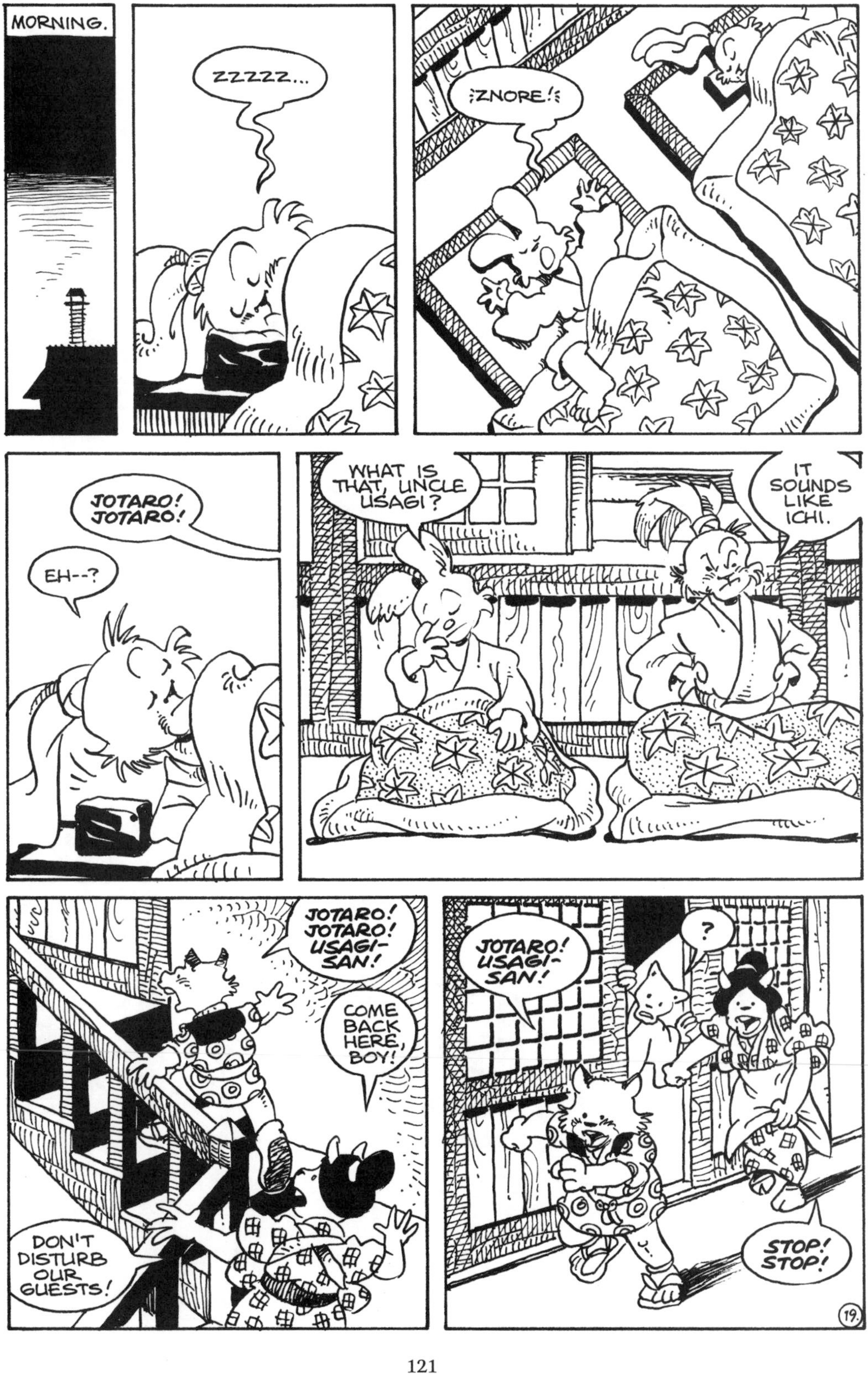
MORNING.
ZZZZZ...
ZNORE!
JOTARO! JOTARO!
EH--?
WHAT IS THAT, UNCLE USAGI?
IT SOUNDS LIKE ICHI.
JOTARO! JOTARO! USAGI-SAN!
COME BACK HERE, BOY!
DON'T DISTURB OUR GUESTS!
JOTARO! USAGI-SAN!
?
STOP! STOP!
19.

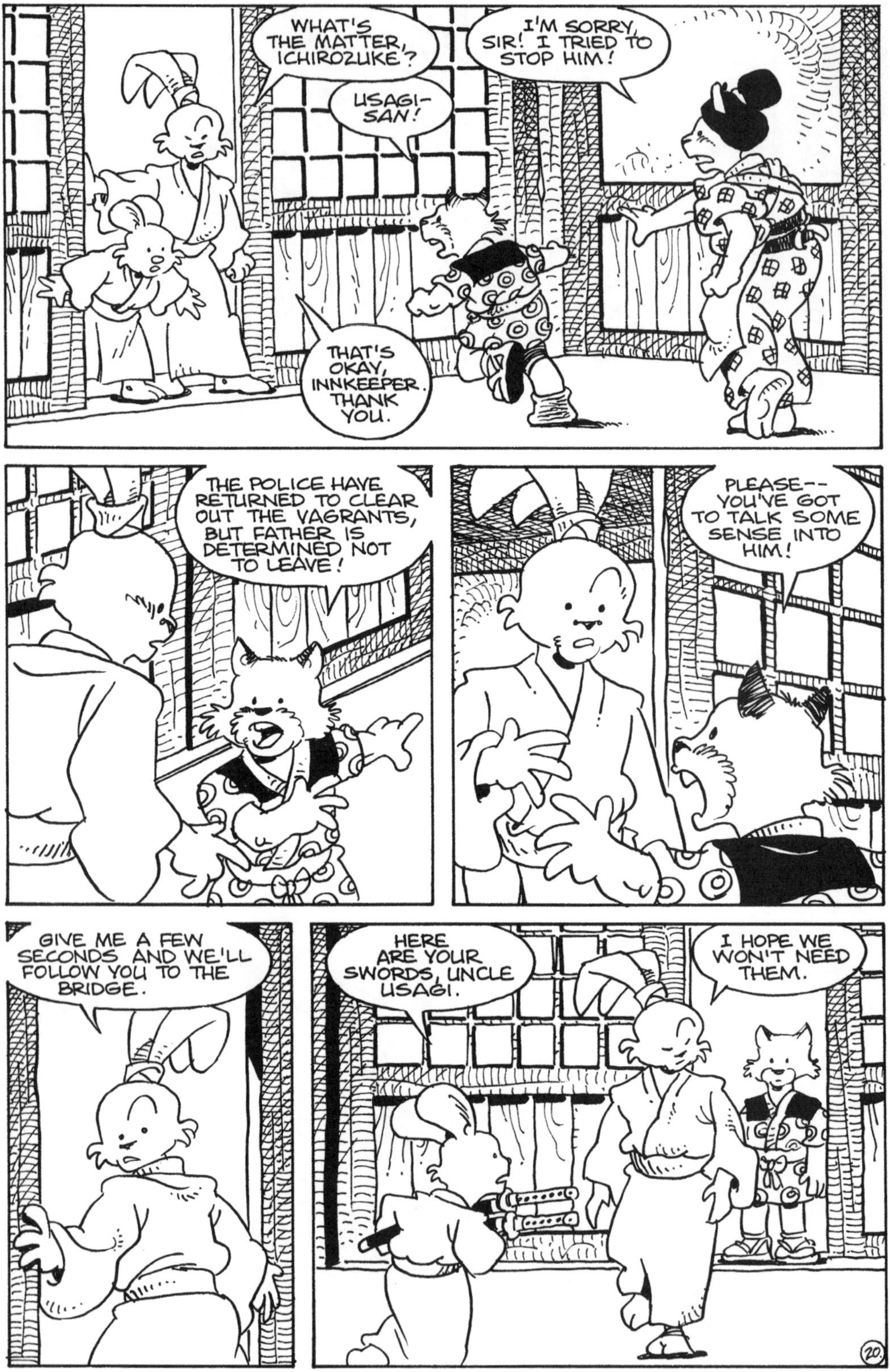
WHAT'S THE MATTER, ICHIROZUKE?
USAGI-SAN!
I'M SORRY, SIR! I TRIED TO STOP HIM!
THAT'S OKAY, INNKEEPER. THANK YOU.
THE POLICE HAVE RETURNED TO CLEAR OUT THE VAGRANTS, BUT FATHER IS DETERMINED NOT TO LEAVE!
PLEASE-- YOU'VE GOT TO TALK SOME SENSE INTO HIM!
GIVE ME A FEW SECONDS AND WE'LL FOLLOW YOU TO THE BRIDGE.
HERE ARE YOUR SWORDS, UNCLE USAGI.
I HOPE WE WON'T NEED THEM.
20

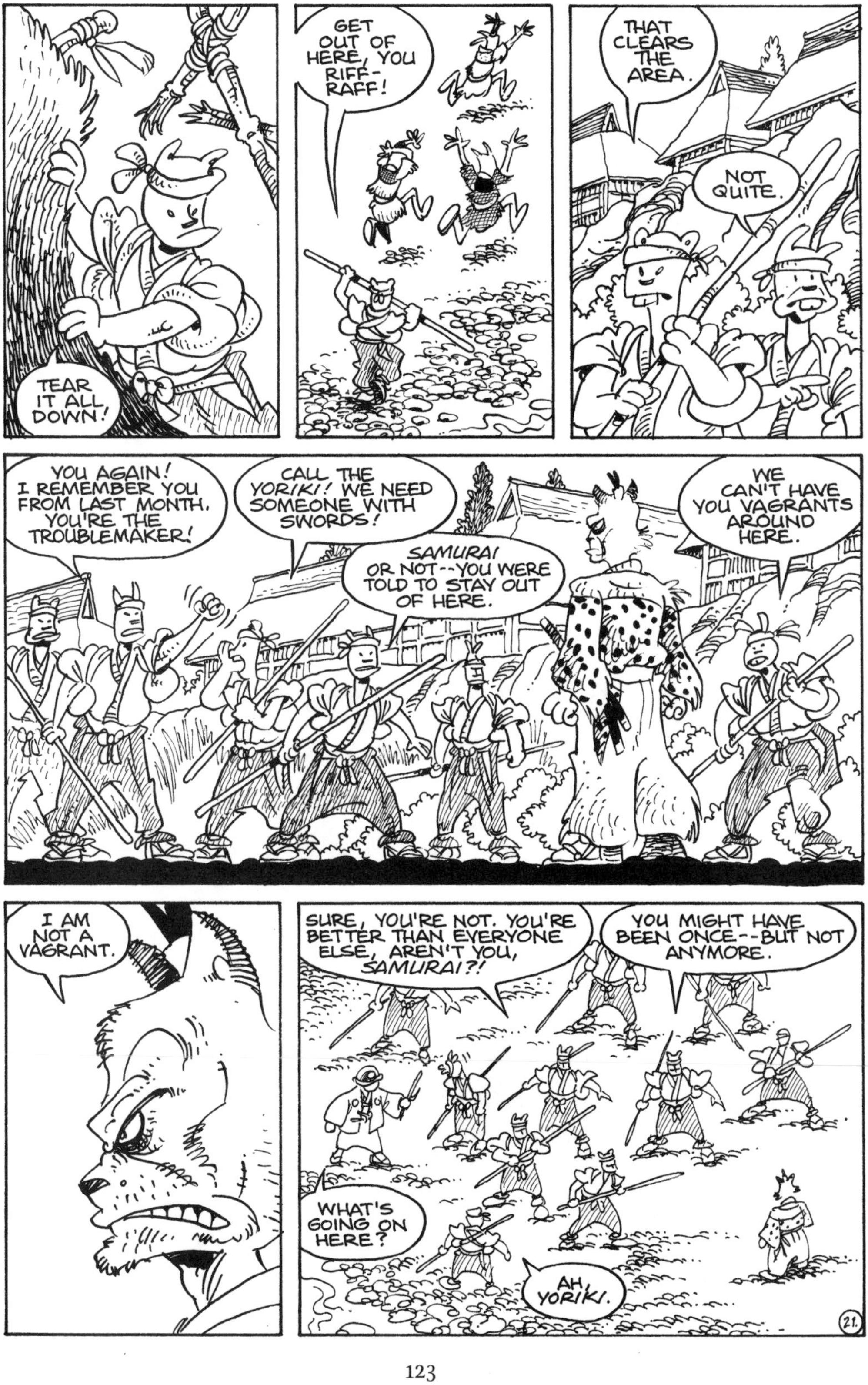
TEAR IT ALL DOWN!
GET OUT OF HERE, YOU RIFF-RAFF!
THAT CLEARS THE AREA.
NOT QUITE.
YOU AGAIN! I REMEMBER YOU FROM LAST MONTH. YOU'RE THE TROUBLEMAKER!
CALL THE YORIKI! WE NEED SOMEONE WITH SWORDS!
SAMURAI OR NOT--YOU WERE TOLD TO STAY OUT OF HERE.
WE CAN'T HAVE YOU VAGRANTS AROUND HERE.
I AM NOT A VAGRANT.
SURE, YOU'RE NOT. YOU'RE BETTER THAN EVERYONE ELSE, AREN'T YOU, SAMURAI?!
YOU MIGHT HAVE BEEN ONCE--BUT NOT ANYMORE.
WHAT'S GOING ON HERE?
AH, YORIKI.
21.

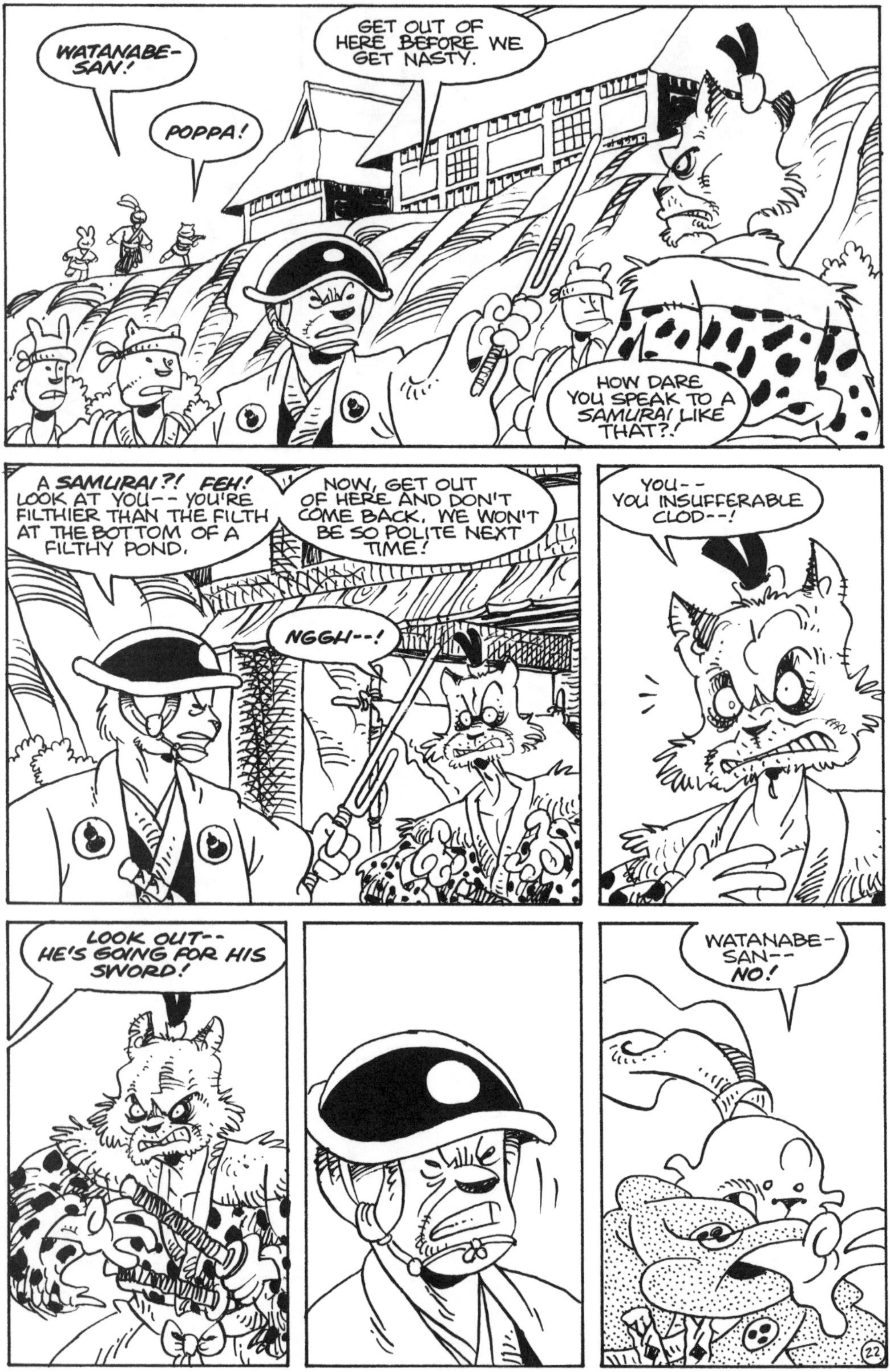
WATANABE-SAN!
POPPA!
GET OUT OF HERE BEFORE WE GET NASTY.
HOW DARE YOU SPEAK TO A SAMURAI LIKE THAT?!
A SAMURAI?! FEH! LOOK AT YOU-- YOU'RE FILTHIER THAN THE FILTH AT THE BOTTOM OF A FILTHY POND.
NOW, GET OUT OF HERE AND DON'T COME BACK. WE WON'T BE SO POLITE NEXT TIME!
NGGH--!
YOU-- YOU INSUFFERABLE CLOD--!
LOOK OUT-- HE'S GOING FOR HIS SWORD!
WATANABE-SAN-- NO!
22

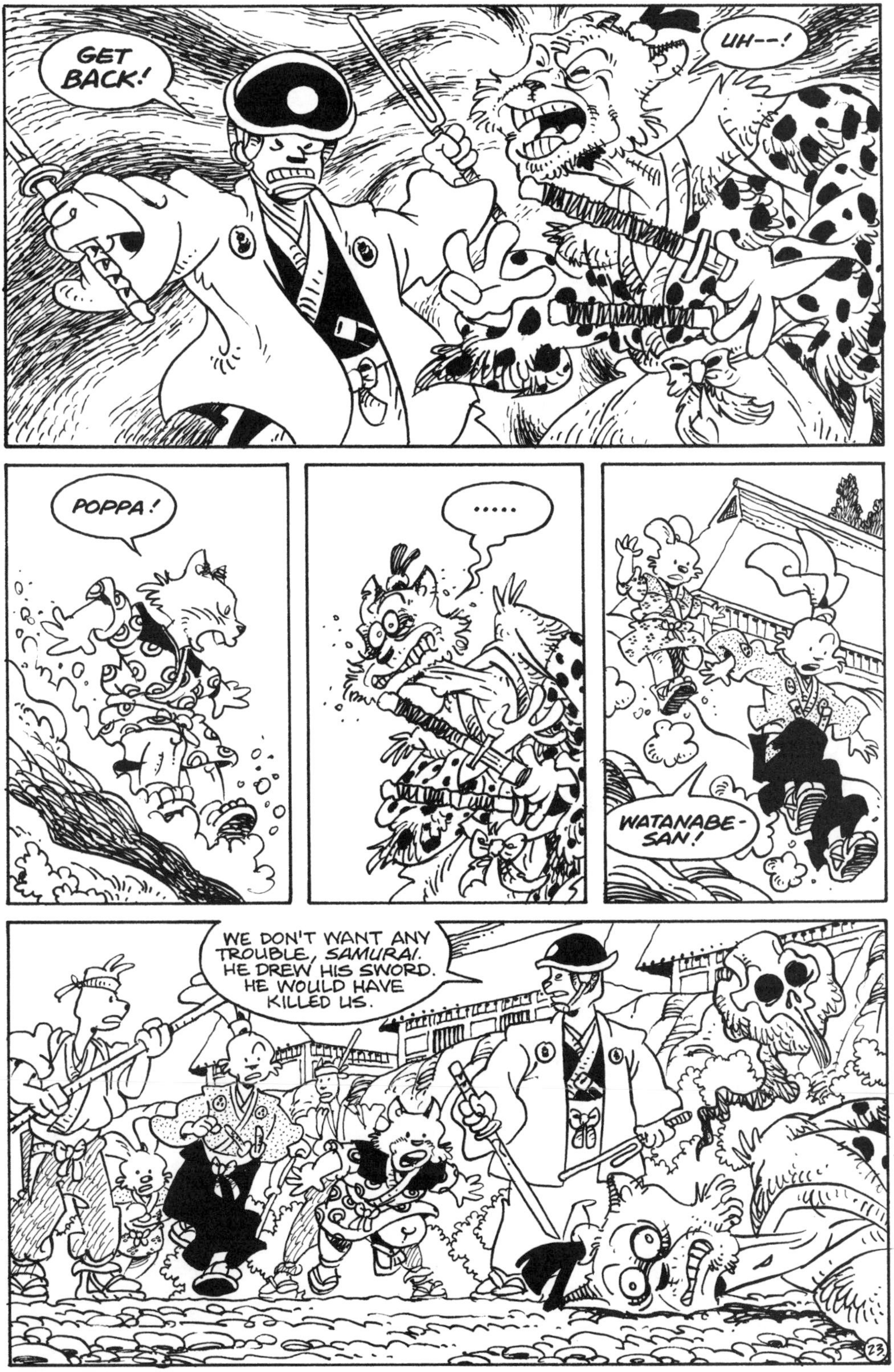
GET BACK!
UH--!
POPPA!
.....
WATANABE-SAN!
WE DON'T WANT ANY TROUBLE, SAMURAI. HE DREW HIS SWORD. HE WOULD HAVE KILLED US.
23

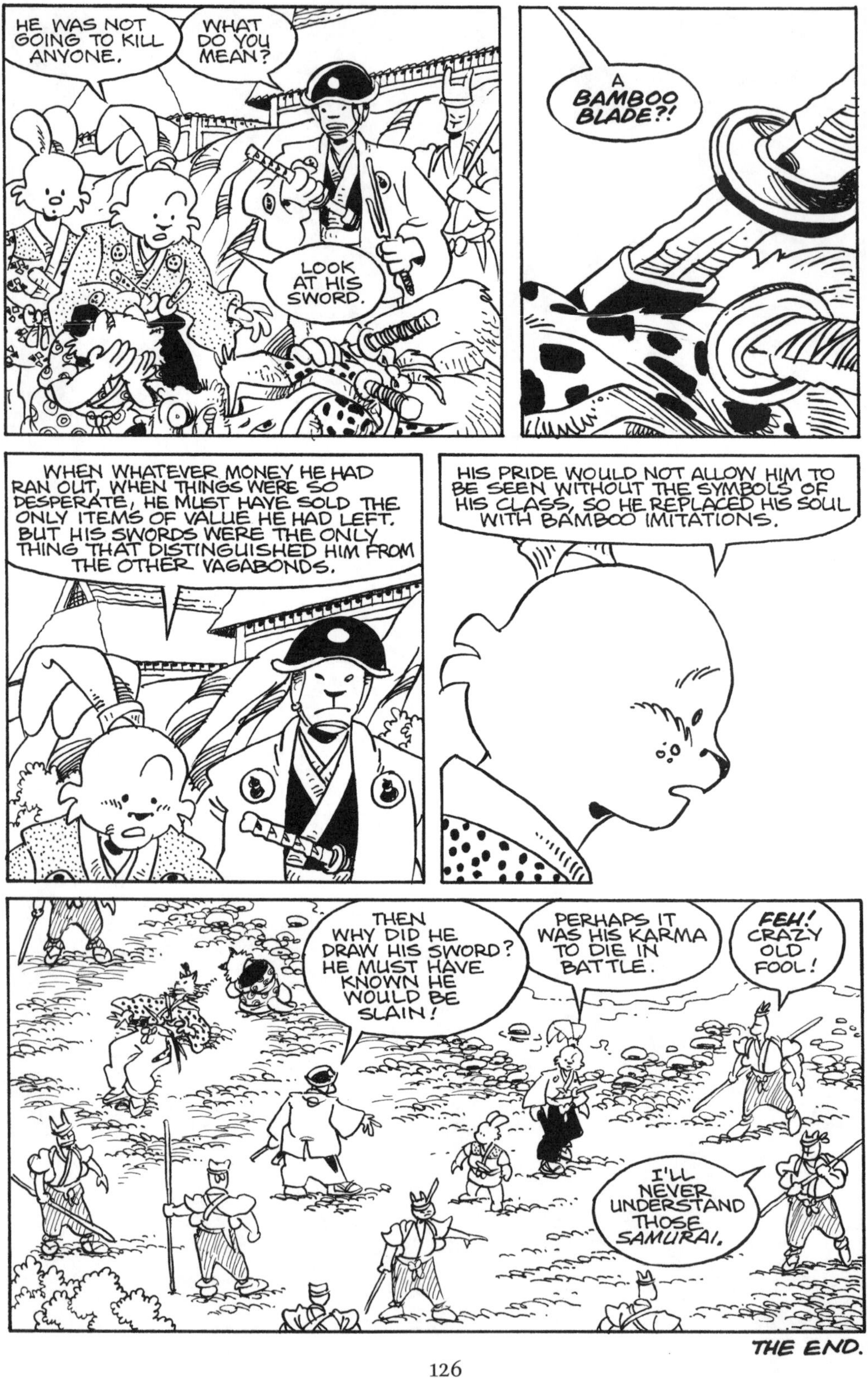

HE WAS NOT GOING TO KILL ANYONE.
WHAT DO YOU MEAN?
LOOK AT HIS SWORD.
A BAMBOO BLADE?!
WHEN WHATEVER MONEY HE HAD RAN OUT, WHEN THINGS WERE SO DESPERATE, HE MUST HAVE SOLD THE ONLY ITEMS OF VALUE HE HAD LEFT. BUT HIS SWORDS WERE THE ONLY THING THAT DISTINGUISHED HIM FROM THE OTHER VAGABONDS.
HIS PRIDE WOULD NOT ALLOW HIM TO BE SEEN WITHOUT THE SYMBOLS OF HIS CLASS, SO HE REPLACED HIS SOUL WITH BAMBOO IMITATIONS.
THEN WHY DID HE DRAW HIS SWORD? HE MUST HAVE KNOWN HE WOULD BE SLAIN!
PERHAPS IT WAS HIS KARMA TO DIE IN BATTLE.
FEH! CRAZY OLD FOOL!
I'LL NEVER UNDERSTAND THOSE SAMURAI.

THE END.

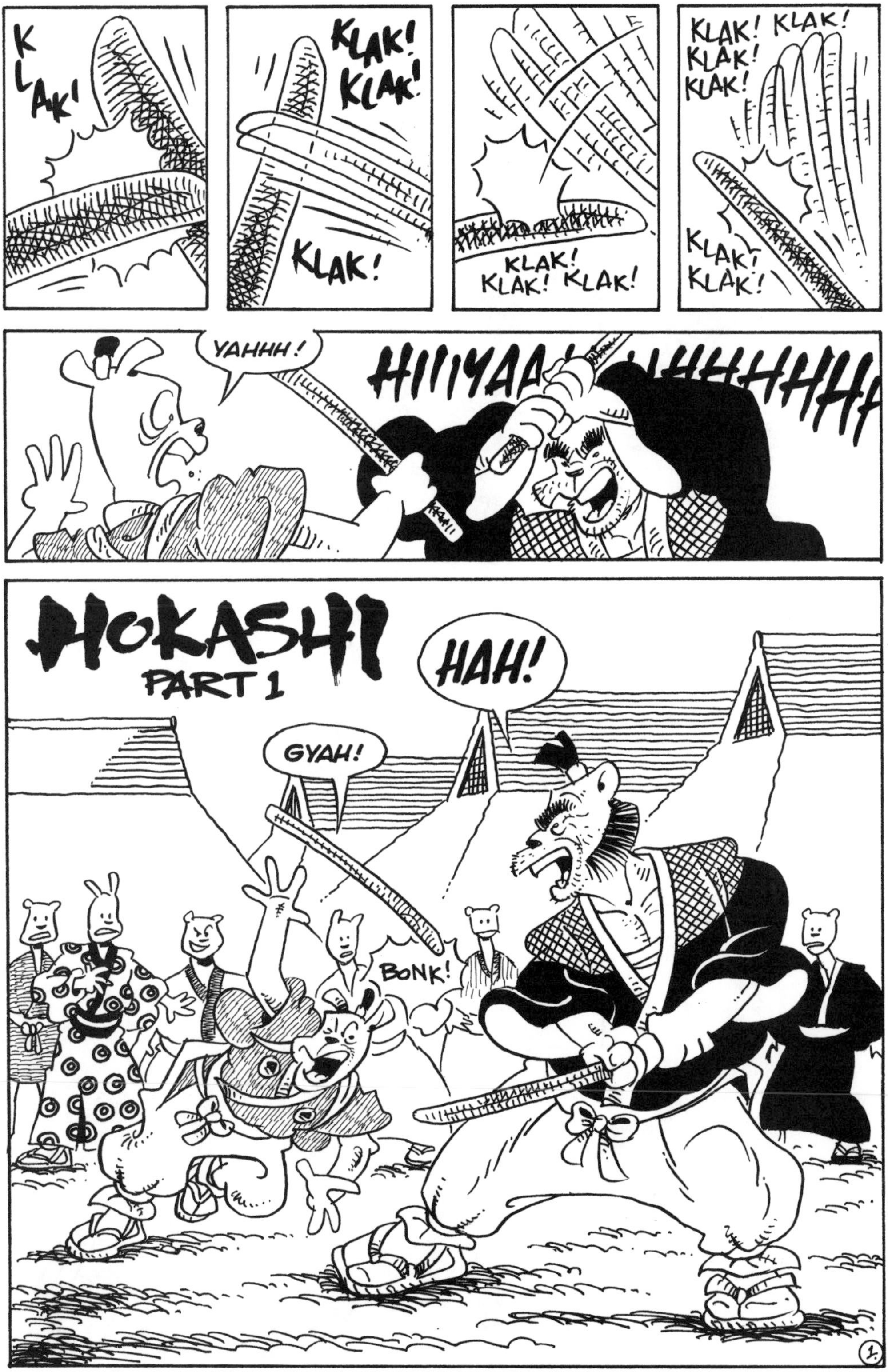
KLAK!
KLAK! KLAK!
KLAK!
KLAK! KLAK! KLAK!
KLAK! KLAK! KLAK! KLAK!
KLAK! KLAK!
YAHHH!
HIIIYAAHHHHHHHH
HOKASHI
PART 1
HAH!
GYAH!
BONK!
1

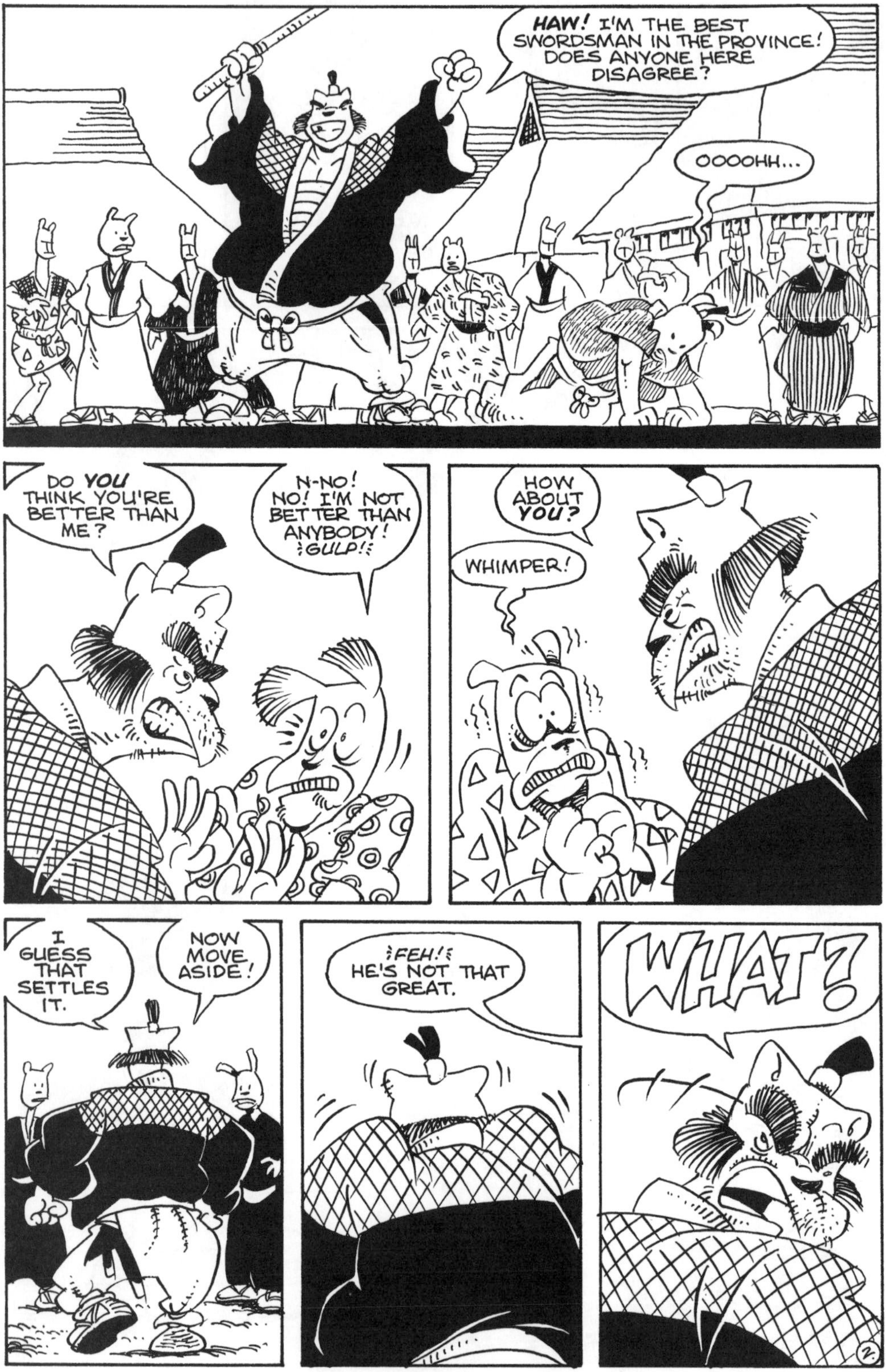
HAW! I'M THE BEST SWORDSMAN IN THE PROVINCE! DOES ANYONE HERE DISAGREE?
OOOOHH...
DO YOU THINK YOU'RE BETTER THAN ME?
N-NO! NO! I'M NOT BETTER THAN ANYBODY! GULP!
HOW ABOUT YOU?
WHIMPER!
I GUESS THAT SETTLES IT.
NOW MOVE ASIDE!
FEH! HE'S NOT THAT GREAT.
WHAT?
2.

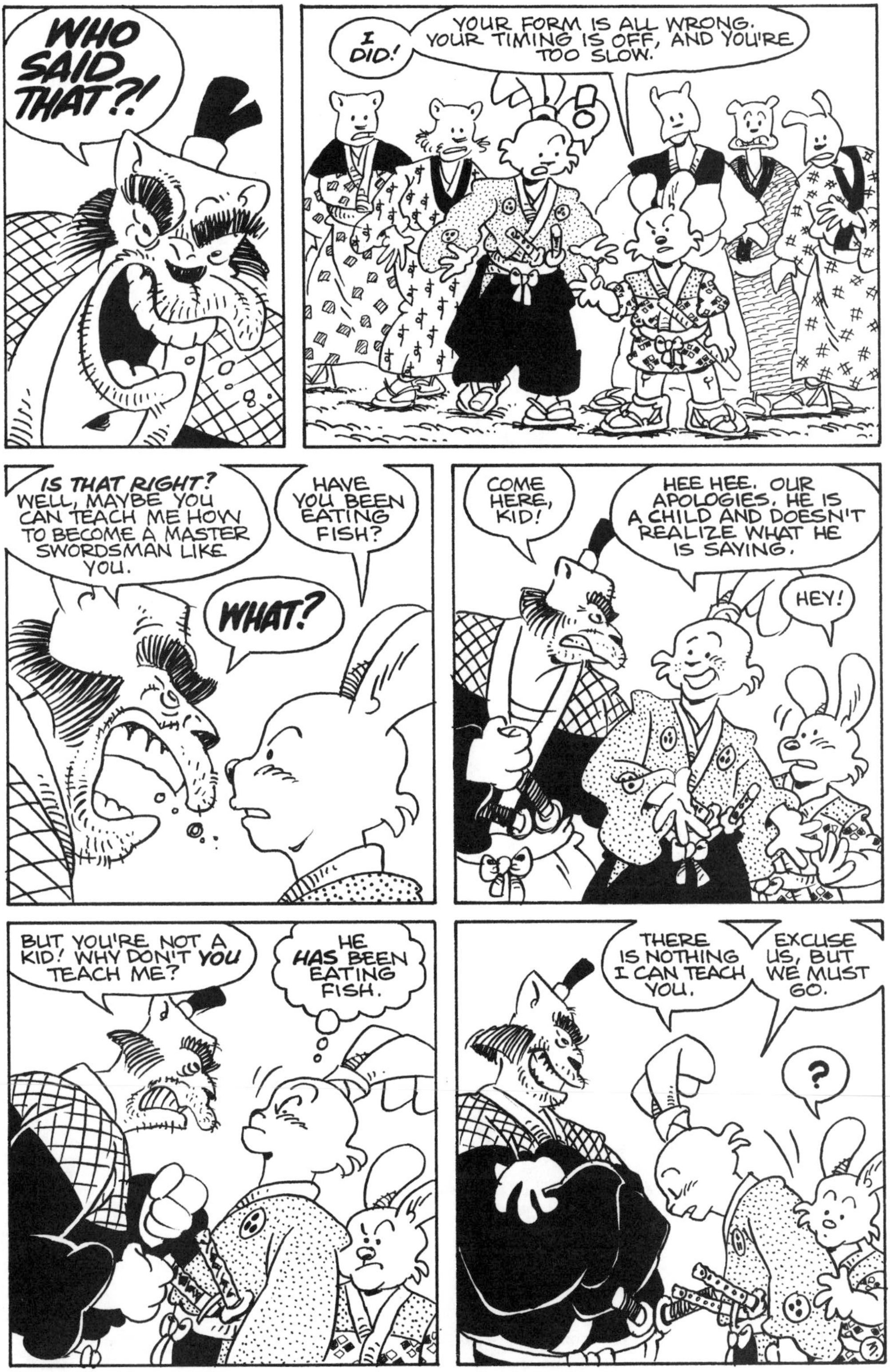
WHO SAID THAT?!
I DID!
YOUR FORM IS ALL WRONG. YOUR TIMING IS OFF, AND YOU'RE TOO SLOW.
!
IS THAT RIGHT? WELL, MAYBE YOU CAN TEACH ME HOW TO BECOME A MASTER SWORDSMAN LIKE YOU.
HAVE YOU BEEN EATING FISH?
WHAT?
COME HERE, KID!
HEE HEE. OUR APOLOGIES. HE IS A CHILD AND DOESN'T REALIZE WHAT HE IS SAYING.
HEY!
BUT YOU'RE NOT A KID! WHY DON'T YOU TEACH ME?
HE HAS BEEN EATING FISH.
THERE IS NOTHING I CAN TEACH YOU.
EXCUSE US, BUT WE MUST GO.
?

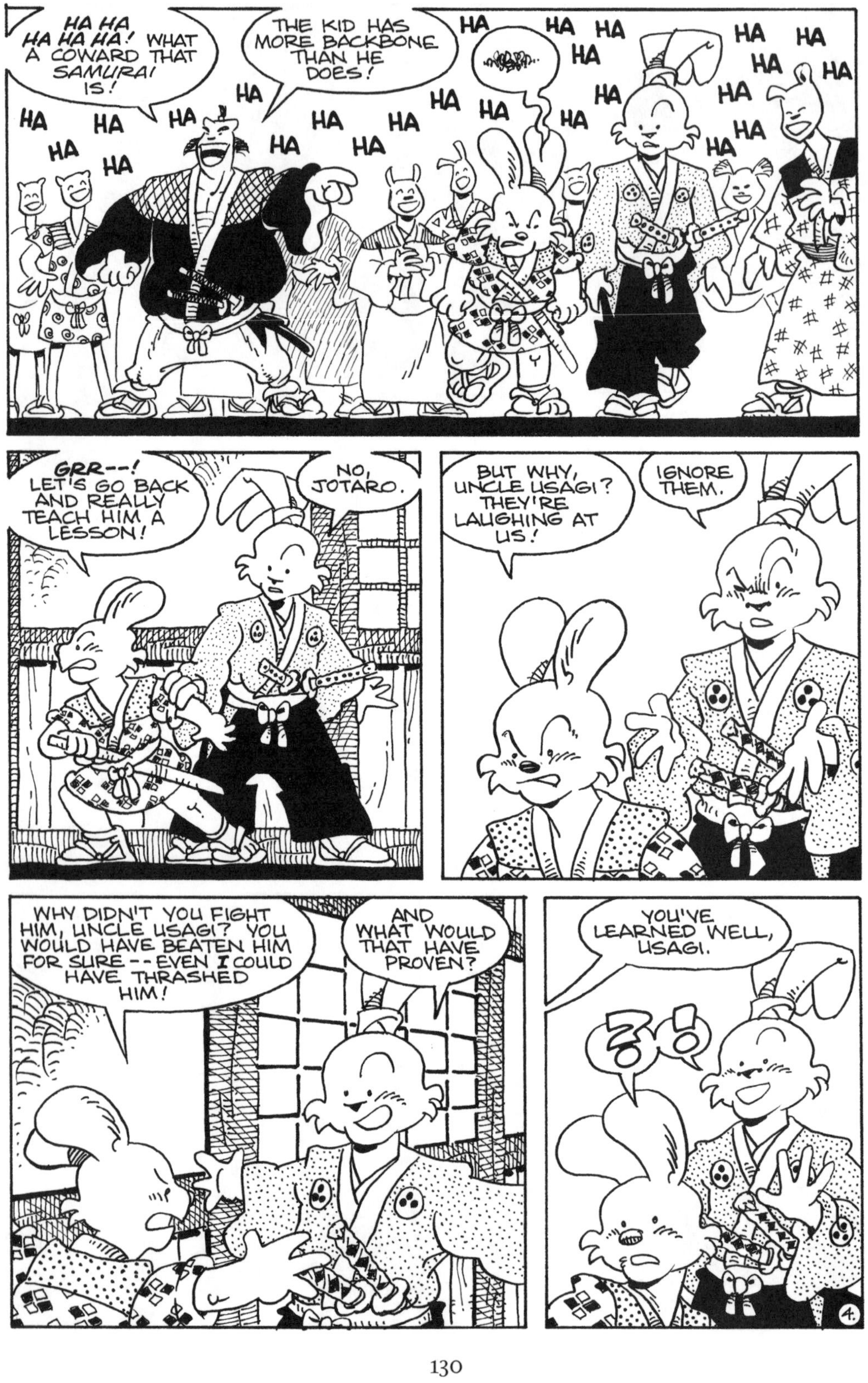
HA HA, HA HA HA! WHAT A COWARD THAT SAMURAI IS!
THE KID HAS MORE BACKBONE THAN HE DOES!
HA HA HA HA HA HA HA HA HA HA HA HA HA HA HA HA HA HA HA HA HA HA HA
GRR--! LET'S GO BACK AND REALLY TEACH HIM A LESSON!
NO, JOTARO.
BUT WHY, UNCLE USAGI? THEY'RE LAUGHING AT US!
IGNORE THEM.
WHY DIDN'T YOU FIGHT HIM, UNCLE USAGI? YOU WOULD HAVE BEATEN HIM FOR SURE--EVEN I COULD HAVE THRASHED HIM!
AND WHAT WOULD THAT HAVE PROVEN?
YOU'VE LEARNED WELL, USAGI.
?!
4.

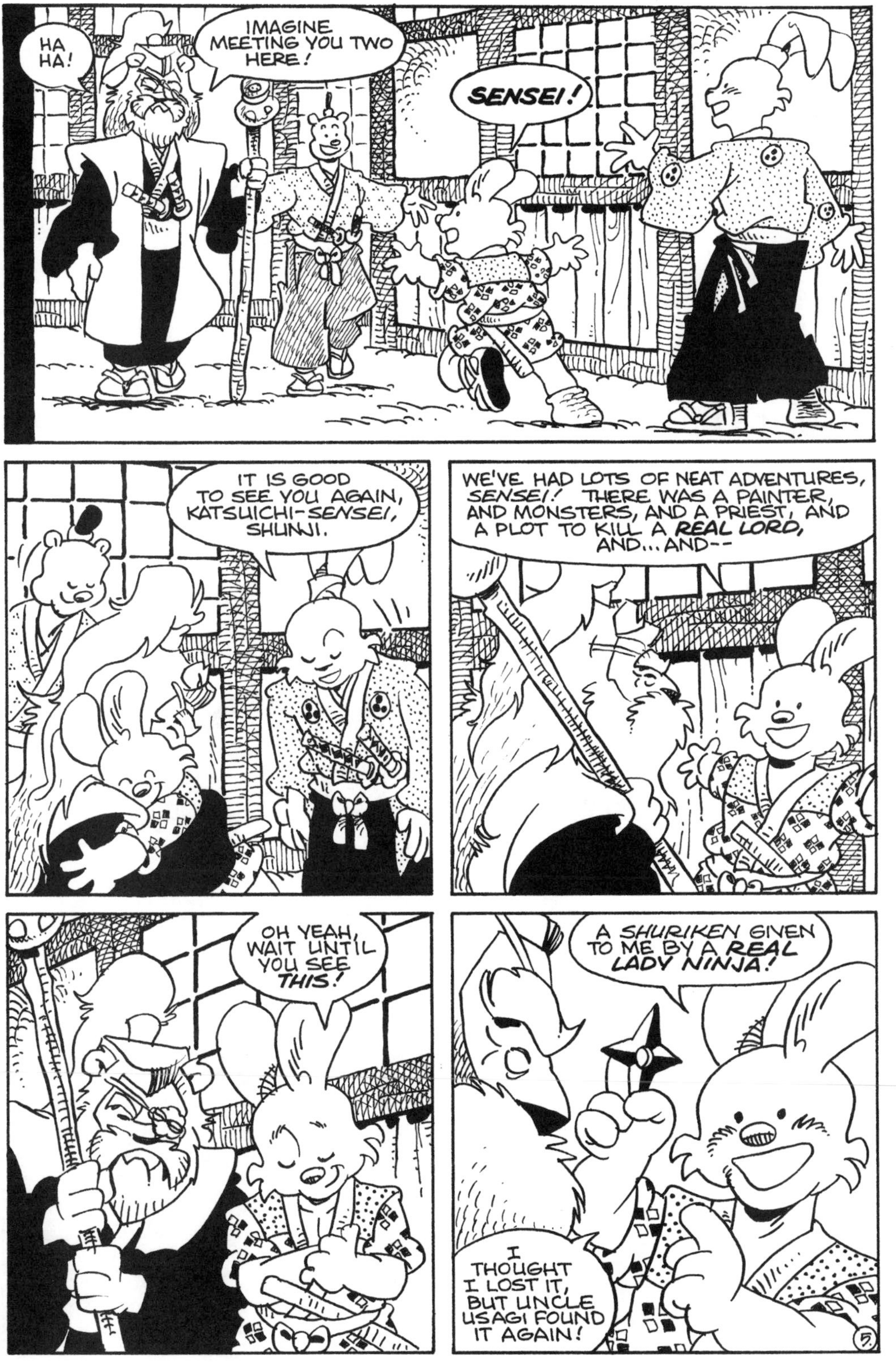
HA HA!
IMAGINE MEETING YOU TWO HERE!
SENSEI!
IT IS GOOD TO SEE YOU AGAIN, KATSUICHI-SENSEI, SHUNJI.
WE'VE HAD LOTS OF NEAT ADVENTURES, SENSEI! THERE WAS A PAINTER, AND MONSTERS, AND A PRIEST, AND A PLOT TO KILL A REAL LORD, AND... AND--
OH YEAH, WAIT UNTIL YOU SEE THIS!
A SHURIKEN GIVEN TO ME BY A REAL LADY NINJA!
I THOUGHT I LOST IT, BUT UNCLE USAGI FOUND IT AGAIN!
5.

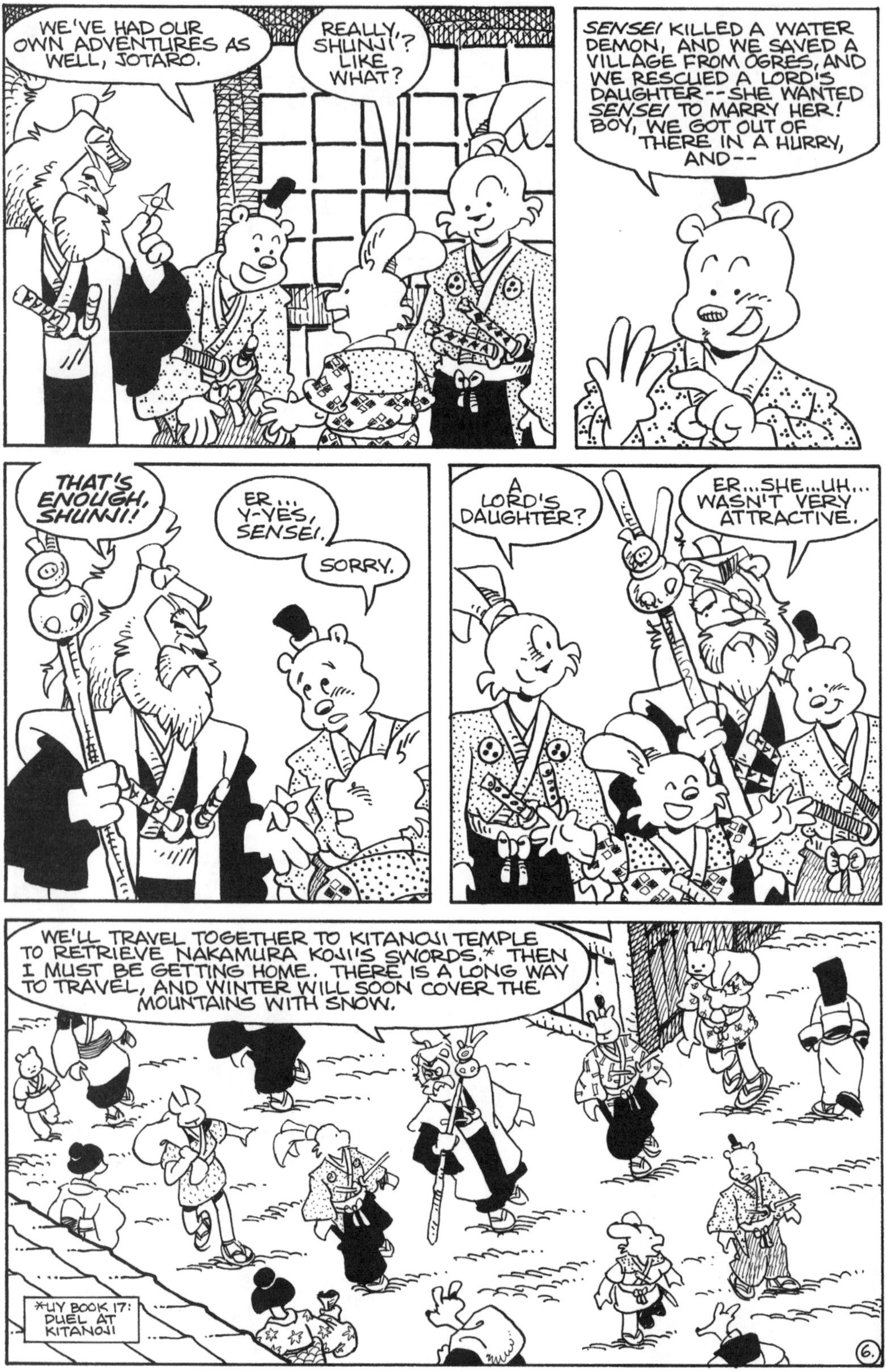
WE'VE HAD OUR OWN ADVENTURES AS WELL, JOTARO.
REALLY, SHUNJI? LIKE WHAT?
SENSEI KILLED A WATER DEMON, AND WE SAVED A VILLAGE FROM OGRES, AND WE RESCUED A LORD'S DAUGHTER--SHE WANTED SENSEI TO MARRY HER! BOY, WE GOT OUT OF THERE IN A HURRY, AND--
THAT'S ENOUGH, SHUNJI!
ER... Y-YES, SENSEI.
SORRY.
A LORD'S DAUGHTER?
ER...SHE...UH... WASN'T VERY ATTRACTIVE.
WE'LL TRAVEL TOGETHER TO KITANOJI TEMPLE TO RETRIEVE NAKAMURA KOJI'S SWORDS.* THEN I MUST BE GETTING HOME. THERE IS A LONG WAY TO TRAVEL, AND WINTER WILL SOON COVER THE MOUNTAINS WITH SNOW.
*UY BOOK 17: DUEL AT KITANOJI
6.

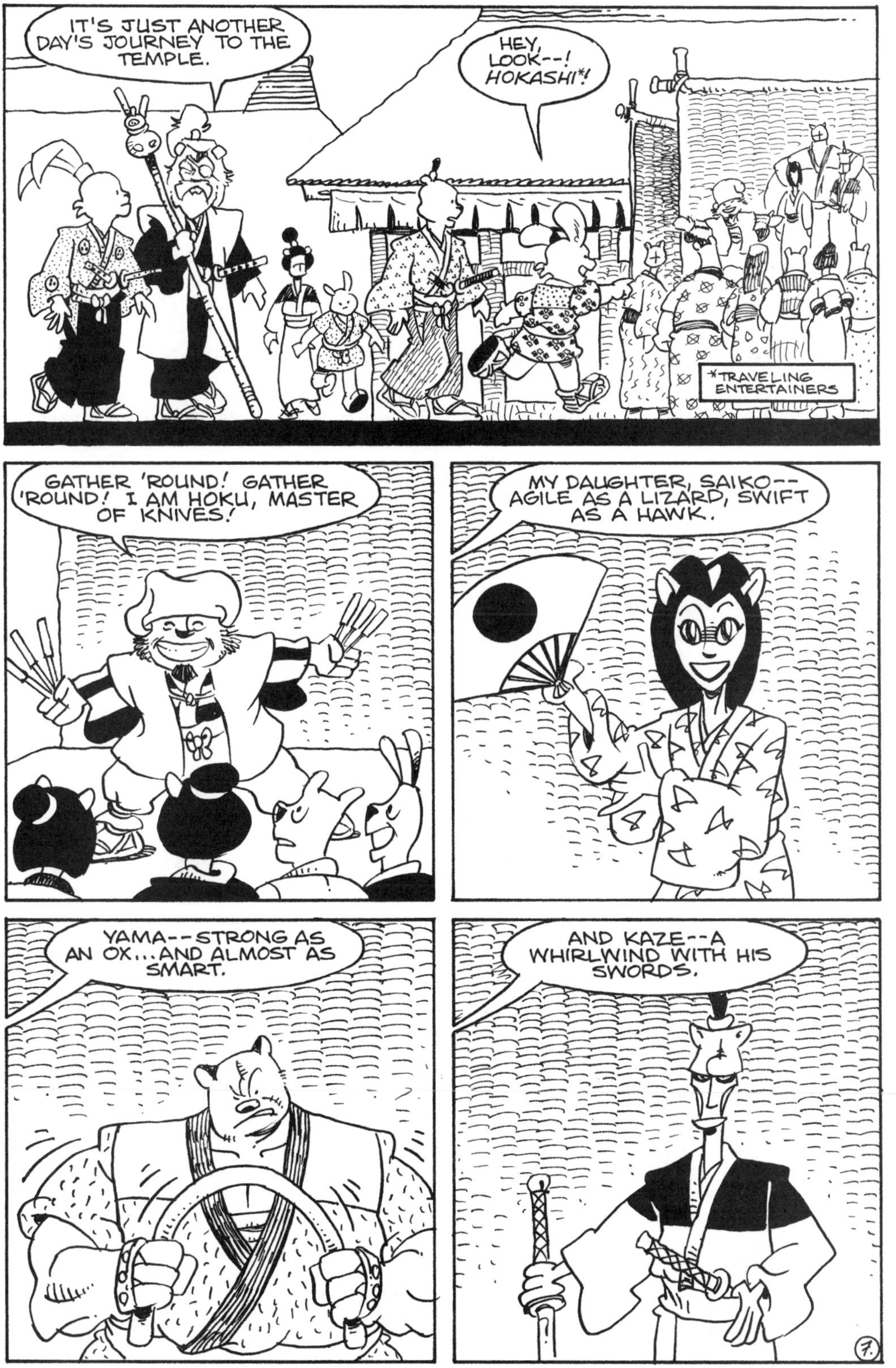
IT'S JUST ANOTHER DAY'S JOURNEY TO THE TEMPLE.
HEY, LOOK--! HOKASHI*!
*TRAVELING ENTERTAINERS
GATHER 'ROUND! GATHER 'ROUND! I AM HOKU, MASTER OF KNIVES!
MY DAUGHTER, SAIKO-- AGILE AS A LIZARD, SWIFT AS A HAWK.
YAMA--STRONG AS AN OX...AND ALMOST AS SMART.
AND KAZE--A WHIRLWIND WITH HIS SWORDS.
7.

GATHER 'ROUND AND SEE A PREVIEW OF OUR ACT!

I WANT TO SEE! LET'S GET TO THE FRONT!

MARVEL AT KAZE'S SKILL!

A PEACH-- THE IMPERIAL FRUIT!

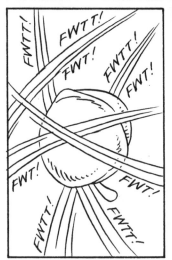

FWTT! FWT! FWTT! FWT! FWT! FWTT! FWT!

HA! HE MISSED!

THUD!

PLOP! PLOP! PLOP! PLOP! PLOP! PLOP!

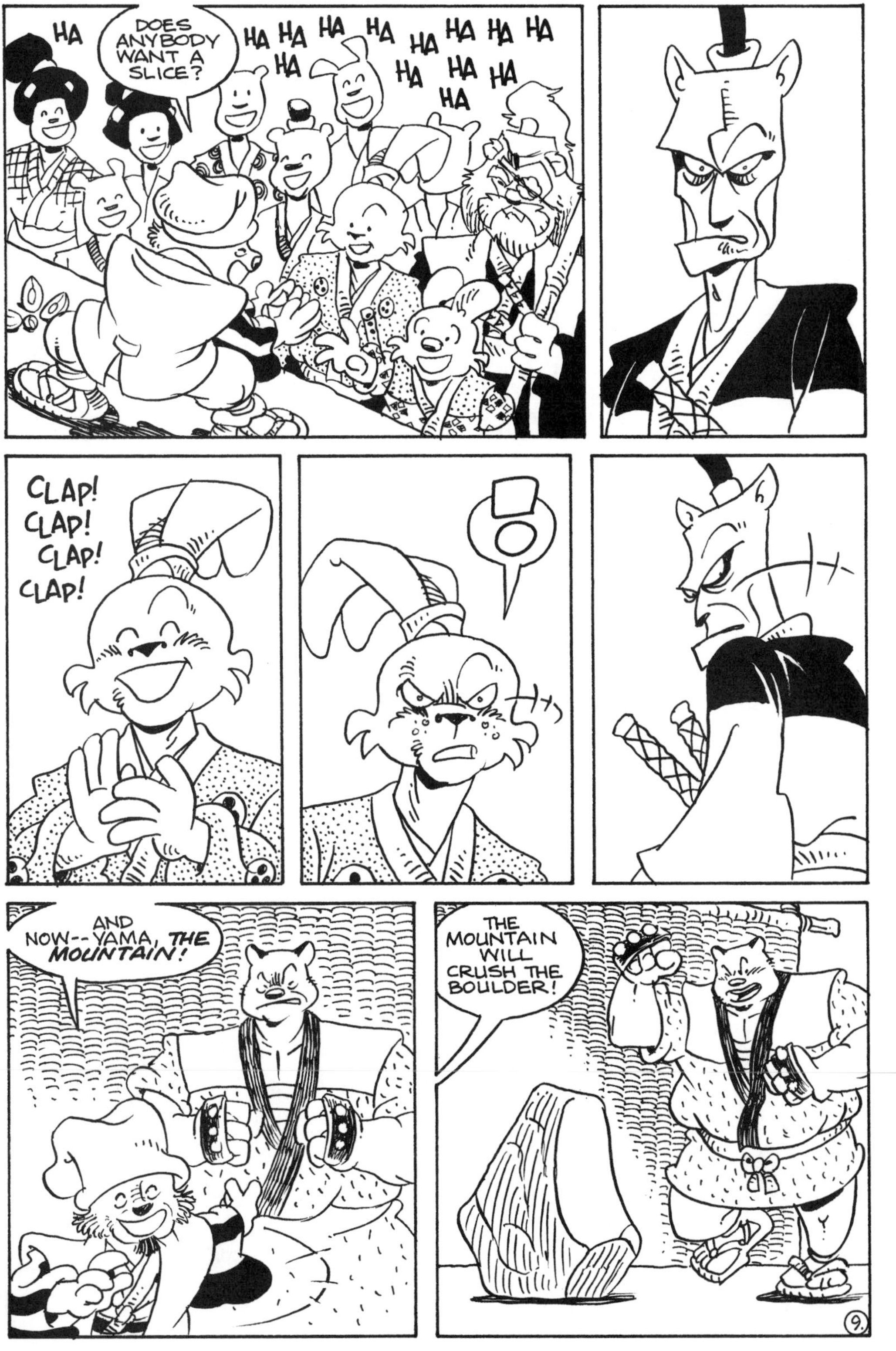
HA
DOES ANYBODY WANT A SLICE?
HA HA HA HA HA HA HA HA HA HA HA HA HA
CLAP! CLAP! CLAP! CLAP!
AND NOW--YAMA, THE MOUNTAIN!
THE MOUNTAIN WILL CRUSH THE BOULDER!
9.

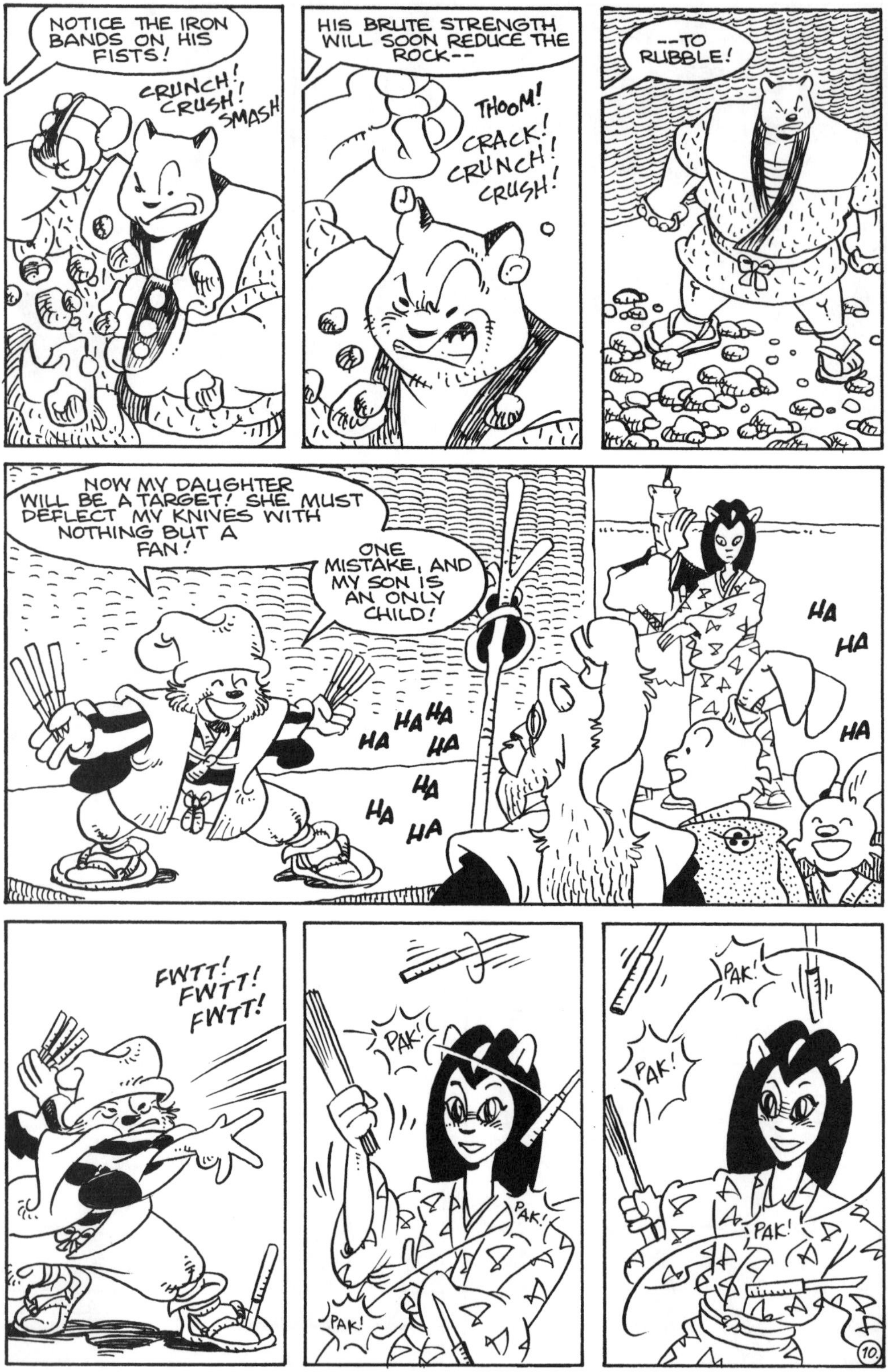
NOTICE THE IRON BANDS ON HIS FISTS!
CRUNCH! CRUSH! SMASH!
HIS BRUTE STRENGTH WILL SOON REDUCE THE ROCK--
THOOM! CRACK! CRUNCH! CRUSH!
--TO RUBBLE!
NOW MY DAUGHTER WILL BE A TARGET! SHE MUST DEFLECT MY KNIVES WITH NOTHING BUT A FAN!
ONE MISTAKE, AND MY SON IS AN ONLY CHILD!
HA HA HA HA HA HA HA
HA HA HA
FWTT! FWTT! FWTT!
PAK! PAK! PAK!
PAK! PAK! PAK!
10.

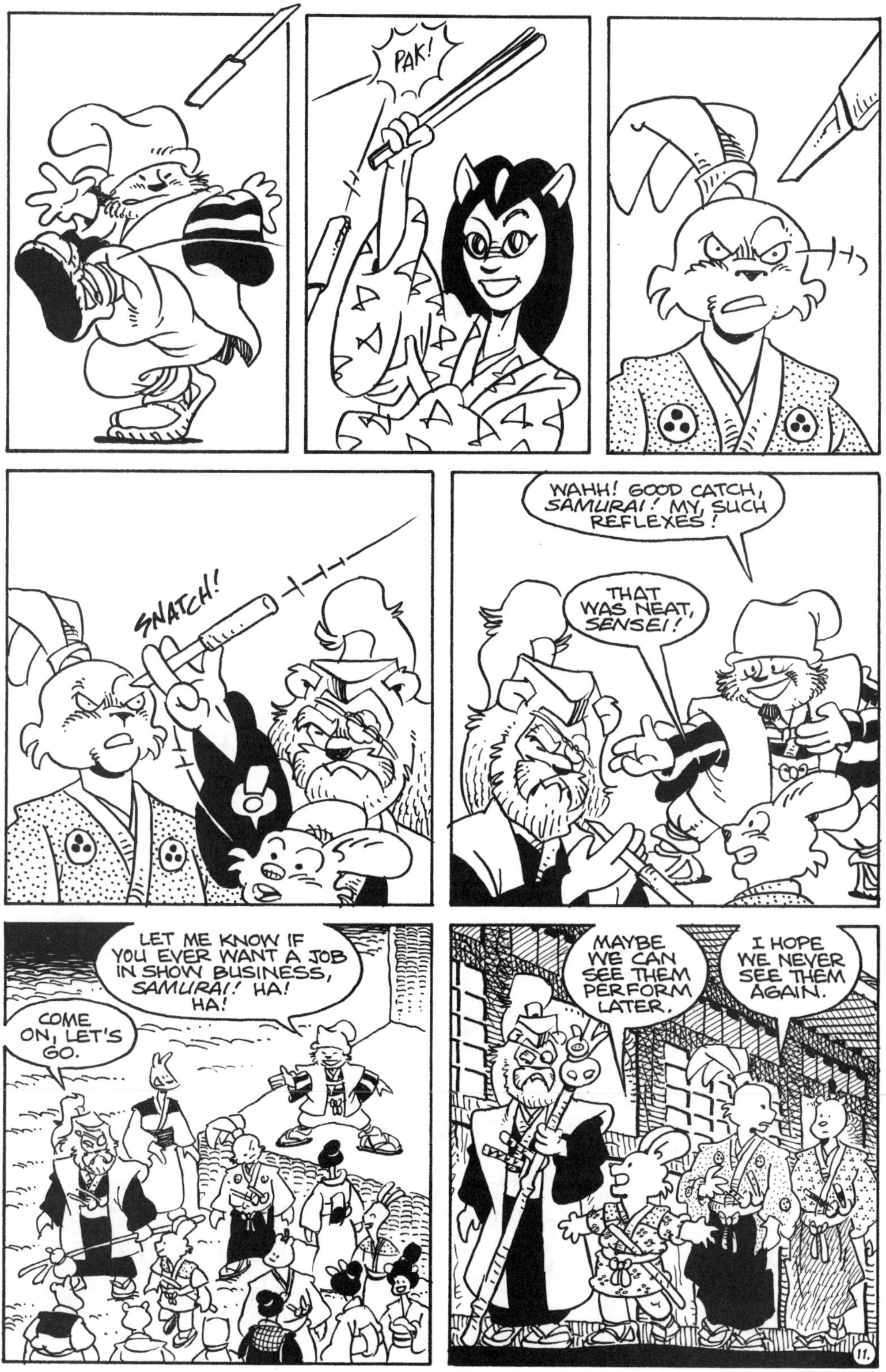
PAK!
SNATCH!
WAHH! GOOD CATCH, SAMURAI! MY, SUCH REFLEXES!
THAT WAS NEAT, SENSEI!
LET ME KNOW IF YOU EVER WANT A JOB IN SHOW BUSINESS, SAMURAI! HA! HA!
COME ON, LET'S GO.
MAYBE WE CAN SEE THEM PERFORM LATER.
I HOPE WE NEVER SEE THEM AGAIN.
11.

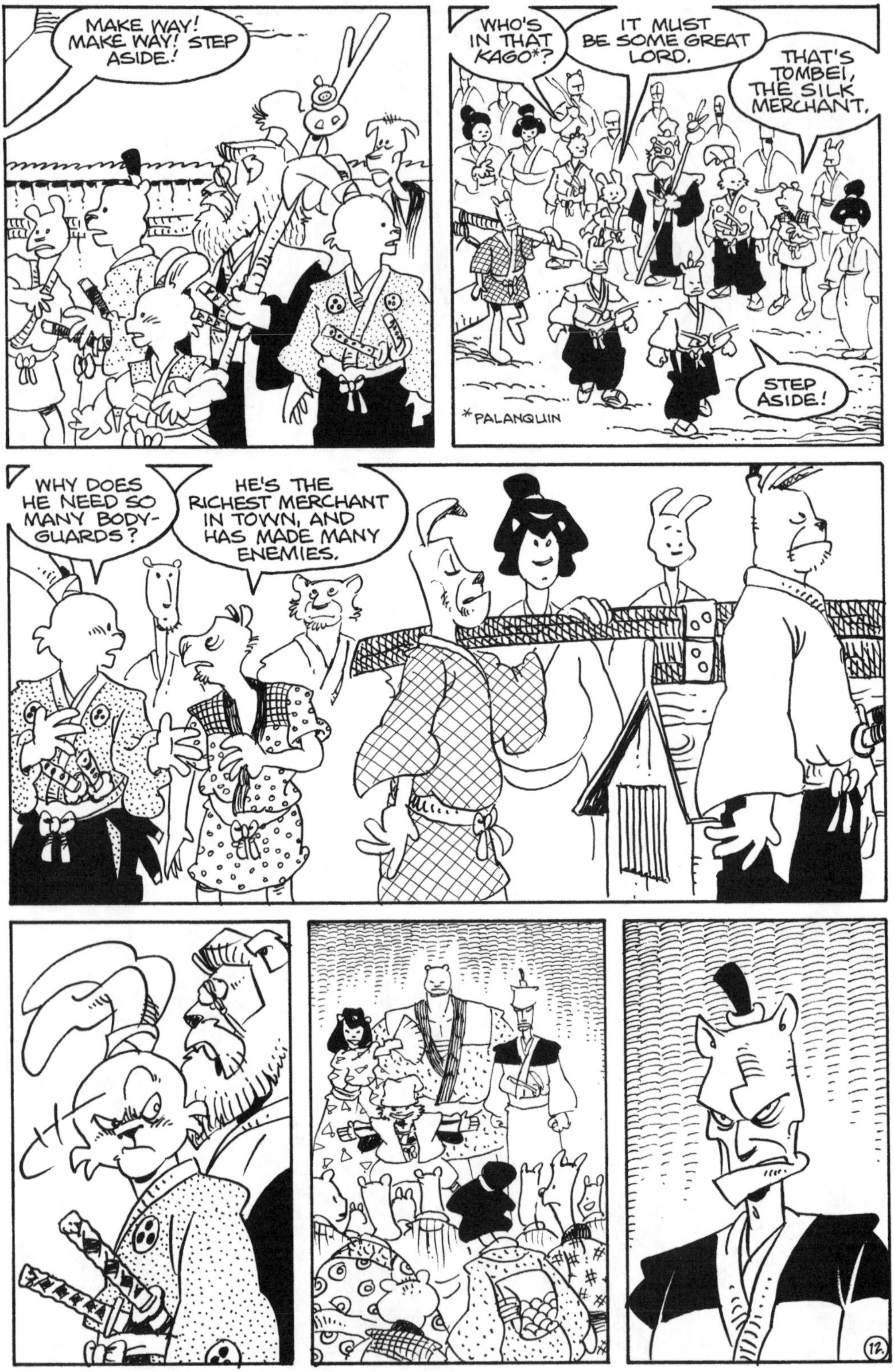
MAKE WAY! MAKE WAY! STEP ASIDE!
WHO'S IN THAT KAGO*?
IT MUST BE SOME GREAT LORD.
THAT'S TOMBEI, THE SILK MERCHANT.
STEP ASIDE!
*PALANQUIN
WHY DOES HE NEED SO MANY BODY-GUARDS?
HE'S THE RICHEST MERCHANT IN TOWN, AND HAS MADE MANY ENEMIES.
12.

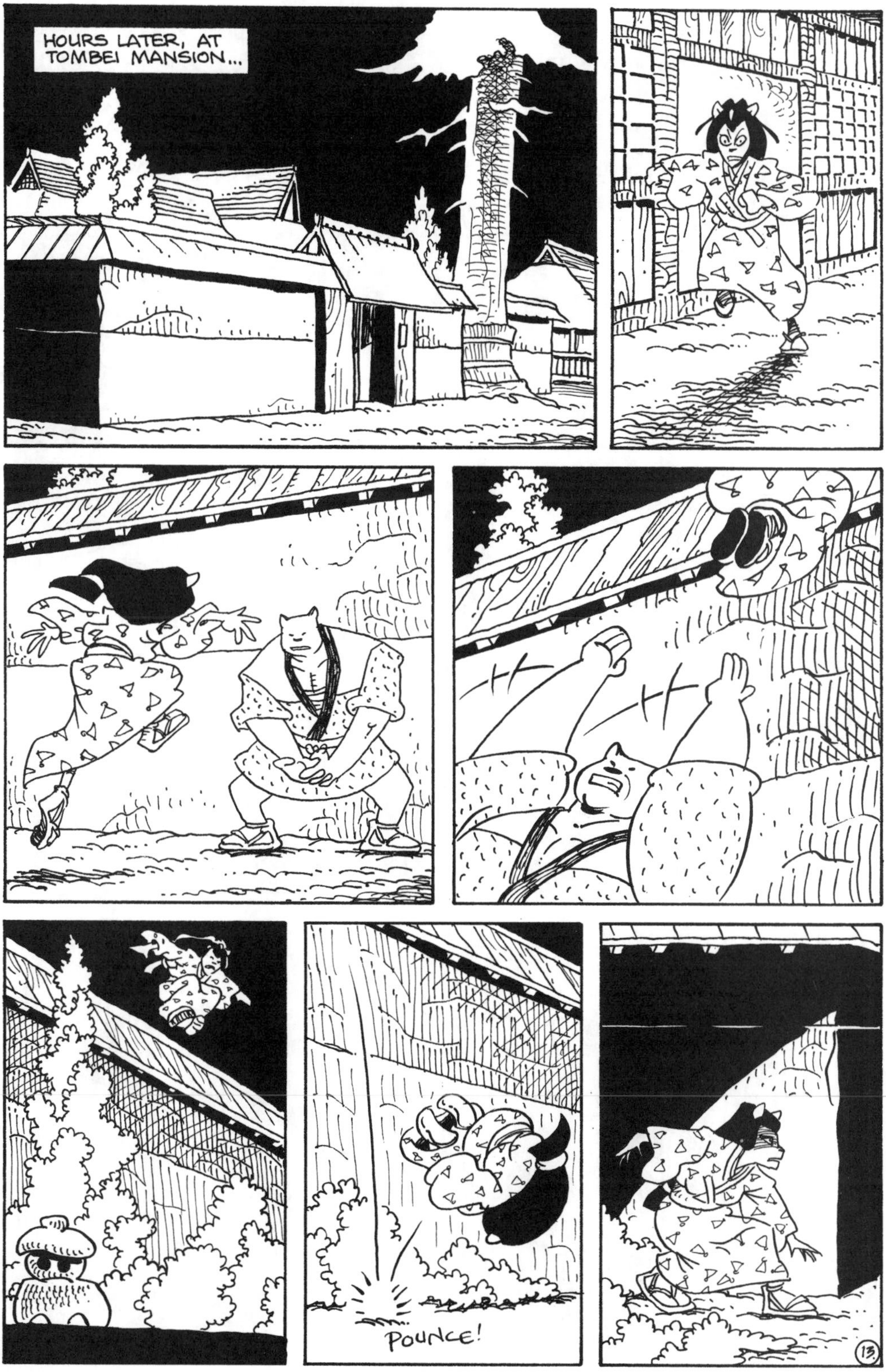
HOURS LATER, AT TOMBEI MANSION...
POUNCE!
13

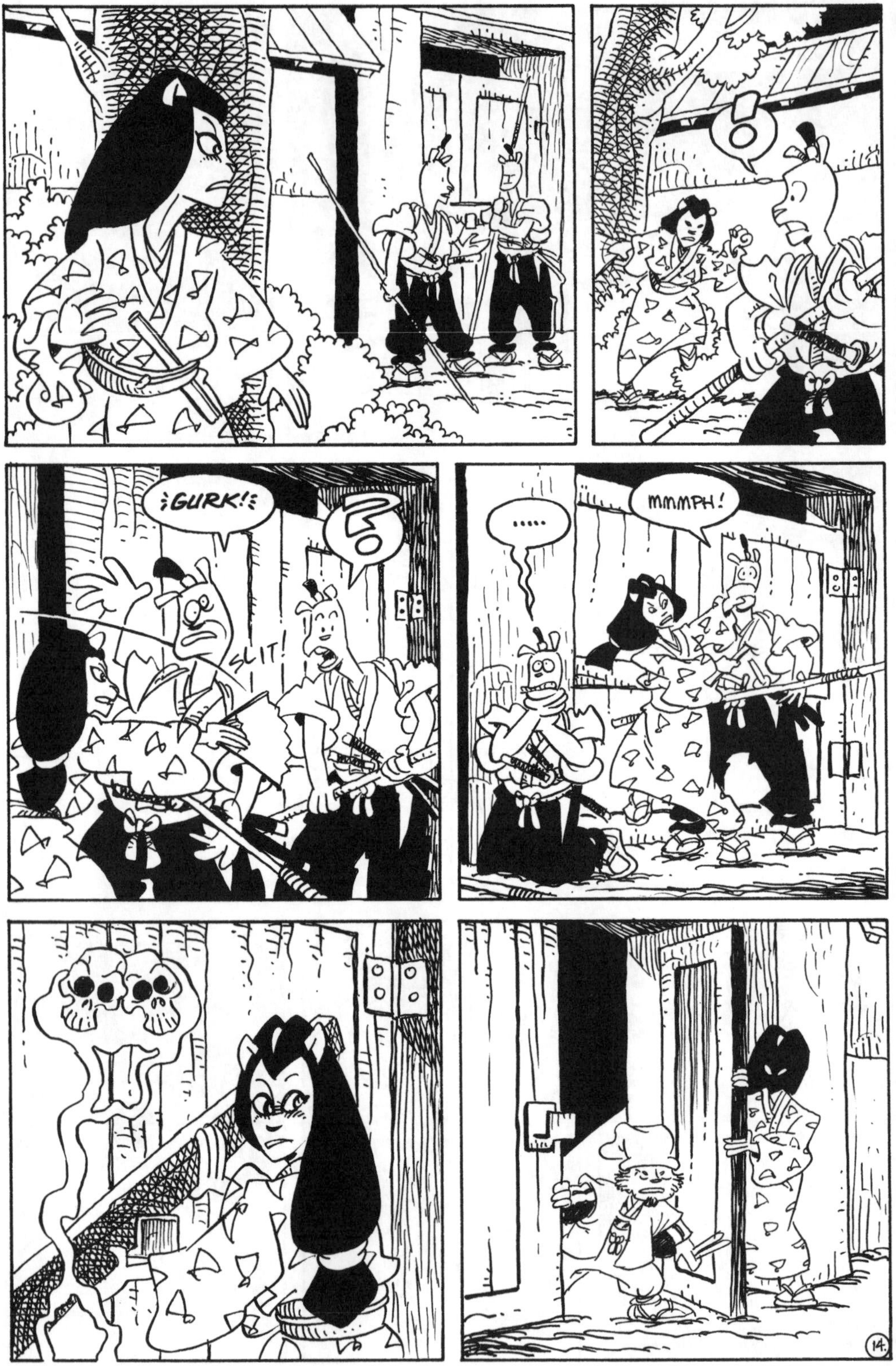
!
?
¡GURK!¡
?
SLIT!
.....
MMMPH!
14.

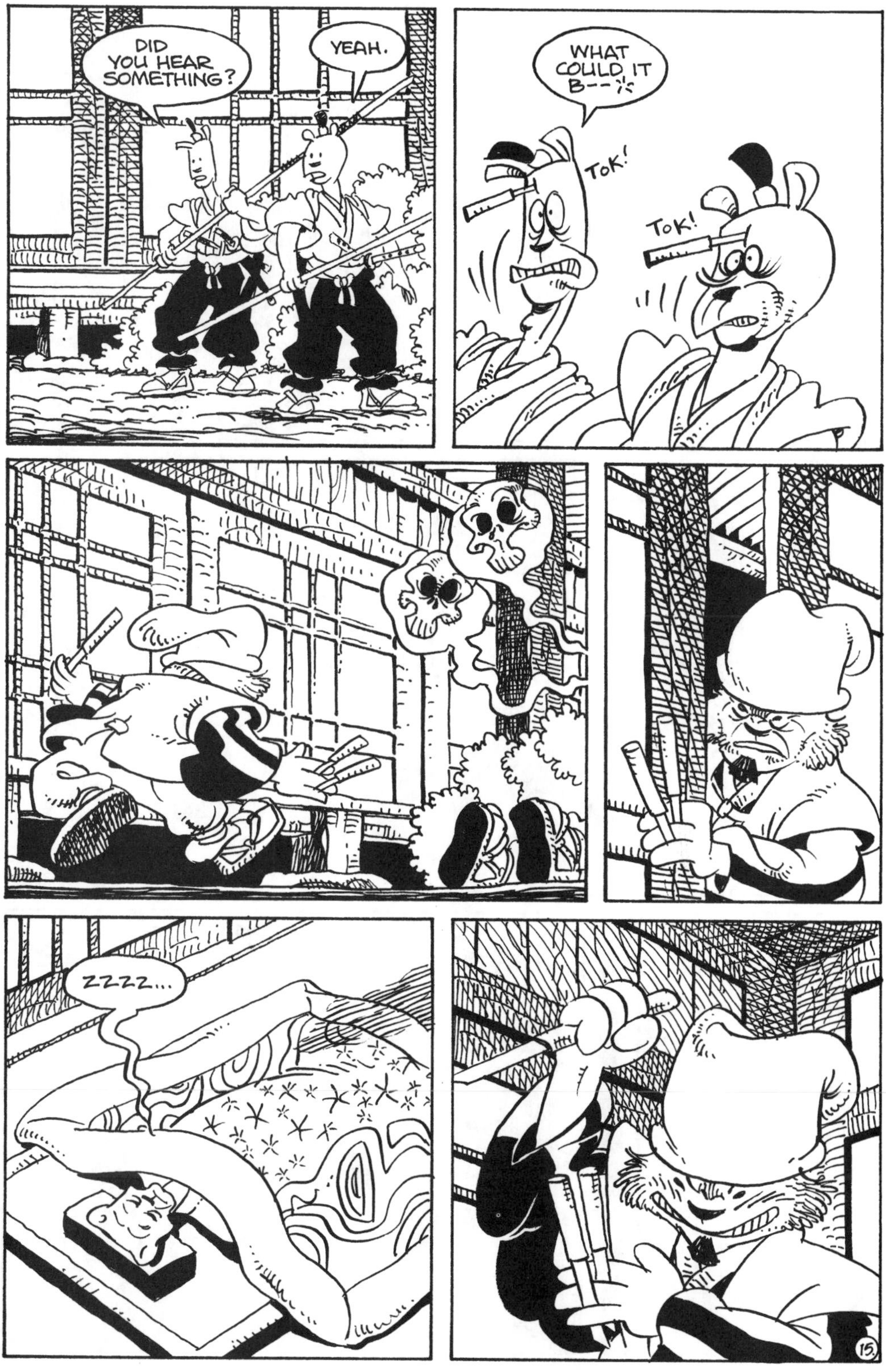
DID YOU HEAR SOMETHING?
YEAH.
WHAT COULD IT B--
TOK!
TOK!
ZZZZ...
15

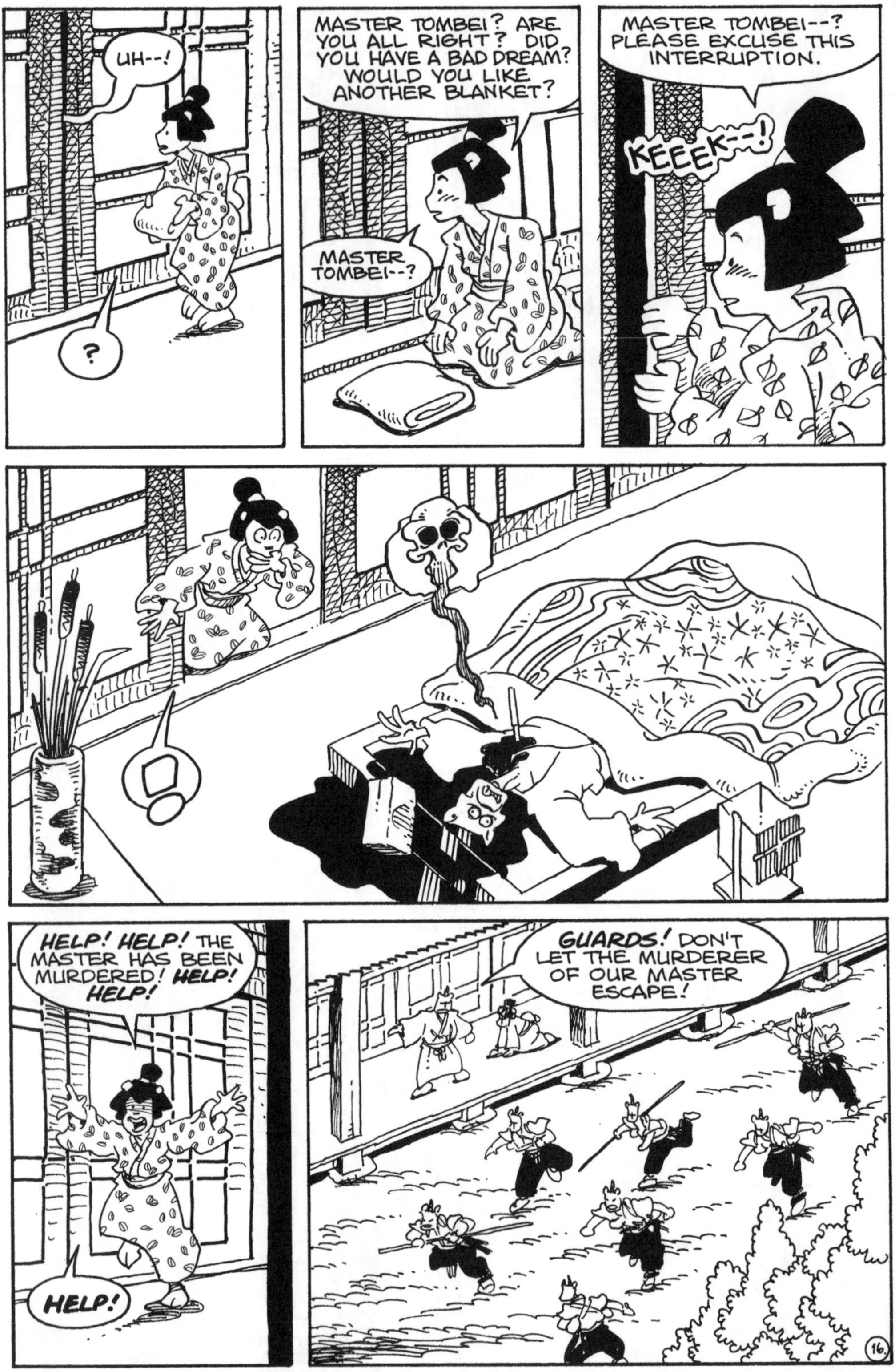
UH--!
?
MASTER TOMBEI? ARE YOU ALL RIGHT? DID YOU HAVE A BAD DREAM? WOULD YOU LIKE ANOTHER BLANKET?
MASTER TOMBEI--?
MASTER TOMBEI--? PLEASE EXCUSE THIS INTERRUPTION.
KEEEK--!
HELP! HELP! THE MASTER HAS BEEN MURDERED! HELP! HELP!
HELP!
GUARDS! DON'T LET THE MURDERER OF OUR MASTER ESCAPE!
16.

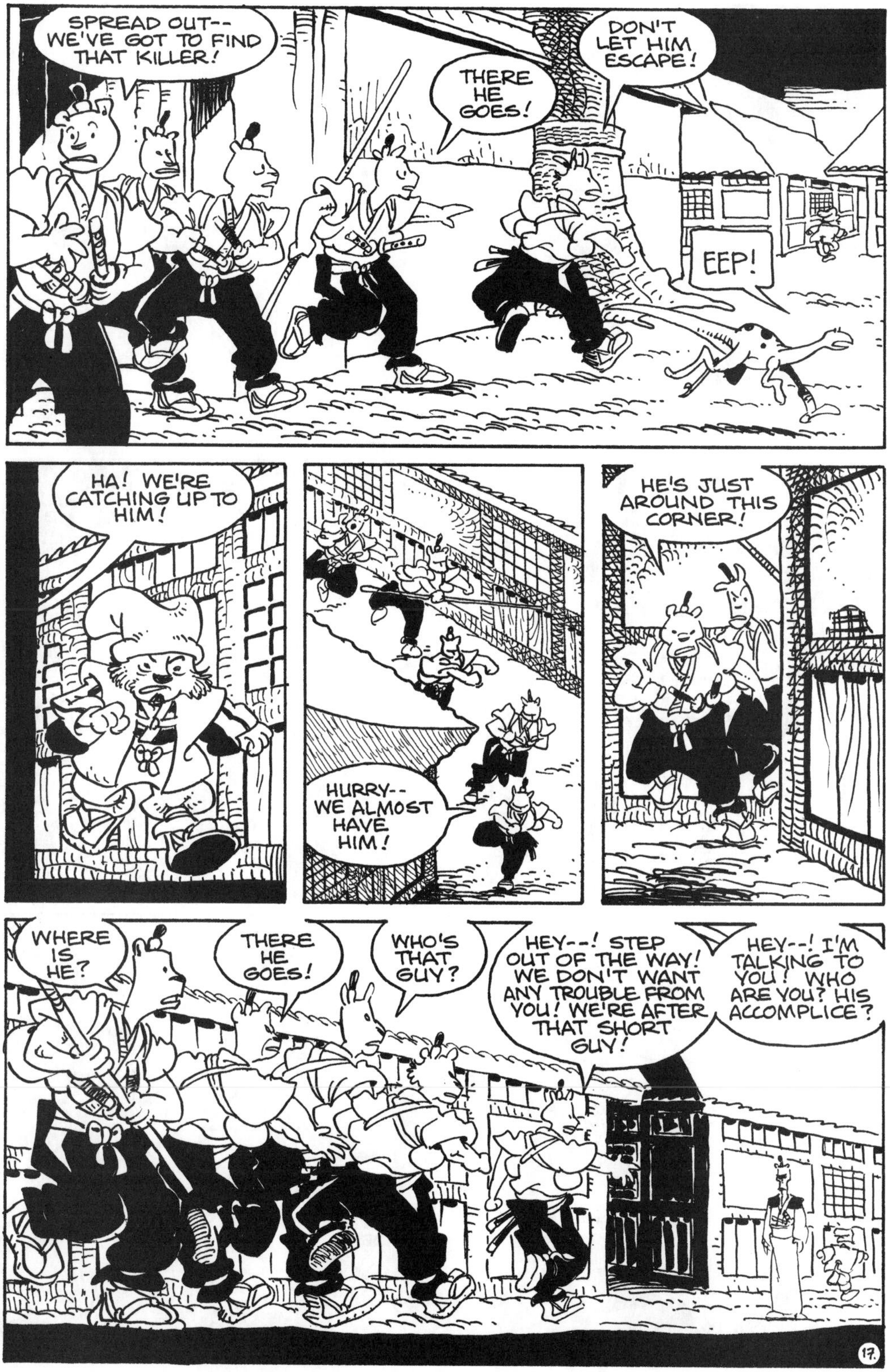
SPREAD OUT-- WE'VE GOT TO FIND THAT KILLER!
THERE HE GOES!
DON'T LET HIM ESCAPE!
EEP!
HA! WE'RE CATCHING UP TO HIM!
HURRY-- WE ALMOST HAVE HIM!
HE'S JUST AROUND THIS CORNER!
WHERE IS HE?
THERE HE GOES!
WHO'S THAT GUY?
HEY--! STEP OUT OF THE WAY! WE DON'T WANT ANY TROUBLE FROM YOU! WE'RE AFTER THAT SHORT GUY!
HEY--! I'M TALKING TO YOU! WHO ARE YOU? HIS ACCOMPLICE?
17.

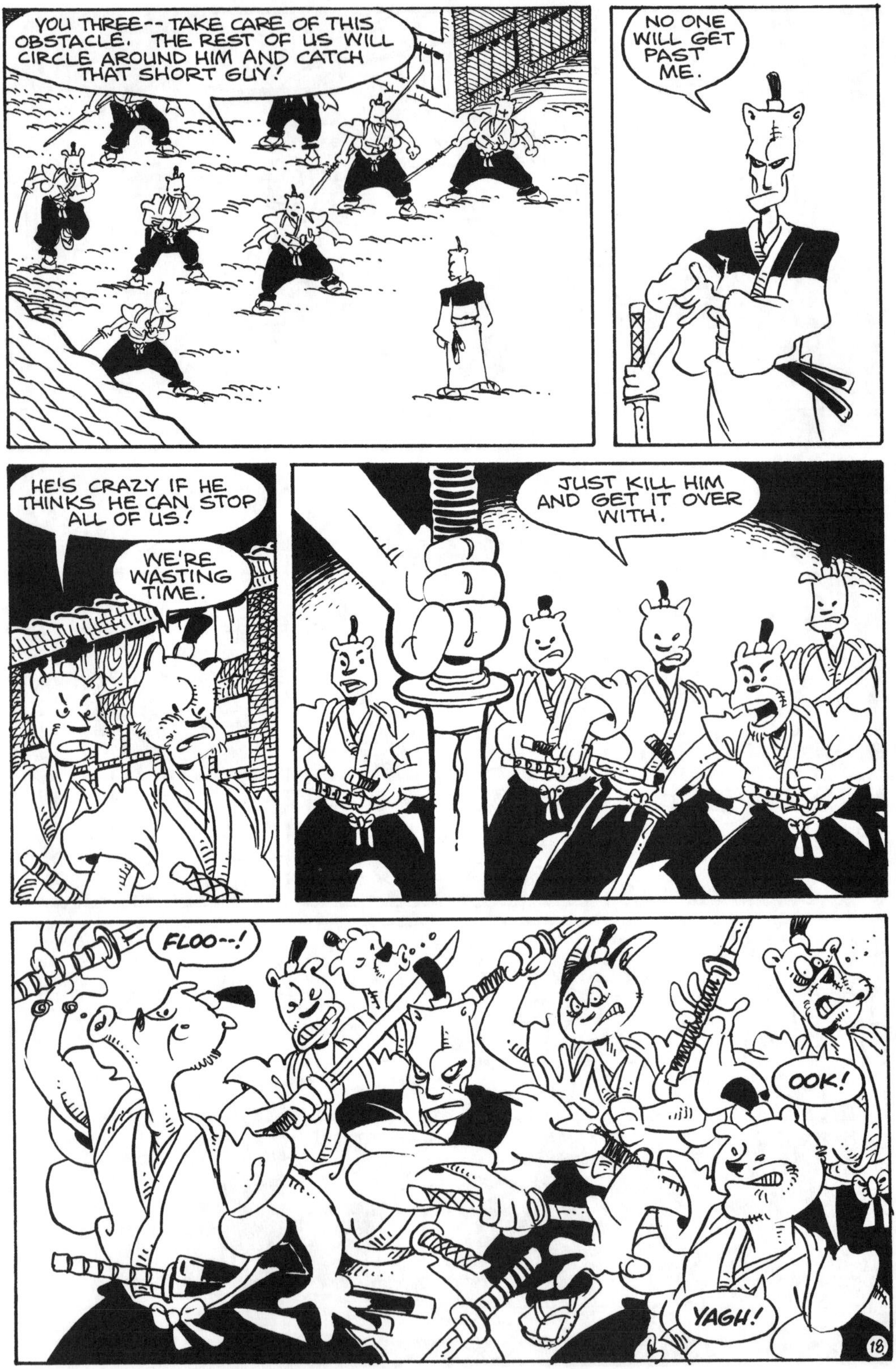
YOU THREE-- TAKE CARE OF THIS OBSTACLE. THE REST OF US WILL CIRCLE AROUND HIM AND CATCH THAT SHORT GUY!
NO ONE WILL GET PAST ME.
HE'S CRAZY IF HE THINKS HE CAN STOP ALL OF US!
WE'RE WASTING TIME.
JUST KILL HIM AND GET IT OVER WITH.
FLOO--!
OOK!
YAGH!
18

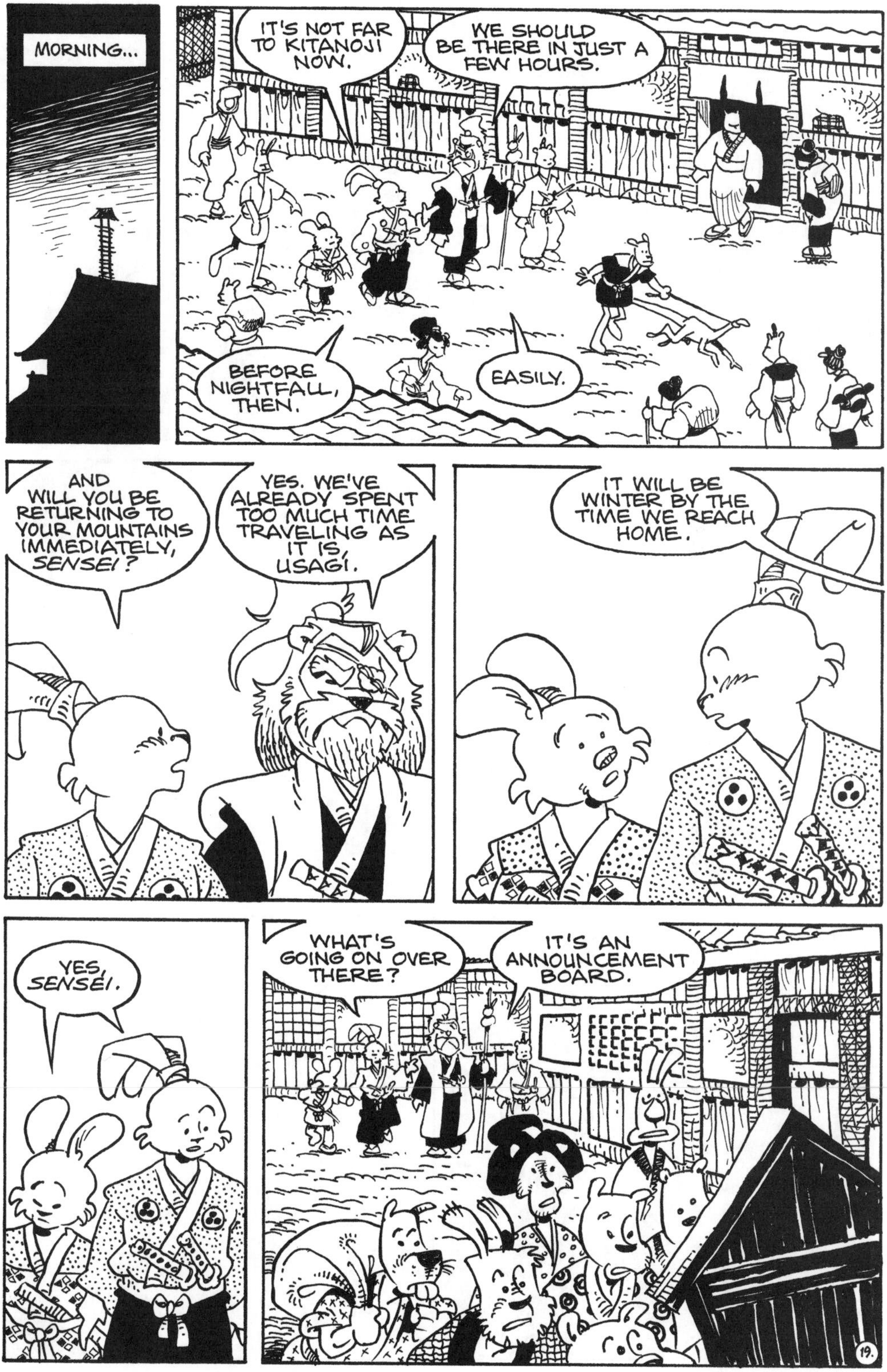
MORNING...
IT'S NOT FAR TO KITANOJI NOW.
WE SHOULD BE THERE IN JUST A FEW HOURS.
BEFORE NIGHTFALL, THEN.
EASILY.
AND WILL YOU BE RETURNING TO YOUR MOUNTAINS IMMEDIATELY, SENSEI?
YES. WE'VE ALREADY SPENT TOO MUCH TIME TRAVELING AS IT IS, USAGI.
IT WILL BE WINTER BY THE TIME WE REACH HOME.
YES, SENSEI.
WHAT'S GOING ON OVER THERE?
IT'S AN ANNOUNCEMENT BOARD.
19.

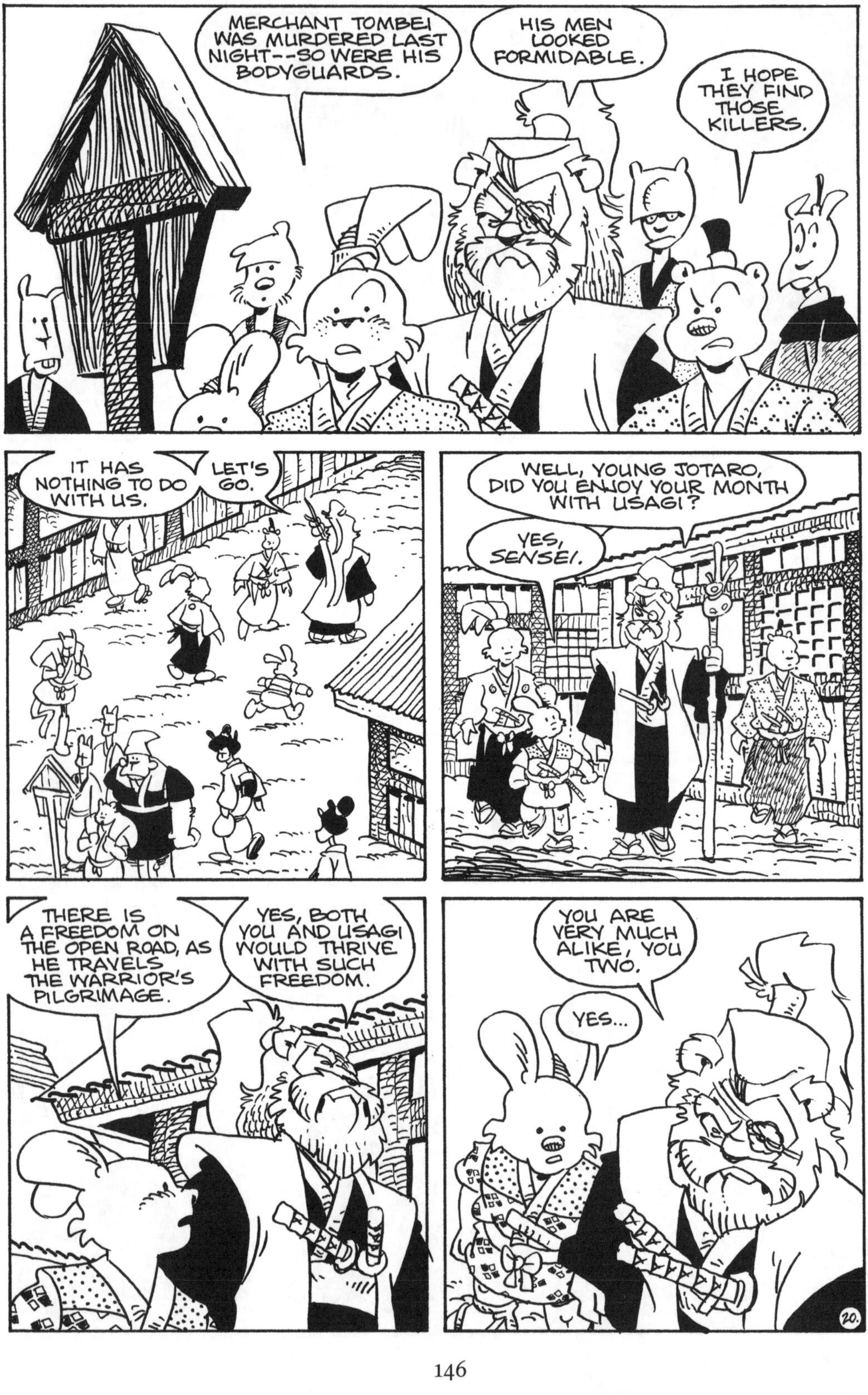

MERCHANT TOMBEI WAS MURDERED LAST NIGHT--SO WERE HIS BODYGUARDS.
HIS MEN LOOKED FORMIDABLE.
I HOPE THEY FIND THOSE KILLERS.
IT HAS NOTHING TO DO WITH US.
LET'S GO.
WELL, YOUNG JOTARO, DID YOU ENJOY YOUR MONTH WITH USAGI?
YES, SENSEI.
THERE IS A FREEDOM ON THE OPEN ROAD, AS HE TRAVELS THE WARRIOR'S PILGRIMAGE.
YES, BOTH YOU AND USAGI WOULD THRIVE WITH SUCH FREEDOM.
YOU ARE VERY MUCH ALIKE, YOU TWO.
YES...
20.

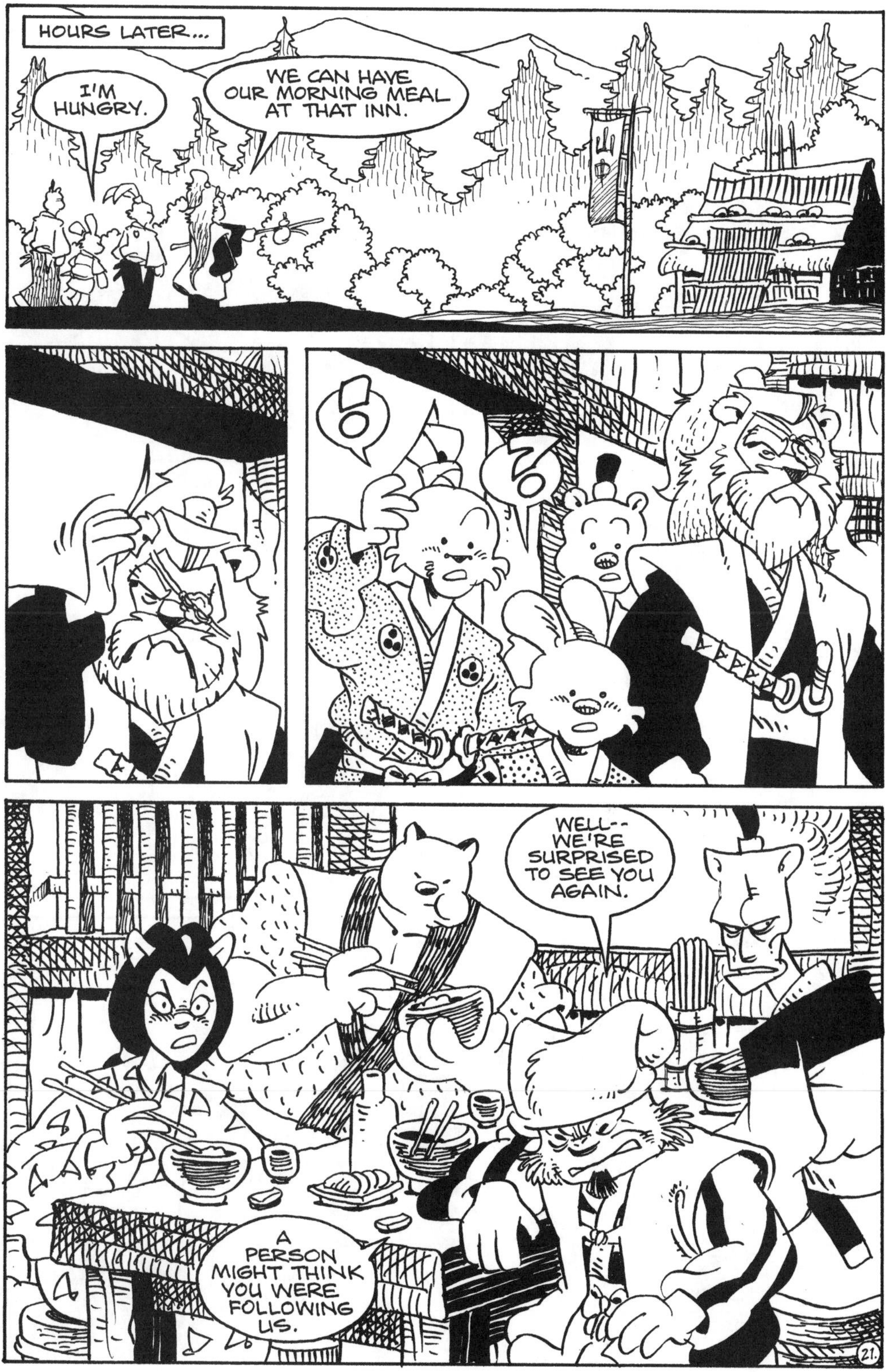
HOURS LATER...
I'M HUNGRY.
WE CAN HAVE OUR MORNING MEAL AT THAT INN.
WELL-- WE'RE SURPRISED TO SEE YOU AGAIN.
A PERSON MIGHT THINK YOU WERE FOLLOWING US.
21.

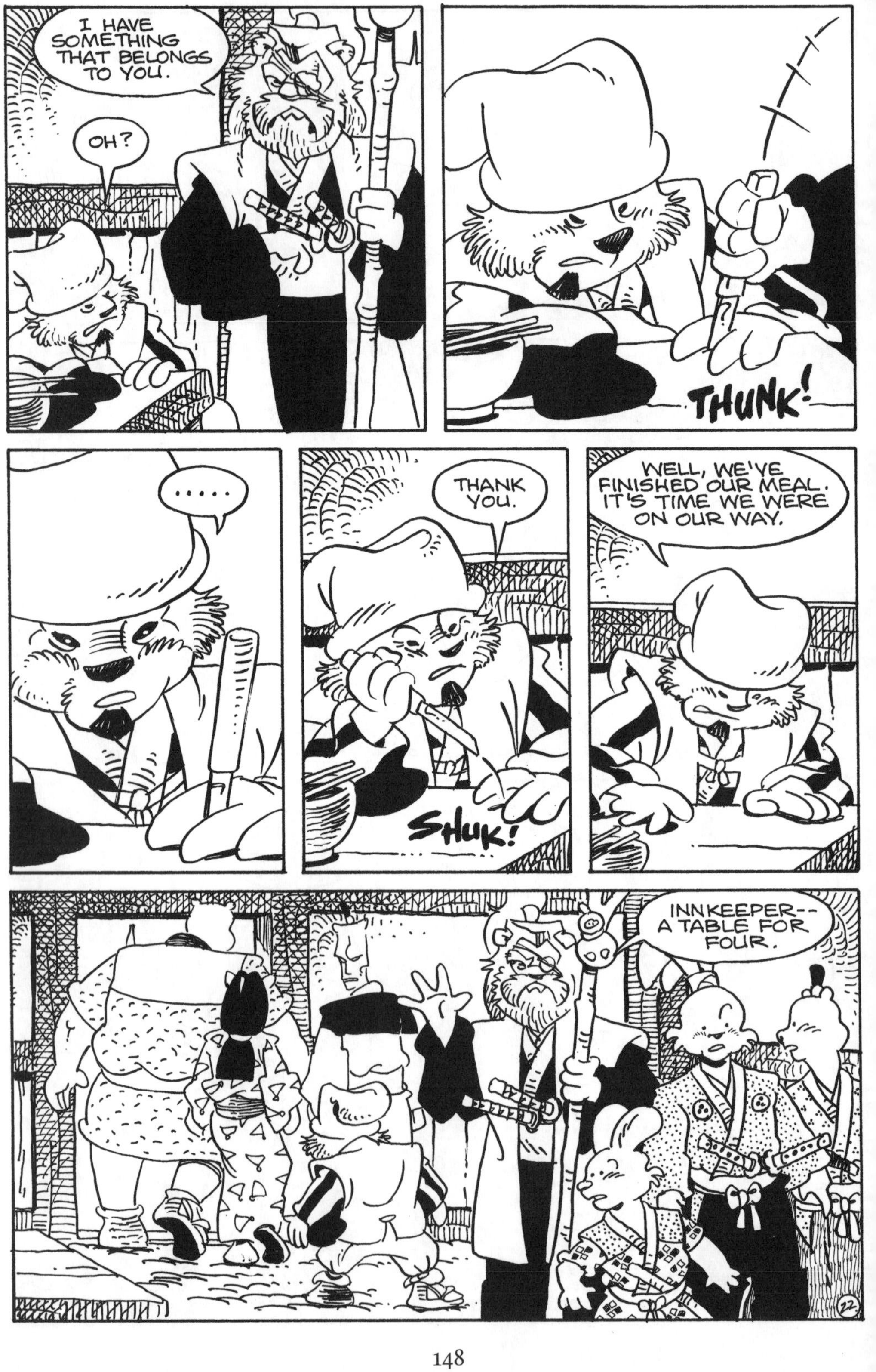
I HAVE SOMETHING THAT BELONGS TO YOU.
OH?
THUNK!
.....
THANK YOU.
SHUK!
WELL, WE'VE FINISHED OUR MEAL. IT'S TIME WE WERE ON OUR WAY.
INNKEEPER-- A TABLE FOR FOUR.
22

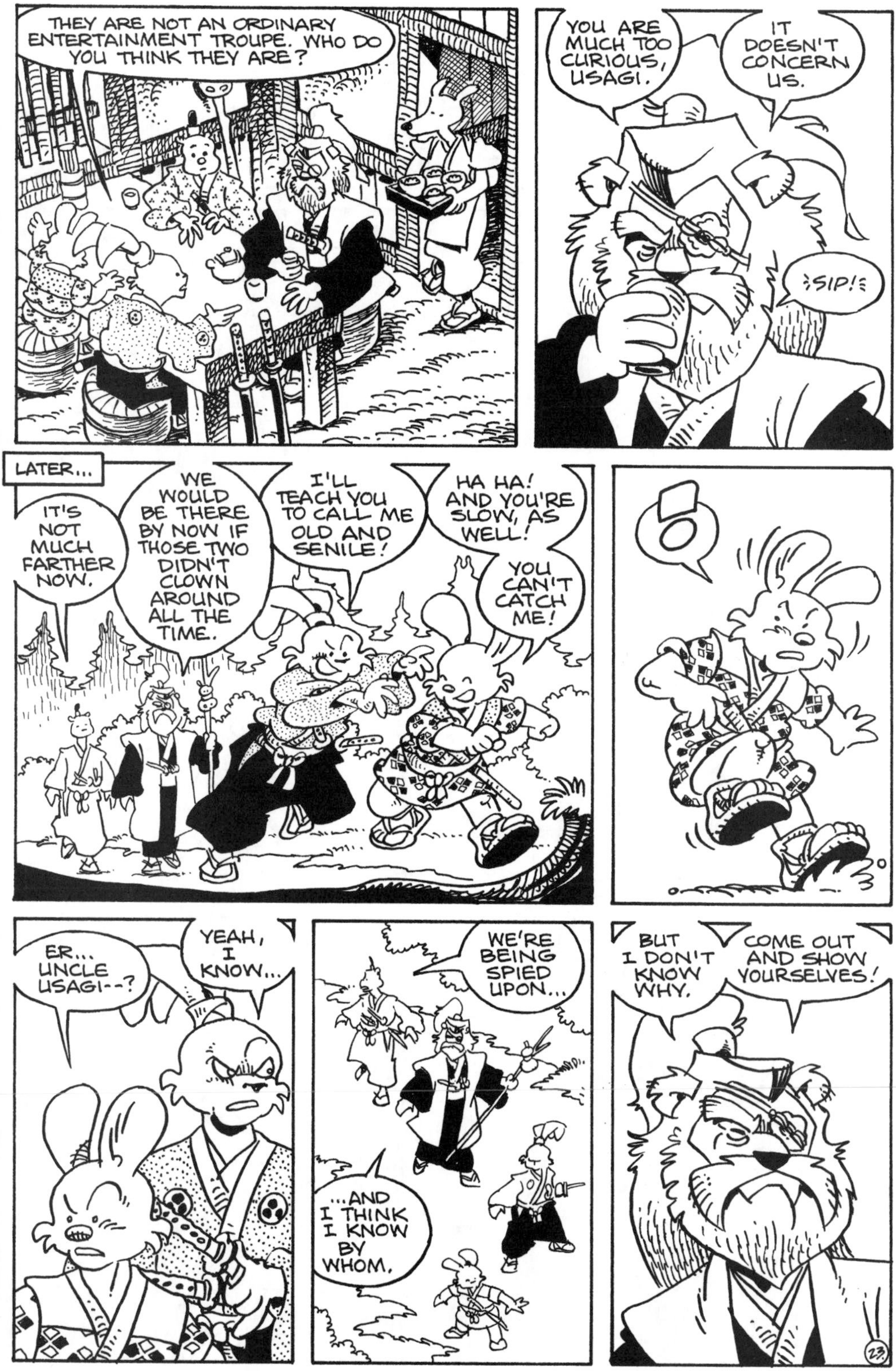
THEY ARE NOT AN ORDINARY ENTERTAINMENT TROUPE. WHO DO YOU THINK THEY ARE?
YOU ARE MUCH TOO CURIOUS, USAGI.
IT DOESN'T CONCERN US.
SIP!
LATER...
IT'S NOT MUCH FARTHER NOW.
WE WOULD BE THERE BY NOW IF THOSE TWO DIDN'T CLOWN AROUND ALL THE TIME.
I'LL TEACH YOU TO CALL ME OLD AND SENILE!
HA HA! AND YOU'RE SLOW, AS WELL!
YOU CAN'T CATCH ME!
ER... UNCLE USAGI--?
YEAH, I KNOW...
WE'RE BEING SPIED UPON...
...AND I THINK I KNOW BY WHOM.
BUT I DON'T KNOW WHY.
COME OUT AND SHOW YOURSELVES!
23

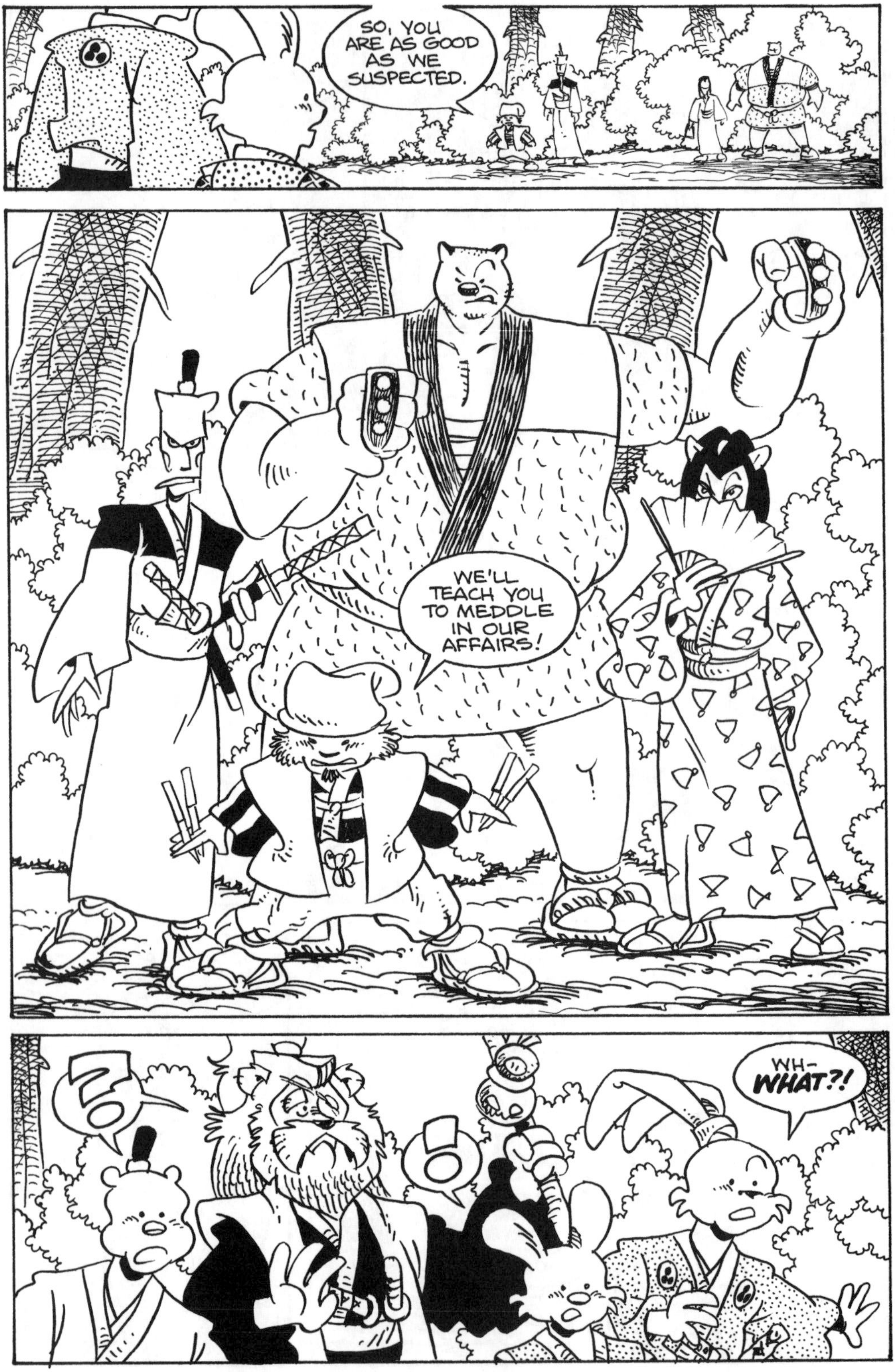
SO, YOU ARE AS GOOD AS WE SUSPECTED.
WE'LL TEACH YOU TO MEDDLE IN OUR AFFAIRS!
?
!
WH- WHAT?!

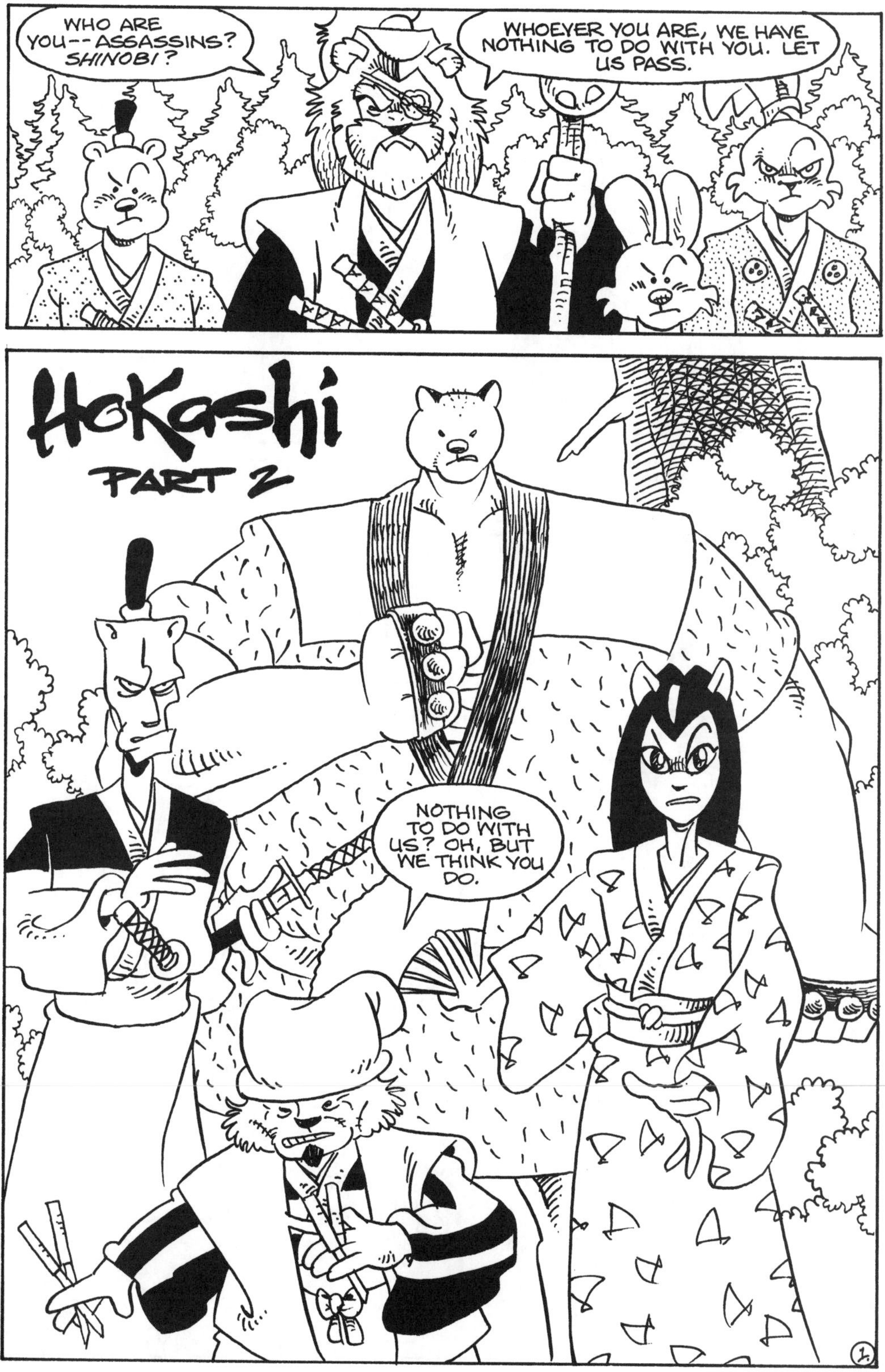
WHO ARE YOU--ASSASSINS? SHINOBI?
WHOEVER YOU ARE, WE HAVE NOTHING TO DO WITH YOU. LET US PASS.
HoKashi
PART 2
NOTHING TO DO WITH US? OH, BUT WE THINK YOU DO.
1.

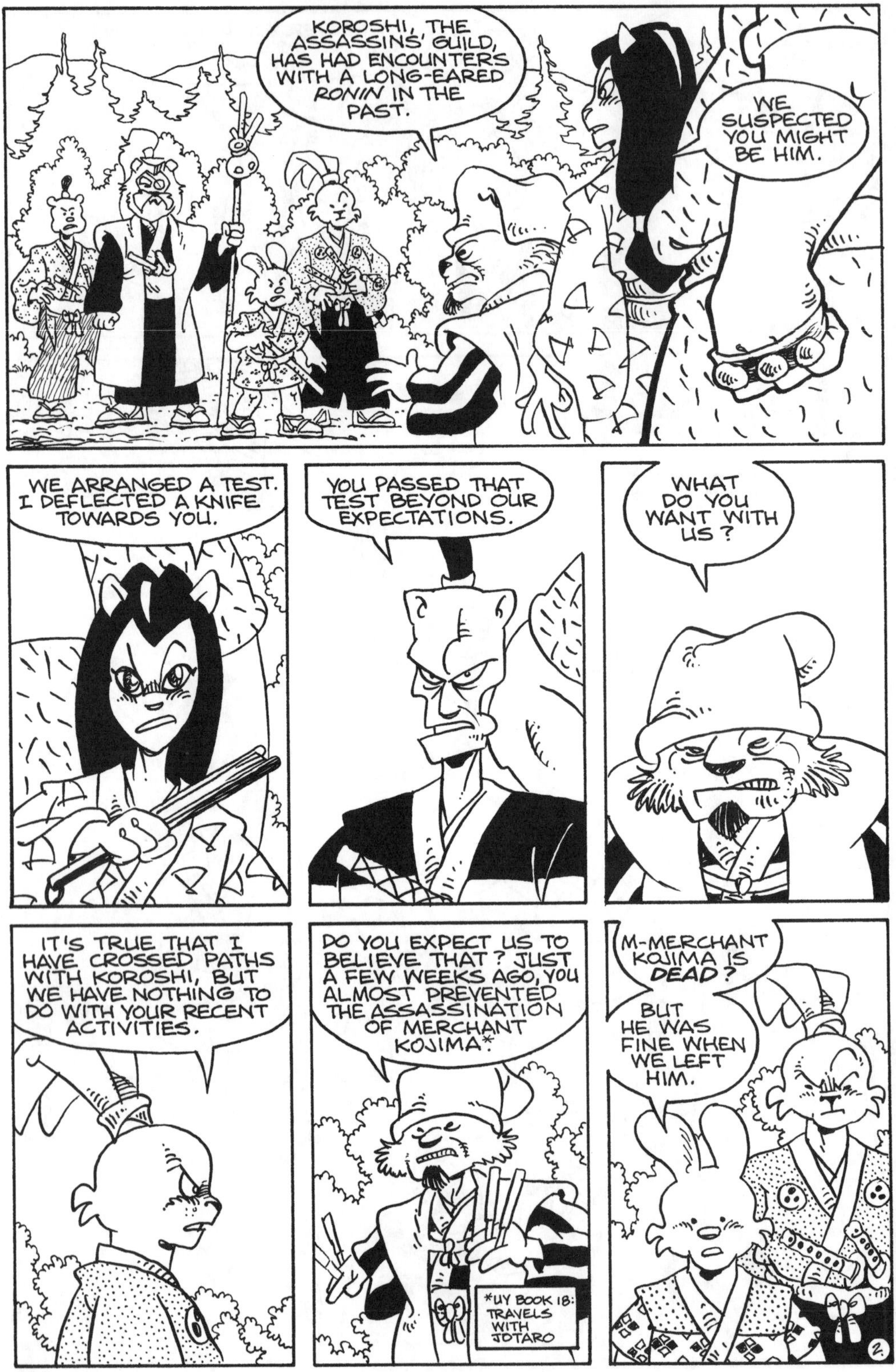
KOROSHI, THE ASSASSINS' GUILD, HAS HAD ENCOUNTERS WITH A LONG-EARED *RONIN* IN THE PAST.
WE SUSPECTED YOU MIGHT BE HIM.
WE ARRANGED A TEST. I DEFLECTED A KNIFE TOWARDS YOU.
YOU PASSED THAT TEST BEYOND OUR EXPECTATIONS.
WHAT DO YOU WANT WITH US?
IT'S TRUE THAT I HAVE CROSSED PATHS WITH KOROSHI, BUT WE HAVE NOTHING TO DO WITH YOUR RECENT ACTIVITIES.
DO YOU EXPECT US TO BELIEVE THAT? JUST A FEW WEEKS AGO, YOU ALMOST PREVENTED THE ASSASSINATION OF MERCHANT KOJIMA*.
*UY BOOK 18: TRAVELS WITH JOTARO
M-MERCHANT KOJIMA IS **DEAD**?
BUT HE WAS FINE WHEN WE LEFT HIM.
2.

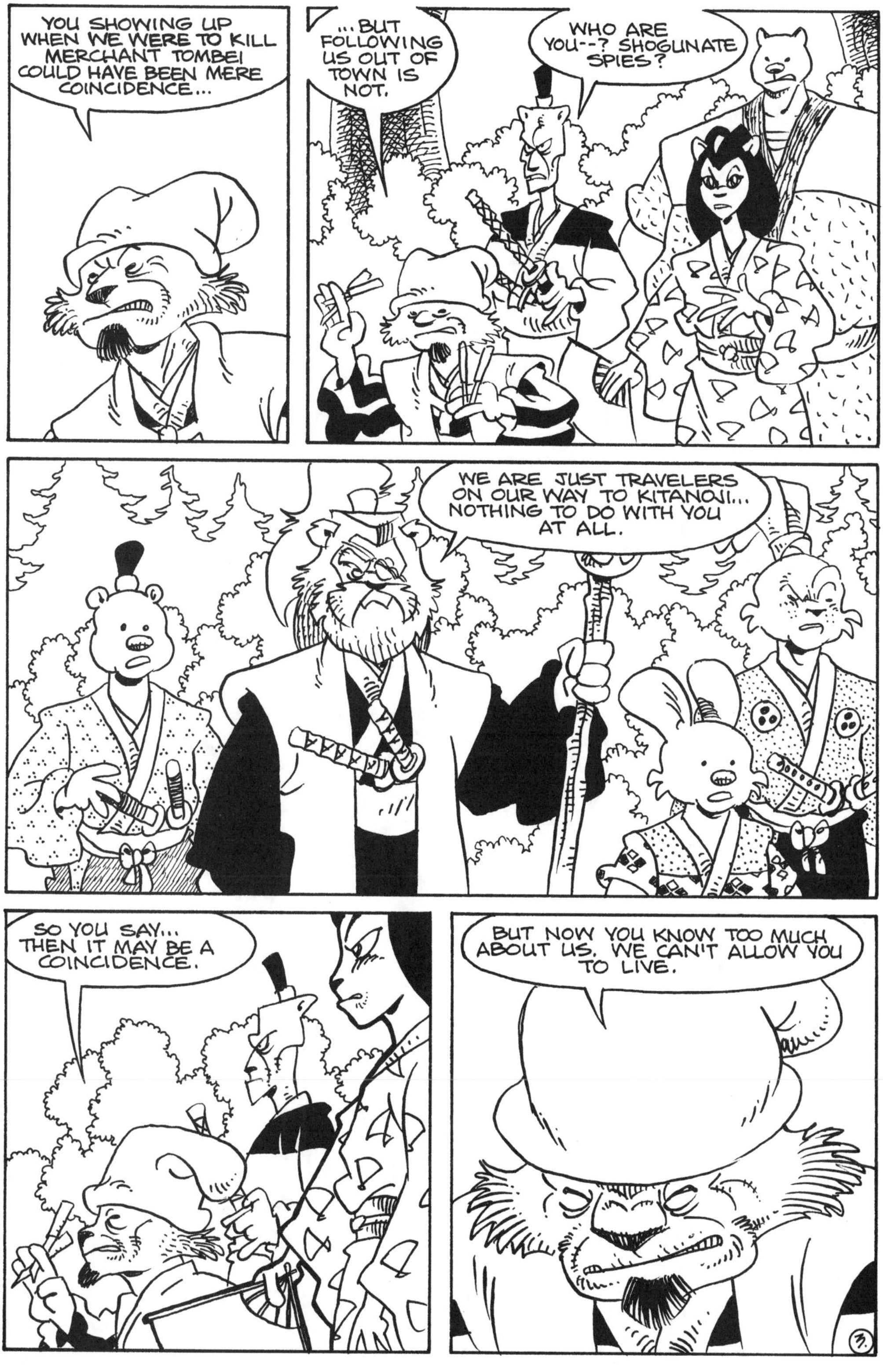
YOU SHOWING UP WHEN WE WERE TO KILL MERCHANT TOMBEI COULD HAVE BEEN MERE COINCIDENCE...
...BUT FOLLOWING US OUT OF TOWN IS NOT.
WHO ARE YOU--? SHOGUNATE SPIES?
WE ARE JUST TRAVELERS ON OUR WAY TO KITANOJI... NOTHING TO DO WITH YOU AT ALL.
SO YOU SAY... THEN IT MAY BE A COINCIDENCE.
BUT NOW YOU KNOW TOO MUCH ABOUT US. WE CAN'T ALLOW YOU TO LIVE.
3.

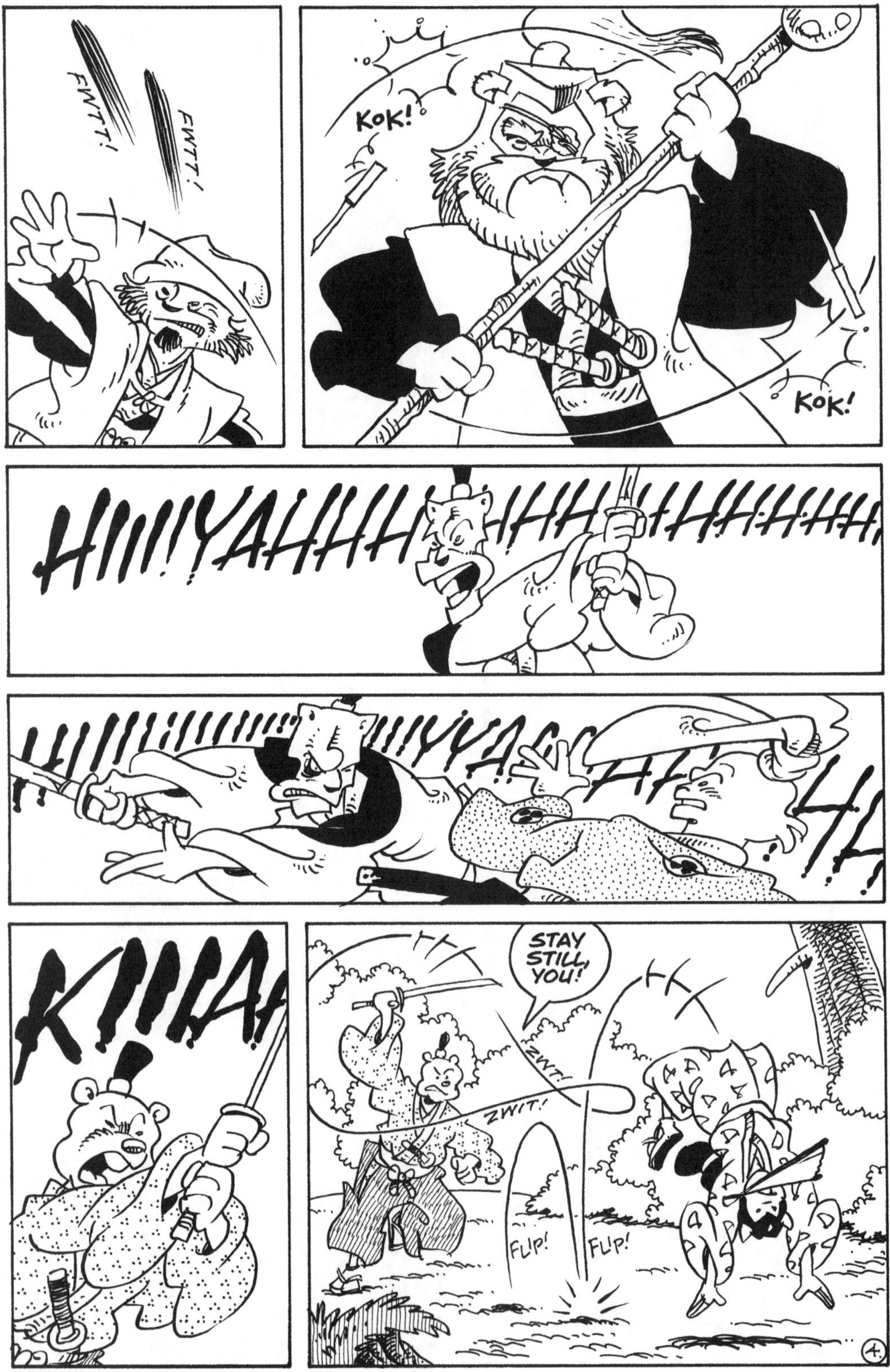
FWTT!
FWTT!
KOK!
KOK!
HIIIYAHHHHHHHHHHHHHH
HIIIIIIIIIIIIIIYYAAAHHH!
KIIIAA
STAY STILL, YOU!
ZWIT!
ZWIT!
FLIP!
FLIP!
4.

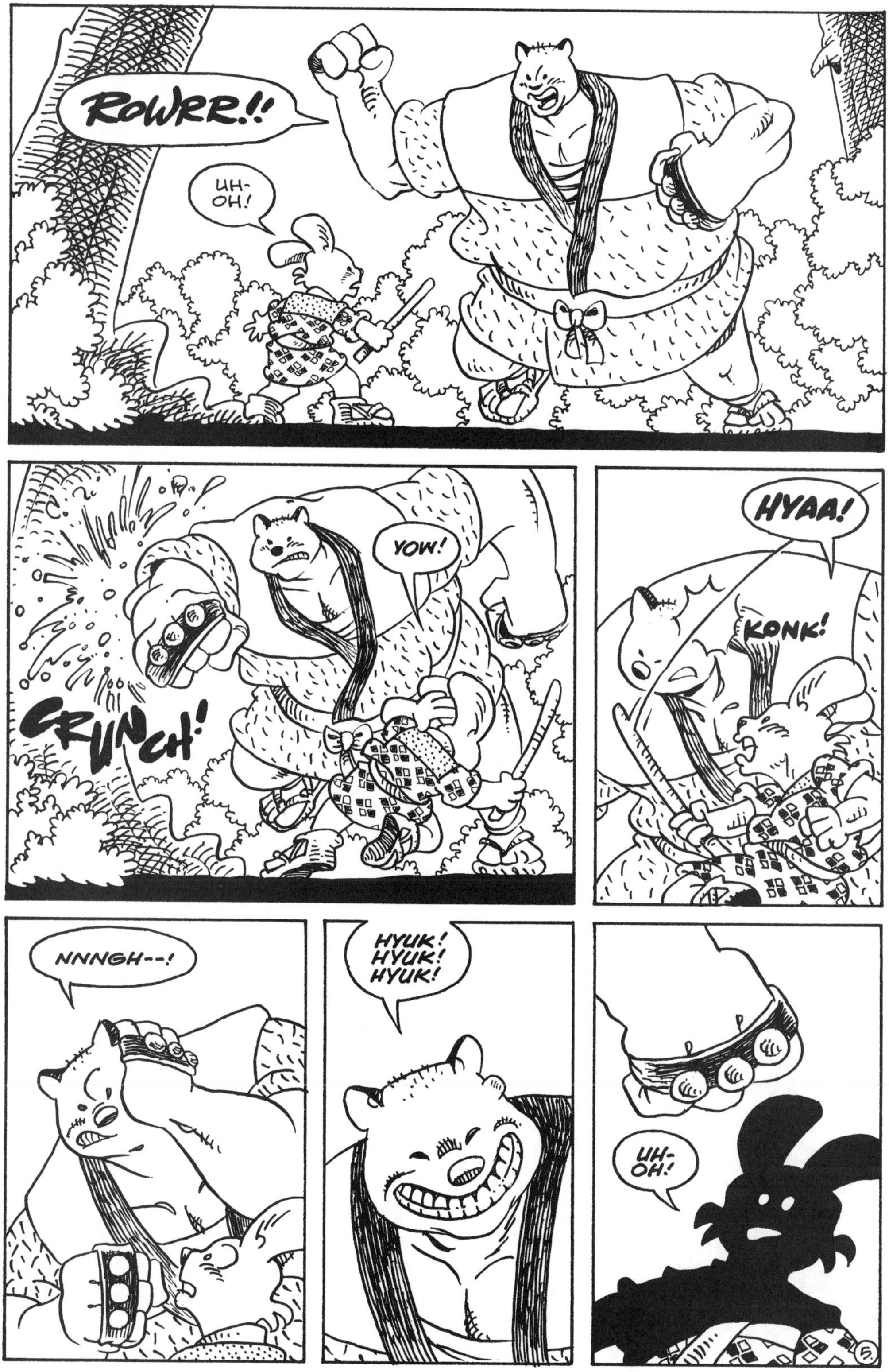
ROWRR!!
UH-OH!
YOW!
CRUNCH!
HYAA!
KONK!
NNNGH--!
HYUK! HYUK! HYUK!
UH-OH!

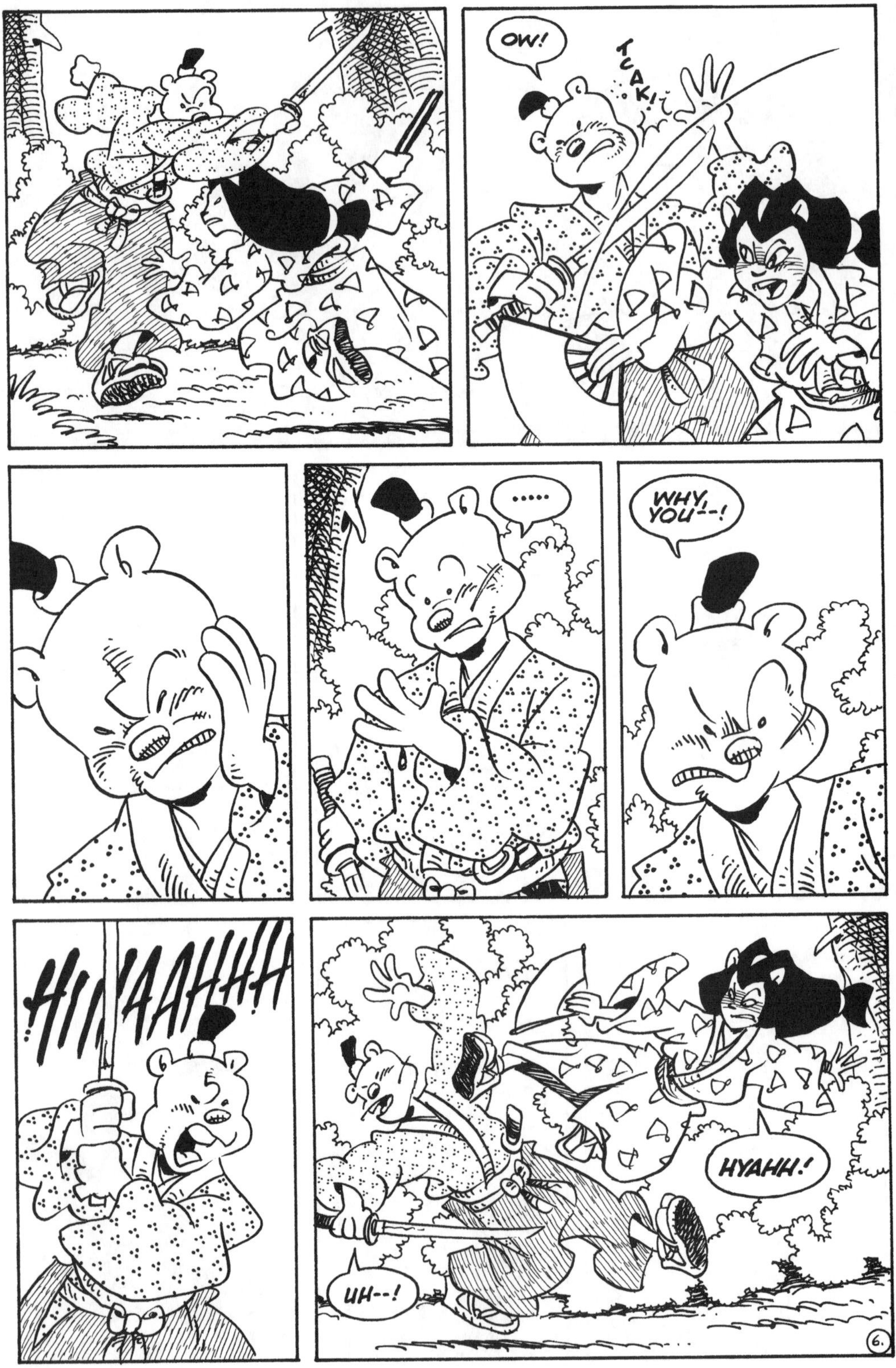
OW!
TCAK!
.....
WHY, YOU--!
HIYAAHHH
HYAHH!
UH--!
6.

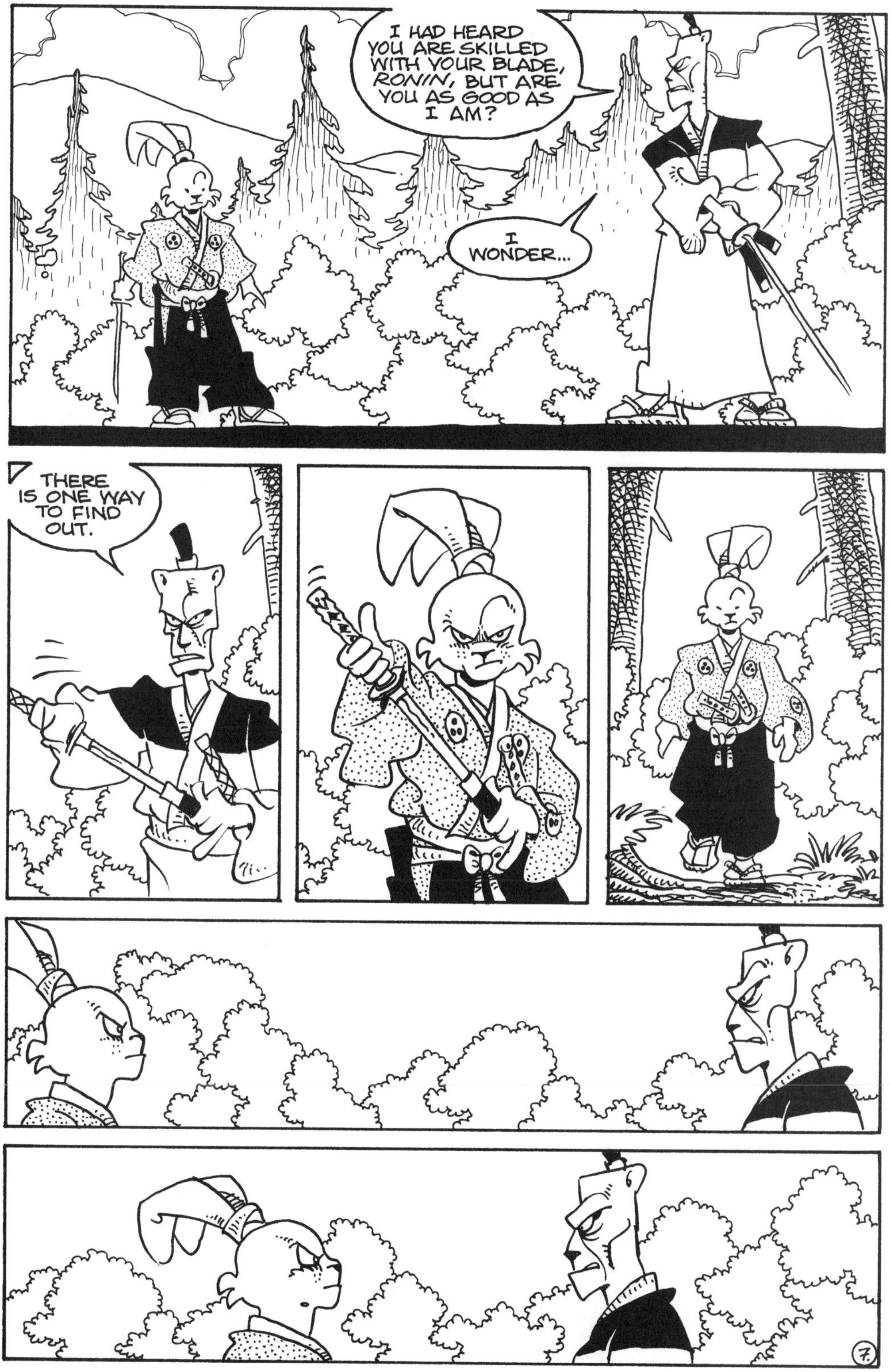
I HAD HEARD YOU ARE SKILLED WITH YOUR BLADE, *RONIN*, BUT ARE YOU AS GOOD AS I AM?
I WONDER...
THERE IS ONE WAY TO FIND OUT.
7.

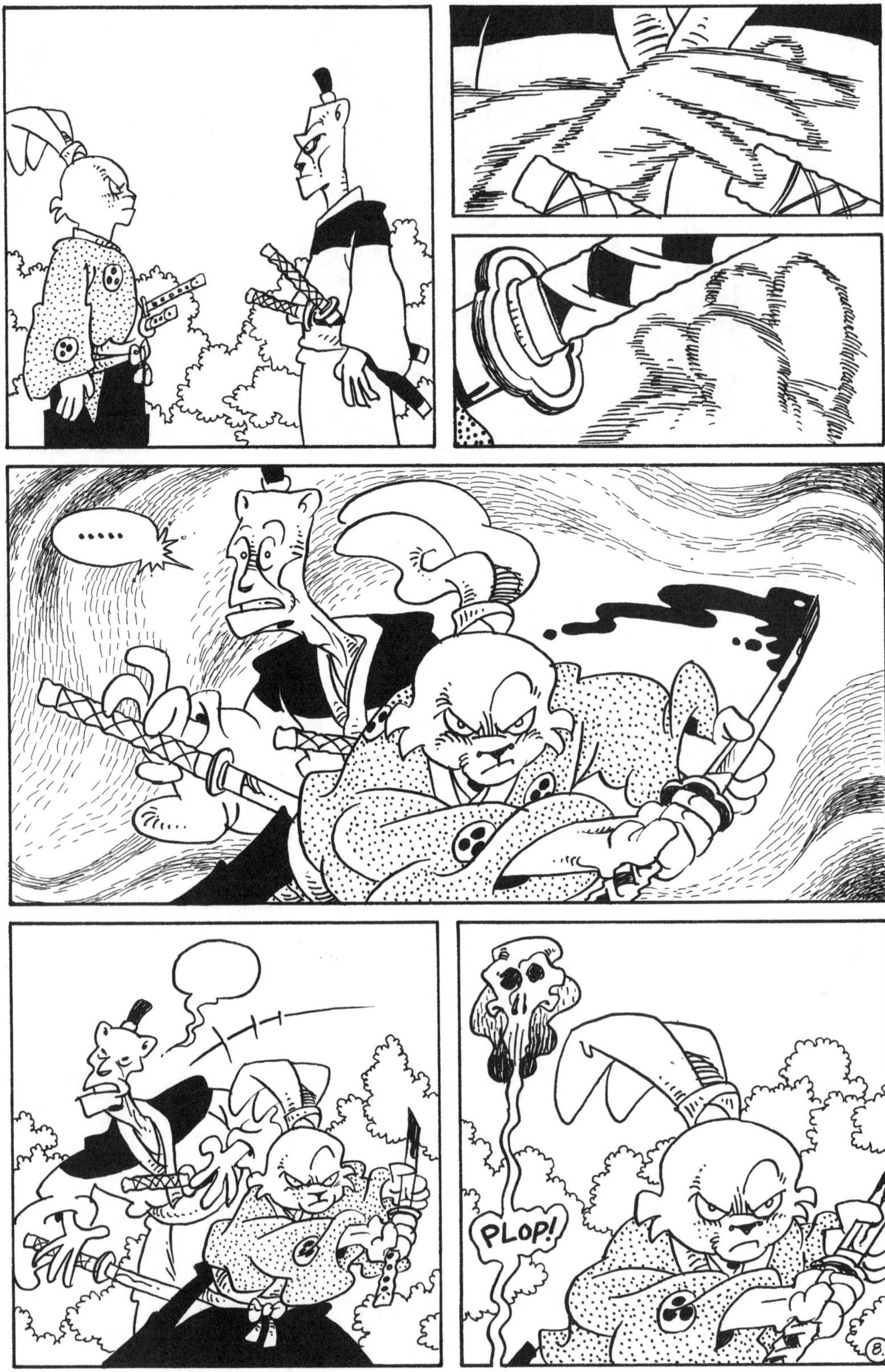
.....
PLOP!
8.

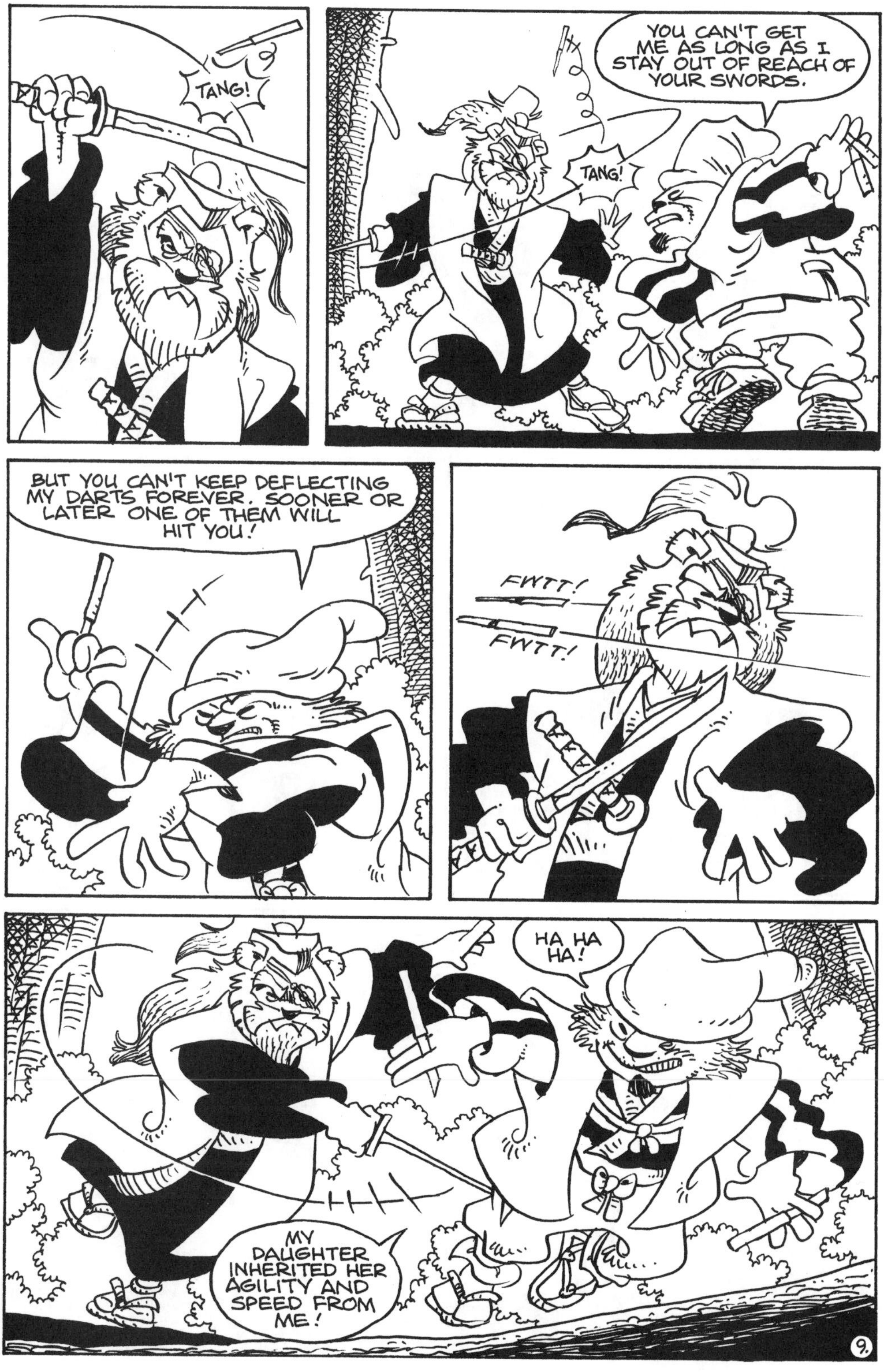
TANG!
YOU CAN'T GET ME AS LONG AS I STAY OUT OF REACH OF YOUR SWORDS.
TANG!
BUT YOU CAN'T KEEP DEFLECTING MY DARTS FOREVER. SOONER OR LATER ONE OF THEM WILL HIT YOU!
FWTT!
FWTT!
HA HA HA!
MY DAUGHTER INHERITED HER AGILITY AND SPEED FROM ME!
9.

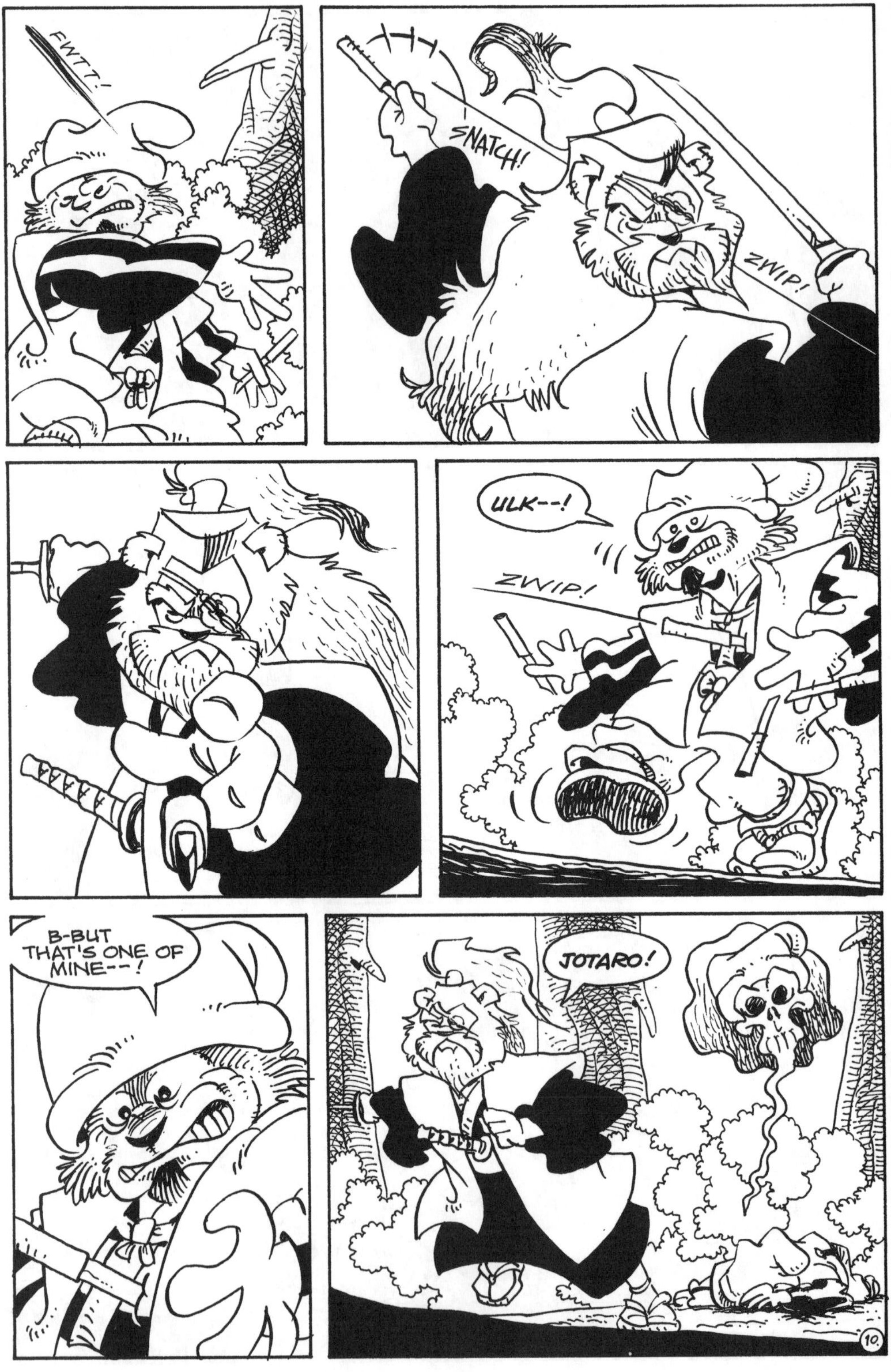
FWTT!
SNATCH!
ZWIP!
ULK--!
ZWIP!
B-BUT THAT'S ONE OF MINE--!
JOTARO!
10.

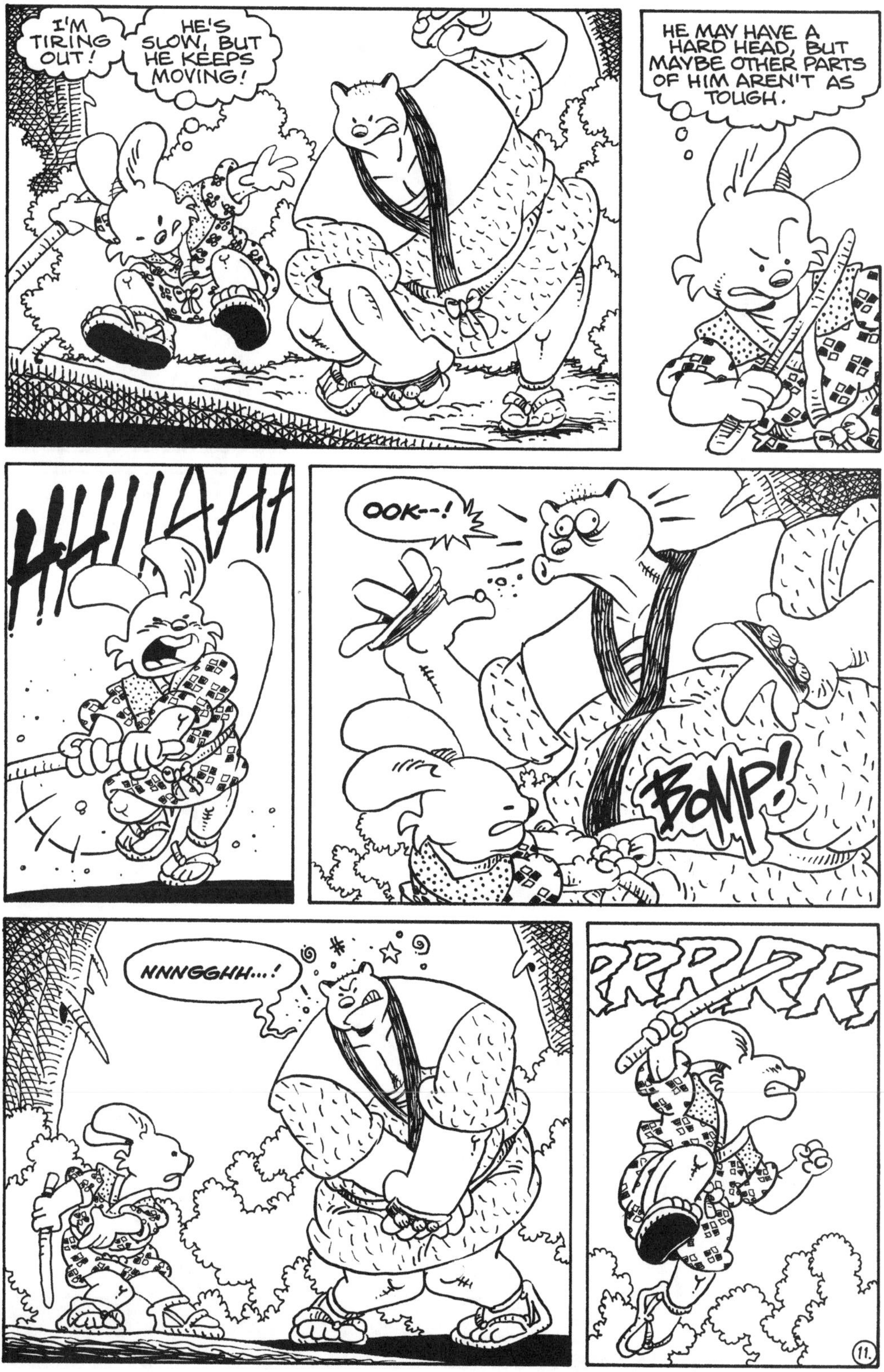
I'M TIRING OUT!
HE'S SLOW, BUT HE KEEPS MOVING!
HE MAY HAVE A HARD HEAD, BUT MAYBE OTHER PARTS OF HIM AREN'T AS TOUGH.
HHIIAAH
OOK--!
BOMP!
NNNGGHH...!
RRRRRR
11.

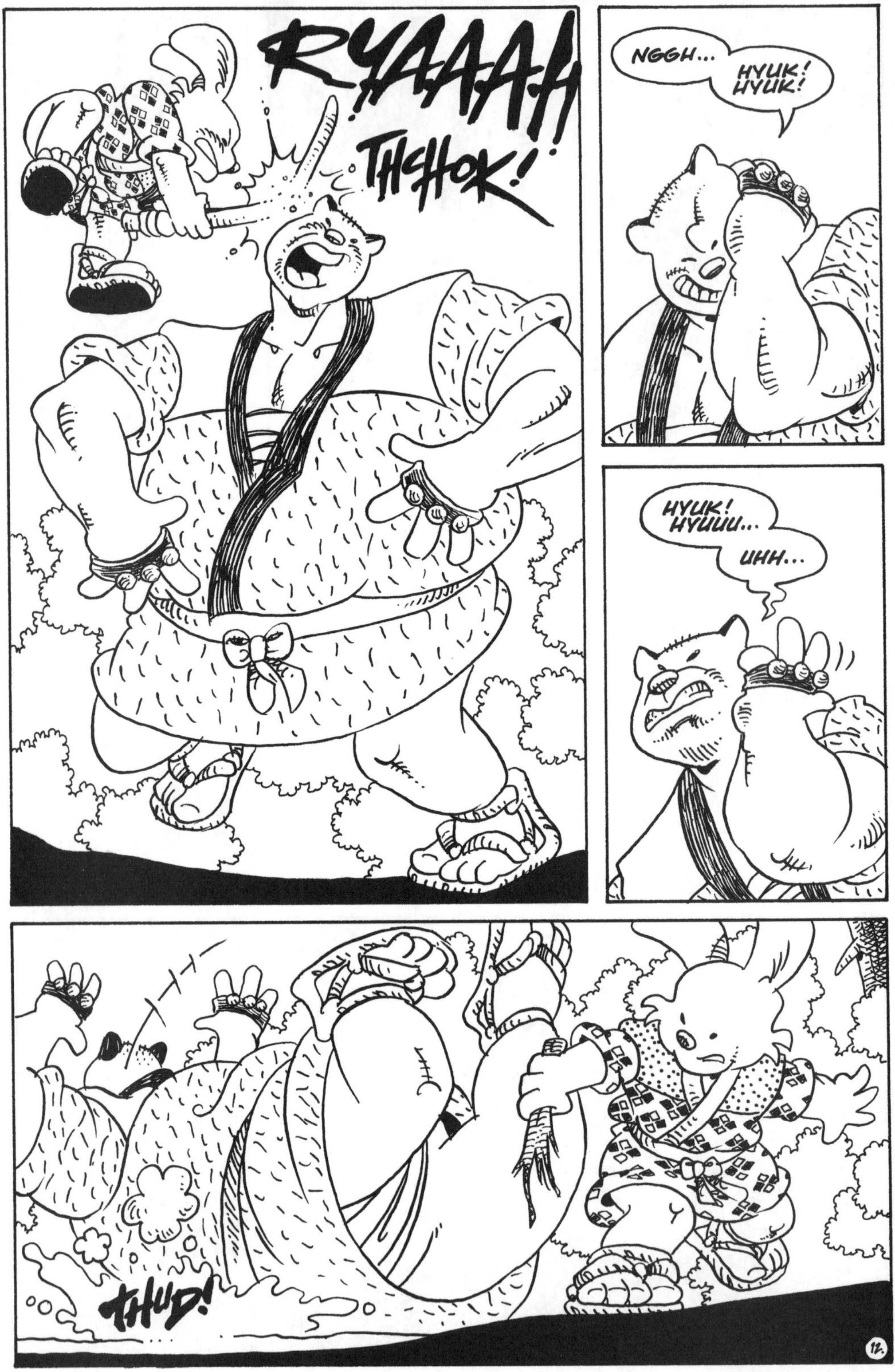
RYAAAH
THCHOK!
NGGH...
HYUK! HYUK!
HYUK! HYUUU...
UHH...
THUD!
12.

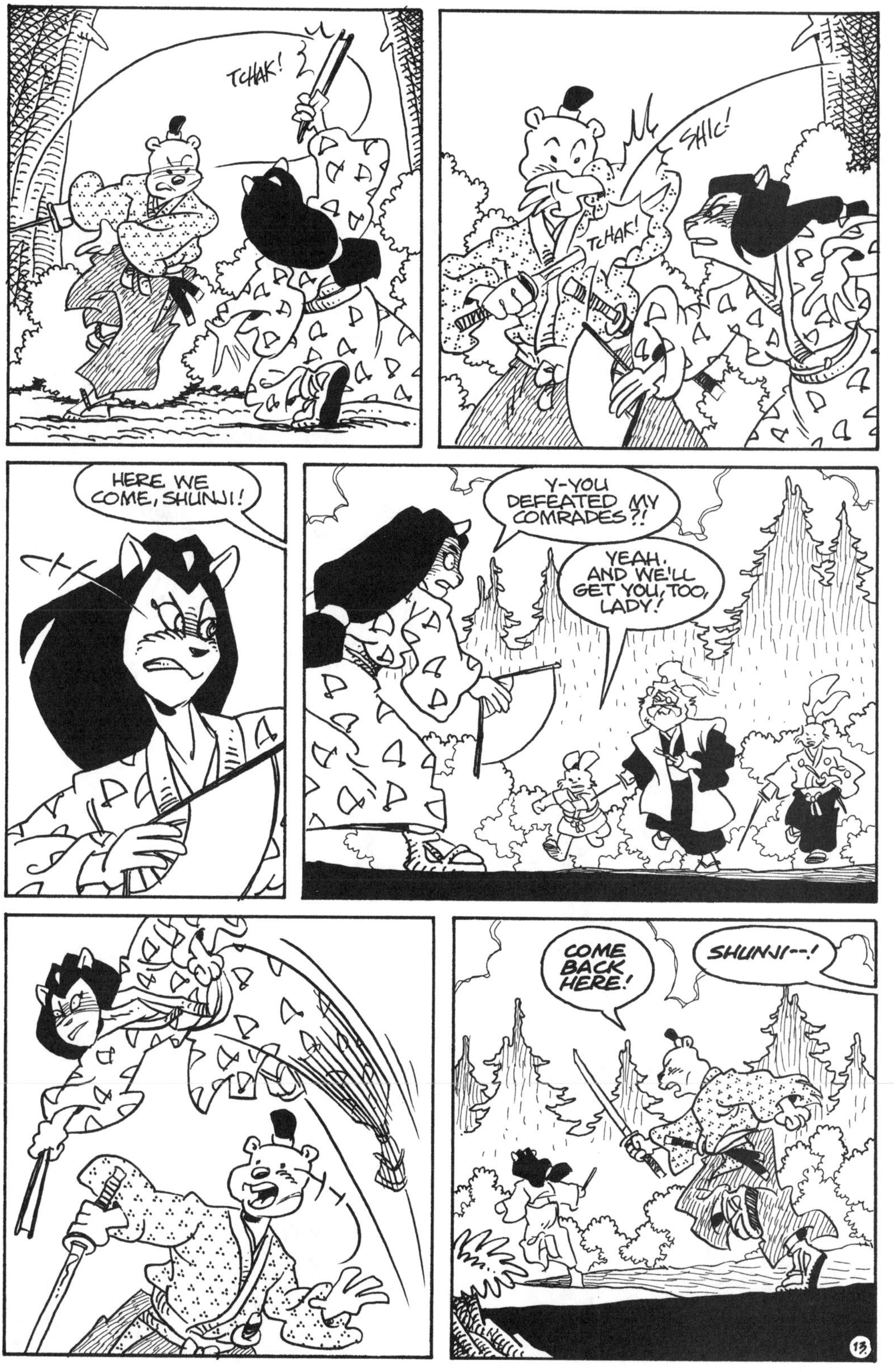
TCHAK!
SHIC!
TCHAK!
HERE WE COME, SHUNJI!
Y-YOU DEFEATED MY COMRADES?!
YEAH. AND WE'LL GET YOU, TOO, LADY!
COME BACK HERE!
SHUNJI--!
13.

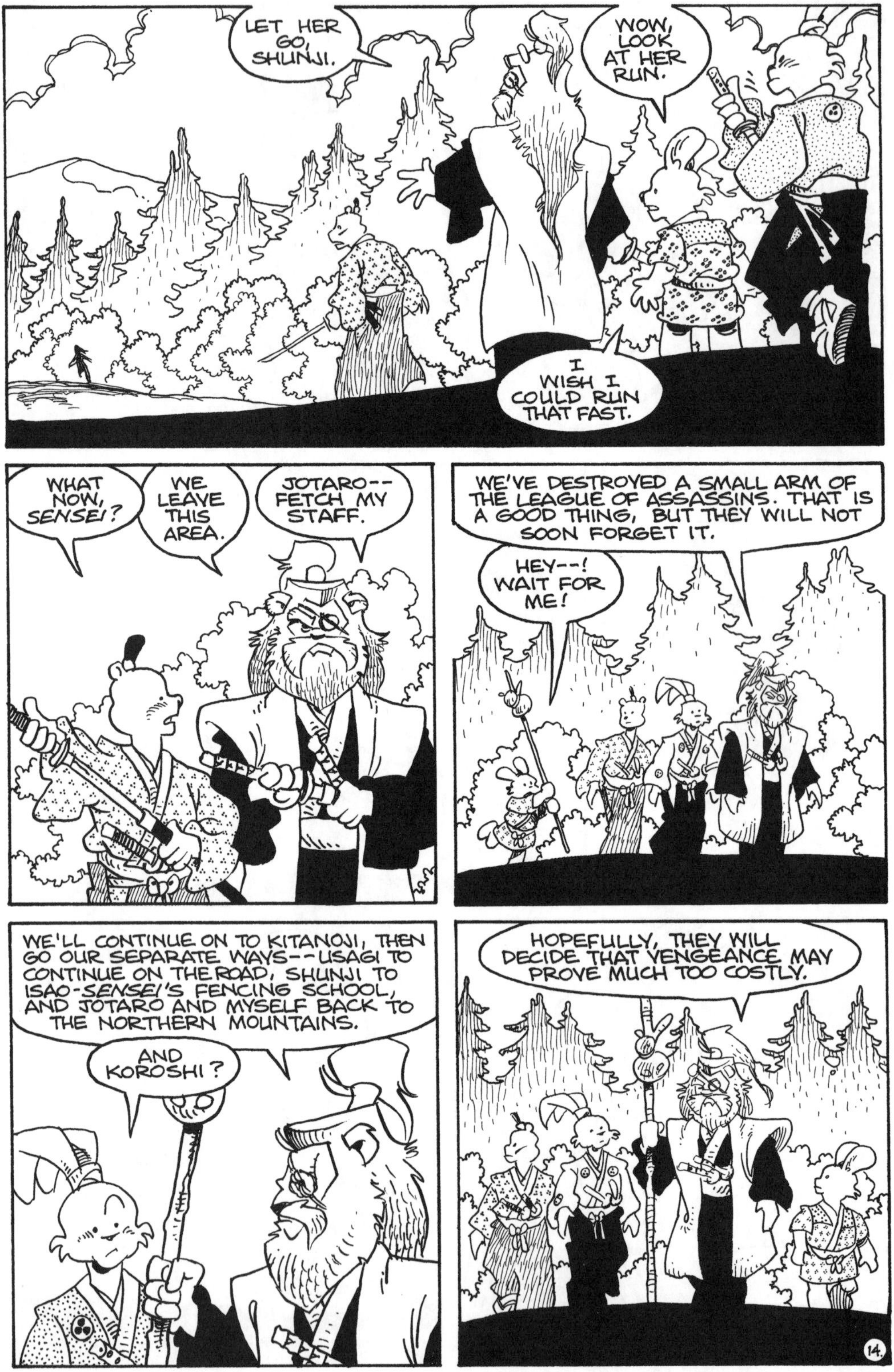
LET HER GO, SHUNJI.
WOW, LOOK AT HER RUN.
I WISH I COULD RUN THAT FAST.
WHAT NOW, SENSEI?
WE LEAVE THIS AREA.
JOTARO--FETCH MY STAFF.
WE'VE DESTROYED A SMALL ARM OF THE LEAGUE OF ASSASSINS. THAT IS A GOOD THING, BUT THEY WILL NOT SOON FORGET IT.
HEY--! WAIT FOR ME!
WE'LL CONTINUE ON TO KITANOJI, THEN GO OUR SEPARATE WAYS--USAGI TO CONTINUE ON THE ROAD, SHUNJI TO ISAO-SENSEI'S FENCING SCHOOL, AND JOTARO AND MYSELF BACK TO THE NORTHERN MOUNTAINS.
AND KOROSHI?
HOPEFULLY, THEY WILL DECIDE THAT VENGEANCE MAY PROVE MUCH TOO COSTLY.
14.

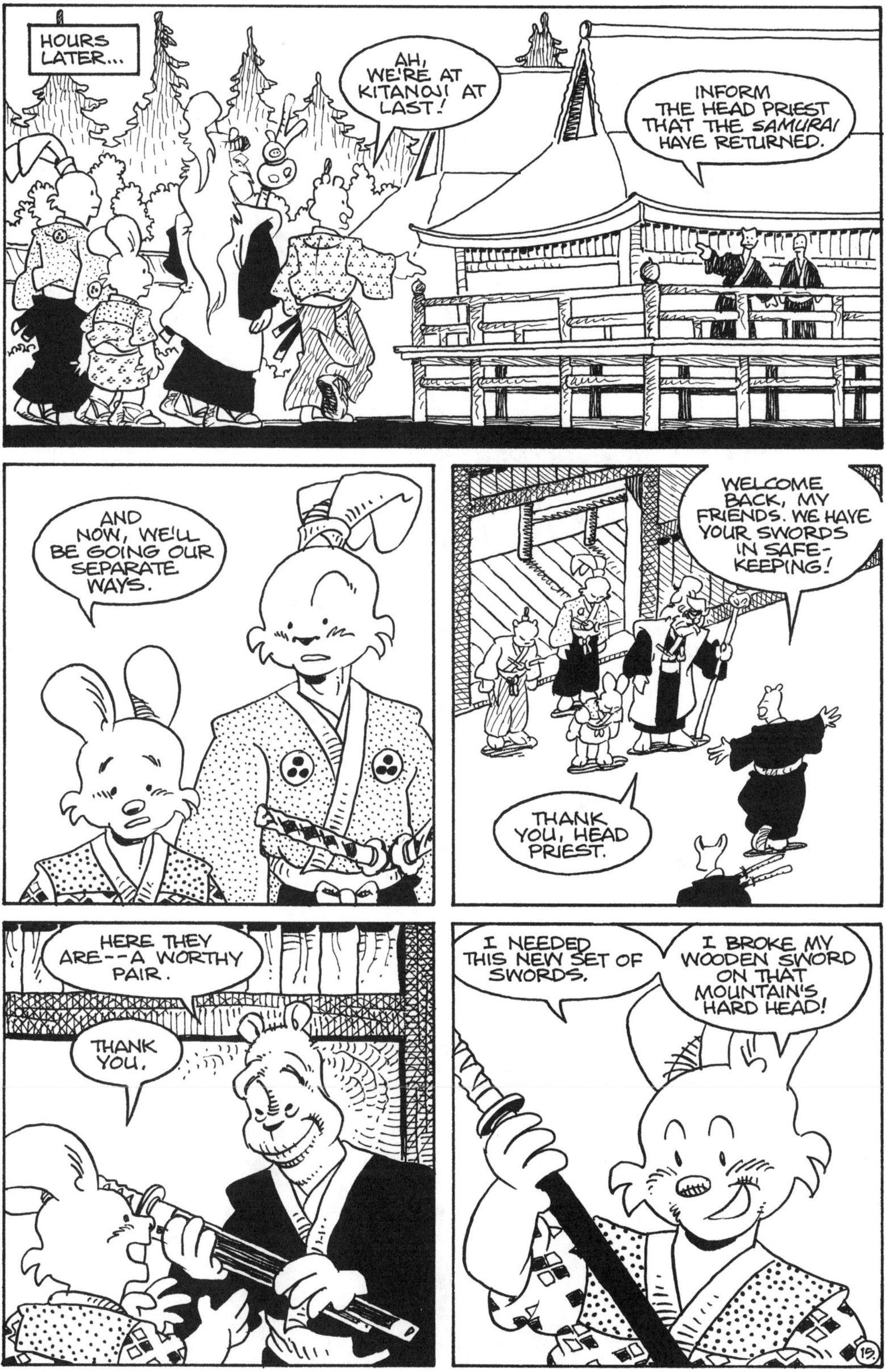
HOURS LATER...
AH, WE'RE AT KITANOJI AT LAST!
INFORM THE HEAD PRIEST THAT THE SAMURAI HAVE RETURNED.
AND NOW, WE'LL BE GOING OUR SEPARATE WAYS.
WELCOME BACK, MY FRIENDS. WE HAVE YOUR SWORDS IN SAFE-KEEPING!
THANK YOU, HEAD PRIEST.
HERE THEY ARE--A WORTHY PAIR.
THANK YOU.
I NEEDED THIS NEW SET OF SWORDS.
I BROKE MY WOODEN SWORD ON THAT MOUNTAIN'S HARD HEAD!
15.

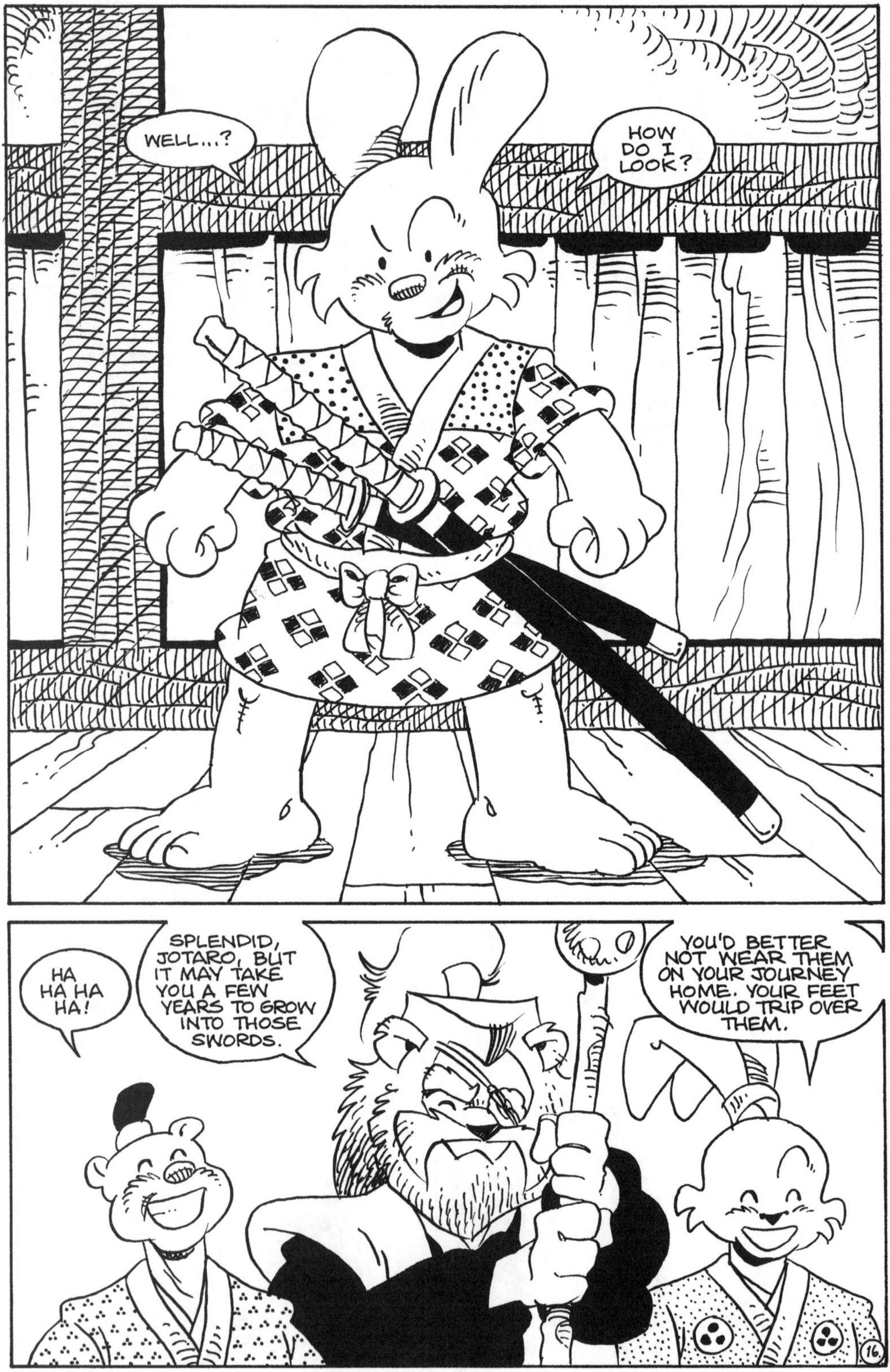
WELL...?
HOW DO I LOOK?
HA HA HA HA!
SPLENDID, JOTARO, BUT IT MAY TAKE YOU A FEW YEARS TO GROW INTO THOSE SWORDS.
YOU'D BETTER NOT WEAR THEM ON YOUR JOURNEY HOME. YOUR FEET WOULD TRIP OVER THEM.
16.

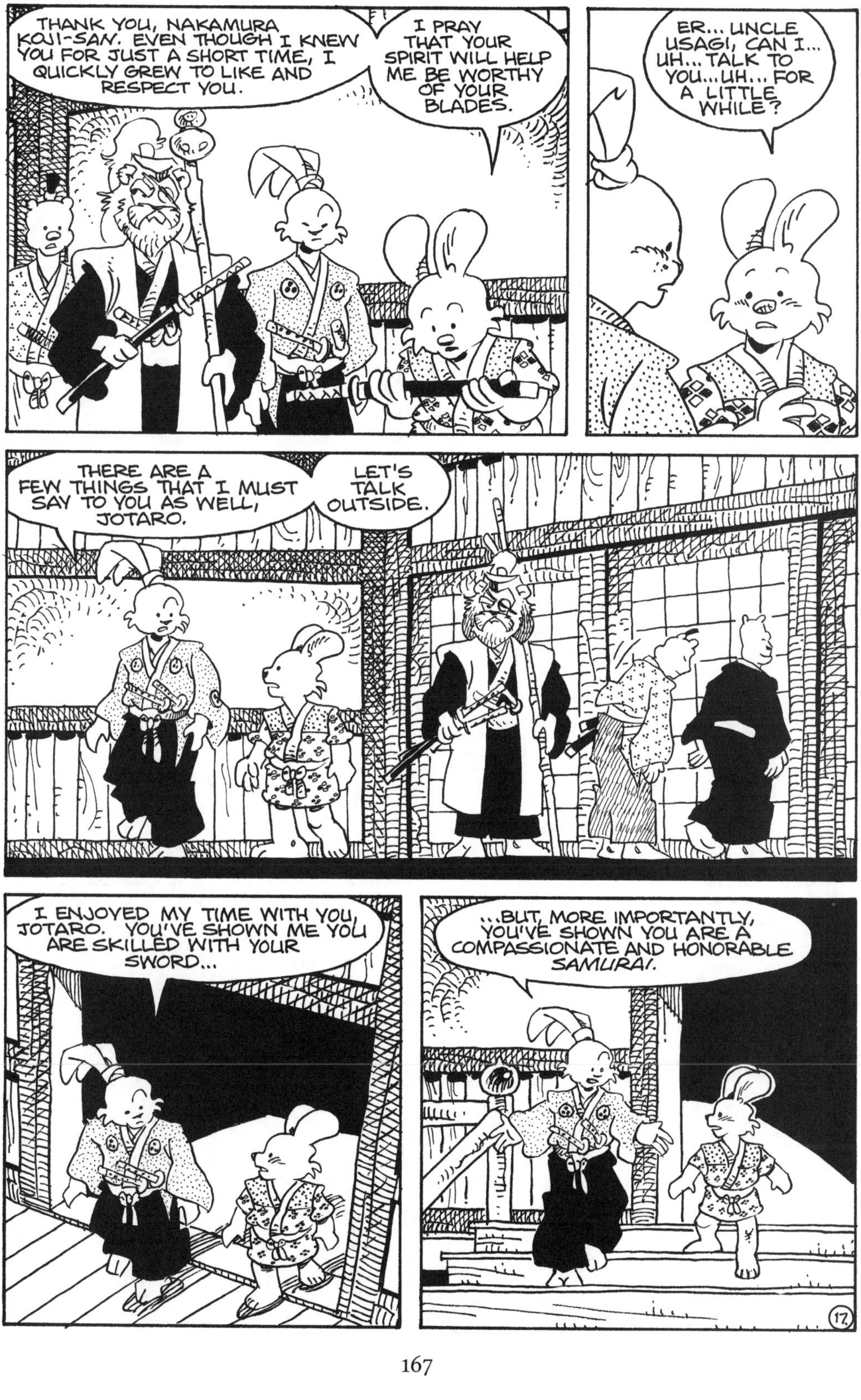
THANK YOU, NAKAMURA KOJI-SAN. EVEN THOUGH I KNEW YOU FOR JUST A SHORT TIME, I QUICKLY GREW TO LIKE AND RESPECT YOU.
I PRAY THAT YOUR SPIRIT WILL HELP ME BE WORTHY OF YOUR BLADES.
ER... UNCLE USAGI, CAN I... UH... TALK TO YOU... UH... FOR A LITTLE WHILE?
THERE ARE A FEW THINGS THAT I MUST SAY TO YOU AS WELL, JOTARO.
LET'S TALK OUTSIDE.
I ENJOYED MY TIME WITH YOU, JOTARO. YOU'VE SHOWN ME YOU ARE SKILLED WITH YOUR SWORD...
...BUT, MORE IMPORTANTLY, YOU'VE SHOWN YOU ARE A COMPASSIONATE AND HONORABLE SAMURAI.
17

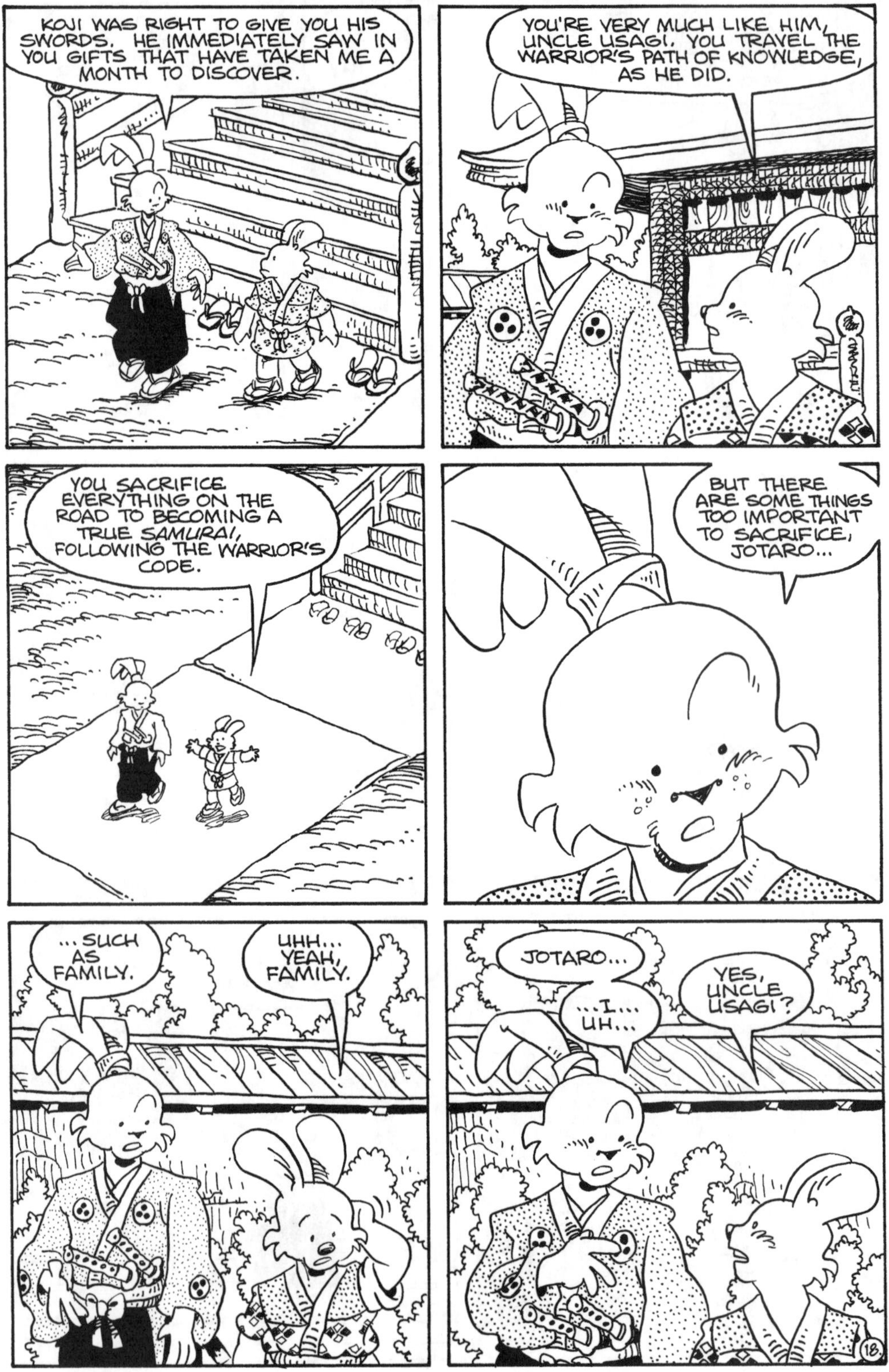
KOJI WAS RIGHT TO GIVE YOU HIS SWORDS. HE IMMEDIATELY SAW IN YOU GIFTS THAT HAVE TAKEN ME A MONTH TO DISCOVER.
YOU'RE VERY MUCH LIKE HIM, UNCLE USAGI. YOU TRAVEL THE WARRIOR'S PATH OF KNOWLEDGE, AS HE DID.
YOU SACRIFICE EVERYTHING ON THE ROAD TO BECOMING A TRUE *SAMURAI*, FOLLOWING THE WARRIOR'S CODE.
BUT THERE ARE SOME THINGS TOO IMPORTANT TO SACRIFICE, JOTARO...
...SUCH AS FAMILY.
UHH... YEAH, FAMILY.
JOTARO...
...I... UH...
YES, UNCLE USAGI?
18

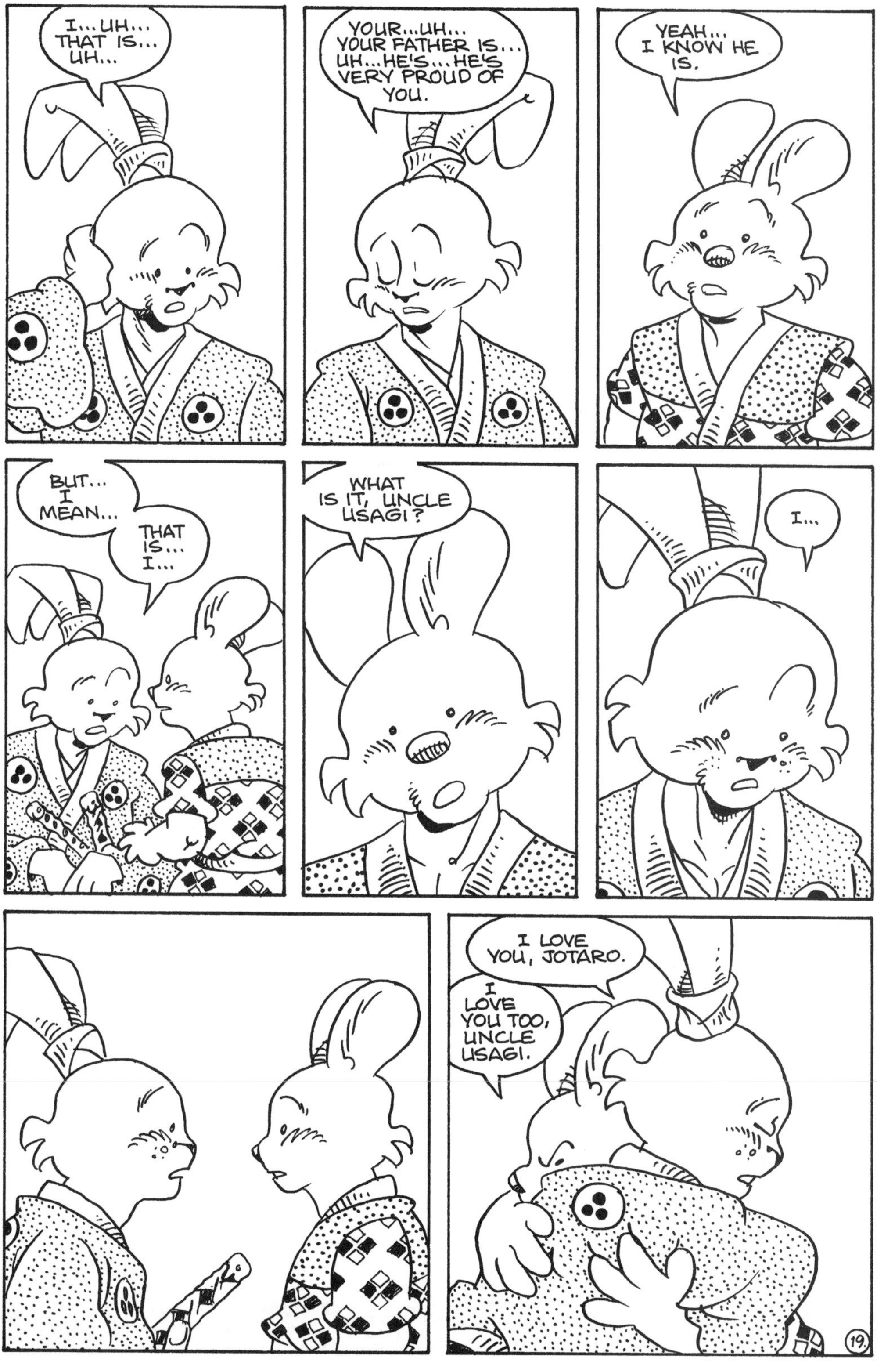

I...UH...
THAT IS...
UH...
YOUR...UH...
YOUR FATHER IS...
UH...HE'S...HE'S
VERY PROUD OF
YOU.
YEAH...
I KNOW HE
IS.
BUT...
I
MEAN...
THAT
IS...
I...
WHAT
IS IT, UNCLE
USAGI?
I...
I LOVE
YOU, JOTARO.
I
LOVE
YOU TOO,
UNCLE
USAGI.
19.

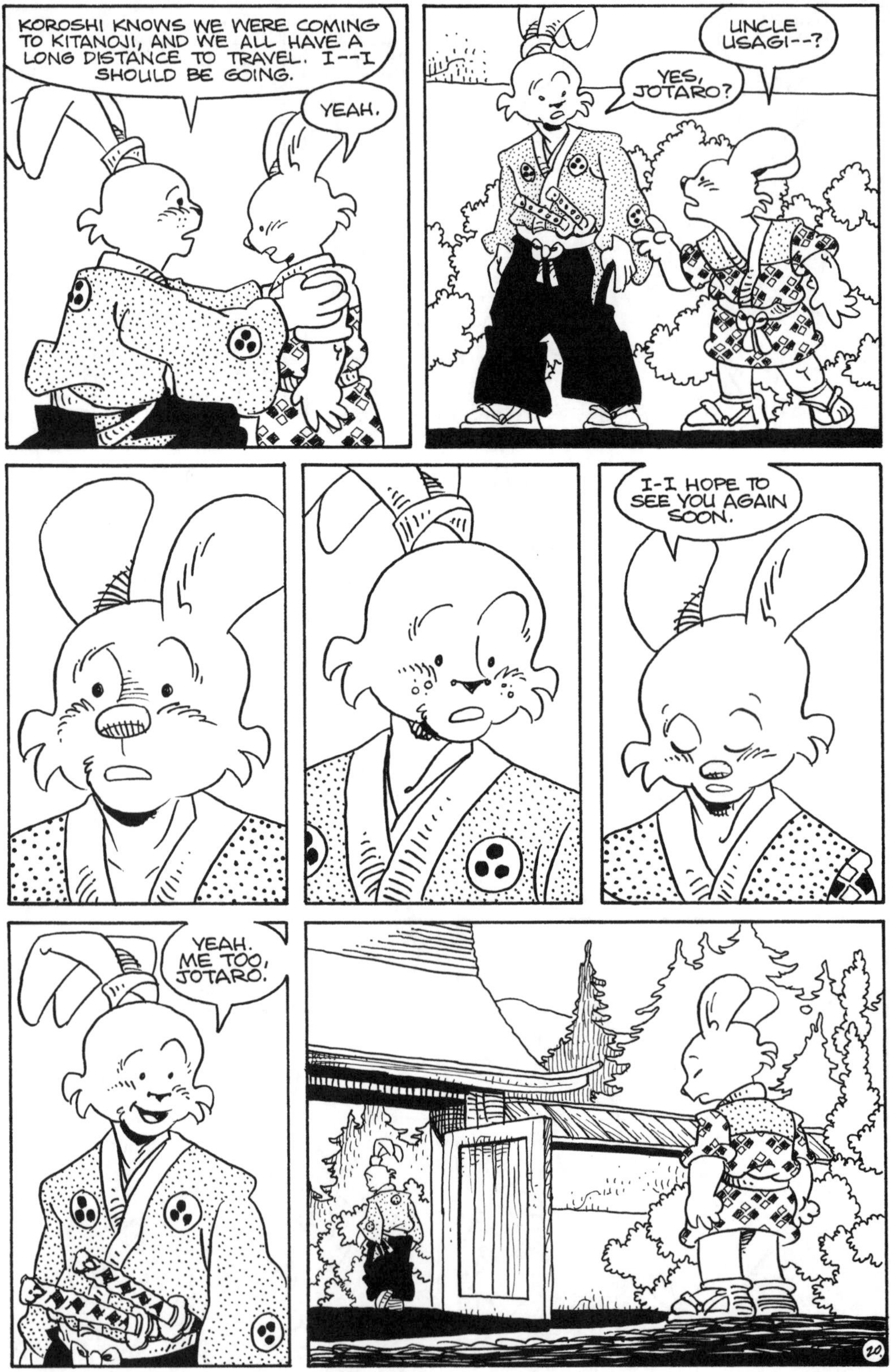
KOROSHI KNOWS WE WERE COMING TO KITANOJI, AND WE ALL HAVE A LONG DISTANCE TO TRAVEL. I--I SHOULD BE GOING.
YEAH.
UNCLE USAGI--?
YES, JOTARO?
I-I HOPE TO SEE YOU AGAIN SOON.
YEAH. ME TOO, JOTARO.
20.

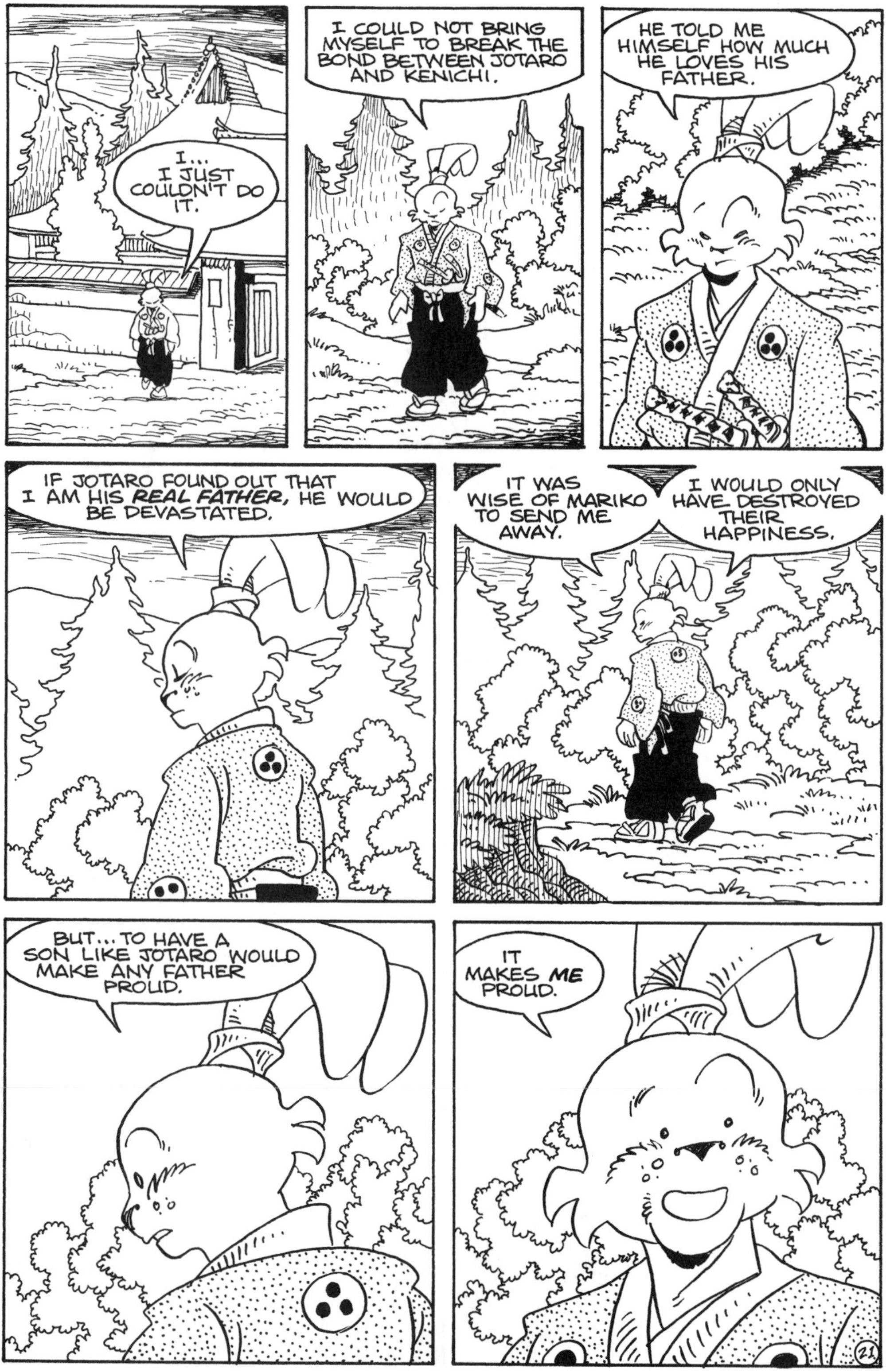
I... I JUST COULDN'T DO IT.
I COULD NOT BRING MYSELF TO BREAK THE BOND BETWEEN JOTARO AND KENICHI.
HE TOLD ME HIMSELF HOW MUCH HE LOVES HIS FATHER.
IF JOTARO FOUND OUT THAT I AM HIS **REAL FATHER,** HE WOULD BE DEVASTATED.
IT WAS WISE OF MARIKO TO SEND ME AWAY.
I WOULD ONLY HAVE DESTROYED THEIR HAPPINESS.
BUT... TO HAVE A SON LIKE JOTARO WOULD MAKE ANY FATHER PROUD.
IT MAKES **ME** PROUD.
21

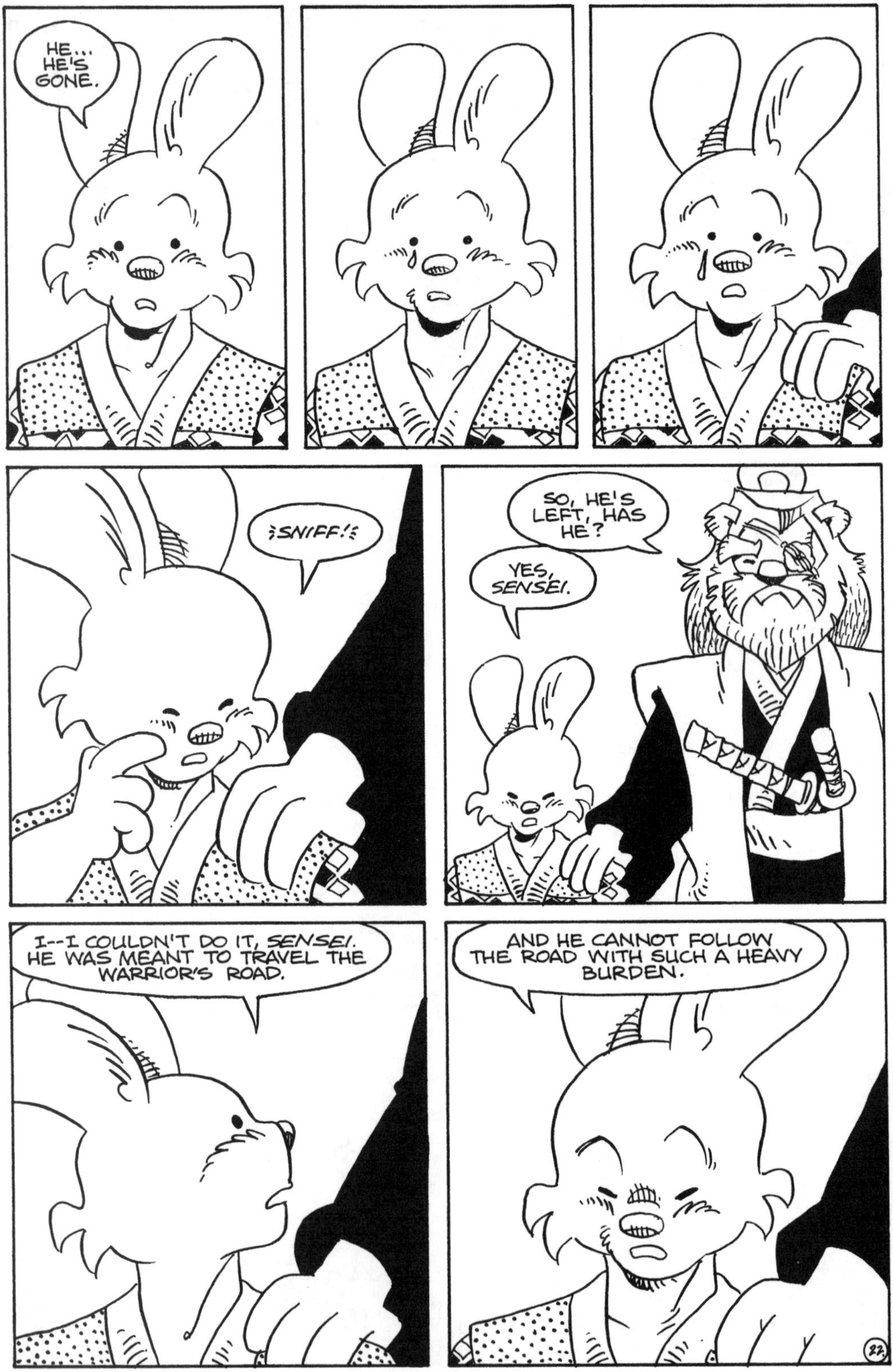
HE... HE'S GONE.
;SNIFF!;
SO, HE'S LEFT, HAS HE?
YES, SENSEI.
I--I COULDN'T DO IT, SENSEI. HE WAS MEANT TO TRAVEL THE WARRIOR'S ROAD.
AND HE CANNOT FOLLOW THE ROAD WITH SUCH A HEAVY BURDEN.
22.

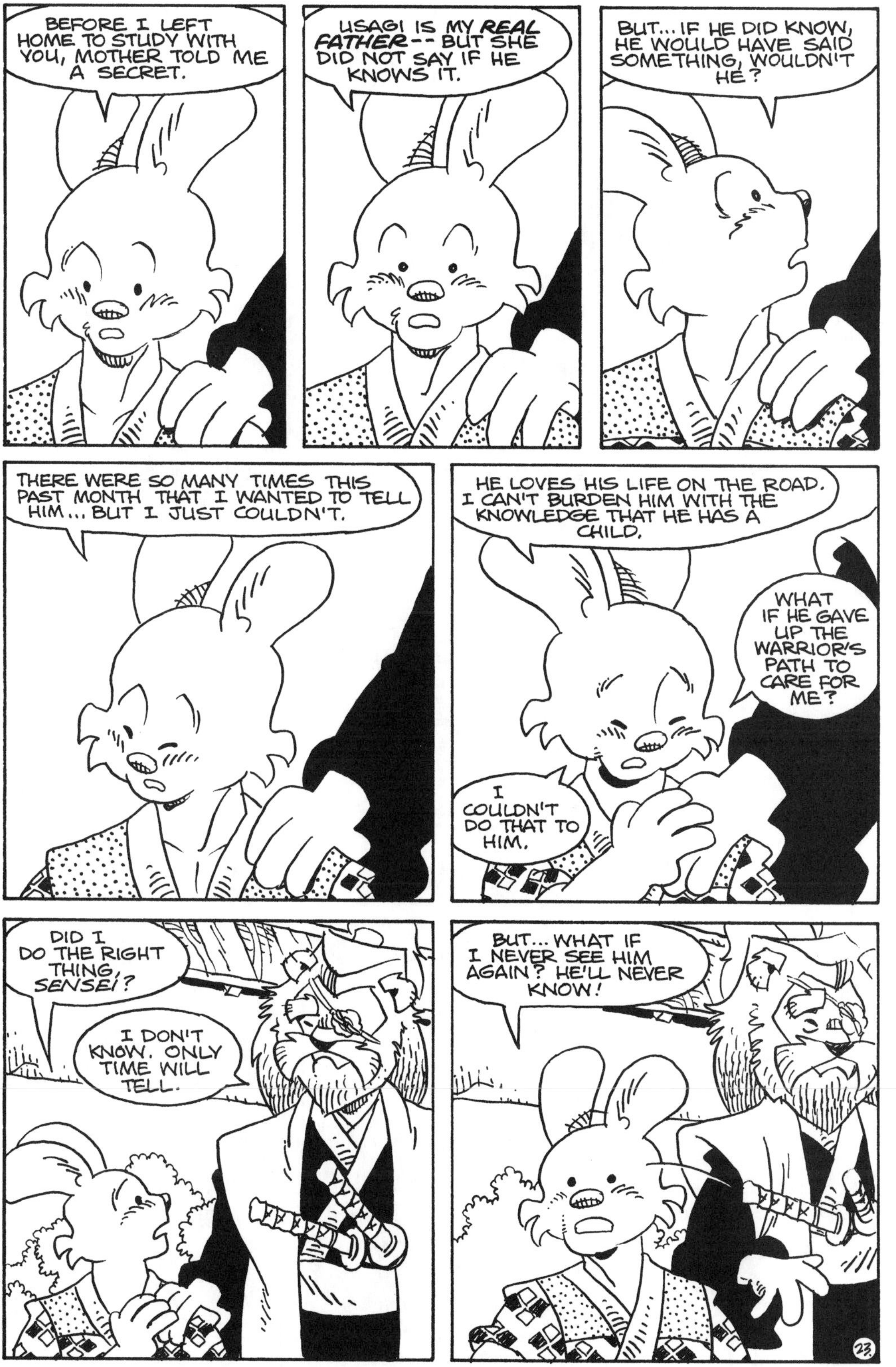

BEFORE I LEFT HOME TO STUDY WITH YOU, MOTHER TOLD ME A SECRET.
USAGI IS MY **REAL FATHER**-- BUT SHE DID NOT SAY IF HE KNOWS IT.
BUT... IF HE DID KNOW, HE WOULD HAVE SAID SOMETHING, WOULDN'T HE?
THERE WERE SO MANY TIMES THIS PAST MONTH THAT I WANTED TO TELL HIM... BUT I JUST COULDN'T.
HE LOVES HIS LIFE ON THE ROAD. I CAN'T BURDEN HIM WITH THE KNOWLEDGE THAT HE HAS A CHILD.
WHAT IF HE GAVE UP THE WARRIOR'S PATH TO CARE FOR ME?
I COULDN'T DO THAT TO HIM.
DID I DO THE RIGHT THING, *SENSEI*?
I DON'T KNOW. ONLY TIME WILL TELL.
BUT... WHAT IF I NEVER SEE HIM AGAIN? HE'LL NEVER KNOW!
23.

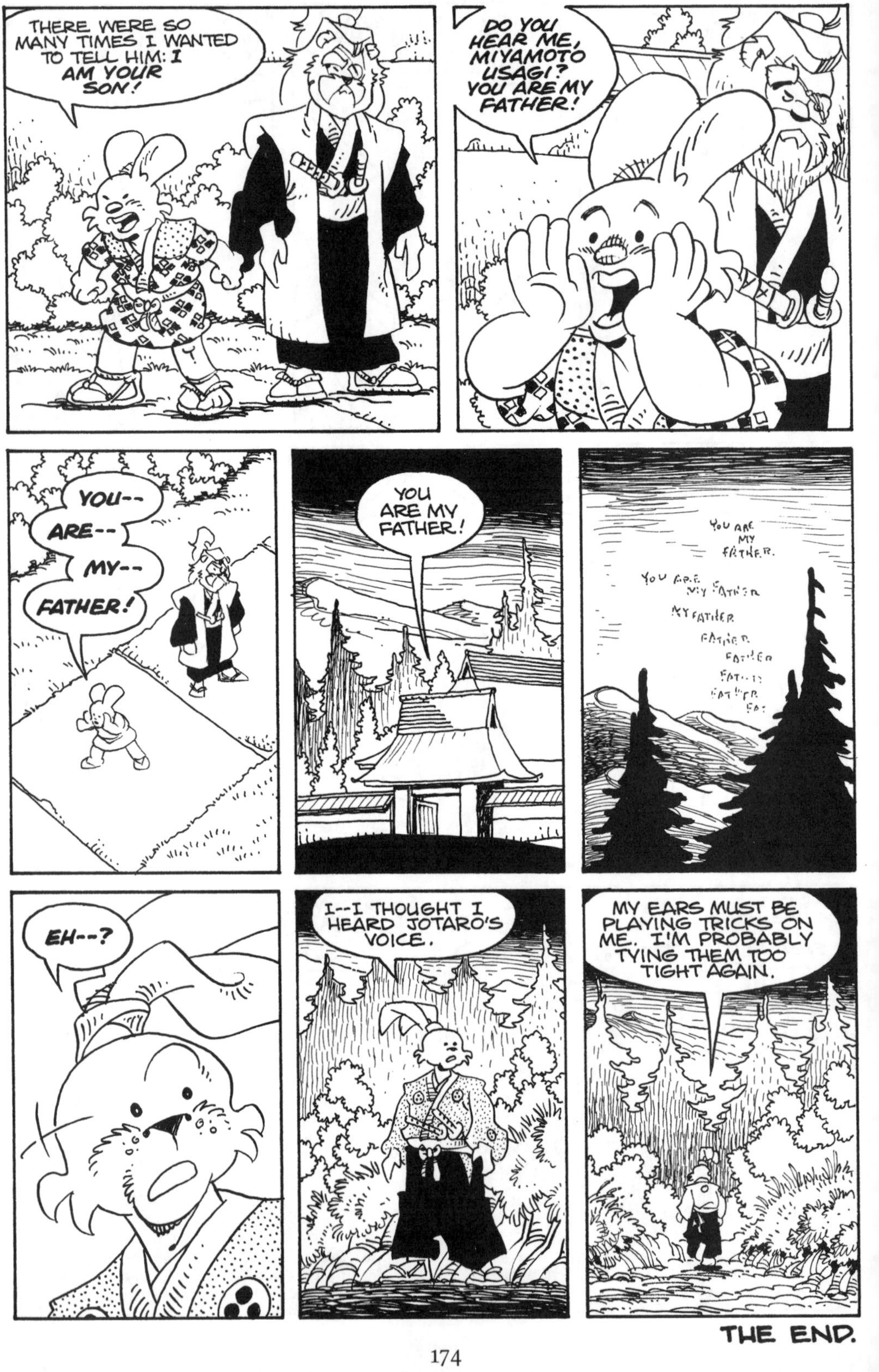
THERE WERE SO MANY TIMES I WANTED TO TELL HIM: I AM YOUR SON!
DO YOU HEAR ME, MIYAMOTO USAGI? YOU ARE MY FATHER!
YOU-- ARE-- MY-- FATHER!
YOU ARE MY FATHER!
YOU ARE MY FATHER.
YOU ARE MY FATHER
MY FATHER
FATHER
FATHER
EH--?
I--I THOUGHT I HEARD JOTARO'S VOICE.
MY EARS MUST BE PLAYING TRICKS ON ME. I'M PROBABLY TYING THEM TOO TIGHT AGAIN.
THE END.

Usagi Yojimbo

Story Notes

Bells

There are three kinds of Japanese bells. Smaller bells are called *suzu*, meaning "cool and refreshing." They are round and hollow, with tiny metal pellets inside. They give a clear ringing when they are moved. *Kane* are generally larger and "bell-shaped." They emit a ringing when struck. *Suzu* are associated with Shinto shrines, while *kane* are connected with Buddhist temples and ceremonies. The *furin*, or wind bell, is bell-shaped with a striker suspended underneath, to which a rectangular cardboard is attached to catch the breeze.

Children, both boys and girls, often have tiny *suzu* attached to their sashes as an ornament. Girls also wear them on their *geta*, or wooden clogs. Mothers attach them to scissors and other utensils, and cats and dogs wear them on their collars to tell their owners where they are. Shinto shrine maidens will shake clusters of them during ritual dances. They are attached to ropes over the offering boxes in shrines to attract the attention of the *kami*.

The larger *kane* are found in temples. The technique of making a good bell is difficult, and there were many famous bell casters. Though there are many *kane* throughout the country, there are only a few considered to have the right clear and pleasant tone. They are struck on the exterior, always on the same spot, called the *tsukiza*, which is traditionally lotus-shaped. They are rung slowly, so that each ring sounds just as the preceding ring fades away. The bell at the Chion-in temple in Kyoto is 18 feet high. The one at the Daibutsu in Nara is 15 feet high. The largest bell was at Shitenoji in Osaka, and was 26 feet high and cast in 1902. It was improperly cast, however, and was said not to give out any sound at all. Bells were also used to announce the time by their hourly ringing. Unfortunately, many temple bells were scrapped for their iron in WWII.

Information for this story came from *Quaint Customs and Manners of Japan* by Mock Joya, published circa 1951 by The Tokyo News Service, Ltd., Tokyo, Japan.

Kill The Geishu Lord!

The use of a *kagemusha* was not unheard of in feudal Japan. The most famous double was used by Takeda Shingen (1521-'73), one of the three major lords during the "time of warring

states." On his deathbed, Takeda had recommended that his death be kept a secret for three years. The clan kept up the deception for two years, by employing an impersonator and by a series of brilliant Shingen-like military campaigns by Takeda's son and brother.

The 1980 Akira Kurosawa film *Kagemusha* was inspired by this impersonator. Oda Nobunaga and Tokugawa Ieyasu have formed an alliance against the Takeda clan. A condemned criminal is found to have an astonishing resemblance to Shingen and is hired as an impersonator when the great lord is shot by a sniper and dies. The ex-thief must not only deceive the enemy, but also his own armies, family, and wives. After he is thrown from his horse, the "lord" is examined for injuries and it is discovered that he does not have the familiar scars. The secret is out, and there is no more need for pretense. The impostor is dismissed, and Shingen's son Katsuyori becomes leader of the clan. He orders an attack against Oda and Tokugawa that ends in disaster. The thief is drawn to the battlefield where he picks up a fallen banner, advances upon the enemy, and is shot. He sees the clan flag floating upon the river, tries to reach it, and dies.

The Pride Of The Samurai

In 1603, Tokugawa Ieyasu was proclaimed *shogun*, or military dictator, a title his family would hold for the next two and a half centuries. Toyotomi Hideyoshi, the most serious threat to the Tokugawa, was defeated in 1615 at the siege of Osaka Castle. The *samurai* became a standing army with no real enemies to fight, and so spiraled into a decline, in comparison to the rising merchant class.

Trade was becoming more important to the feudal economy. Coinage had been in use for many centuries, but Japan had been primarily a barter economy based on rice. However, to keep growing cities supplied with food and goods from farther away required a less cumbersome system than rice. By 1600, gold and silver coins were in wide use. The merchant class

understood the intricacies of finance, and soon grew rich speculating in rice and making loans to the *samurai*. Turnbull cites one example of a *samurai* whose annual stipend was 300 *koku*. (One *koku* was the amount of rice required to feed a man for a year — about five bushels.) This yearly stipend was equivalent to 75 *ryo*. But in a year, the *samurai* spent 38 *ryo* on salaries, 10 for his horse, 12 for firewood, 18 for oil, food, and other daily needs, and 30 for clothes and other expenses, for a total of 108 *ryo*. According to one estimate, by 1700 the debts of the *samurai* class were one hundred times as great as all the money in the country. The poverty of some *samurai* forced them to sell their swords, substituting them with bamboo replicas or borrowing a pair from a friend to wear on duty. One way for a *samurai* to receive a larger stipend was to advance in rank — very difficult for a warrior to do in peacetime. He could also take on a part-time job such as making paper lanterns, umbrellas, fishhooks, or toothpicks, or raising crickets or vegetables. In Saga province, samurai became farmers. Debt-ridden *samurai* would even charge to adopt a merchant or townsperson's son into his family to raise the boy's class status.

The martial arts gradually fell into neglect in favor of office work, as more and more warriors were trained as civil servants for peacetime. However, they still wore their two swords on the job.

It was not only the *samurai* who suffered, but many tradesmen did as well. A sword created by the smith Kiyomitsu Shichiemon could cost as much as one *koku*. Kiyomitsu was used to getting orders for twenty swords at one time. However, in just the space of two generations, his grandson Chobei was forced to live in a poorhouse. Many swordsmiths earned more money from making pots and pans than swords.

In 1871 the wearing of two swords became optional, and in 1876 it was banned except for members of the armed forces.

The bulk of the research for this story came from *The Samurai: A Military History* by Stephen Turnbull, 1977, Macmillan Publishing Co., Inc., New York.

Gallery

The following pages feature Stan Sakai's cover art from issues sixty-nine through seventy-five of Dark Horse's Usagi Yojimbo Volume Three *series.*

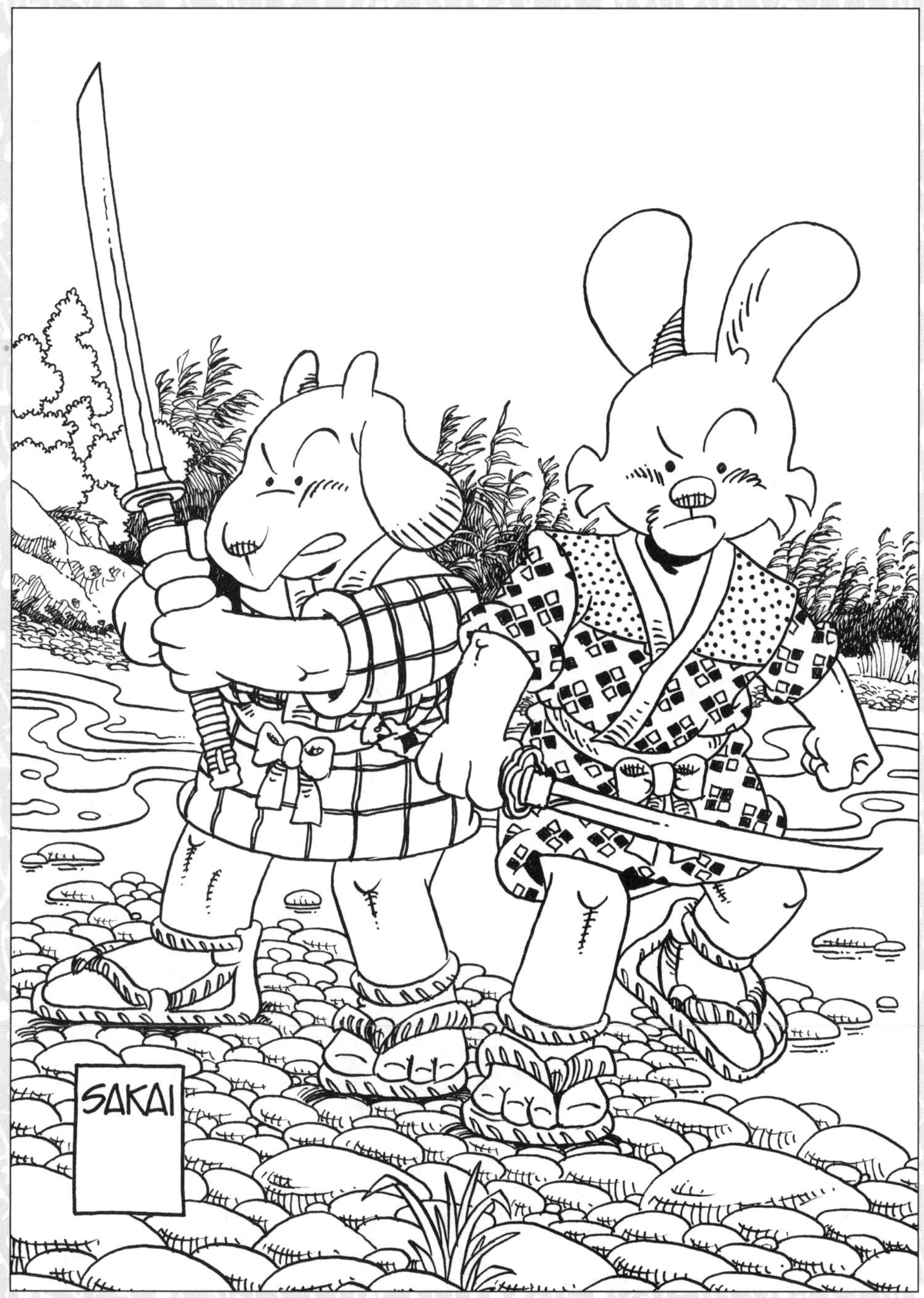
SAKAI

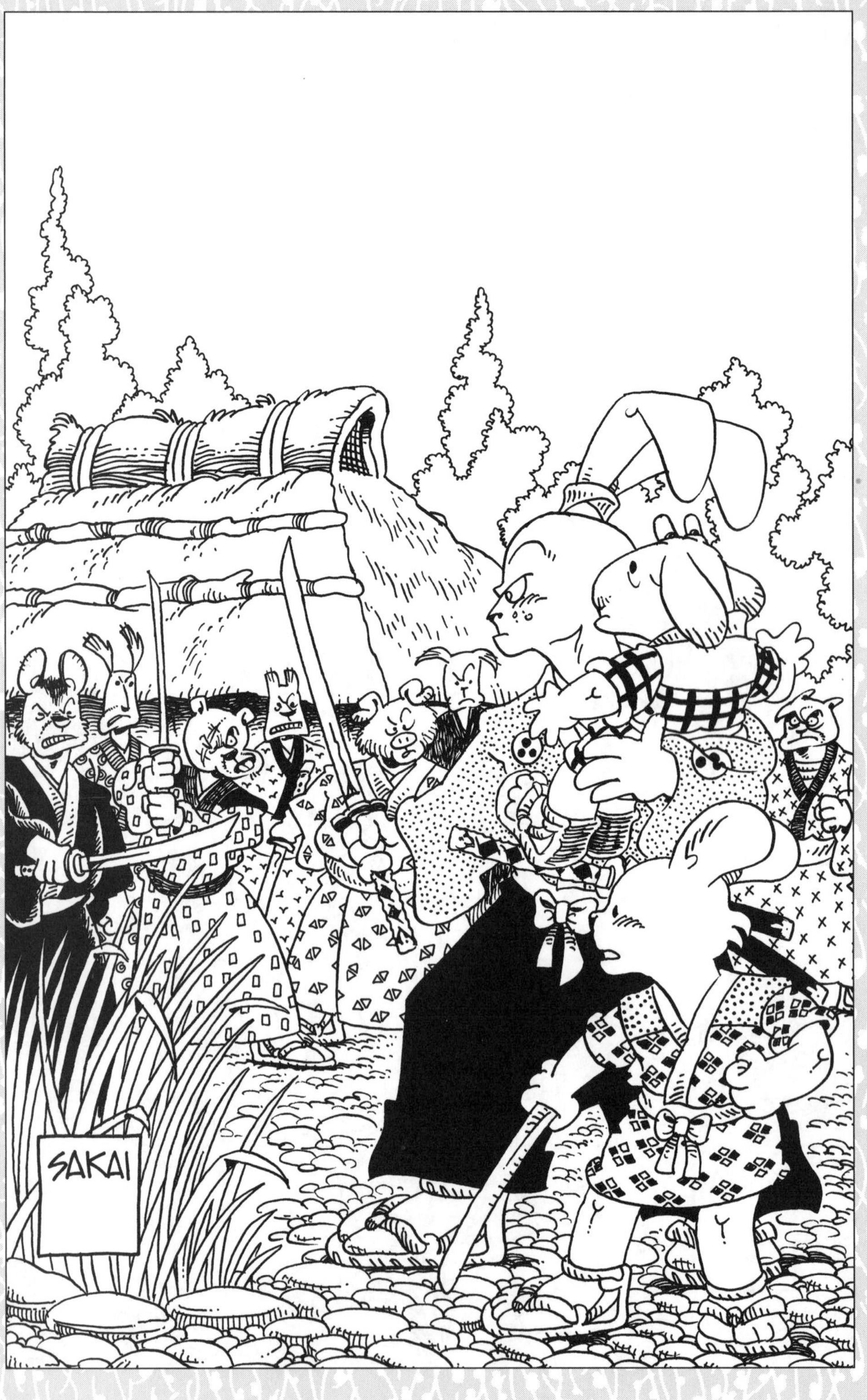
SAKAI

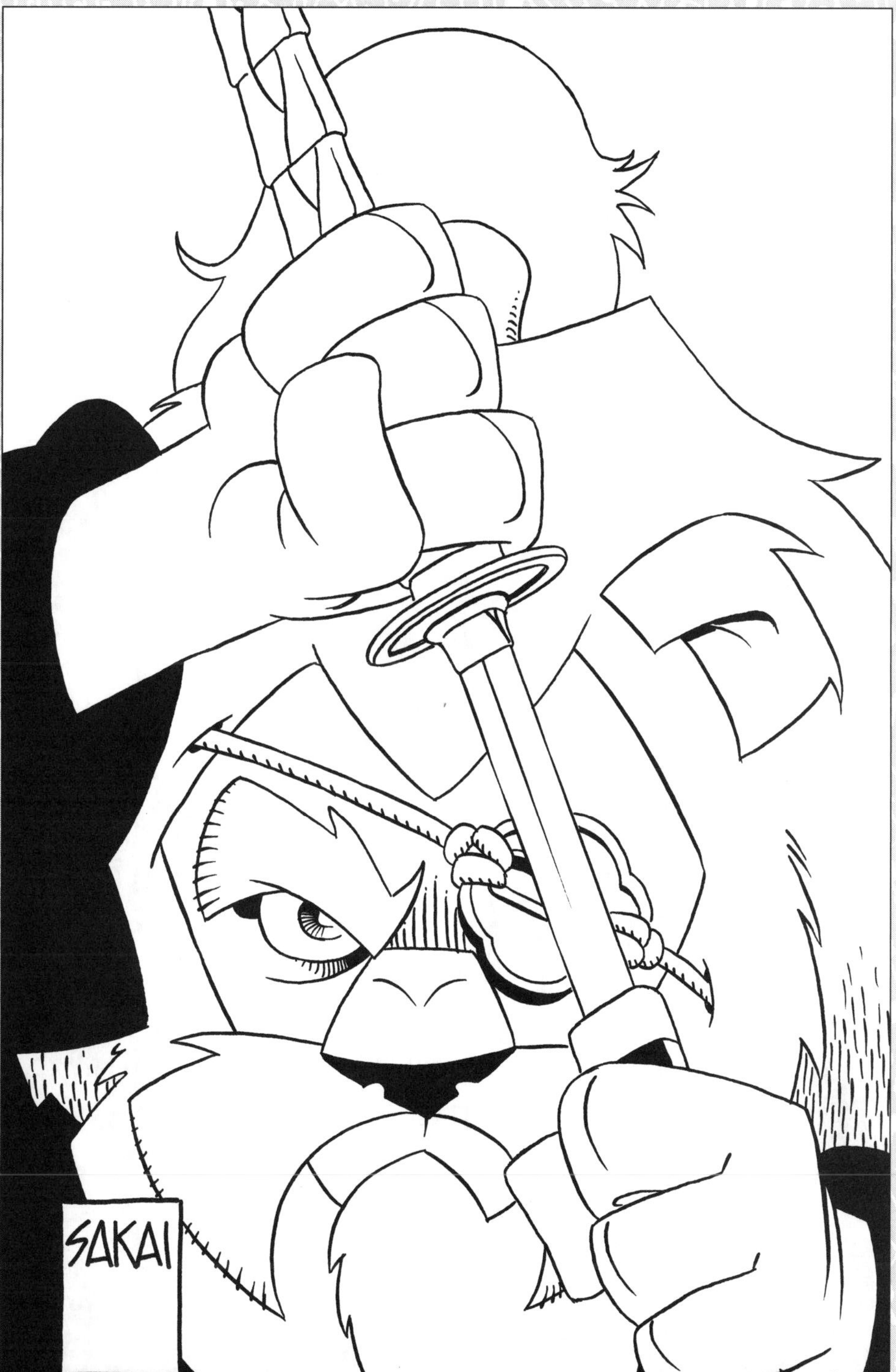
SAKAI

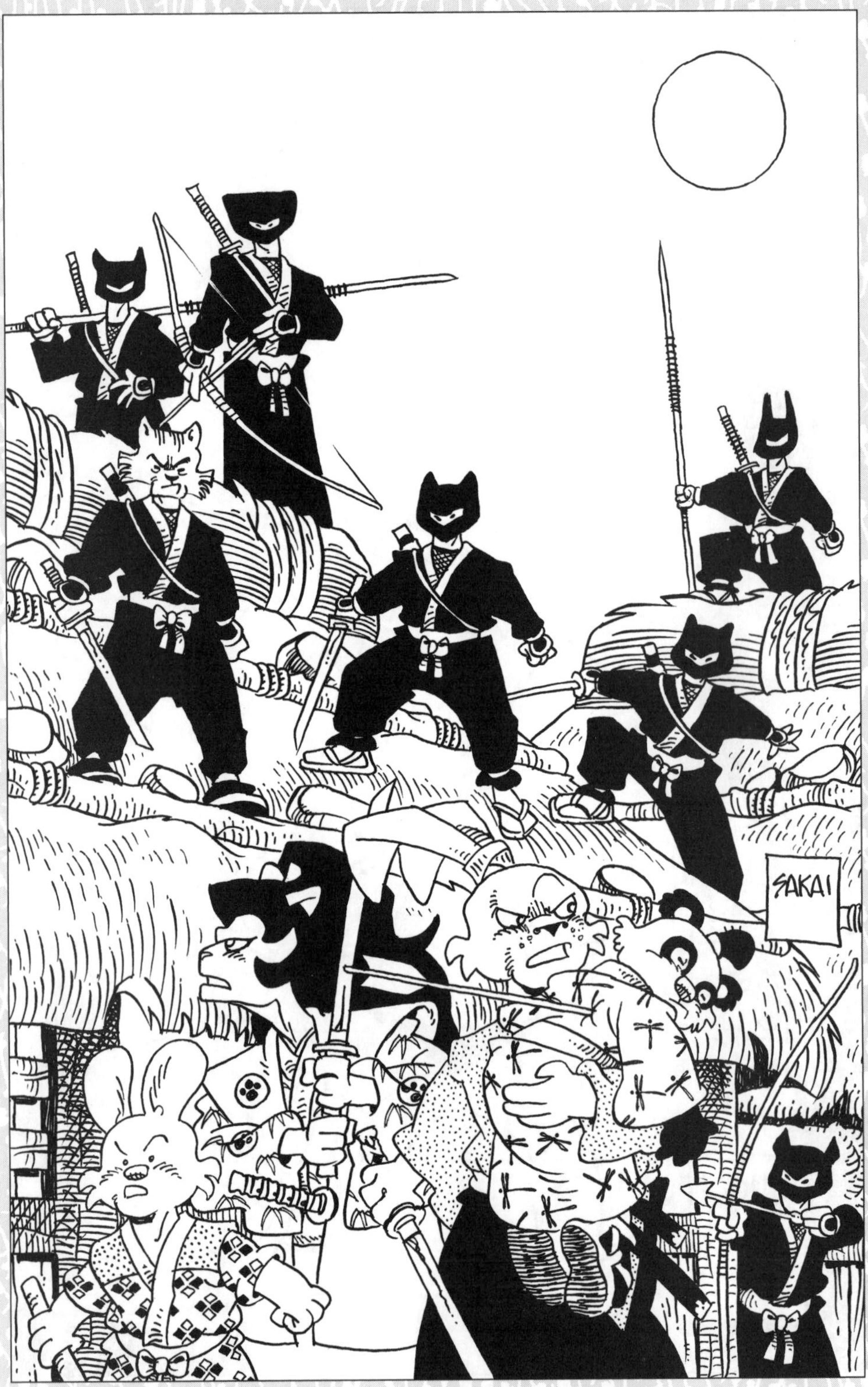
SAKAI

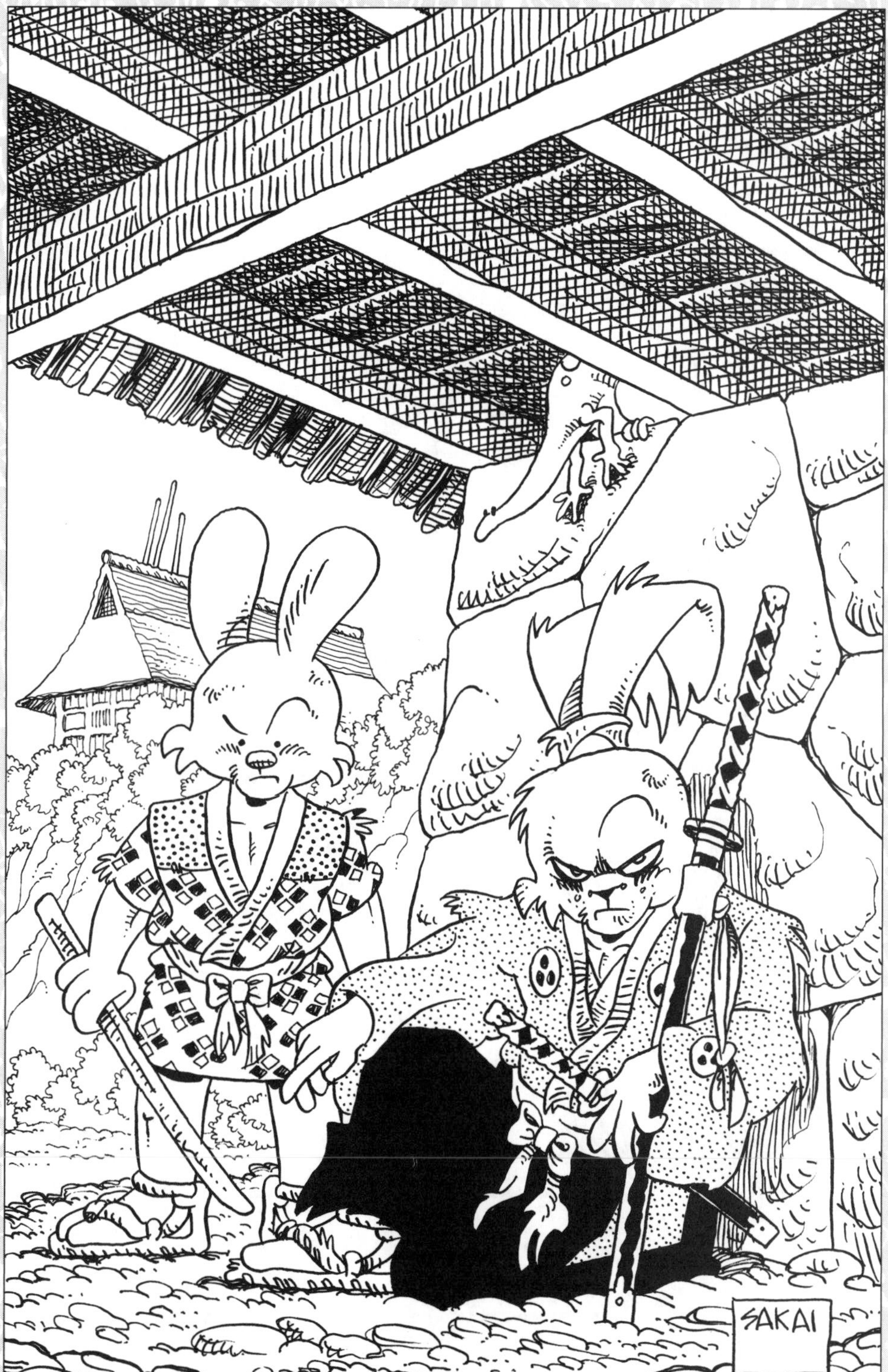
SAKAI

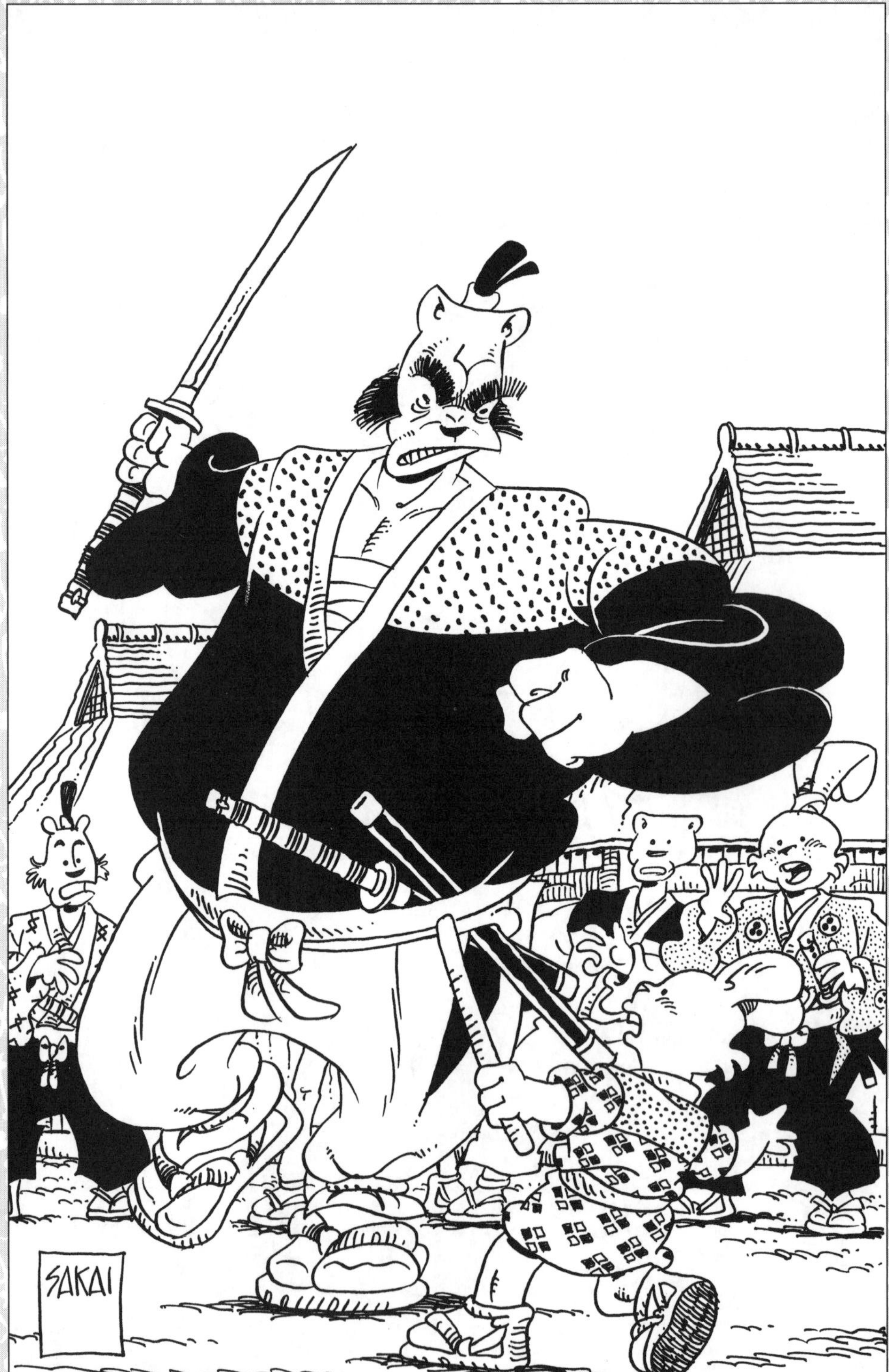
SAKAI

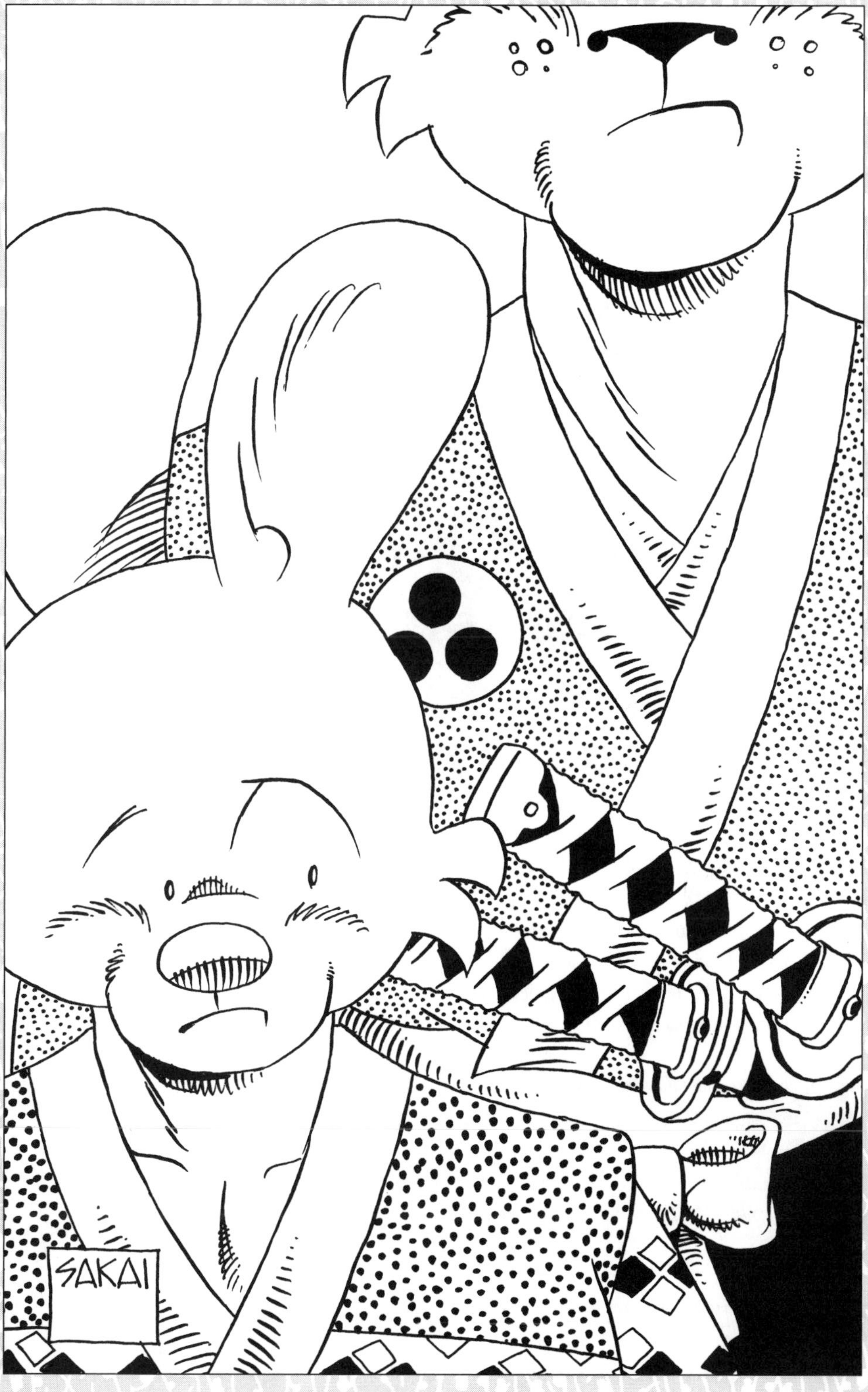
SAKAI

BIOGRAPHY
Stan Sakai

Stan Sakai with his son, Matthew, at Niagara Falls.
Photo by Sharon Sakai

STAN SAKAI was born in Kyoto, Japan, grew up in Hawaii, and now lives in California with his wife, Sharon, and children, Hannah and Matthew. He received a Fine Arts degree from the University of Hawaii and furthered his studies at Art Center College of Design in Pasadena, California.

His creation, Usagi Yojimbo, first appeared in comics in 1984. Since then, Usagi has been on television as a guest of the Teenage Mutant Ninja Turtles and has been made into toys, seen on clothing, and featured in a series of trade-paperback collections.

In 1991, Stan created *Space Usagi*, a series about the adventures of a descendant of the original Usagi that dealt with *samurai* in a futuristic setting.

Stan is also an award-winning letterer for his work on Sergio Aragonés' *Groo*, the "Spider-Man" Sunday newspaper strips, and *Usagi Yojimbo*.

Stan is a recipient of a Parents' Choice Award, an Inkpot Award, an American Library Association Award, two Spanish Haxtur Awards, and several Eisner Awards. In 2003 he received the prestigious National Cartoonists Society Comic Book Division Award.